Crisis
and
Reform

Crisis
and
Reform

Current Issues
in American
Punishment

Alexis M. Durham III
University of Tampa

Little, Brown and Company
Boston New York Toronto London

Library of Congress Catalog Card No. 93-79051

ISBN 0-316-19710-6

CCP

Published simultaneously in Canada
by Little, Brown & Company (Canada) Limited

Printed in the United States of America

This book is dedicated to Earl, whose intellectual energy
and enthusiasm during my undergraduate years fostered the
developments that have ultimately led to this book

and

to all those victims and offenders who simply
do not stand a chance.

Summary of
Contents

Contents

Contents

5   Women in Prison   105

8   Alternatives to Incarceration: Fines, Restitution, Community Service, and Day-Reporting Centers   205

9   Shock Incarceration: The Prison Boot Camp   231

10 The Privatization of Prisons 259

Contents

Acknowledgments

I would like to thank the following authors and publishers for permitting me to include excerpts from these works:

Mark T. Carleton, Politics and Punishment: The History of the Louisiana State Penal System. Reprinted by permission of Louisiana State University Press. Copyright © 1971 by Louisiana State University Press.

Potter & Mahlburg, *Pay counties for inmates, state is told*, Fort Worth Star-Telegram, June 2, 1990. Reprinted courtesy of the Fort Worth Star-Telegram.

Von Drehle, *Price Tag Changes Minds in Kansas*, The Miami Herald, July 13, 1988. Reprinted with permission of The Miami Herald.

I would also like to express my appreciation to several important individuals involved in the production of this book. Although a number of people at Little, Brown have helped bring this project to fruition, and I am grateful to them all, Patty Bergin was especially invaluable for her work on the manuscript. I also want to thank Betsy Kenney, Carolyn O'Sullivan, and Cate Rickard for the attention they devoted to the project, and Rick Heuser for his willingness to support the project from the very outset.

Lastly, I want to convey my gratitude to the many dedicated scholars and criminal justice system practitioners whose efforts have provided the basis for the work contained in this volume.

Crisis
and
Reform

1

Introduction

"More inmates could be back on streets early."
Tampa Tribune—January 30, 1993

Up to 7,000 inmates would be eligible for early release under a rec-
ommendation made Friday at a summit called by Gov. Lawton
Chiles to deal with the swelling prison population. The inmates
would include some drug-traffickers and non-violent habitual
offenders. . . .[1]

Prison crowding in Florida, and in many other states, has forced public
officials to consider a wide range of remedies, some of which are regarded
by the general public with a considerable lack of enthusiasm. Early
release is one such remedy. Of course, the reality is that Florida's prison
system is "almost 33 percent over capacity—the maximum allowed by
the federal government."[2] A further reality is that a majority of the states
are under court orders relating to prison crowding or conditions. With
official crime rates remaining at relatively high levels,[3] political leaders
are struggling to find solutions.

This is not to suggest that our leaders have not been making efforts
to address crime during the past two decades. They have. For evidence of
this one need only consider that the incarceration rate in the United
States has tripled since the early 1970s and more than doubled since the
early 1980s.[4] During the second half of the 1980s criminal justice system
expenditures increased by 24 percent in constant dollars. The percentage
increase in correctional system expenditures alone was double this overall figure. In 1990 dollars, annual per capita correctional expenditures
have gone from slightly more than $30 per capita in 1971 to more than
$90 in 1990.[5] Moreover, "[s]tate government expenditures for building
prisons increased 593 percent in actual dollars between 1979 and 1988."[6]
In 1988 and 1989 alone the increase in correctional expenditures was 29
percent. It is interesting to note that this contrasts with a mere 7.3 per-

1

cent increase in elementary and secondary education expenditures over the same period.[7]

Despite all of this effort, crime has not disappeared, and political leaders remain locked in a struggle to find solutions. Unfortunately, their "new" solutions seem very much like the "old" solutions. To continue with the case of Florida, Governor Lawton Chiles has proposed creating 21,000 more prison beds, an enormous increase of about 40 percent over current capacity.[8] This solution is proposed despite what has taken place during the past decade. An analysis conducted by the National Council in Crime and Delinquency concluded that

> [o]f the states, Florida has most dramatically increased the use of imprisonment—especially for drug crimes. . . . The data show that Florida has increased the number of offenders sentenced to prison by over 330 percent. . . . But despite this impressive and unprecedented increase in the use of imprisonment, the crime rate (reported serious crime to the police, excluding all drug crimes, per 100,000 population) has not been reduced.[9]

Florida's predicament is partially the result of increased use of mandatory minimum sentences. Such sentences have substantial appeal to the general public, but have also had the effect of dramatically increasing the use of early release.[10] Florida has continued to use such mandatories despite evidence described in an analysis by the United States Sentencing Commission that they do not work.[11]

The past decade has been characterized by continuing concern with crime, increased use of imprisonment, enormous hikes in correctional expenditures, and no discernable gains in terms of public perceptions of increased safety. How is this possible? After 300 years of the American struggle with crime and punishment-related issues, the nation seems less able to deal with them now than at perhaps any other time in its history.

This book is designed to explore some of the most significant aspects of the continuing crisis in corrections. In general, it will examine a number of the most serious problems currently afflicting the correctional system, as well as consider a number of solutions that have received substantial attention in recent years. Problems such as prison crowding, high recidivism rates, and AIDS in prison, as well as difficulties associated with the growing numbers of elderly and female inmates, will be examined. It is clear that these problems have already had considerable consequences, and there is every reason to believe that the worst is yet to come.

We will also examine some of the most highly touted reforms proposed to address some of these problems. Intensive supervision programs, house arrest, electronic monitoring, day-fines, community service, restitution, prison boot camps, and correctional privatization will be considered. Supporters of each of these initiatives argue that correctional problems, as well as the more general problem of crime, can be addressed through expanded use of such approaches and programs. Naturally, detractors of these programs are also plentiful, and we will discuss the shortcomings along with the potential benefits of such correctional innovations. In addition, although it is neither new nor innovative, but because of its high level of visibility and public interest and its apparent symbolic importance, we will examine the death penalty. Not all of the important issues confronting the correctional system could be included in this book, but those that have been included reflect high levels of concern and interest among the general public and in the criminological community.

The chapters which follow contain descriptive material on correctional problems, including substantial amounts of data on correctional processes and outcomes. Numerous innovations are described, and both correctional problems and solutions are placed in ideological and historical contexts in the hope of communicating the full complexity of the correctional reform process. In addition, data on public sentiment regarding correctional issues are presented, some of which sharply contradict popular impressions of what the public really wants from the correctional system.

That this book exists is in part testimony to the failure of the initiatives of the past two decades. Despite plentiful and often heated political rhetoric about getting serious about solving the crime problem, and even though many billions of dollars have been devoted to the problem, there is little evidence that significant progress has been made. As will soon become evident, although some of the initiatives described in the chapters to follow may have promise, there is reason to regard them with a sharply critical eye, and to recognize that too often those approaches that appear to have the most immediate and self-evident value and appeal are in fact among the most utterly ineffective.

Thus one objective of this book is to create a healthy skepticism about so-called landmark correctional reforms. Although skepticism is sometimes regarded as an expression of high levels of pessimism, this need not be the case. Skepticism can act as a restraining influence, often keeping us from throwing good money after bad on programs of dubious value, such as the highly publicized, but questionably effective, Scared Straight Program. It can also motivate us to continue the search for solid answers to difficult questions, to treat as improbable those solutions that promise everything at little expense or effort, and to maintain a careful critical posture in evaluating correctional reforms. Although maintenance of a scrupulous critical approach to correctional reform provides no guarantee that we will be able to solve the major correctional problems that confront us today, failure to sustain a critical posture surely dooms us to a continuing string of intransigent problems and fruitless reforms.

Notes

[1]Thompson, Stephan (1993) "More inmates could be back on streets early," *Tampa Tribune*, Jan. 30, Florida/Metro, p. 4.

[2]Id.

[3]*Law Enforcement News* (1992) "Largest-ever violent crime jump leads 1991 UCR stats," Sept. 30, p. 3.

[4]Flanagan, Timothy J. and Maguire, Kathleen (1992) *Sourcebook of Criminal Justice Statistics—1991*, Washington, D.C.: U.S. Department of Justice, p. 635.

[5]Lindgren, Sue A. (1992) "Justice expenditure and employment, 1990," Washington, D.C.: Bureau of Justice Statistics, pp. 4-5.

[6]Chambliss, William J. (1991) "Trading textbooks for prison cells," Alexandria, VA: National Center on Institutions and Alternatives, p. 4.

[7]Id. at p. 7.

[8]Lavelle, Louis (1993) "Proposal would add 21,000 prison beds," *Tampa Tribune*, Feb. 17, Florida/Metro, p. 1.

[9]Austin, James (1991) "Escalating the use of imprisonment: The case study of Florida," San Francisco, CA: National Council on Crime and Delinquency, pp. 1 & 3.

[10]Peterson, Sigrid C. (1991) "Florida mandatories backfire," *Overcrowded Times* 2(6).

[11]Tonry, Michael (1991) "Mandatory sentencing laws don't work, says U.S. Sentencing Commission," *Overcrowded Times* 2(6).

2

Theory, Ideology, and Rationales for Punishment

The vast majority of this book will be concerned with a variety of correctional issues, events, and practices. We will examine prison crowding, AIDS in prison, problems of female and elderly inmates, and a host of other pressing difficulties. We will also discuss the wide range of responses to these problems, such as prison construction, alternatives to incarceration, and involvement of the private sector in corrections. Before proceeding to these subjects, however, it is crucial that we prepare the groundwork for what we will ultimately encounter. Part of this preparation includes gaining a thorough appreciation of how so-called practical problems and solutions depend on theoretical concepts and formulations. Thus in this chapter we will explore the linkages between theory, ideology, and the world of practical affairs.

There are four reasons why this brief preparation is necessary. First, it is important to understand how theory in general, and ideology in particular, makes it possible for us to understand, as well as to act in, the everyday world. Second, the political context of corrections and correctional reform is impossible to grasp without an adequate feel for ideological influences. Third, a theoretical sensitivity is required to appreciate how correctional conditions and events come to be regarded as problems meriting attention. Finally, in any examination of issues that are highly charged with emotion it is useful to try and lay bare the biases and predispositions that may interfere with development of a full understanding of the dilemmas. All of us who seek to understand complex social problems are to some extent incapacitated by the prejudgments we bring to our personal deliberations. Effort invested at this point in our discussion to come to grips with some of these often well disguised biases may prove fruitful in making most effective use of the material presented in subsequent chapters.

We will begin with discussions of theory and ideology and how they make it possible for us to understand the world. More specifically, it will become clear how both theory and ideology influence our view of crime, and form the basis for the rationales used to justify punishment. The remaining portion of the chapter will describe these rationales and their relationship to the punishments employed by society to respond to crime.

Understanding the World: Theory

In the normal course of daily affairs each of us encounters a wide range of events, objects, and experiences. We somehow manage to negotiate our way through the course of each day, and we are rarely left with the sense that we do not understand what transpired. We may not always be satisfied with how our day went, but generally we are not confused about what took place.

How is this possible? Even though our day may include visiting places we have never been before, meeting people who were previously unknown, and engaging in activities that are essentially novel, we nonetheless manage to make our way without breaking down under the accumulated weight of such new experiences. Furthermore, we rarely think about how we did it.

In a sense, of course, all experiences are different. Each day at work, each approach to a stop light, each meal, each game of tennis, all are to some extent unique. What makes it possible for us to ignore the unique quality of each experience is the human ability to selectively process experience. A mundane example will help clarify this point. A driver approaching a traffic signal at one intersection will treat it the same way the signal at the previous intersection was treated. The intersections are not identical, and each intersection approach experience is unique. However, the driver is able to abstract out of what is being experienced those features that pertain to the significance of the situation. The driver recognizes the signal as a traffic control device, accords this device primary significance over the other aspects of the intersection, and responds to the approaching intersection largely on the basis of his or her understanding of the importance of the traffic signal.

Of course, the hanging traffic signal and the color of the light are but two of scores of potentially observable physical features that might be noted at the intersection. The vast majority of these features go unnoticed, or if noticed, unattended to. The waste receptacle on the corner, the bus stop sign on the curb, and the man waiting on the sidewalk for the bus's arrival are all essentially ignored. They are all there to be observed and attended to, yet typically only the traffic signal captures the driver's attention. The driver has learned that different colored lights mean that she or he may pass through the intersection or that it is necessary to stop and await the illumination of a different color light.

This obvious point is useful in illustrating that we do not simply respond to an objective, external world, but rather that we select, often unconsciously, among various aspects of what we are exposed to. This kind of selection process conditions everything that we do, and ultimately has an important impact on how we regard criminal justice-related issues. A simple model may be useful in clarifying this point.

A Model of Reality

We can use a model of various levels of reality to more clearly represent the constituent parts of this example. In this model the **EXTERNAL WORLD** is the physical environment within which the driver operates (the streets, bus stop, pedestrian, "BIG SALE" sign in a store window, waste receptacle, traffic signal, for example). Only some aspects of this world are even potentially observable. A small child hidden behind the waste receptacle will not be visible to the driver. The **OBSERVED WORLD** is the world the driver *does* receive information about, even if only a small portion of such information is noticed. The person awaiting the bus is observed by the driver but not noticed or attended to. (We have all had the experience of noticing for the first time a building situated on a route we regularly travel. We are amazed that we never noticed the structure before, despite the fact that we must have observed it many times on our daily trips.) The **NOTICED WORLD** consists of the objects that we both observe and take note of. In our example the traffic light and the "BIG SALE" sign fall into this category. Finally, some of the objects that we notice comprise the **ACTED-UPON WORLD**. It is this last level of reality that forms the basis for our behavior. The driver observes the traffic signal, becomes aware of the red light, and then acts upon this visual information by bringing the car to a halt. Other aspects of the NOTICED WORLD, such as the "BIG SALE" sign, may have been noticed but not acted upon.

Figure 2-1
A Model of Reality:
The Traffic Intersection

EXTERNAL WORLD

Traffic signal, dog in yard, man reading newspaper,
bus stop sign, "BIG SALE" sign in store window,
waste receptacle, small child hidden by waste receptacle

↓

OBSERVED WORLD

Traffic signal, dog in yard, man reading newspaper,
bus stop sign, "BIG SALE" sign in store window, waste
receptacle

↓

NOTICED WORLD

Traffic signal, "BIG SALE" in store window

↓

ACTED-UPON WORLD

Traffic signal

In reality, we may not always be sharply aware of the objects that form the basis for our actions. Drivers approaching a traffic signal automatically note the color of the light, and reflexively respond to the color without anything that could be characterized as conscious deliberation. Nonetheless, the main point is that the EXTERNAL WORLD exists for us through a variety of personal psychological processes that select out only a subset of theoretically possible worlds that are available for observation. A Kalahari Bushman might approach the intersection and not notice the traffic signal at all, but instead notice the person standing still holding a large white object in front of his or her face. (Our bus-awaiting executive reading the Wall Street Journal.) We attend to and classify the world based on our experiences, and the Bushman's experience simply does not include driving or the need to be attentive to colored lights hanging above roadways. To the Bushman the light may be observed but neither noted nor attended to.

Naturally, this brief description of how human beings come to experience their world is subject to a variety of criticisms and modifications. Philosophers and social scientists remain hard at work in pitched battles over the processes by which human beings come into meaningful possession of their experiences. For our purposes it is important to understand that what we experience as the world is conditioned by a variety of factors that have little to do with an external, objective, outside world.

Moreover, the explanations that are devised to explain various aspects of the world reflect this slippage between what is "out there," what we experience, and what we do. Human beings bring to each experiential situation a collection of interests, motives, sensitivities, and abilities that affect how the "objective" world will be experienced.

One final example will further extend this point. Imagine for a moment getting into your car on a cold morning, turning the key, and finding that the car will not start. You may notice only that the car will not start. You go back into the house and call the tow truck.

Of course, what actually transpired would have been somewhat more complicated. Perhaps the key was turned, and a groaning noise was emitted from the engine compartment, followed by silence. Alternatively, perhaps the key was turned and a single click was heard, then silence. Or the key was turned, the engine started, but then died with a loud whine. Each of these scenarios represents what would in common parlance be referred to as "the car wouldn't start."

In fact, different people will note different things about the "car not starting" phenomena. Those utterly unfamiliar with even the most elementary details of automotive functioning may notice only that when

11

the key was turned the car failed to run in its normal manner. Others might notice an unusual groaning noise but fail to detect the single click. Still others might notice that the dashboard indicator lights failed to come on when the key was turned. One's experience and knowledge will heavily influence what details of the actual process will be noted and attended to.

The significance of this little scenario is that what is noticed will likely influence the motorist's *explanations* for the vehicle's failure to start and ultimately his or her actions to remedy the problem. A driver knowledgeable about automobiles who notes that the dashboard indicator lights did come on is unlikely to theorize that the car failed to start because the battery was completely dead. A driver who noted that the engine turned over and over without starting likewise would not hold a completely dead battery at fault. A driver who neglected to note the smell of gasoline would not likely be able to attribute the failure to start to a flooded carburetor. Drivers who possess an understanding of how an automobile works will be sensitive to the various signs that indicate the source of trouble. They will observe and *notice* occurrences that others will merely observe.

The explanation, or in other words the theory, advanced to account for the vehicle's failure to start thus depends on both what is noticed and how what is noticed is interpreted in the light of knowledge of automotive functions. In a general sense, a *theory* is a systematic effort to account for some process, event, or object. Although many theories are complex, sophisticated, multidimensional conceptual structures, at their heart they are essentially explanations. We use theories regularly in our everyday lives, even though we may not always be aware that we are using them. For instance, we use theories to account for the ill behavior of those we know ("He's had a tough week"; "He's just a mean person"; "His parents never taught him any manners"; "She just lost her job"; "He's undergoing a divorce"). These little theories help us to understand the world we inhabit, and make it possible to design appropriate courses of action. An ill-behaving individual thought to be acting rudely due to special stresses associated with the loss of a job would likely be treated more indulgently than would one thought to possess an intentionally abrasive personality.

The driver of the vehicle may devise a theory to account for the car's failure to start and then act in accord with that theory. If the problem is identified as electrical, the battery terminals may be inspected for corrosion. If the carburetor is thought to be at fault, the butterfly plate in the throat of the carburetor may be wedged open. If these steps do not solve the problem, the initial theories may be discarded in favor of as yet untested explanations.

The four-level model of reality demonstrates that our actions ultimately depend on many factors that go beyond the characteristics or features of the "EXTERNAL WORLD." We selectively experience and interpret this world, and this process influences our behavior. This is not a one-way process, for our behavior itself also influences our subsequent processing of the world. As we will see, the theories and ideologies we hold make a significant contribution to this processing in the context of crime and justice issues. Before turning to ideology let us briefly consider the four-level model as it relates to efforts to account for crime.

Explaining Crime

As Figure 2-2 shows, the EXTERNAL WORLD of crime may be comprised of a wide variety of offenses. Holding aside issues associated with the process by which various harmful acts are designated as crimes, these offenses range from simple public intoxication to homicide to price-fixing. Some kinds of crimes comprising the external world of crime, price-fixing for example, are never witnessed by the general public, are poorly reported in the press, and have consequences that are so difficult to identify as to be essentially unobservable to the average citizen. There is usually no knowing victim because the public is unaware that prices have been fixed. The few pennies per fixed-price product added to consumer costs will generally not be noticed by consumers. The press, if it covers the case at all, may relegate it to a back page of the paper. In a loose sense, then, price-fixing is analogous to sounds that are beyond the perceptual capabilities of human beings. They exist but are usually not directly observable by human beings.

Other white collar crimes, such as embezzlement, tend to be more easily observed. Such crimes are more frequent, and although only a small fraction end up being described in the press, the relatively large number of embezzlements assures that the public is not entirely unaware of embezzlement. However, such offenses, though observed, tend not to be noticed by the public.

Homicide, though relatively rare statistically (less than 1 percent of all F.B.I. Crime Index offenses), is both observed and *noticed* by the public. Homicide incidents and homicide offender trials, as well as death penalty appeal processes, receive substantial media attention. In addition, homicide is an *acted-upon* offense. When citizens are asked about the crime problem, and about appropriate remedies for the problem, images of lower socioeconomic status homicide offenders, rather than of upper-class white collar offenders, tend to form the basis for their thoughts on such issues.

Figure 2-2
A Model of Reality:
Crime

EXTERNAL WORLD OF CRIME

Homicide, rape, armed robbery, unarmed robbery,
price-fixing, public intoxication, kidnapping,
shoplifting, embezzlement

OBSERVED WORLD OF CRIME

Homicide, rape, armed robbery, unarmed robbery,
embezzlement

NOTICED WORLD OF CRIME

Homicide, rape, armed robbery, unarmed robbery

ACTED-UPON WORLD OF CRIME

Homicide, rape, armed robbery

Of course, what is noticed depends on many variables, and to some extent the process is circular. If a citizen is suddenly made aware of price-fixing through an unusual circumstance like the conviction of a family member for fixing prices, he or she will thereafter likely notice virtually every future reference to price-fixing, no matter how minor. The OBSERVED and NOTICED WORLDs for that individual are changed forever. Moreover, the theories devised by that individual to explain crime will likely be quite different from those created by citizens who are largely unaware of the financial crimes of the wealthy.

Theories devised to account for crime thus reflect specific kinds of awareness of crime. Even within criminology, until the late 1960s explanations of crime tended to focus upon certain kinds of crimes, notably conventional street crimes. This interest in street crime to the exclusion of crimes such as white collar offenses has been reflected more recently by the Attorney General's Task Force on Violent Crime under President Reagan. The objective of this task force was to address serious crime, and this was defined as conventional street violence. Extremely serious forms of white collar crime, including those associated with significant physical harm to citizens, were excluded from the purview of the inquiry.[1] The public exposure to such definitions, through mechanisms such as a Presidential task force, may heavily influence development of public perceptions of what constitutes serious crime. Thus, theories both reflect selective processes and further reinforce these processes.

Responding to Crime

Of equal importance is the relationship between theories of crime and theories of response to crime. Perceptions of why individuals become involved in crime condition and limit the kinds of social responses deemed appropriate and effective in dealing with crime. The correctional system is based upon a number of theories that provide the foundation for the various correctional strategies and activities employed by the system. Some of these theories pertain to the fundamental nature of humankind, while others are more narrowly concerned with accounting for criminal behavior. For instance, one well regarded theory of human decision-making states that human beings possess free will and the capacity for rational thought. Human decisions are viewed, therefore, as the product of the exercise of this rationality and free will. In accord with this viewpoint, crimes result when citizens decide that the benefits of committing a crime outweigh the risk of significant punishment.[2] In situations within which this theory of human behavior is accepted the

15

response of the correctional system to criminal behavior will generally be to impose sanctions of sufficient severity so as to provide reason for free-acting rational individuals to ultimately come to the rational decision that the price of crime is simply too high to make it worthwhile.

If, at the other extreme, one explains human behavior by asserting that debilitating social conditions drive men and women to the actions they commit, then a morally acceptable and practically useful response to crime might be to rearrange socioeconomic conditions in order that such circumstances have more desirable influences on citizens. Basic education and job training programs are typical of correctional strategies based on this theory of criminality.

The selective process discussed earlier clearly has influence upon the correctional remedies chosen by the justice system. For instance, if the exclusion of white collar crime in the Attorney General's Task Force on Violent Crime's definition of serious crime influences public perceptions of serious crime, then the public view of serious criminals will focus upon an offender group that is disproportionately young, minority, poor, and uneducated. Publicly supported correctional remedies designed to respond to these offenders may thus include employment skills training and education programs. Such programs obviously have no relevance to price-fixers, who are typically well-educated, occupy the upper end of the socioeconomic scale, and do not commit crimes out of the personal scramble for economic survival. This selective defining of the notion of serious crime effectively precludes commitment of energy to designing strategies that make sense in addressing price-fixing problems.

The nature of the response to crime thus reflects some theory or set of theories about *why* people commit crimes. In the upcoming discussion of rationales for punishment, it will be important to bear in mind that theories of human nature underpin the justifications for punishment. This is no minor matter because such theories ultimately justify the state's right to intrude into the lives of citizens and inflict pain and suffering on those convicted of crimes.

Understanding the World: Ideology

Related to theory is the notion of ideology. Ideology refers to the belief system adopted by a group and consists of assumptions and values. The assumptions are beliefs about the way the world is constituted, organized, and operates. They may include factually-based beliefs, such as the belief that fire is hot, as well as beliefs that do not rest upon an obvious empirical basis, such as the religious belief that humans are inherently sinful or good. Values, on the other hand, are beliefs about what is moral and desirable. The premium placed on individual liberty and the interest in acquisition of material wealth are examples of modern American values.

Ideologies are important because they provide a relatively cohesive explanation of the world, and in so doing create a basis for action. A capitalist ideology, for instance, assumes that human beings are essentially free-acting individuals whose careful decisions and hard work can reap a variety of rewards. It tends to minimize social structural factors, such as poverty, which may put severe limits on what can be achieved, even with hard work and careful attention to decision-making. The capitalist ideology not only provides an account of human nature, but in addition suggests personal and public courses of action. Laws that provide tax incentives for the wealthy, for instance, may be justified on the basis that such incentives will encourage hardworking, rational individuals to put their resources to work through various kinds of investment. According to this view, such investment ultimately will lead to benefits for the individual capitalist, but will also benefit society at large. Jobs may be created, new technology may become available, and breakthroughs in knowledge may occur. Ideologies, therefore, are not merely abstract concepts which play no role in the world of everyday affairs.

There are numerous ways to classify ideologies. A basic classification, and one that can be applied easily to crime and punishment, includes conservative, liberal, and radical ideologies. A brief description of each of these will be useful in setting the framework for what follows in the remainder of the book. It is important to note that these descriptions oversimplify the character of each of the three ideologies. There are no clear boundaries between them. Furthermore, individuals or groups that generally adhere to one ideological position may sometimes find themselves attracted to positions that do not appear to fit their normal ideological posture. (Conservative William Buckley's endorsement of the legalization of drugs is a good example of such variation.)

Conservative Ideology

Conservative ideology tends to accept the proposition that human beings are possessed of free will and are capable of making rational choices. It is relatively supportive of already existing values and institutions, somewhat suspicious of social change, and generally receptive to the idea that people succeed or fail as a result of their own initiative. The world is viewed largely as an opportunity that can be taken advantage of if citizens will simply put their nose to the grindstone. Contemporary conservative political causes, such as national defense and the hotly debated proposal for a constitutional amendment banning flag desecration, typify the interest in maintaining the status quo. Conservative opposition to progressive tax schedules has traditionally represented the belief that the wealthy have achieved their economic status as a result of their own efforts, and thus should not be penalized for their achievements.

Conservative ideology views crime as the result of the behavior of individuals who freely elect to commit crimes, and who can therefore be held to account for their behavior. It is less sympathetic to the idea that criminals are driven to their criminality by a confluence of social circumstances beyond the control of the individual. In this light, punishment ought to be designed to increase the costs of crime such that rationally acting individuals will no longer have incentives to commit crimes. In addition, conservative ideology also tends to be comfortable with the idea that punishment should be imposed to inflict suffering on the criminal, suffering that is *deserved* because of the calculated victimization of society by the offender. Finally, because of its view of the roots of human behavior, conservative ideology generally finds rehabilitation to be a less attractive objective of punishment.

Liberal Ideology

Liberal ideology views human behavior as more than just a function of free will. Human behavior is influenced by social circumstances such as one's upbringing, material affluence, education, occupational experience, peer relationships, mishaps and successes, and many other variables. Although most adherents to liberal ideology would not insist that human beings are altogether lacking in the capacity to make free choices, they do acknowledge that there are individuals whose decisions are highly influenced by experiences over which those individuals have no control.

Thus, success or failure in life is more than a simple expression of one's enterprise and diligence. Having had good parental upbringing, high quality schooling, proper peers, and a bit of good fortune

18

increases the likelihood of success. As might be expected, therefore, adherents to liberal ideology tend to be supportive of publicly assisted and financed policy measures, such as social welfare programs (Medicare, Aid to Families with Dependent Children, Job Corps, and food stamps, for example). They tend to be relatively enthusiastic about programs that reflect clearly the belief that antecedent events sharply constrain and condition current and future events. Affirmative Action employment programs represent a tangible political expression of this belief.

Criminal behavior also tends to be regarded as more than simply a product of free choices made by evil individuals. All of the influences we have noted above, along with many others, are seen as important factors in the progression of events that leads one into crime. Viewing crime as a product of social, as well as individual, circumstances inclines adherents of liberal ideology to accept more readily responses to crime that include rehabilitative, as well as purely punitive, measures. To no small extent this interest in rehabilitation reflects the moral understanding that if individuals cannot be held solely responsible for what they become and what they do, society has an obligation to try to correct the influences or conditions which may have led an individual into crime. This concern with rehabilitation does not, however, mean that other aims of punishment, such as deterrence, are considered valueless. Liberals tend to be receptive to a wider range of explanations of criminal behavior, and that range does include some of the free will-based explanations put forth by conservatives. Because of this, they also tend to be more supportive of a wider range of aims for punishment as well.

Radical Ideology

Although the views associated with conservative and liberal ideology tend to occupy opposite ends of the scale in terms of the beliefs and values *commonly* expressed in society, the views typical of radical ideology generally call into question the very existence of the existing social order. For instance, although conservatives and liberals will differ on the extent to which government ought to be involved in assisting citizens to acquire private property (through tax breaks, business incentive programs, and welfare, for example), radicals may reject the notion of private ownership of property altogether. Radical ideology certainly rejects the notion that free-acting rational individuals simply make choices that determine their position in society. It is in accord with liberal ideology in placing great weight on social influences as determinants of human behavior, but it rejects the notion that improvements in the human condition can be achieved within the existing economic, ideological, and sociopolitical framework. Radical ideology tends to be supportive of a restructuring of the socioeconomic relations of society, such as the extent to which workers own the businesses in which they work. Radical ideology is uncomfortable with the competitive ethic of capitalist society, and generally views personal success as a product of a series of fortunate coincidences, such as having been raised in a caring and competent family and sent to the proper schools.

Crime is viewed as a natural consequence of the conventional social system. Street crimes, which are typically regarded as crimes of the disadvantaged, are committed in response to degrading and often impoverished conditions under which many people are forced to live. White collar crimes, on the other hand, are regarded as the crimes of the privileged. The fact that white collar crimes have traditionally been accorded minor punishments is taken as evidence of the way the system is stacked in favor of the advantaged.

According to the radical ideology the proper response to crime entails more than imposing severe punishments or exposing offenders to rehabilitative programs. Because crime is seen as a clear reflection of social conditions, it is those conditions themselves that must be altered. Individual culpability plays little role in radical ideology. Unlike liberal ideology, however, the altering of conditions must go beyond merely restoring family values, providing job opportunities, or making minor adjustments in the distribution of wealth. Fundamental changes in the socioeconomic basis of society, such as re-conceptualization of the role of private property or ownership of the means of production, is required to make any significant progress in efforts to control crime.

Ideology: Summary

How one understands the world depends heavily on the ideology through which the world is viewed. Well-meaning, intelligent, capable people look at the same circumstances and events and derive very different meanings from what they observe. Ideologies help us to order, organize, and interpret the world, and in so doing make it relatively easy for us to develop theories of human experience. At the same time, however, ideologies blind us to aspects of reality that are important. Although it is not possible to view the world from an ideology-free posture, being aware of ideology in general, and the ideology one tends to feel most comfortable with in particular, may be useful in helping to move beyond the constraints that limit our ability to grapple with important issues.

The remaining chapters of this book will discuss a number of extremely serious problems and issues. The success of this volume in addressing these issues will depend in part on the extent to which sensitivity to ideological considerations remains a part of the analysis. Before moving to consideration of these issues we must first examine the major rationales for punishment, each of which reflects various ideological perspectives.

Rationales for Punishment

When individuals are convicted of crimes it seems natural and proper that they should receive some sort of punishment. In theory, of course, that need not be the case. It would be possible to have a proceeding to assess the facts of a case, determine guilt, but then conclude proceedings with no further action. The mere identification of the responsible party, and their public exposure, might be deemed a sufficient response. Society is, however, generally not satisfied with discovering who is responsible for criminal acts. Additional action to respond to the crime is considered necessary. (In practice, suspended sentences and sentences of probation often closely resemble a criminal justice process without punishment.) There is a wide range of responses that might, in theory, be made. Offenders can be lectured, tortured, provided with economic incentives to stay out of trouble in the future, executed, publicly humiliated, imprisoned, educated, put to hard labor, deported, or subjected to any of numerous other sanctions.

The range of sanctions incorporated in law is, however, relatively narrow. Moreover, the sanctions *regularly* used by a society is even more circumscribed. This narrow range reflects many factors, including a society's rationales for punishment.

In the context of this discussion a rationale is an underlying reason for a social practice. With regard to punishment, rationales justify the basis for the state's intrusion into the lives of citizens subsequent to conviction for commission of a crime. Rationales for punishment provide the general justification for intrusion and influence which punishments are deemed suitable for particular offenders.

21

There are five main rationales for punishment. These rationales include revenge, retribution, deterrence, incapacitation, and rehabilitation. Although we can distinguish between them, punishments imposed to satisfy one rationale may also help achieve objectives associated with other rationales. This will become more evident as we discuss each rationale in turn.

Rationales for punishment can be classified into two general categories. *Backward-looking* rationales are those which are concerned solely with a morally proper response to an offense. Both retribution and revenge fall into this category and are past-oriented in the sense that the nature of the response to crime is typically based on the character of the offense, a past event. An offender receives a punishment that is suited to the offense perpetrated.

Forward-looking, or utilitarian, rationales are concerned with future crimes, either those of the offender or those of other individuals. Deterrence, incapacitation, and rehabilitation are utilitarian rationales which view punishment as a device to minimize the likelihood of future offenses. Under this perspective, a serious crime might be met with a relatively minor sanction if it is believed that a gentle punishment is all that is required to prevent future crimes. The relatively mild punishments accorded many white collar offenders is a good example of this kind of sentencing.

▦ Revenge

Perhaps the most fundamental rationale is *revenge*. Revenge refers to the punishment of offenders in order to avenge the criminal act of an offender. Although the term "getting even" is sometimes applied to revenge, "getting back" is probably a more accurate term. Getting even implies a balancing of the ledger, equal harm returned for the initial harm done. Such constraints do not apply to revenge. The infliction of harm on an offender need not be merely to the extent of the harm associated with the offender's crimes. The harm of a revenge-based punishment may be well in excess of the harm created by the original offense. In accord with the lack of measured commensurability, revenge is generally associated with an emotional, unrestrained response, free from well-defined legal constraints and limits. In Emile Durkheim's view "[P]unishment consists of a passionate reaction. This character is especially evident in less cultivated societies. In effect, primitive peoples punish for the sake of punishing, making the culpable suffer particularly for the sake of making him suffer".[3] With revenge the passions drive the punitive response. This occurs without particular regard for instrumental objectives, such as the effect of the punishment on the offender's future character and actions.

▨ *Retribution*

Retribution is fundamentally a moral rationale for punishment. It justifies punishment because morality demands that the harm perpetrated by the criminal be offset by harm imposed on the offender through punishment. The offender should be punished not because it will scare other potential offenders, nor because it may have a rehabilitative effect on the criminal, but because it is the morally correct social response. Kant argued that the imposition of punishment is necessary to restore the moral balance in the universe, a balance that is upset by the offender's act.[4] Others point out that punishment provides satisfaction to those victimized by the crime or that punishment annuls the offensive act.[5]

Retribution is often confused with revenge, in large part because both are concerned primarily with providing punishments that derive their form and force from an already transpired event, the crime. Like revenge, the retributive rationale is not concerned with the impact of punishment on the offender's future behavior or on the future behavior of others. Unlike revenge, however, retributive sanctions attempt to match the severity of the punishment to the seriousness of the crime. Passions alone cannot determine this match, and often carefully specified rules govern the kinds of punishments that may be imposed for various offenses. The Biblical "eye for an eye . . . and tooth for a tooth" is a retributive response because it places limits on the kinds of punishment that can be imposed. The "eye for an eye" rationale is usually cited as an example of a harsh approach to punishment, but in fact it is less harsh than revenge-based systems which do not rule out "two eyes for an eye" forms of punishment.

Modern expressions of retribution generally do not rely upon Biblical guidance, but do reflect an interest in matching the severity of the punishment to the seriousness of the crime. Recent theoretical work on punishment has attempted to address the issue of measuring the seriousness of crime as an approach to establishing appropriate punishments.[6] In addition, during the recent movement to develop and implement determinate sentencing systems many states have invested significant resources into trying to determine the proper match between crime and punishment. In the absence of a single authoritative source for guidance, this matter is not easily decided. The adoption of the "just deserts" model of punishment, about which more will be said later, has led to energetic debate over the nature of this matching process.

As might be expected, ideological considerations influence what is regarded as the proper punishment match for various crimes. Furthermore, punishment based solely on retribution is not supposed to reflect other interests or objectives. In practice, however, policymakers are seldom concerned with a single objective. They may be strongly interested in giving the offender what he or she deserves but likely are also interested in other objectives, such as deterrence.

Deterrence

There are a number of rationales for punishment that focus heavily on future outcomes rather than past crimes. Perhaps the most well-known of these is deterrence. Punishments based upon deterrence are designed to create fear of future punishment in offenders or would-be offenders. *Specific deterrence* refers to deterring a convicted offender who considers the painfulness of the punishment he or she has experienced, decides to avoid additional punishments in the future, and thus refrains from future involvement in crime. *General deterrence* refers to deterring individuals other than the offender. These others learn about the punishment of the offender and experience fear that such suffering might befall them if they engage in criminal conduct. In both cases it is fear of future suffering that motivates rational, free-acting citizens to decide to avoid involvement in crime.

With deterrence, the appropriate magnitude and nature of the punishment to be imposed does not depend solely on the nature of the offense but on what is required to achieve deterrent effects. An individual may commit a serious crime but feel so badly about his or her act as to require only a modest sanction to assure that no further crimes will be committed. For instance, homicide offenders who kill family members as a result of family-related problems are generally not likely to kill again and, thus, may not require severe fear-producing sanctions to create motivation to abstain from future involvement in crime. On the other hand, a career shoplifter, whose individual offenses are relatively minor, may require severe punishment to dissuade the offender from continuing his or her career in crime.

Incapacitation

Another important future-oriented rationale is *incapacitation*. This involves disabling the offender so that even should the offender desire to commit additional offenses he or she is prevented from doing so. Imprisonment is the most obvious modern method for incapacitation. Historically there have been other prominent methods. Exile of offenders out of communities and nations was one popular approach to isolating the offender from the citizens. Cutting off body parts, such as the hands of a pickpocket, was another incapacitative method. In recent times castration has been proposed as a method for incapacitating rapists.

Incapacitation is an attractive rationale for punishment because it requires little understanding of why individuals commit crimes. Its focus is generally on physically disabling the offender. Enthusiasts of incapacitation do not have to be concerned with the social conditions that led to an offender's involvement in crime, why the individual freely elected to commit crimes, or what psychological processes operate in the minds of criminals. Of course, incapacitative punishments may also be attractive because many such sanctions are harsh and thus would seem to have potential general deterrent capabilities. As will become evident, incapacitation is currently quite popular as a rationale for punishment, and many of the problems discussed in this book are at least partially the result of vigorous use of incapacitative punitive strategies.

There are two important variations on the incapacitative theme. Collective incapacitation refers to sanctions applied to offenders without regard to their personal characteristics. For instance, all offenders in specific crime categories, such as violent felons, might receive lengthy prison sentences. It would not matter whether an offender had an alcohol problem, had family ties in the community, or was a high school graduate. Being a violent felon would be sufficient to qualify for a lengthy prison sentence.

Selective incapacitation refers to incapacitation of special groups of individuals who have been identified as high risk offenders. Some research has shown, for instance, that robbers with a previous record of incarceration, history of drug use, *and* prior conviction for robbery have an increased probability of recidivating subsequent to release from custody.[7] Under a strategy of selective incapacitation individuals possessing these features would be selected for longer sentences than would individuals convicted of the same crimes who had no previous history of conviction, drug use, or imprisonment. Unlike the retributivist rationale, the purpose here is to reduce the number of offenses committed in the future by the offender. The moral concerns associated with retributivism are not as important as the reduction of future victimization.

Rehabilitation

The final major rationale for punishment is *rehabilitation*. This rationale focuses on modification of the offender so as to reduce the individual's inclination to return to further criminal involvement. The focus is on the individual offender, and in this respect it is similar to specific deterrence. It differs from specific deterrence in that the rehabilitated offender is not kept from further criminality merely by fear, but by modifications in the individual's character such that crime appears as a morally unacceptable or practically undesirable option. A rehabilitated offender may be one who has overcome substance abuse problems, a shortage of self-esteem, inadequate educational preparation, deficient social skills, or barren occupational prospects. This might be accomplished through a variety of educational, occupational, counseling, substance abuse, or other programs. Of course, if an individual does manage to avoid further involvement with the law it is not always easy to determine if rehabilitation or special deterrence is responsible.

As is the case for other future-oriented rationales, under the rehabilitative rationale the punishment deemed appropriate for a particular offender will have less to do with the nature of the offense than with what is perceived to be necessary to prevent future involvement in crime. This means paying careful attention to the characteristics of the offender, for example, family background, educational experience, occupational history, previous criminal activity, psychological adjustment, economic status. Depending on these attributes, an offender might receive a more lenient or more severe sanction than would otherwise be imposed if the seriousness of the crime were the sole basis for the sentence.

During the past 15 years rehabilitation has been largely abandoned in the major reforms overtaking the correctional system. For a major part of the twentieth century rehabilitation was given at least lip service as a legitimate and important goal of punishment. The shift to the past-oriented retributively based just deserts model of punishment has to no small extent displaced rehabilitation-based punitive strategies.

▨ *Rationales for Punishment: Summary*

The most important modern rationales for punishment are retribution, deterrence, incapacitation, and rehabilitation. The first three have lengthy histories of use, while rehabilitation is a historically recent rationale. In practice, and as we will see in future chapters, when considering the appropriate punishment for criminals, citizens generally rely on more than a single rationale to justify punishment.

In view of the enormous resources committed to punishment, it is important to have a sense of whether punishment is having the desired effects. Of the four important modern rationales, retribution seems least suitable for empirical evaluation. Retribution is concerned with a measured return of punishment for the harm created by a crime. How much punishment is enough punishment to achieve this measured return is ultimately a moral question. Deterrence, incapacitation, and rehabilitation, on the other hand, are somewhat different. Although the task is complicated, many analysts believe that it is possible to measure whether punishment deters, incapacitates or rehabilitates. The criminological literature contains thousands of studies on such effects. We will look further at the results of such studies in future chapters.

Theory, Ideology, and Punishment

In this chapter we have attempted to accomplish three main objectives. First, we discussed theory and how it makes it possible for us to understand a world comprised of several layers of reality. Theory helps us to classify and organize the world we encounter, to interpret events that would be otherwise unintelligible, and to devise plans of action to respond to situations. Second, we considered ideology. Ideology, the more or less integrated belief systems which represent particular views of the world, is both an expression of and instrument for the further development of theories of how the world operates. Moreover, rationales for punishment reflect ideologies directly, and theories more indirectly. Finally, we discussed the major rationales for punishment.

Before concluding this chapter, a brief word on the relationship between ideology, theory, rationales for punishment, and punishments themselves is in order. Figure 2-3 presents a graphic representation of this relationship. Although this representation is an oversimplification, it is useful in showing how ideology and theory influence the social response to crime. The offense example used is robbery, and the figure shows how the various ideologies may lead to different theories of human behavior, rationales for punishment, and actual punishment decisions. In reality, of course, the causal process is not so cleanly linear. Theories of human behavior, for instance, may influence the selection of ideology. What can be seen from this example, however, is that ideology, theory, rationales for punishment, and punishments themselves are linked together.

Figure 2-3

Ideology, Theory, and Rationales for Punishment: Robbery, Retribution, and Rehabilitation

Offense: Robbery

IDEOLOGY	THEORY of BEHAVIOR	RATIONALE for PUNISHMENT	PUNISHMENT
Conservative	• Free will • Rationality	• Retribution	• Lengthy prison term • No parole
Liberal	Mixture: • Social forces • Free will	• Rehabilitation	• Prison with rehabilitative programs • Parole
Radical	• Socio-political conditions determine behavior	• None—reform law and society	• None

The importance of theory in general, and ideology more specifically, simply cannot be ignored in efforts to come to grips with the debilitating problems currently confronting the correctional system. Practices which have led to these problems, as well as solutions devised to address the difficulties, reflect a variety of theories and ideologies which may or may not do a good job of accurately identifying and isolating current conditions. Thus it is crucial that a sensitivity to these ideologies be maintained as we examine the various correctional dilemmas. Failure to adopt this critical posture will result in a mechanical approach to the issues which essentially limits our capacity to think creatively about correctional problems and potential remedies.

Notes

[1]United States Attorney General's Task Force on Violent Crime (1981) *Attorney General's Task Force on Violent Crime: Final Report*, Washington, DC: Government Printing Office.

[2]Beccaria, Cesare (1963) *On Crimes and Punishments* (orig. 1764) trans. H. Paolucci, New York: Bobbs-Merrill Co., Inc.

[3]Durkheim, Emile (1964) *The Division of Labor in Society*. New York: The Free Press, pp. 85-86.

[4]Kant, Immanuel (1965) *The Metaphysical Elements of Justice*, trans. John Ladd, New York: Bobbs-Merrill.

[5]Cottingham, John (1979) "Varieties of retribution," *Philosophical Quarterly* 238.

[6]E.g., von Hirsch, Andrew (1976) *Doing Justice: The Choice of Punishments*, New York: Hill and Wang; von Hirsch, Andrew (1985) *Past or Future Crimes: Deservedness and Dangerousness in the Sentencing of Criminals*, New Brunswick, NJ: Rutgers University Press.

[7]Greenwood, Peter (1982) *Selective Incapacitation*, Santa Monica, CA: Rand Corporation.

3

Overcrowding: A Modern Correctional Nightmare

Perhaps the most consistently visible item in the media regarding American prisons is the fact that they are endemically overcrowded. News stories on crowding are numerous and include accounts of inmates sleeping on floors, inmate misbehavior made possible by staff shortages, early release of inmates to relieve crowding, and packed local jails refusing to continue to hold inmates awaiting transfer to crowded state prisons. Crowding in a number of state prisons is so severe that some state prison convicts never make it to state prison.

> Dennis Allen Huff of Hurst [Texas] served only 11 months of his three four-year concurrent state prison sentences for burglary, forgery, and possession of a controlled substance—and he never left Tarrant County. Huff is but one of hundreds of state prisoners who have been granted "parole in absentia": a safety valve to relieve pressure on a prison system so crowded that critics say it no longer works.[1]

Whatever the benefits of doing time in state prison might be, Mr. Huff was never provided with the opportunity to experience them. Mr. Huff is far from alone.

Even when inmates do make it to state prison, it is not unusual for them to serve relatively small percentages of their potential maximum sentence. A study of sentences for state felony offenders found that murderers, rapists, robbers, and those convicted of aggravated assault served less than 45 percent of their potential maximum sentence.[2] A study of Florida, one of the states most afflicted with crowding, found that the average percentage of sentences served declined from 52.8 percent in 1987 to only 32.7 percent in 1990.[3] Data from an analysis of federal pris-

31

ons provide further confirmation that only rarely do inmates serve out their entire potential sentence.[4] Crowding has played an increasingly important role in the shortening of sentences for incarcerated offenders.

These kinds of difficulties are being encountered in states across the nation, and there appears to be little immediate prospect of relief. The number of inmates in state and federal prisons reached 883,593 at the beginning of 1993, a 7.2 percent increase over the previous year. The additional 59,460 prisoners pushed the number of inmates per capita to a record high 329 prisoners per 100,000 citizens.[5] Institutional crowding represents perhaps the most serious direct threat to the mission of the correctional system. As we will see, it has potential consequences for the ability of wardens to maintain institutional order, the capacity of the system to rehabilitate offenders, the creation of deterrent and incapacitative effects, and the effectiveness with which prisons are able to dispense the appropriate measure of retributively-based punishment. In this chapter we will discuss crowding in the state and federal systems, consider the situation in both prisons and jails, examine the causes of overcrowding, examine crowding in historical perspective, look at the effects of crowding, and briefly look at the political obstacles to finding solutions. We begin with an examination of the concept of penal overcrowding.

What Is Penal Overcrowding?

In very general terms, crowding refers to filling a structure, such as a room or building, beyond what it can accommodate. A classroom with 30 desks but holding 45 students, 15 of whom must sit on the floor, would be regarded as overcrowded. We have all been on buses or in restaurants that we have viewed as overcrowded. One key feature of an overcrowded situation is that the structure can physically hold the number of individuals, but somehow the manner in which they are held violates our sense of what is appropriate. The social context often determines exactly what this sense is.

For instance, part of the charm of some environments is that they are densely populated. The excitement of a popular discotheque is that it is packed with gyrating dancers. If you were to arrive at a highly touted disco only to find that there was more than ample space to dance without running the risk of jostling other dancers you might be disappointed that the spot was not all that popular after all, and thus you might question the attractiveness of the place, and the merit in your being there. A party at someone's house that is not packed with people might be regarded as a failure, even if the social density of the party was well beyond what would be comfortable in other contexts (e.g., a quiet night at home, a normal day at work).

The main point is that the notion of overcrowding is a social, not a mathematical, concept. In Japan subway packers physically cram riders into subway cars to maximize the number of riders transported on each trip. Such a practice would be unthinkable in American culture, where values of personal privacy and appropriate social and physical distance need not be responsive to the crowded conditions of a geographically small but densely populated country such as Japan. Highways into New York City will be viewed as overcrowded by a newly arrived midwesterner from a small town. Native New Yorkers will not find such conditions to represent overcrowding; they are merely how things work at rush hour.

Thus, although overcrowding does involve physical capacity and numbers of occupants, the ratio of capacity to occupants that represents overcrowding is socially determined. This principle certainly applies to prisons and jails. Although prisons and jails are residential institutions, they differ in many ways from other similar institutions, such as houses, apartments, and hotels. Most importantly they differ in the types of occupants they accommodate, and the reasons why the occupants are in such facilities. The fact that prison inmates are convicted criminals institutionalized to be punished makes us less concerned that conventional standards for personal space and privacy are not observed. The American Correctional Association standard of not less than 60 square feet of floor area for inmates spending no more than ten hours per day in their cells is very little personal space by contemporary standards. Nonetheless, in practice many jurisdictions now place two inmates in such space. Many citizens are unwilling to define such conditions as overcrowded because discomfort is thought to be part of the nature of punishment. The same can be said about inmates sleeping on mattresses in corridors, another practice devised to handle too many inmates confined in too little space. There are other institutional environments within which limited personal space is regarded as acceptable, college dormitories and military quarters being among the most common examples.

Nonetheless, there is some point beyond which virtually all of us would be willing to agree conditions are overcrowded. The American Correctional Association has promulgated standards for inmate living space. Multiple standards for determining institutional capacity have been identified in government documents and reports. Moreover, during the last two decades the courts have become ever more willing to become involved in specifying how much occupancy represents overcrowded occupancy. Thus, although what constitutes crowding is a conceptual matter, and although citizens may differ on how much occupancy represents overcrowding, a number of standards have now been articulated that have a significant influence on the operation and effectiveness of the correctional system.

In order to make a determination that a facility is overcrowded, a formal standard for facility capacity must be operationalized. Again, this is no different than the process for other kinds of structures. Ballrooms and restaurants, for instance, commonly have a rated capacity and typically display signs specifying that capacity. There are several major kinds of capacity ratings used in corrections. *Rated capacity* is the capacity (in inmates or beds) that is determined by a rating official. The number of prisoners that can be handled based upon the staff size, program availability, and institutional services offered is *operational capacity*. *Design capacity* is the number of institutional residents for whom facility designers and architects created the institution.[6] As might be expected, these methods for rating capacity yield different results. Measures of overcrowding will, therefore, be influenced by the rating system used.

The capacity rating method used will heavily influence the exposure of a facility to formal legal liability. Moreover, there are political reasons why some methods are favored over others. A jurisdiction which has just revised its criminal code to increase sentence lengths, and which thus is incarcerating greater numbers of prisoners in its institutions, will be more receptive to the most generous capacity rating system. Use of such a system will make it possible to claim that the state is getting tougher on crime, but that its facilities are not overcrowded. In fact, the federal government is now considering revising its current rating method in an effort to slash the cost of constructing new facilities to handle projected inmate populations through the remainder of the 1990s.[7]

It is not difficult to see how ideology is related to standards for crowding. Conservatives tend to be more interested in the punitive aspect of criminal sanctions than are liberals. Consequently, they are likely to be more tolerant of uncomfortable prison living conditions and, thus, probably more willing to use the operational capacity rating system. Liberals, who typically have more interest in the rehabilitative component of punishment, are likely to regard high population density as antithetical to establishment of an effective rehabilitative environment. They will not be enthusiastic about capacity ratings that permit higher population densities and likely will prefer the design capacity system.

To some extent the concept of overcrowding may obscure the problems associated with various levels of population density. Debate over what constitutes unreasonable occupancy may deflect attention away from the issues associated with various occupancy levels, whether or not such levels represent overcrowding. From a liberal political point of view, a population density of less than 60 square feet per inmate may represent overcrowding, while those sympathetic to conservative perspectives may not regard it in the same light. But irrespective of the dispute over labeling the density level, various levels may nonetheless be associated with different levels of social disruption within the institution (for example, assaults and disciplinary infractions). Although the political and legal questions regarding what constitutes overcrowding are important, a prison that exceeds the density level associated with high rates of assault will experience such assaults whether or not the institution is labeled as overcrowded. Energetic and visible debate over the definitional issue may thus divert attention away from the effects of population density in penal institutions.

From an analytic perspective, it may be more reasonable to view penal institutions as occupying points on a population density continuum rather than as either overcrowded or not overcrowded. Analysis of the effects of various levels of population density does not require that penal institutions be dichotomized into crowded and non-crowded facilities. From a public policy perspective, however, it is difficult to establish practices to minimize the ill effects of high population density without establishing at least a working definition of overcrowding. The promulgation of such standards provides certainty to correctional officials seeking to operate facilities within the limits of the Eighth Amendment protection against cruel and unusual punishment. It also provides guidance to courts attempting to examine lawsuits over conditions of confinement.

It is important to understand that the debate over the amount of population density permissible under various ideological conceptions of punishment is a somewhat different debate than that over the nature of the effects of various levels of population density. One might acknowledge that the probability of institutional disturbances increases with densities in excess of 60 square feet, but argue that such densities are acceptable in light of what punishment for commission of a crime entails.

One final point merits mention before turning to consideration of crowding in state prisons. The term "crowding" is sometimes distinguished from "overcrowding," while at other times the two terms are used interchangeably. Crowding can be regarded as a population density that exceeds what is desirable or intended, but which nonetheless falls within what is tolerable. Overcrowding may refer to densities that are beyond what is tolerable. In the discussion which follows, however, we will not distinguish between the two terms.

State Prisons

In 1960 there were about 200,000 individuals held in state prisons. That number decreased to less than 190,000 in 1970, then increased to about 300,000 in 1980.[8] Thus the overall population increase during the sixties and seventies was about 50 percent.

The growth in state prison populations during the last decade has been especially dramatic. At the beginning of 1990 there were 650,883 inmates in state prisons. This represents an increase of almost 13 percent over the previous year[9] and double the inmate count for 1980.[10] Contrary to popular opinion, this increase has not merely been fueled by increases in the crime rate. During the first half of the decade official crime rates actually decreased. In 1980 the Uniform Crime Reports Crime Index rate per 100,000 population was 5,521. By 1985 it had slipped to 5,206, a decrease of about 6 percent.[11] Nonetheless, prison populations increased substantially during this period.[12] From 1980 through 1985 the state prison population increased by almost 50 percent. At the beginning of 1993 state prisons held 803,334 inmates.[13]

Of course, the raw population figures are somewhat deceiving. The population of the United States has been steadily increasing. The ratio of state prison inmates to population takes this population growth into consideration. At the beginning of 1990 the number of state prison inmates per 100,000 population was 255, an increase of almost 200 percent over the 86.2 rate for 1971, and an increase of 123 percent over the figure for 1980.[14] As we have already seen, the rate has continued to rise and now exceeds 300 per 100,000 population.

Increases in prison populations do not necessarily mean increases in crowding. In fact, institutional capacity has increased substantially during the past decade. Between 1979 and 1984, 138 new state prisons were opened. This new space, in addition to renovations of existing facilities, represented a 29 percent increase in facility space. Unfortunately, this increase was outstripped by a 45 percent increase in inmates during the same period.[15]

This pattern continued through the second half of the 1980s. In 1989 alone, 34 states added almost 18,000 new beds to their systems.[16] At the beginning of 1990, 171,000 new beds were either under construction or in the planning stages.[17] Such additions ultimately will bring prison space to almost 800,000 beds. Data released in 1992 show that the design capacity of state prisons increased 52 percent from 1984 to 1990, while rated capacity increased by 61 percent. Nonetheless, the 67 percent increase in inmates during this time period outstrips these facility capacity increases.[18]

Additional evidence indicates that capacity increases have not solved the overcrowding problem. At the beginning of 1990, 39 states reported operating at 100 percent or more of their *most liberal* population capacity rating.[19] Thirty-eight jurisdictions were under court order regarding conditions of confinement, typically related to overcrowding.[20] More than 18,000 state prisoners were being held in local jails because of the unavailability of space in state prisons.[21] Some states, such as Texas, were engaged in lawsuits filed by counties seeking compensation for state prisoners left in their jails.[22] About 30 percent of the states had court appointed monitors, masters, overseers, or court order compliance coordinators at the beginning of 1990.[23]

Grim as this overall picture of state prisons is, many individual states are confronting far more serious levels of difficulty. Massachusetts, for instance, reported being at almost 170 percent of its highest capacity rating at the beginning of 1990. New York was at 156 percent, Ohio at 154 percent, Nebraska at 146 percent, and Indiana at 136 percent. Using the lowest capacity rating system, California and Colorado were at 181 percent and 195 percent respectively.[24] (In fact, California has now topped the 100,000 inmate mark and currently confines more citizens than any country in the western world, excepting the United States of course.[25]) Clearly the problem is not limited to any one region of the country. Projections for the 1990s provide little reason to think the overcrowding problem in state prisons will soon abate.

Federal Prisons

The federal prison system is experiencing problems at least as serious as those being endured by the states. From 1950 to 1980 the average annual increase in the inmate population in the federal system was less than 1.5 percent. In those 30 years the population increased only about 40 percent. Recent years have seen a dramatic shift in this modest trend.

In 1980 the federal prison population was 24,162 and was operating at only 1 percent over capacity[26]. At the beginning of the current decade the federal prison population had more than doubled, reaching 54,644 inmates. This figure does not include another 5,717 inmates being held in local jails.[27] Although the federal system did expand its capacity during the 1980s, the percent over design capacity figure rose from 1 percent to almost 70 percent by the beginning of the 1990s.[28] Problems continue as the federal system now confines a record high 80,259 inmates.[29]

Current plans are for the federal system to expand its capacity to 64,000 by 1995. Obviously, this is not enough. This expansion will cost the taxpayer close to two billion dollars. Despite this massive expenditure, the Bureau of Prisons estimates that the expansion will still leave the system operating at 30 percent over capacity[30]. Of course, since previous population estimates have been too conservative, the population projections upon which 1995 overcrowding is based also may be too conservative. A recent federal study found that 967 new bedspaces will be needed *weekly* to keep pace with the growth in inmates in federal and state prisons.

Jails

Scrutiny of the historical experience with incarcerative institutions reveals that jails, rather than prisons, have often been the most ill-equipped facilities. Designed to hold prisoners only while awaiting trial or serving very short sentences, public funds have sparingly been committed to maintenance of adequate conditions within these institutions. The modern experience mirrors this history in many ways.

The 1989 Survey of Inmates in Local Jails collected data on a nationally representative sample of jail inmates. This recently published survey reveals that in 1989 about 400,000 inmates were being held in American jails. This represents an increase of more than 40 percent over the 1983 population[31]. Although jail capacity has also been increasing in the last few years, like prisons it has not been able to keep pace with population increases. Jail bedspace increased 30 percent from 1983 to 1988, not enough to keep pace with the population increase.[32] From 1988 through 1989 jail capacity increased only half as much as jail populations.[33]

More recent data from the Bureau of Justice Statistics indicate that at midyear of 1991, 426,479 inmates were being held in local jails. This figure represents an increase of 5.2 percent over midyear 1990 and makes clear that the upward spiral in the jail population is continuing into the 1990s.[34]

As was the case for prisons, local conditions are often much worse than the national average. An analysis of the largest 25 U.S. jails revealed that almost 70 percent were at or above capacity.[35] Some of these large jails, such as the one in Orange County, California, have long traditions of jail overcrowding. The Orange County jail has been the target of legal action since 1975 when the ACLU first filed a lawsuit. A court order was imposed in 1978 to force alleviation of overcrowded conditions. Adequate action had not been taken by 1985; thus a fine of $50,000 was levied against the Board of Supervisors, and a population cap was imposed. Although the court order was lifted in 1988, the population cap remains in effect.[36]

Court orders are far from rare. Even in the mid-1980s more than a fifth of the country's largest jails were under court order to reduce overcrowding.[37] A survey of 268 jail managers revealed that 38 percent of their facilities were under court orders regarding unconstitutional conditions of confinement most typically related to overcrowding.[38] This is not surprising in light of the fact that 55 percent of the facilities hold populations in excess of their rated capacity.[39] As might be expected, the largest cities were beset by the most significant crowding difficulties.[40]

Although in some jurisdictions levels of crowding are less than what can be found in state prisons, in some respects merely approaching facility capacity creates more problems for jails than prison managers. Because inmates are confined for relatively short periods of time, jails experience much higher turnover rates than prisons. In addition, they handle a much wider range of offenders. While prisons are typically classified as maximum, medium, or minimum security facilities, and therefore confine relatively narrow ranges of offender types within each institution, jails confine offenders ranging from murderers to traffic violators. Confining such diverse kinds of prisoners requires more space for intra-institutional inmate segregation. A shortage of space severely restricts the ability of jails to properly segregate such radically different offender types. As Harry Allen and Clifford Simonsen note, "Most jail administrators acknowledge that all flexibility in a jail, in regard to classification and housing, is lost when the jail is at 90 percent of capacity."[41]

In addition to prisoners serving short terms and inmates awaiting trial, jails have recently begun to hold increasing numbers of inmates awaiting transfer to state prisons. At the beginning of the 1990s more than 6,400 state prison inmates were being held in jails because crowding in state prisons made it impossible for the state systems to accommodate them.[42] At the beginning of 1992 this figure increased to more than 12,000 inmates.[43] This national problem has resulted in a variety of efforts to cope with the back-up. A sheriff in Massachusetts moved 15 inmates out of his overcrowded jail into the local National Guard Armory. Although the National Guard protested the action, the sheriff insisted that his action was justified by a seventeenth century law authorizing the seizure of property whenever a serious danger to public peace exists.[44] During the summer of 1991 the overcrowded jail in Fort Worth, Texas simply stopped accepting prisoners when the population exceeded its capacity.[45] focus 3-1 describes another response to the problem of prison inmates backed up in local jails.

Focus 3-1
Counties vs. the State: Jail Litigation in Texas

In Texas 12 counties filed suit against the state, demanding compensation for the costs of maintaining state prison inmates in local jails. These counties claimed to be confining about 6,000 inmates who had been sentenced to state prison. In 1990 the court ruled that the state must reimburse these counties for the costs of the state prisoners held in local facilities. The Travis County District judge ruled that a fee of $40 per day for each inmate must be paid by the state to the counties to defray the costs of maintaining prison inmates in local jails. Nueces County Attorney Carlos Valdez said, "We're losing money paying for the state's responsibilities.

This is not like shifting responsibility to the state. We're just asking them to take responsibility for what is legally theirs."

The fees are retroactive and extend back to cover inmates held from September 1987 to the present. According to some estimates, the court ruling could cost the state more than $100 million. Assistant Attorney General Robert Ozer, who represented the state in the lawsuit, insisted, "We don't have the money." Moreover, a spokesman for the state argued that such payments would actually make the jail crowding problem worse. "This order is going to aggravate the problem of overcrowded jails because counties are going to be making money off this. They'll be making $40 a day when it costs $12 a day. It encourages them [the counties] to put them in jail rather than look for less expensive alternatives."[46]

Not all counties involved in the suit have agreed to the terms of the settlement. The governor was forced to get involved in an effort to draft a compromise that would satisfy counties reluctant to agree to drop the litigation in exchange for the state's compensation plan.[47]

An April 1, 1991 U.S. Supreme Court decision further extended the state's responsibility. The ruling required the state "to deposit $750,000 in a special fund to pay Harris County for the costs of relocating jail inmates. The state must reimburse the county because approximately 2,000 jail inmates are awaiting transfer to the state prison system, which is operating under a court-ordered population ceiling."[48] The Governor complied with the order, but only under protest.

Causes of Institutional Crowding

Penal analysts have argued that a number of factors account for the increase in crowding. Most of these explanations focus on the growth in the inmate population rather than on the failure to allocate adequate resources to create new facility space.

Perhaps the most well-publicized explanation is that an increase in crime has resulted in more arrests and convictions and thus an increase in the institutionalized population. In fact, the FBI's Uniform Crime Reports does show an increase in crime from 1980 through the end of 1990. However, in light of the fact that the prison population increased by 134 percent during this period,[49] it is surprising that the number of Crime Index offenses known to police increased only about 7 percent.

Of course, it must be remembered that the numbers forming the basis for the percentages is much larger for crimes known to police. There were more than 14 million Index crimes in 1990[50] compared to only about 1 million inmates in prisons and jails. A brief example will illustrate the importance of this fact.

Suppose that in 1992 there were 10 inmates in the prison system, and that the number of crimes committed in 1992 was 1,000. For purposes of simplicity let us assume that each crime is committed by a different offender and that 20 percent of criminals end up in prison for their crimes. In 1993 the number of crimes increases only 5 percent. Five percent of 1,000 is 50; 50 crimes committed by 50 individuals. Because we have agreed that 20 percent of criminals end up in prison, this means that 10 individuals are sent to prison in 1992 (50 individuals x .20 = 10). Adding these 10 convicts to the 10 already in prison results in a total of 20 inmates, a 100 percent increase in the prison population in a single year. This increase is the result of a mere 5 percent increase in the number of crimes.

This simple example demonstrates how even a small percentage increase in crimes may result in a large percentage increase in the prison population. Because the numerical bases on which the respective percentages are calculated differ so greatly in magnitude, a small percentage increase in crimes may result in a very large percentage increase in the prison population. Thus it is somewhat deceptive to counterpose the small increase in total crimes against the enormous increase in prison inmates. A better measure is the ratio of crimes per 100 population against the number of inmates per 100 crimes. Graphically represented (Figure 3-1) this reveals that as crime fell during the first half of the 1980s, as well as when it rose during the second half, the number of inmates per 100 crimes increased faster than the crime rate. In other words, irrespective of the movement of crime rates during the past decade, the number of inmates per 100 crimes has increased. Thus the overall movement of crime rates alone cannot account for swelling prison populations.

Figure 3-1
Crime Rates and Prison Risks: 1960-1985

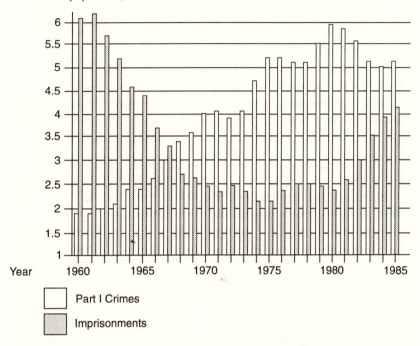

Crimes/100 population; inmates/100 crimes

Part I Crimes

Imprisonments

From: Zedlewski, Edwin W. (1987) "Making Confinement Decisions." National
Institute of Justice — Research in Brief, Washington, D.C.: U.S. Department
of Justice.

Of course, the F.B.I. Crime Index includes large numbers of relatively minor offenses, such as larcenies, which may not be strongly associated with imprisonment for convicted offenders. Examining only violent crimes, however, we find that the number of violent crimes increased more than 20 percent during the 1980s. Thus it is likely that at least some of the increase in inmates is the result of the increase in violent crime.

A related explanation for penal crowding is that prison population increases reflect changes in demographic attributes. That is, an increase in the numbers of citizens who are at the high-risk ages (late teens, early adult) results in more crime, and ultimately greater numbers of prisoners. Although criminologists generally acknowledge that shifts in the population age structure have had an impact on the movement of crime rates, it is not completely clear what effect this relationship has had on incarceration rates. A study conducted in Louisiana, for instance, failed to find evidence that increases in the state prison population could be traced to age shifts. The authors of the study pointed instead to changes in behavior of justice-system decisionmakers and the enactment of more severe penal laws as causes of Louisiana's population increase.[51]

Shifts in sentencing practices may be especially important. This explanation holds that the general shift toward conservative public policy in the 1980s, with its renewed interest in enhanced punishments for crimes, accounts for increased numbers of offenders being sent to prison. In fact, a survey of state correctional officials found that increased public desire for law and order was rated as the most significant cause of penal overcrowding. Longer minimum sentences was ranked second.[52]

The shift in sentencing practices is exemplified by the processing of drug offenders. Almost 80 percent of new admissions to the federal system between fall 1986 and fall 1988 were for drug offenses. The number of inmates incarcerated for non-drug crimes increased only 5 percent during this period as compared to a 31 percent increase in the population of drug offenders.[53] Although it can be argued that at least some kinds of drug law violations have increased, this population increase is in part the result of tougher sentences for federal drug offenders, such as those resulting from the enactment of the Anti-Drug Abuse Act of 1988.[54] About 38 percent of federal inmates are now being held subsequent to conviction for drug violations, a percentage likely to increase if the current trend continues.[55]

Many states experienced similar events. Washington, for instance, experienced a significant increase in felony convictions in general, and drug convictions in particular. Drug convictions skyrocketed 438 percent during the 1980s at the same time that sanctions for such offenses were toughened.[56] The number of individuals imprisoned in either jail or prison for drug offenses in Delaware during the 1980s increased fivefold. In his analysis of the Delaware experience, John O'Connell notes that "trends in the detained and incarcerated drug offenders population shows the special burden on the prison system resulting from changes in drug laws and increased law enforcement. Reductions in the amount of drugs required for mandatory commitment to prison and increases in police manpower have had a significant impact on the prison population, especially since 1985."[57]

The situation for jails is very similar. A report issued by the Bureau of Justice Statistics in the spring of 1991 revealed that "drug offenses accounted for 23 percent of the charges against nearly 400,000 men and women held in local jails in 1989."[58] This represents an increase of more than 150 percent over the 9 percent figure for 1983, when the previous jail survey was conducted by the Bureau. Moreover, more than "40 percent of the 1983-to-1989 rise in the jail population resulted from increases in the number of jail inmates accused or convicted of drug offenses."[59]

Beyond changes in the number of crimes and increased willingness to use imprisonment for certain kinds of offenders, recently amended laws have changed practices for releasing inmates from prison. Backdoor population control mechanisms, such as parole, have a history of effectiveness in helping correctional officials regulate prison populations. New legislation, however, has now extended the minimum percentage of sentence that an inmate must serve before becoming eligible for parole, thereby keeping inmates in longer once they are admitted to the system. In the previously noted survey of correctional officials' views of the causes of crowding, out of 18 causes identified reductions in the granting of parole trailed only desire for law and order and longer minimum sentences.[60]

This has not had altogether happy consequences. In Alabama, for instance, the state passed legislation increasing the percentage of sentence state prisoners must serve before being eligible for release. This modification naturally increased the population pressure in the system and forced the system to find backdoor methods of moving inmates out of the prisons. The organizational adjustment to the new rules had not been anticipated by the legislature, and to some extent this adjustment defeated its objectives.[61] Such adjustments are fairly typical of organizations subjected to pressures that are not manageable using conventional management methods.

Finally, it must also be noted that legislators have lagged behind in their efforts to create space to hold new inmates. It is a politically simple matter to come down hard on crime and to support tough laws and sanctions. It is quite another matter to advocate the enormous expenditures required to *support* tougher measures. A decade of neglect in Texas, for instance, has left the state in a major crisis. The emergency has now resulted in drastic measures. The state house and senate have each approved different bills to create badly needed prison space. While the senate passed a bill approving a $1.1 billion bond package for prison construction, the house bill called for less than half the senate amount.[62] Although the final bill mirrored the senate figure, both initial versions called for extraordinary expenditures as part of a desperate effort to get a grip on the state's prison crisis. The political enthusiasm for cracking down on crime, coupled with a typical political reluctance to provide resources to manage the increased inmate flow, has left the state with an enormous problem. Needless to point out, Texas is far from alone. A survey of state correctional budget requests for 1991-1992 revealed that the states were requesting a 25 percent increase in total budget for corrections. Funds requested for prison construction exceeded $3.5 billion, with California leading the way with a $1 billion construction budget.[63]

A 1990 plan for the federal system called for doubling the federal system capacity by 1995, at a cost of $1.8 billion.[64] At the state level, facilities under construction or immediately anticipated will increase prison space by about 40 percent. The costs for such construction will run into the billions of dollars.[65] Nobody believes, however, that these planned and in-progress increases will eliminate the crowding problem. Estimates made after the 1990 federal plan was submitted, for instance, concluded that population growth would exceed that upon which the 1990 expansion plan was based.[66] At both the state and federal level these current extraordinary budgetary figures reflect in part the failure of political leadership to commit new resources to the penal system despite enacting changes in law that assured significant increases in prison populations. In light of the extensive historical experience the United States has had with crowding (see Focus 3-2), this lack of consolidated political will is both surprising and troubling.

Thus the movement of crime rates, changes in sentencing laws (especially for drugs), and failure to create more prison space all seem to have contributed to the current overcrowding crisis. As might be expected, there are a number of important potential consequences of crowded penal conditions.

Focus 3-2
Crowding in American Prisons — The Nineteenth-Century Experience

Although we are often tempted to regard ourselves as modern and progressive, a brief look at the nineteenth-century prison experience reveals that we have not come very far in handling at least one major correctional problem—prison crowding. At the very dawn of the American prison system crowded institutions were too often the rule. In Philadelphia, for instance, the inspector of Philadelphia's Walnut Street Jail resigned in frustration over crowded conditions.[67] In New York State, Newgate Prison became overcrowded within a single decade of its opening in 1797. To relieve some of the pressure, Auburn Prison was constructed and began accepting its first inmates in 1816. This merely provided temporary relief, and New York continued to struggle with crowding throughout the nineteenth century.[68]

In the South, states such as Georgia struggled with overcrowded facilities after the Civil War. Georgia tried to solve this problem by leasing out the convicts to private entrepreneurs.[69] This model was followed by other southern states, such as Alabama.[70] In the West, Texas adopted a similar solution.[71] Even Eastern State Penitentiary in Pennsylvania, which was founded on the concept of inmate solitude and contemplation, was forced to abandon the single inmate cell as a result of crowding.[72]

Prison crowding during the nineteenth century was an endemic problem, affecting every region of the growing nation. It is somewhat remarkable that, although two centuries have now passed since the beginning of the American penitentiary era, and despite enormous advances in correctional technology, this difficulty continues to bedevil modern correctional operations.

The Effects of Penal Crowding

Identifying the effects of crowding in the penal setting is a complicated matter. Because so many of the features of prison life differ from conventional life it is not an easy matter to separate those difficulties that derive from crowding from those that result from other conditions. In addition, although it is possible to compare crowded institutions with uncrowded institutions, they often differ in numerous other ways. Crowded prisons may, for instance, tend to hold higher proportions of offenders convicted of violent crimes. Narrowing down the effects of crowding is thus confounded by other variables. Moreover, some of the effects of crowding may not manifest themselves within the institution. The psychological impact of living in crowded conditions may not appear until after the inmate has returned to society and is no longer under careful observation.

In the remainder of this section we will briefly examine the impact of crowding on prison violence and discipline, recidivism, inmate well-being, and early release practices.

Prison Violence and Disciplinary Infractions

Of all the potential consequences of crowding, increased prison violence seems perhaps most unavoidable. Every undergraduate student who takes elementary psychology learns that the behavior of rats changes when they are forced to live in high density population cages. Rats appear to become more aggressive, and have an elevated level of altercations with other rats.[73] In our own personal lives many of us have experienced circumstances where we felt hemmed in by the crush of too many people, such as in a crowded bus, a packed party, or a jammed rest room. And, of course, many of our large cities have the reputation of being crowded as well as generally aggressive and hyperactive places. Although people often visit New York City for pleasure, with few exceptions no one goes there for an atmosphere of relaxed tranquility.

Some analysts argue that crowding creates elevated levels of uncertainty, unpredictability, and interference with goal achievement. This in turn creates heightened anxiety and fear, which lead to acts of aggression.[74] Obie Clayton and Tim Carr examined prison rule infractions, including those involving violence, and found them to be strongly related to crowding.[75] An examination of rates of misconduct and population density in the federal prison system discovered that the most crowded institutions had the highest misconduct rates.[76] A study of the Mississippi prison at Parchman found that inmate-on-inmate assaults decreased when the prison population dropped significantly. Based on their study of six federal prisons the authors concluded that "[i]ncreases in population in prisons where facilities were not increased proportionally were associated with increased death, suicide, disciplinary infractions, and psychiatric commitment rates."[77] Gerald Gaes and W.G. McGuire com-

48

pared inmate age composition and rate of inmate turnover with population density as explanations for prison violence and found that crowding was the most significant factor.[78] In his review of the research on crowding and prison violence, Gerald Gaes concluded that "prisons housing significantly more inmates than a design capacity based on sixty square feet per inmate are likely to have high assault rates."[79]

Of course, most of these studies have been challenged, and not all the research finds overcrowding to be the major factor responsible for increasing rates of prison violence. In his study of the overcrowded Texas penal system, Sheldon Ekland-Olson compared two possible explanations for increases inmate violence: overcrowding and the breakdown in social control. The research used official data on prison homicides, disciplinary and incident reports, field observations, and other data sources. It concluded that both inmate-on-inmate and inmate-on-staff assaults were more heavily influenced by the breakdown in social control subsequent to court-ordered changes in prison conditions and operations than by crowding alone.[80]

Nonetheless, the weight of the current evidence does suggest that prison violence and crowding are related.

▨ Recidivism and Overcrowding

As is well known, recidivism rates for ex-prison inmates are far from what the public would like them to be. In general, although there are some promising exceptions, there appears to be little clear evidence of dramatically consistent effects on recidivism produced by the prison experience. The effectiveness of imprisonment in deterring or rehabilitating depends upon both the integrity and quality of prison programs designed to rehabilitate, as well as on the level of discipline and control achieved in the more punitive aspects of the prison experience. It seems reasonable to consider, therefore, that institutional crowding may well interfere with achievement of both punitive and rehabilitative goals. This is a serious concern because, as Gaes notes, "a cycle of crowding and recidivism would be tantamount to releasing individuals from crowded prisons only to ensure their eventual return to the same or worse conditions."[81]

In fact, the literature on crowding and recidivism is not very substantial. Compared to other aspects of crowding, little research has been conducted. One of the more cited studies examined British prisons and found that crowding and staying out of prison were negatively related.

Furthermore, the authors of this research concluded that this relationship was not likely an artifact of other untested variables. "[I]n view of the high negative correlation between overcrowding and effectiveness, it seems unlikely that this relationship could be explained away by the operation of some third variable. It seems more likely that in some direct way overcrowding produces ineffectiveness."[82]

These findings have been criticized by Gaes, who pointed out that the British study fails to adequately control for variables such as criminal history. The most crowded prisons may be those containing the worst offenders, thus the apparent relationship between crowding and recidivism may actually reflect a relationship between criminal history and recidivism.

Gaes' concerns were addressed in an examination of the relationship between crowding and recidivism using data from the Georgia state prison system.[83] The researchers conducted a two-year follow-up of inmates released from prison, and controlled for variables such as inmate age, prior arrest history, and race. These control variables have been shown in other research to be related to recidivism. The findings of this research revealed that "prison density is a poor predictor of recidivism. The results cast suspicion upon research that suggests prison overcrowding is strongly related to recidivism."[84] The researchers discovered that age, not overcrowding, was more closely related to recidivism. Younger inmates may have higher rates simply because of their incomplete personal maturation.

As it currently stands, despite the paucity of research on crowding and recidivism, and although Gaes made a number of methodological suggestions to improve the research on crowding and recidivism, there has been surprisingly little effort committed toward researching this issue. The mixed nature of the research that does exist does not permit confident assertions about the ultimate impact of crowding on recidivism. In light of the increasingly crowded conditions in the American penal system, and the fact that in the years to come ever-larger numbers of inmates from crowded institutions will be completing their terms and returning to society, it is imperative that this vacuum in our understanding be filled.

Overcrowding and Inmate Well-being

The first studies conducted on the effects of crowded living conditions on physical and mental health were not conducted in prison environments. Some of the earliest research focused on military environments.

I.W. Brewer's study of a 1918 influenza outbreak, for instance, found that as density of beds per unit living space increased, rates of infection also increased.[85] A review of the non-prison literature led Bailus Walker and Theodore Gordon to conclude that "there are data available from which it can be inferred that crowding people into small areas where they are forced to breathe and too often to cough into each other's face favors the transmission of disease-producing organisms because it increases the likelihood of the organisms finding a new person and reduces the distance they—the germs—must travel between persons."[86]

Other non-prison research has suggested that there exists a relationship between stress and physical well-being. Physical responses to stress include a wide range of physical maladies, such as suppression of the immune system, blood pressure variation, and illness (as reflected by sick call records).[87]

There have been a few studies examining various aspects of inmate well-being, including studies of physical health, suicide, and psychological health. A survey of federal prisons discovered that population increases without facility expansion were related to psychiatric commitments. The authors of this study also reported that in the Mississippi state prison inmate population reduction was related to a decline in attempted suicides and self-mutilations.[88]

It is important to remember that, in addition to the fact that the majority of research on crowding and health has not been conducted within the prison setting, there are a number of methodological constraints which limit much of the research that has been conducted in prisons.[89] Controls for variables such as the kinds of inmates held in different facilities have not always been used in the research.

Moreover, the findings of the prison research have not been unequivocal. One relatively recent prison study examined data in a California prison complex. When prison population fluctuation was related to sick call data for the entire complex, evidence emerged that supported the notion that crowding and illness are related. Examination of data at the individual unit level (within the four facility prison complex) did not, however, support the relationship. An analysis of the 1984 Prison Census revealed that suicide rates were highest in densely populated maximum security facilities. Inmate-on-inmate assault rates, however, were highest in the lowest density facilities. The study concludes that "[i]n general, no consistent pattern emerges from these data to indicate that the incidence or prevalence of these negative events increases with greater population densities."[90] Such mixed findings are all too typical of the research on the effects of crowding.

51

Again, because of the increase in crowding and the increase in the number of inmates held in prisons, it is critical that this issue be more closely studied. If a strong relationship exists between crowding and various aspects of physical and mental health, the costs of responding to health problems may eventually dwarf current expenditures. Moreover, the indirect costs of widespread health problems among inmates, such as those associated with lawsuits against the government, may be substantial.

▓▓▓ Overcrowding and Early Release

One of the traditional methods for reducing prison overcrowding has been the "back-door" method of early release on parole. Inmates who have served the minimum percentage of their sentences required by law may be released earlier than they otherwise would, not because it is clear that the inmate has been adequately punished or rehabilitated, but because early release makes room for new inmates. At a time when many states have reduced their reliance on parole, or even eliminated parole altogether, crowding has forced states to adopt other early release methods.

As of 1991, 14 states had emergency release programs, the majority of which were established by state legislatures. Washington, D.C. led all jurisdictions in making use of early release, freeing more than 2,200 inmates prematurely in 1990.[91] In fact, these figures are an underestimate due to the accelerated use of good time possible under determinate sentencing law.[92] Although the early release safety valve clearly has made it possible for states to accommodate thousands of new prisoners they could not otherwise have handled, the public has not always been delighted with the practice. The Willie Horton issue raised during the 1988 Presidential campaign is perhaps the most visible expression of negative public sentiment toward the early release of inmates under any circumstances. George Bush challenged the Democratic candidate from Massachusetts, Michael Dukakis, to explain why Massachusetts released Horton on furlough before the conclusion of his sentence. Horton went to Maryland and committed serious crimes during his furlough. Although furlough is generally not permanent early release, the negative public reaction was based upon a powerful general concern with criminals being released before serving full sentences.

In a Florida case the early release of a state prisoner concluded with the killing of a police officer in Miami and provoked a statewide expression of outrage at the state's early release policy. In the early summer of 1990, a Texas convict released from prison a full year before his parole date shot to death a Houston police officer during a traffic stop.[93] In explaining the release decision, a Texas Board of Pardons and Paroles spokesperson explained, "When the [prison] population approaches the critical point, we begin to review those cases granted tentative parole. Tentative parole, in effect, creates a buffer pool of inmates whose release has been approved by the board."[94] The early release policy was adopted to prevent Texas from exceeding its court-ordered population cap.

The effectiveness of early release in creating new space to handle incoming inmates has not been subjected to thorough rigorous review. When an inmate leaves a prison it is obvious that a space opens up. However, if inmates who are released too early then go on to commit new crimes they would not have committed had they served a full sentence, the net effect in terms of cost savings and even prison crowding may well be obviated. A detailed analysis of the impact of early release was conducted in Illinois. The study looked at more than 21,000 inmates released from prison under the state's early release program. These inmates were released on average about 105 days early, a reduction of about 12 percent of the expected sentence.[95] An examination of the post-release experience of early-release inmates revealed that they did not commit new crimes at a rate higher than that for inmates who served their full terms. When the economic losses sustained by the victims of crime-committing early-releasees were considered, it was still less expensive to release these inmates than it would have been to have them serve their full sentence. Despite these findings supportive of early release, the study author argues that early release is at best a temporary measure, and that there are more productive long-term approaches to addressing prison overcrowding.

The Effects of Overcrowding: Conclusions

Although the effects of overcrowding are varied and potentially dramatic, there has been relatively little effort to estimate the full extent of this impact. As we have seen with prison violence and recidivism, the amount of solid research committed to developing our understanding of the effects of crowding has been disappointingly minimal. Moreover, new hazards are appearing on the horizon. For instance, the National Commission on AIDS has recently concluded that American prisons are not meeting the health and education needs of inmates who have AIDS.

The commission concluded that "no other institution in this society has a higher concentration of people at substantial risk of HIV infection" than prison inmates.[96] AIDS transmission was currently minimal, the Commission acknowledged, although it may be wondered whether transmission rates of the fatal disease will increase as crowding continues unabated. Tuberculosis, which is even more easily transmitted, represents yet another menace associated with overcrowding. In light of the fact that more than 95 percent of inmates are eventually released back into society, both AIDS and TB could become major problems.

Another less visible consequence of overcrowding is the potential for expensive litigation. As conditions in crowded institutions deteriorate, the threat of potentially costly inmate suits against the state may increase. Court rulings nationwide have created a variety of legal obligations to meet basic living standards within penal institutions. Violations of these standards, ever more likely under crowded conditions, may accelerate the pace of lawsuits. A recent Justice Department report has now advised that population caps should be imposed by the courts only as a last resort in meeting crowding-related difficulties. The report cites increasing litigation as one of the major consequences of lower court decisions establishing population caps, and warns penal administrators that signing consent decrees may commit them to performance standards that they cannot meet, thereby exposing them to liability.[97]

As matters currently stand, insufficient effort has been committed to studying the full effects of overcrowding. Both long-standing problems, as well as new difficulties such as AIDS, may have enormous impact on the economic costs of operating the penal system, the incapacitative and deterrent capacity of the penal system, and the effectiveness of the system in rehabilitating offenders. Part of the explanation for this relative lack of research effort undoubtedly involves the methodological difficulties of measuring this impact. Other factors may play a role as well, however. In a political climate where the use of prison is being expanded in a number of offense areas, such as for drug-related crimes, overcrowding is simply going to be a fact of life. The political realities of overcrowding are such that, although political rhetoric contains significant amounts of tough talk, most state legislatures have yet to display the political will to seek out real solutions to crowding, either in the form of the creation of adequate prison capacity or through alternatives to incarceration. As noted earlier, in Texas the state senate passed a bill authorizing creation of 35,000 new beds. The state house, on the other hand, authorized less than half that amount. Although ultimately the larger bill was passed, the lack of firm political consensus reflected by these dramatically different bills reflects the ongoing absence of clear will and direction.

Solving the Overcrowding Crisis

The correctional system has very little control over the flow of inmates into the system. In a sense it has been victimized by decisions, processes, and practices enacted at other points in the criminal justice system process. Nonetheless, the correctional system has not been able to sit back and wait until a foolproof solution to crowding is devised and implemented. It has used every trick at its disposal, including jail backlogging, system expansion, parole, early release, and graduated release.[98] Obviously, none of what has been done thus far has handled the problem, and the dilemma grows worse with each passing month.

One analyst has suggested that there are four common kinds of strategies currently used to address crowding. These include using alternatives to incarceration at more places in the criminal justice process, use of incarceration for only a select group of offenders and persons awaiting trial, increasing the punitive nature of non-incarcerative sanctions, and restructuring the way in which correctional programs are used.[99]

Much of the remainder of this book will discuss potential remedies for crowding and its concomitant effects. In view of the mission of this book, our main focus will be on crowding-reduction strategies that can be adopted within the correctional system. We will not, therefore, commit much discussion to remedies such as fundamental changes in sentencing law or development of mental health and drug treatment facilities that could serve to handle offenders now mired in the correctional system. We will examine alternatives to incarceration such as fines, electronic monitoring, and house arrest. We will discuss new forms of incarceration such as the highly publicized and touted boot camp. We will look at the potential contribution that can be made by the private sector.

One approach to solving crowding, which we will not explore in detail, is massive construction of new facilities. A controversial analysis by Edwin W. Zedlewski concluded that, although imprisonment is expensive, the costs of not imprisoning serious offenders are much greater. He argues that the average imprisoned offender committed 187 crimes per year while on the outside, and that the economic costs associated with such crimes far exceed the costs of imprisonment.[100] His study has been criticized by a number of analysts, including Marc Mauer of The Sentencing Project. Mauer identified a number of errors in the analysis, including the use of an average figure of 187 crimes per year for each offender who is left in the community instead of imprisoned.[101] A more recent cost-benefit assessment conducted in Wisconsin found that the expense of imprisonment is about half of that to permit criminals to remain in the community. This analysis has been severely criticized by the National Council on Crime and Delinquency (NCCD). NCCD calls into question several of the assumptions used in the analysis, including the figure used for the cost of each crime to society. Moreover, NCCD has conducted research showing that community-based sanctions can result in significant savings when compared to imprisonment.[102]

Despite the fact that there is no conclusive research to suggest that imprisonment is a cost-effective remedy to crime, U.S. Attorneys General such as William P. Barr under President Bush have continued to argue for building more prisons, in part on cost-effectiveness grounds.[103] Nonetheless, political realities are such that even many conservative political leaders now acknowledge that it is simply not possible to build our way out of the crowding crisis. Other approaches simply must be tried, and tried soon.

Of course, all the approaches to reducing overcrowding that we will be discussing are approaches to achieving other goals as well. Reduction of correctional costs, enhancement of rehabilitative, punitive, deterrent, and incapacitative effects, and satisfaction of the public interest in crime control are but a few of these other goals. As might be expected, significant ideological baggage is associated with any approaches that purport to achieve these objectives. To conservatives, solutions to overcrowding that rely heavily upon deinstitutionalization are far less attractive than solutions that expand the use of serious punitive measures. They anticipate that such punitive measures will produce deterrent and incapacitative effects which ultimately will reduce the demand for prison space. Liberals are likely to have severe reservations about expanded use of imprisonment, and see enhancement of alternatives to incarceration as a more productive route to reducing crowding and accomplishing the other major goals of punishment.

Focus 3-3
The Public's View of
Prison Crowding

A common perception is that the public is far less concerned with crowding in prisons than it is with reducing crime. This may be true, but it does not mean that the public is not concerned with crowding. A study of citizens in one large state found that almost 90 percent of respondents believed that prison crowding was a "very important" or "somewhat important issue." Almost two-thirds rated it as a "very important issue."[104]

Citizens are also interested in a variety of approaches to address the problem. A study of Texas citizens found that "while Texans believe that more prisons should be built, they are equally in favor of simultaneously developing community corrections programs."[105] National polls show a similar willingness to build new prisons, but also reveal an interest in developing alternatives to incarceration to relieve crowding.[106] A study of California citizens presented respondents with 25 hypothetical offense situations and asked whether the appropriate punishment should be prison or probation. Respondents selected prison for 60 percent of the offenders. The respondents were then given additional information about current prison population levels, the costs of incarceration, and about alternatives to conventional incarceration or probation. The percentage of offenders given prison dropped dramatically to only 27 percent. The study author concluded that "the public, properly informed, is sufficiently accepting of community-based sanctions that a much lower prison rate would be quite acceptable."[107]

The issue of a properly informed public is important. In his focus group research, John Doble found that many Americans understand neither the full extent of crowding nor the potential consequences. He also found that Americans tend to believe that crowding is simply the result of increase in crime. Even when presented with data on the first half of the 1980s showing that crime actually declined, many respondents had difficulty accepting this fact. Nonetheless, Doble's work also revealed that Americans were receptive to alternatives to incarceration when they were presented with data on the costs of constructing and operating prisons.[108]

Finally, a recently published study of citizen preferences for solutions to crowding found that only 31 percent of respondents favored building new prisons to address the crowding problem. Fifty-seven percent favored shorter prison sentences for non-dangerous offenders, and 76 percent favored placing non-dangerous convicts in community-based correctional programs. Respondents in this study were permitted to indicate enthusiasm for more than a single alternative. Less than 10 percent only favored building new prisons, while about 6 percent only favored shorter sentences. About 18 percent only favored community-based sentences. Thus, respondents generally were willing to try more than a single approach to reduce crowding, and adoption of non-incarcerative sanctions was the most popular option.[109]

Despite political rhetoric to the contrary, therefore, it appears that the public possesses significant interest in further development of non-incarcerative sanctions. Unfortunately, policymaker perceptions often underestimate this interest,[110] thus politicians are reluctant to aggressively pursue non-incarcerative solutions to overcrowding. Given the current expenses associated with prison construction and maintenance, this reluctance could well prove extremely costly. In view of the evidence suggesting that policymakers themselves are not disinclined to give serious consideration to alternatives to incarceration,[111] clarifying the public's real view on the matter for political leaders could well lead to some significant political enterprise focusing on non-incarcerative sanctions.

Unfortunately, even were political support for public desires more forthcoming, a study of citizen attitudes in Cincinnati and Columbus provides little evidence that the public has a realistic sense of the problem. Although community-based programs received significant support, the kinds of offenders served in such programs would not be of the kind currently populating American prisons, thus adoption of community programs would have little impact on crowding. The public was vigorously opposed to shortening incarcerative sentences. In their analysis of this opposition the study authors concluded that "[t]he public generally rejects policies that have the greatest potential for reducing prison crowding and supports those that provide smaller amounts of relief from crowding."[112] Like the above-mentioned Doble study, this research suggests that public education about the nature of the crowding problem is a must if the public is to become an important source of effective guidance in addressing the crowding crisis.

In fact, to some extent these ideology-based positions are straw persons for public display, the main purpose of which is to influence voters. The facts suggest that although we have expanded the prison population significantly over the past decade, the size of the captive population held under state control in alternative programs is also at an all-time high. In 1983 the percentage of all persons under correctional supervision who were serving sentences in the community under conditions of parole or probation was 73.1 percent. At the beginning of the 1990s the figure was an almost identical 71.6 percent.[113] While the prison population increased during this time period the number of convicts under probation or parole also increased by a staggering 675,000.[114] The pie, in other words, has simply gotten much larger. Reductions in crowding, apart from the many other traditional objectives of the correctional system, are not likely to occur merely by establishing more vigorous use of alternatives to incarceration. We will return to this general point in a subsequent chapter.

As a practical matter, one major correctional concern is with reducing the probability that inmates will commit new crimes subsequent to release and be returned to prison to further clog the system. A substantial reduction in recidivism may make a significant contribution toward reducing prison crowding. We turn now to consideration of what we know about changing the behavior of individuals who have come under the supervision of the correctional system.

Notes

[1]"Short sentences—Overcrowding leads to paroles for criminals who have never been to prison," *Fort Worth Star-Telegram* 31 March 1991, p. B1.

[2]Lanagan, Patrick (1989) "Felony sentences in state courts," Washington, D.C.: U.S. Department of Justice, p. 6.

[3]Austin, James (1991) "The consequences of escalating the use of imprisonment: The case study of Florida," San Francisco, CA: National Council on Crime and Delinquency, p. 5.

[4]Bureau of Justice Statistics (1987) "Sentencing and time served," Washington, D.C.: U.S. Department of Justice, p. 4.

[5]Gilliard, Darrell K., Bureau of Justice Statistics (1993) *Prisoners in 1992*, Washington, D.C.: U.S. Department of Justice, 1993.

[6]Bureau of Justice Statistics (1990) "Prisoners in 1989," Washington, D.C.: U.S. Department of Justice, p. 6.

[7]Government Accounting Office (1991) "Federal prisons—Revised design standards could save expansion funds," Report to Congressional requesters, March, Washington, D.C.: U.S. Government Printing Office.

[8]Allen, Harry E. and Simonsen, Clifford E. (1989) *Corrections in America— An Introduction*, New York: MacMillan Publishing Co., p. 232.

[9]Bureau of Justice Statistics (1990) "Prisoners in 1989" Washington, D.C.: U.S. Department of Justice, p. 2.

[10]Flanagan, Timothy and Maguire, Kathleen (1990), p. 581.

[11]Federal Bureau of Investigation (1981 and 1986) *Uniform Crime Reports*, Washington, D.C.

[12]Zedlewski, Edwin M. (1987) "Making confinement decisions," Washington, D.C.: U.S. Department of Justice, p. 5.

[13]Flanagan, T. (1989) *Sourcebook of Criminal Justice Statistics—1988*, Washington, D.C.: U.S. Department of Justice, Bureau of Justice Statistics, p. 612; see Gilliard, note 5 above.

[14]Bureau of Justice Statistics (1990) "Prisoners in 1989." Washington, D.C.: U.S. Department of Justice, p. 2.; Flanagan, T. and Maguire, K. (1990) *Sourcebook of Criminal Justice Statistics—1989*, Washington, D.C.: U.S. Department of Justice, Bureau of Justice Statistics, p. 583; Snell, Tracy L. and Morton, Danielle (1992) "Prisoners in 1991," Washington, D.C.: U.S. Department of Justice, p. 2.

[15]Innes, Christopher A. (1986) "Population density in state prisons,"

Bureau of Justice Statistics Special Report, Washington, D.C.: U.S. Department of Justice, p. 4.

[16]Camp, George M. and Camp, Camille G. (1990) *The Corrections Yearbook*, Salem, NY: Criminal Justice Institute, p. 33.

[17]Id. at 32.

[18]Bureau of Justice Statistics (1992) "National Update," July, Washington, D.C.: U.S. Department of Justice, p. 9.

[19]Bureau of Justice Statistics (1990) "Prisoners in 1989," Washington, D.C.: U.S. Department of Justice, p. 7.

[20]See Camp and Camp, note 16 above at 6.

[21]Bureau of Justice Statistics (1990) "Prisoners in 1989," Washington, D.C.: U.S. Department of Justice, p. 5.

[22]"Jail limits intake of prisoners," *Fort Worth Star-Telegram* 12 July 1991, p. B1; "Pay counties for inmates, state is told," *Fort Worth Star-Telegram*, 2 June 1990, p. A1.

[23]See Camp and Camp, note 16 above at 3.

[24]Bureau of Justice Statistics (1990) "Prisoners in 1989," Washington, D.C.: U.S. Department of Justice, p. 6.

[25]"California reaches 100,000," *Corrections Compendium* 16, p. 13.

[26]Government Accounting Office (1989) "Prison Crowding—Issues Facing the Nation's Prison System," Washington, D.C.: U.S. Government Accounting Office, p. 2.

[27]See Camp and Camp, note 16 above at 3.

[28]See Camp and Camp, note 16 above at 29.

[29]See Gilliard, note 14 above.

[30]Government Accounting Office (1989) "Prison Crowding—Issues Facing the Nation's Prison System," Washington, D.C.: United States Government Accounting Office, p. 3.

[31]Beck, Alan J. (1991) "Profile of state inmates," Bureau of Justice Statistics Special Report, Washington, D.C.: U.S. Department of Justice, p. 3.

[32]Landes, Alison, Siedel, Mark A., and Foster, Carol D. (1990) *Crime—A Serious American Problem*, Wylie, TX: Information Plus, p. 73.

[33]Id.

[34]Jankowski, Louis W. (1992) "Jail inmates 1991," Washington, D.C.: Department of Justice.

[35]Champion, Dean (1990) Corrections in the United States, Englewood Cliffs, NJ: Prentice Hall, Inc., p. 177.

[36]Welsh, Wayne N., Pontell, Henry N., Leone, Matthew C., and Kinkade, Patrick (1990) "Jail overcrowding: An analysis of policymakers' perceptions," *Justice Quarterly* 7(2), p. 349.

[37]Hall, Andy (1987) "Systemwide strategies to alleviate jail crowding," National Institute of Justice Research in Brief, Washington, D.C.: United States Department of Justice, p. 1.

[38]Guynes, Randall (1988) "Nation's jail managers assess their problems," National Institute of Justice—Research in Action, Washington, D.C.: U.S. Department of Justice, p. 7.

[39]Id. at 1.

[40]Id. at 7.

[41]Allen, Harry E. and Simonsen, Clifford E. (1989) *Corrections in America*, New York: MacMillan Publishing Co., p. 553.

[42]Camp, George M. and Camp, Camille G. (1990) *The Corrections Yearbook*, Salem, NY: Criminal Justice Institute, p. 86.

[43]See Snell and Morton, note 14 above at 5.

[44]*Criminal Justice Newsletter* (1990) 21, pp. 5-6.

[45]"Jail limits intake of prisoners," *Fort Worth Star-Telegram*, 12 July 1991, p. B1.

[46]All material to this point is based on Potter, Karen and Mahlburg, Bob, "Pay counties for inmates, state is told," *Fort Worth Star-Telegram*, 2 June 1990, p. A1.

[47]"Richards seeks way to implement jail bill," *Fort Worth Star-Telegram*, 8 June 1991, p. B2.

[48]"State of Texas and Harris County in dispute over jail crowding," (1991) *Criminal Justice Newsletter* 22(7), p. 5.

[49]Proband, Stan C. (1991) "American prison population—134 percent increase in 10 years," *Overcrowded Times* 2(4), p. 1.

[50]Federal Bureau of Investigation (1991) *Uniform Crime Reports*, Washington, D.C.: U.S. Department of Justice.

[51]Mackenzie, Doris L., Tracy, George S. and Williams, George (1988) "Incarceration rates and demographic changes: A test of the demographic change hypothesis," *Journal of Criminal Justice* 16, pp. 241-253.

[52]Holbert, Fred and Call, Jack E. (1989) "The perspective of state correctional officials on prison overcrowding: Causes, court orders, and solutions," *Federal Probation* 53(1), pp. 25-32.

[53]United States General Accounting Office (1989) *Federal Prisons—Trends in Offender Characteristics*, GAO/PEMD-90-4FS, Washington, D.C.: U.S.

Government Accounting Office.

[54]"Government Accounting Office (1989) "Prison Crowding—Issues Facing the Nation's Prison System," (1989) Briefing Report to Congressional Requester, Washington, D.C.: Government Accounting Office, GAO/GGD-90-1BR, p. 15.

[55]Id. at 2.

[56]Lieb, Roxanne (1991) "Washington State: A decade of sentencing reform," *Overcrowded Times* 2(4), p. 7.

[57]O'Connell, John P. (1991) "Delaware releases incarceration factbook," *Overcrowded Times* 2(4), p. 4.

[58]"Proportion of jail inmates doing time for drugs is up," (1991) New York Times, 25 April 1991, p. A9.

[59]Bureau of Justice Statistics (1991) "National Update," Washington, D.C.: U.S. Department of Justice, p. 8.

[60]See Holbert and Call, note 52 above at 27.

[61]McCarthy, Bernard J. (1988) "Responding to the prison crowding crisis: The restructuring of a prison system," *Criminal Justice Policy Review* 2, pp. 3-20.

[62]"Huge Texas prison bill passes," (1991) *Fort Worth Star-Telegram*, July 19, p. A1.

[63]"Corrections' budget requests up 25 percent," *Corrections Compendium* 16, p. 6.

[64]"Prison Crowding—Issues facing the nation's prison system," (1991) GAO/GGD-90-1BR, Washington, D.C.: U.S. Government Accounting Office, p. 1.

[65]See Camp and Camp, note 42 above at 32-34.

[66]"Prison crowding—Issues facing the nation's prison system," (1991) GAO/GGD-90-1BR, Washington, D.C.: U.S. Government Accounting Office, p. 1.

[67]Mullen, Joan (1987) "State responses to prison crowding: The politics of change," in Gottfredson, S.D. and McConville, S. (eds.) *America's Correctional Crisis: Prison Populations and Public Policy*, New York: Greenwood Press, p. 102.

[68]Lewis, W. David (1965) *From Newgate to Dannemora*, Ithaca, NY: Cornell University Press.

[69]Ayers, Edward L. (1984) *Vengeance and Justice—Crime and Punishment in the 19th century American South*. New York: Oxford University Press.

[70]Going, Allen J. (1951) *Bourbon Democracy in Alabama—1870-1890*, Birmingham, AL: University of Alabama Press.

[71]McKelvey, Blake (1977) *American Prisons: A History of Good Intentions*, Montclair, NJ: Patterson Smith.

[72]Rothman, David (1971) *The Discovery of the Asylum*, Boston: Little, Brown and Company.

[73]Calhoun, J.B. (1962) "Population density and social pathology," *Scientific American* 206, pp. 139-148.

[74]Cox, Verne C., Paulus, Paul B., and McCain, Garvin (1984) "Prison crowding research: The relevance for prison housing standards and a general approach regarding crowding phenomena," *American Psychologist* 39, pp. 1148.

[75]Clayton, O. and Carr, T. (1984) "The effects of prison crowding upon infraction rates," *Criminal Justice Review* 9, pp. 69-77.

[76]Nacci, P.L., Teitlebaum, H., and Prather, J. (1977) "Population density and inmate misconduct rates in the federal prison system," *Federal Probation* 41, pp. 26-31.

[77]See Cox, note 74 above at 1156.

[78]Gaes, G.G. and McGuire, W.G. (1984) "Prison violence: Crowding versus other determinants of prison assault rates," *Journal of Research in Crime and Delinquency* 22, pp. 41-65.

[79]Gaes, Gerald G. (1985) "The effects of overcrowding in prison," in Morris and Tonry, (eds.), *Crime and Justice—vol. 6*, Chicago: University of Chicago Press.

[80]Ekland-Olson, Sheldon (1991) "Crowding, social control, and prison violence: Evidence from the post-Ruiz years in Texas," *Law and Society Review* 20, pp. 389-421.

[81]See Gaes, note 79 above at 134.

[82]Farrington, David P. and Nuttal, Christopher P. (1985), "Prison size, overcrowding, prison violence, and recidivism," in Braswell, Dillingham, and Montgomery, (eds.) *Prison Violence in America*, Cincinnati, OH: Anderson Publishing Co., p. 128.

[83]Clayton, Obie, Jr. and Carr, Tim (1987) "An empirical assessment of the effects of prison crowding upon recidivism utilizing aggregate level data," *Journal of Criminal Justice* 15, pp. 201-210.

[84]Id. at 208.

[85]Brewer, I.W. (1918) "Report of epidemic of Spanish Influenza which occurred at Camp A.A. Humphreys, Virginia during September and October," *The Journal of Laboratory and Clinical Medicine* 4, pp. 87-111.

[86]Walker, Bailus and Gordon, Theodore (1980) "Health and high density confinement in jails and prisons," *Federal Probation* 44(1), p. 57.

[87]E.g., Rogers, M., Dubey, D., and Reich, P., (1979) "The influence of the psyche and the brain on immunity and disease susceptibility," *Psychosomatic Medicine* 4: 141-63; Cox, V., Paulus, P., and McCain, G. (1984) "Prison crowding research," *American Psychologist* 39, pp. 1148-1160.

[88]See Cox, note 74 above.

[89]Fry, Lincoln (1988) "Continuities in the determination of prison overcrowding effects," *Journal of Criminal Justice* 16: 231-240; see Gaes, note 79 above at 111-127.

[90]Innes, Christopher A. (1987) "The effects of prison density on prisoners," *CJAIN* Spring, The Criminal Justice Archive and Information Network, p. 3.

[91]See Camp, note 42 above at p. 20.

[92]Austin, James (1986) "Using early release to relieve prison crowding: A dilemma in public policy," *Crime and Delinquency* 32, p. 406.

[93]"Man who killed officer got early parole, records show," *Fort Worth Star-Telegram*, 21 April 1991, p. B3.

[94]Id.

[95]See Austin, note 92 above at 406.

[96]Quoted in "AIDS commission reports prisons fail to provide adequate care for HIV-infected inmates," (1991) *Corrections Compendium* 16(4) p. 13.

[97]"Justice Department says prison caps should only be used as a last resort," (1991) *Corrections Compendium* 16(4), p. 13.

[98]McCarthy, Bernard (1989) "Coping with crowding: The prison system response to crowding," *American Journal of Criminal Justice* 13, pp. 240-256.

[99]Harris, Kay (1985) "Reducing prison crowding and nonprison penalties," *Annals of the American Academy of Political and Social Sciences* 478, pp. 150-160.

[100]Zedlewski, Edwin M. (1987) "Making confinement decisions," Washington, D.C.: U.S. Department of Justice, p. 5.

[101]Mauer, Marc (1988) "Briefing sheet: Does building more prisons save money?" Washington, D.C.: The Sentencing Project.

[102]Criminal Justice Newsletter (1991) "Claim that Wisconsin prisons are cost-effective is challenged," 22(4), p. 2.

[103]Criminal Justice Newsletter (1992) "Justice Dept. raises eyebrows with focus on need for prisons," 23(7), p. 2.

[104]Johnson, Bruce and Huff, C. Ron (1988) "Public opinion and criminal justice policy formulation," *Criminal Justice Policy Review* 2, pp. 118-132.

[105]Cullen, Francis T., Clark, Gregory A., and Wozniak, John F. (1985) "Explaining the get tough movement: Can the public be blamed?" *Federal*

Probation 49, p. 19.

[106]Flanagan, Timothy J. and Caulfield, Susan L. (1984) "Public opinion and prison policy: A review," *The Prison Journal* 64, pp. 31-46.

[107]Bennett, Lawrence A. (1989) "Californians accepting of community punishments for criminal offenders," Sacramento, CA: American Justice Institute.

[108]Doble, John (1987) *Crime and Punishment: The Public's View*, The Public Agenda Foundation.

[109]Williams, J. Sherwood, Johnson, Daniel M., and McGrath, John H. (1991) "Is the public committed to the imprisonment of convicted felons? Citizen preferences for reducing prison crowding," *Journal of Contemporary Criminal Justice* 7, pp. 88-94.

[110]E.g., Gottfredson, Stephen D., Warner, Barbara D., and Taylor, Ralph B. (1988) "Conflict and consensus about criminal justice in Maryland," in Walker and Hough (eds.) *Public Attitudes to Sentencing—Surveys from Five Countries*, Brookfield: Gower; Johnson, Bruce A. and Huff, C. Ron (1988).

[111]Hamm, Mark S. (1990) "Legislator attitudes toward policies to reduce prison crowding," *Criminal Justice Policy Review* 3, pp. 220-235.

[112]Skovron, Sandra Evans, Scott, Joseph E., and Cullen, Francis T. (1988) "Prison crowding: Public attitudes toward strategies of population control," *Journal of Crime and Delinquency* 25(2), p. 164.

[113]Clear, Todd R. and Cole, George F. (1986) *American Corrections*, Monterey, CA: Brooks/Cole, 231; Camp, G. and Camp, C. (1990), Criminal Justice Institute, p. 5.

[114]Clear, Todd R. and Cole, George F. (1986) *American Corrections*, Monterey, CA: Brooks/Cole, p. 231; Camp, G. and Camp, C. (1990) *The Corrections Yearbook—Probation and Parole*, South Salem, NY: Criminal Justice Institute, pp. 13, 30.

4

Special Problems: AIDS, Tuberculosis, and the Elderly Inmate

The past decade has been characterized by unprecedented use of imprisonment as a punishment for crime. The leap in prisoners in state and federal prisons from a little over 300,000 in 1980 to more than 880,000 in early 1993, and the increase in jail populations from less than 190,000 at the beginning of the eighties to the current level exceeding 400,000 inmates are clear examples of this increased enthusiasm for incarceration.[1] It is evident from the building construction programs in states such as Texas, which has authorized more than a billion dollars for new prison construction, that this trend will not soon abate. Although there is growing interest in a variety of alternatives to incarceration, and the promises or risks that they contain, the reality is that prisons and jails will continue to hold large numbers of inmates, at least in the near future.

In light of this reality, it is important to consider some of the special problems the correctional system will be facing in dealing with these unprecedented numbers of prisoners. These problems are of unusual importance because of the crowded conditions within which many of these inmates are confined. In this chapter, therefore, we will take up the issues of AIDS and tuberculosis as they affect prison management and operation. In addition, we will examine problems associated with caring for the quickly growing population of elderly inmates.

Whatever problems might otherwise exist in managing these special kinds of inmates, they are exacerbated by the crowded conditions in modern penal institutions. Under optimal circumstances, inmates afflicted with easily communicated contagious diseases might be identified and isolated from the general population. Special hospital wards provide a good example of this approach to disease care and management. Under

67

optimal conditions, elderly inmates who may be at high risk of victimization from younger citizens, like their elderly counterparts on the outside, would be cared for in special settings designed to afford them protection and meet their special needs (for example, health care).

Current crowded conditions, however, do not permit easily such kinds of institutional protective segregation. The absence of both physical space and adequate staff resources places severe constraints on what can be accomplished in dealing with these special inmates.

We begin with a detailed consideration of the problem of AIDS in prison, then present a brief examination of how the looming tuberculosis epidemic is similar to and different from the AIDS problem. The chapter concludes with a section on elderly prisoners and the special correctional challenges they represent.

AIDS in Penal Institutions

Our discussion examines several components of the problem of AIDS as it pertains to institutional corrections. We began with an account of the extent and nature of the current problem and projections for the future. Risks to the major participants in the correctional process will then be considered, followed by a discussion of the full range of potential methods to address such hazards. The section concludes with an examination of the legal rights of those at risk in penal institutions.

AIDS—A Modern Nightmare

Acquired Immunodeficiency Syndrome (AIDS) is a serious communicable disease that compromises the functioning of the human immune system. An individual with AIDS will possess heightened susceptibility to a variety of diseases and infections as a result of the diminished capacity of the body to deflect "opportunistic" threats. Pneumonia, cancer, and a host of other conditions have been associated with individuals whose immune systems have been degraded by AIDS.

AIDS is caused by the Human Immunodeficiency Virus (HIV).

HIV, which contaminates and destroys the white blood cells needed to fight disease and infection, does not always lead quickly to AIDS. Current estimates place the number of infected individuals worldwide at almost 13 million.[2] Many individuals have been HIV-positive for years without developing AIDS symptoms.[3] Of course, AIDS is a deadly condition and has proved fatal to almost all of those who have had the malady for any length of time. In the United States, 85 percent of those with AIDS in 1985 had died by 1988.[4] As of the beginning of 1992, the world death toll for AIDS had reached 2.5 million people.[5] The World Health Organization now predicts that the number of infected persons will increase to more than 30 million by the year 2000. By the fall of 1992, about 250,000 AIDS cases had been reported in the United States, and more than 160,000 people had died from the disease.[6] Not all cases have been reported, and it is estimated that more than one million American citizens are infected.[7] The Centers for Disease Control predict that the death toll will reach 330,000 Americans by 1995. AIDS is "now the leading cause of death among young men 25 to 45 years of age in 5 states and 64 cities."[8]

The progression of the disease begins with HIV infection, then progresses to AIDS-related Complex (ARC), and concludes with fully developed AIDS. ARC refers to the existence of a number of conditions in the infected individual, all relatively minor, that are indicators of deterioration. Weight loss, night sweats, and swollen lymph nodes are examples of such conditions. To be regarded as indicators of AIDS, these conditions must be accompanied by other indicators such as low white blood cell counts. It has been estimated that 90 percent of seropositive individuals (those who test positive for HIV) will show some signs of immunodeficiency within five years of infection.[9]

AIDS, sometimes referred to as "end-stage" AIDS, is indicated by several conditions, the most common of which are Pneumocystis carinii pneumonia and Kaposi's sarcoma.[10] The number of these indicator diseases has increased as researchers have learned more about AIDS, and the definition of full-blown AIDS continues to change. Naturally, the expansion of the conditions indicative of AIDS has increased the number of patients defined as end-stage AIDS patients.[11] Current estimates place the number of individuals with end-stage AIDS at 100,000 worldwide.[12] This is of significant concern because the median length of survival is only about one year from time of diagnosis of end-stage AIDS. Only 15 percent of such patients live five years or more.[13] The development of drugs such as AZT may offer the promise of longer survival periods, though no cure is currently on the horizon.

▒ *AIDS and Inmates*

Although AIDS is a social problem with wide-ranging implications, it represents a special dilemma in incarcerative environments. AIDS is transmitted primarily through sexual contact and intravenous drug use (IDU).[14] It is thus significant that a study of state prison inmates revealed that almost two-thirds of inmates had used drugs on a regular basis at some point in their lives. More than 50 percent used a major drug in the month before the crime for which they were incarcerated, and 31 percent were under the influence of drugs when they committed the crime.[15] The primary exposure mechanism for infected prison inmates thus appears to be intravenous drug use,[16] and it should come as no surprise that increasing numbers of inmates are entering prison HIV-positive.

Although there is variation among incarcerative institutions, homosexual contact in prisons is far from unusual. Estimates of inmate involvement in homosexual activity in male prisons range from 30 percent to 60 percent.[17] Such behavioral practices place prison inmates at special risks because AIDS can be transmitted by sexual contact. (One study of known American AIDS cases reported that 60 percent of AIDS cases resulted from homosexual or bisexual behavior.[18])

The combination of previous involvement in intravenous drug use and in-prison participation in homosexual relations creates enormous potential difficulties for both inmates and correctional staff. Moreover, this potential appears to be growing steadily. A study of state, federal, and some local correctional facilities revealed that the number of AIDS cases in these institutions rose from 766 in 1985 to 6,985 in late 1990. These figures represent conservative estimates. Although some studies suggest that the percentage of offenders entering prison who are HIV-positive is only about 1 percent,[19] the increase in the number of infected inmates represents an extraordinary climb of about 800 percent in five years.[20] A recent study of more than 11,000 inmates in ten prisons and jails placed the percentage at more than 4 percent.[21] Some states may have percentages that far exceed this average. Data from New York State, for example, reveal that in some facilities more than 17 percent of male inmates and approximately 18 percent of female inmates are HIV-positive.[22]

Part of this general increase is the result of better diagnosis and reporting, yet a significant portion reflects changes in the inmate population. It is important to note that the rate of increase for the most recent year reported (1989-1990) is less than the rate of increase in AIDS cases in the population at large. Moreover, the rate of increase during this most recent year was lower than in any year since 1985.[23]

More than 2,000 inmates died from AIDS during the period from 1985 through late 1990, with about 40 percent of these deaths occurring between 1989 and 1990.[24] Nearly 600 inmates died of AIDS in adult correctional facilities in 1990 alone.[25] Although deaths from AIDS have been a continuing problem in some states since the early 1980s,[26] the pace of such deaths will continue to accelerate as the numbers of end-stage inmates increase. In a few states, such as Maryland, AIDS is the leading cause of inmate deaths.[27]

As might be expected, AIDS inmates are predominantly male and minority. In New York, for instance, "96 percent of AIDS cases have been among males, 48 percent among Hispanics, 38 percent among blacks, and 95 percent among IDUs."[28] In North Carolina, although only 57 percent of inmates were black, almost all (88 percent) HIV-positive inmates were black.[29]

The growing number of inmates infected with HIV, and who have reached ARC and end-stage conditions, has raised significant issues for both inmates and correctional personnel. Moreover, these issues have serious consequences for citizens not involved in the correctional system. It is to these issues that we now turn our attention.

Whose Rights Are at Risk?

Despite popular sentiments to the contrary, prisons are not very nice places to live. (After all, how many inmates would choose to remain in prison if the gates were opened?) Part of the lack of desirability of prisons has to do with the reasons why people reside in them. Citizens who have committed serious crimes or who have lengthy criminal records eventually end up in our state and federal prisons. Society has decided that the magnitude of the transgressions of these citizens merits a serious punitive response, and prison conditions represent to some extent that widespread commitment. Thus many prison inhabitants are relatively unpleasant, often violent, citizens.

Apart from the nasty personal characteristics of some prison inhabitants, prisons are undesirable places because they are highly restricted environments. Inmates must conform to a wide range of regulations that do not have to be endured by free citizens. However, the punitive character of prisons falls within socially acceptable limits. We do not consider it appropriate to confine offenders in institutions and simply let them fend for themselves. We do not consider it appropriate to lock inmates away and deny them a basic modicum of food and shelter. We recognize that some offenders may be killed by other aggressive prisoners, thus efforts are made to provide some level of protection. Society recognizes, therefore, that imprisoned offenders still retain some rights, although other rights will have been forfeit by virtue of their involvement in crime.

In light of this it is important to consider the health rights of prison inmates. A long series of court cases have established the rights of inmates to basic health care.[30] Although health care cases continue to be litigated, and the boundaries of what the state must do in meeting their health care obligations continue to change, it is no longer disputed that the state has some obligation in this area. The emergence of AIDS in incarcerative facilities, however, raises questions about the kinds of protections the state is obligated to provide to inmates in order to protect them from the significant health risks posed by exposure to AIDS.

A second group of individuals whose rights are at risk in incarcerative environments is correctional staff. Correctional officers who have routine and regular contact with inmates are obviously at greatest risk of infection. Although there has yet to be a single case of a corrections officer contracting AIDS from an inmate, it would be remarkable if a case did not eventually appear. Most correctional systems now provide testing of staff exposed to high risk conditions (for example, puncture wounds, blood to blood contact).[31]

A third at-risk group is visitors of inmates. Family and friends who visit inmates run a very small chance of infection. It is theoretically possible to transmit the disease through kissing if special conditions are met, such as cuts in the mouths of the participants. Nonetheless, this risk is exceedingly small, and there is no documented case of this kind of transmission in prisons. Of perhaps more concern are conjugal visits, which in some states may include multi-day visits in special on-site conjugal quarters. Sexual contact during such visits may result in infection of either the inmate or the spouse.

Unlike other diseases which may be communicated within the institutional environment, the lethal nature of AIDS imposes special burdens on correctional administrators in their efforts to protect the rights of these three groups. A number of methods have been proposed or are currently in use to address these obligations.

Preventing and Controlling AIDS within Correctional Institutions

There are several important aspects to the prevention and control of AIDS within correctional institutions: testing, segregation, education, training, and use of special apparatus.

Testing

In an institutional environment such as a prison, knowledge that a resident has AIDS is clearly of value. Inmate segregation and provision of special AIDS-related services require information regarding the infection status of prisoners, and AIDS testing can be the first step in handling infected inmates. Testing is an extremely controversial issue, however.

There are three main categories of testing: voluntary, as-needed, and mandatory. Voluntary testing is conducted when inmates volunteer to submit to the test. The willingness of inmates to take the test may depend on a number of factors, such as the inmate's perceived risk of being infected, the level of confidentiality that will be provided, and institutional policy regarding HIV-positive inmates.

As-needed testing is conducted to meet special circumstances. An inmate who has raped or bitten another inmate, and therefore exposed that individual to risk, may be tested. If the offender is found to be positive, the victim may also be tested.

Mandatory testing refers to institution-wide testing of all inmates who reside in a facility. Questions have been raised about the power of the state to conduct such tests in the absence of any compelling reason to believe that an individual has the virus. Nonetheless, 16 states and the Federal Prison System now have some form of mass testing.[32] The national trend has been for increasing numbers of jurisdictions to implement mass screening.

Each of these forms of testing involves issues associated with legal rights of inmates, staff, and the community. We will return to such rights momentarily. For our present purposes, testing is significant only to the extent that it provides information that can be used to formulate policy designed to prevent and control the spread of AIDS in prisons. Inmate segregation is an excellent example of such a policy.

It is important to note that significant opposition exists to mandatory testing policies. Mark Blumberg and Denny Langston point out that the real risk of infection from bites or spitting is simply too low to justify an inclusive testing policy. Contamination of correctional officials attempting to break up fights may be a theoretical possibility, yet there has not been a single documented case of AIDS transmitted in this fashion. Testing of all inmates will thus not enhance the safety of non-infected individuals operating in the prison environment.[33]

Segregation

Probably the most widely discussed proposal to limit the spread of AIDS within prisons and jails is inmate segregation: the separation of infected inmates from all other inmates. This idea has plenty of precedent in other contexts. Most societies utilize legally imposed quarantines to control certain dangerous communicable diseases, and they have some obvious advantages. If inmates are successfully segregated, the risks of infection of non-HIV positive inmates will be very low. Any hostilities that develop between AIDS-infected and other inmates will presumably be minimal simply because they will not be in contact. Reducing the potential for inmate conflict has clear appeal to correctional administors interested in maintaining a safe, nonviolent environment. Furthermore, the state may be able to reduce its risks of legal liability from suits filed by inmates who acquired AIDS while in prison.

There are a number of different forms that segregation may assume:

1. total separation of HIV-positive, ARC, and end-stage AIDS inmates from all other inmates held in the institution
2. separation of subsets of infected inmates (such as end-stage patients only)
3. separation of infected inmates only when illness necessitates special medical attention.[34]

As of 1991, only four states segregated all HIV-positive inmates: Alabama, California, Colorado, and Mississippi.[35] This represents a change from the early days of concern with infected prisoners. "In 1985, 42 percent of State/Federal systems had policies calling for segregation of at least some HIV-infected inmates, while 35 percent had presumptive general population or case-by-case policies. By 1990, these percentages had changed to 18 percent and 78 percent respectively."[36] Recent experience seems to suggest that, with rare exceptions, infected inmates can remain in the general population without a major increase in infection, or a violent backlash from uninfected inmates. As the top medical authority at a California facility noted "there is no medical . . . rational or scientific basis for the segregation of inmates who are HIV-positive."[37]

Focus 4-1
Integrating AIDS-infected Inmates in Prison: The Colorado Experience[38]

Only a few states completely isolate all HIV-positive inmates from other inmates. Like several other states concerned about mixing infected inmates with HIV-negative prisoners, Colorado adopted a policy providing for mandatory screening and segregation. This policy was challenged in the courts, and upheld in the case of Ramos v. Lamm in 1990.

Although this court decision has provided the legal basis for continued segregation, Colorado has tried to move away from its original blanket segregation policy. Colorado continues to maintain residential segregation but has initiated integration in some areas of institutional programming. The process was begun slowly, with only minimal mixing of HIV-positive and negative inmates. For instance, the visiting room was opened to infected inmates, although they were initially required to use a special area of the room. Use of the weight-training facility was then opened to HIV-positive inmates. Although at the outset of the trial period bleach was used by uninfected prisoners to clean weights used by infected prisoners, this practice was eventually abandoned.

Part of the apparent success of the Colorado approach is attributable to the fact that the slow process of integration was accompanied by serious efforts at education of inmates and staff. Misperceptions that might have limited the potential for success of the movement toward integration were corrected through a thorough education program. By the beginning of 1991 segregation was no longer practiced with regard to institutional programs.

Colorado officials anticipate that residential segregation will be reduced in the future. For many inmates segregation simply will not be necessary. These same officials do not, however, anticipate complete residential integration. Some inmates, fearing mistreatment and other liabilities, may prefer segregated housing. Other inmates may require segregation due to their insistence on participation in high-risk behaviors (for example, sexual relations, assaultive behavior).

Colorado represents a state that has the legal authority to use blanket segregation but which has not chosen to do so. Colorado has increased the extent to which infected inmates are able to participate in activities with members of the general inmate population, while at the same time maintaining residential segregation. The limited use of segregation may well turn out to be the most sensible model for most states in the years to come.

In fact, there are a number of reasons why segregation may make matters worse. Segregation may impede development of an accurate understanding of the disease by reinforcing stereotypes about AIDS and infected individuals. It may also heighten inmate fear of the disease. ("After all, why would they be isolated from the rest of us unless it is really a danger to everyone?") Segregation also entails added economic and staff costs. In a prison system already bulging at the seams, construction of special facilities for AIDS-infected inmates or setting aside precious existing space for such offenders may be difficult to justify on pragmatic grounds.

Isolation may also have a debilitating psychological effect on infected inmates. Such prisoners may see their isolation as further confirmation of their coming demise and degrade the quality of the life experience they have remaining. It must be remembered that HIV-positive inmates may live five or ten years before any serious illnesses set in. Finally, segregation may interfere with the ability of such inmates to participate in programs (for example, educational, vocational) offered to the general inmate population.

Some analysts have raised important legal issues associated with segregation policies. Lynn Branham argues that the Constitution imposes restrictions on the circumstances under which segregation might be imposed and the manner in which it might be administered,[39] although it is not clear exactly which directions will be followed in coming court decisions. However, Barbara Belbot and Rolando del Carmen argue that such limits are not likely to be significant. As evidence, they point to the

1990 case of Harris v. Thigpen in which the court "found segregation of prisoners with AIDS constitutional, rejecting the challenge that it violated prisoners' Eighth and Fourteenth Amendment rights."[40] They conclude that "most courts have overwhelmingly upheld the constitutionality of segregation. As with testing, the courts have concluded that the Constitution neither requires nor prohibits segregation."[41]

Education

In 1986 a National Institute of Justice (NIJ) research report noted that

[b]ecause there is no vaccine or cure for the disease, education and training are the cornerstone of efforts to curb the spread of AIDS in prisons and jails, as well as in the population at large. Education and training also provide the opportunity to counteract misinformation, rumors, and fear concerning the disease.[42]

A 1991 National Institute of Justice report reaffirmed the importance of education. A study of intravenous drug users confined in New York's Riker's Island facility found that such individuals were still likely to "engage in extremely risky behaviors: sharing needles, cookers, and rinse water." The research also found that condom use was infrequent. The researchers concluded that education was still an extremely important aspect of AIDS control and prevention.[43]

AIDS education for inmates is now provided in almost all state and federal prisons, as well as in three-quarters of local and county jails.[44] Unfortunately, because many institutions do not require inmate involvement in these educational activities, a significant proportion of prisoners still do not participate in these programs. Only about half of the state and federal prison systems require inmate participation in all AIDS-related educational programs. The figure for city and county jails is only 11 percent.

Education programs consist of a variety of components. Audiovisual and written materials have been developed to provide important information to inmates. Because of the limited reading skills of many inmates, and because of the generally less influential character of such traditional materials, current trends have been toward "live" instruction. This instruction typically consists of technical information about the disease, methods of transmission, safe sex practices, and even the safe use of illegal drugs.

Although most of these live educational sessions are conducted by educators, there has been increasing interest in peer-based education. This approach relies upon inmates to serve as teachers, crisis and peer counselors, and support resources. Despite the reluctance of some correctional administrators who have concerns about institutional control and inmate confidentiality issues, more institutions are turning to peer education approaches.[45] At the Augusta Correctional Medical Institution in Georgia an AIDS/ARC support group was started to involve inmates more heavily in the educational process, as well as to use education as an instrument to address treatment and counseling objectives. An assessment of Georgia's approach to inmate-dominated education found that the group "has successfully met educational, counseling, therapy, and medical goals."[46]

Use of peer educators is not confined to men's prisons. Although most of the attention accorded to the problems of AIDS in prisons has involved institutions for males, there is some evidence that rates of HIV infection may be higher in women's prisons.[47] The National Prison Project reports that a number of effective education programs have now been initiated in women's prisons across the nation. These programs rely heavily upon the use of prisoners as educators and seem to have been successful.[48]

The expected benefit of education programs, whatever might be their content and structure, is that they will help stem the spread of AIDS within prisons and jails. There does appear to be some empirical evidence that AIDS education can have an influence on behavior. A study of IV drug users outside of prison found that education modified their drug using behavior and habits.[49] Rigorously analyzed replications of the effectiveness of such efforts are yet to emerge in the research literature.

Training

In light of the need for staff to be able to accomplish its security-related objectives, as well as the importance of assuring staff safety, training programs have become important in preparing correctional officials to deal effectively with inmates, some of whom may be HIV-positive. Current data reveal that virtually all prison systems in the United States provide AIDS-related education for staff. However, not all systems require staff attendance at these sessions. Furthermore, after initial orientation for new staff, follow-up training sessions to provide new information are not routinely provided in many systems.[50] As might be expected, jails provide even lower levels of training. The primary focus of staff training is on "infection control procedures and infection response."[51]

As is the case with inmates, proper training is vital if rumors and misinformation are to be avoided. This is not merely a matter of creating an accurate understanding of AIDS in the prison environment; it also has clear practical applications.

> One state reported a recent death by asphyxiation of an HIV-infected inmate who was being transferred—in four-point restraints—from one area of the prison to another. The correctional officers so feared that the inmate might spit on them, exposing them to HIV, that they stuffed a towel in his mouth, and he choked to death. This is a clear example of a death that might have been avoided had updated information on HIV risk factors been disseminated to all staff on a regular basis.[52]

Apparatus

Perhaps the most controversial and publicly visible approach to prevention and control of AIDS within institutions entails providing inmates with devices that will protect them from AIDS. Distribution of such devices is controversial because they are typically used in prohibited forms of activity. In particular, condoms and clean needles are used in sexual activity and drug use, both of which are prohibited within prisons. Despite such formal prohibition, the reality is that these forms of behavior do take place within prisons and jails. The question is whether, given this reality, the state ought to be involved in providing condoms and clean needles to inmates.

This is an extremely important issue, because sexual contact and intravenous drug use are the two main mechanisms by which AIDS is transmitted. Medical personnel tend to support condom distribution programs because of the potential medical benefits. Correctional administrators have resisted this approach due to their concern with "enforcement of regulations, the problem of appearing to condone prohibited behavior, and overall maintenance of security and institutional control."[53]

As of 1991, five American correctional systems had made condoms available to inmates. There were no systems providing needles or bleach (for cleaning drug paraphernalia). It is noteworthy that bleach distribution programs have been initiated in Australia, and recommendations have been made to start a needle distribution pilot program.[54] The Australian experience will merit watching for insight into the advantages and disadvantages of such approaches.

Meeting Health Care Needs

Correctional officials will continue to confront increasing challenges as the numbers of infected inmates grow. We have already seen how institutions must find ways of providing a safe environment for both infected and uninfected inmates. In addition, resources and methods must be found to address escalating health care needs. The National Commission on AIDS held hearings to assess the current state of affairs within prisons and learned that matters are in a deplorable state. According to prison health expert Robert Cohen, "a dangerously inadequate prison health care system is being overwhelmed by two epidemics: one, the mass incarceration of poor black and Hispanic drug users, and the other, the extraordinary medical demands of the AIDS epidemic."[55] The increasing numbers of infected inmates will place special demands on institutions to provide adequate health care. The expense of providing such care will be enormous, but it is a reality that will have to be met.

In New York State alone it is estimated that $6 million has been spent just to purchase AZT for infected inmates. Such costs, while substantial, represent a mere fraction of what will be required to provide basic medical care for inmates with end-stage AIDS. In addition, there are a number of other hidden costs. For instance, Alabama was sued by inmates for its failure to provide competent treatment for AIDS patients. (Patients were not given AZT until they were near death). The costs of defending itself against such suits must be included in estimates of the total AIDS-related costs to the correctional system. Moreover, psychological support services will have to be supplied to assist inmates and staff in coping with the disease.

The correctional system is currently at the frontier in terms of developing means to provide for the health care needs of infected inmates. It is not yet clear what the economic costs for providing such care will turn out to be. What is clear is that the costs will be substantial.

▒ *Legal Issues*

Although AIDS has been an important problem in prisons and jails for less than a decade, a wide range of legal issues has emerged during that time. Some of these matters were anticipated early on, while others developed out of unforseen circumstances. In this section we discuss several issues that have already received some level of recognition by the courts.

The first issue involves whether inmates have the right to refuse mandatory screening upon admission. Critics of mandatory screening argue that the blood test represents an intrusive procedure that is unjustified in the absence of reason to believe an individual is infected. These critics further argue that the results of such tests may be used in ways that further violate inmates' rights. Results may become known to guards and the general inmate population, resulting in difficulties for the inmate that would otherwise not exist. In the Nevada case of Walker v. Sumner, the Ninth Court of Appeals ruled that Fourth, Eighth, and Fourteenth Amendment rights were violated by the state's mandatory testing policy.[56] Previous cases had resulted in decisions which *upheld* mandatory testing provisions (for example, in Colorado). Because the Nevada case was the first to overturn a state's mandatory testing policy, it is expected that at least some other cases will follow which result in similar rulings. However, an important recent federal appeals court decision in an Alabama case affirmed that state's mandatory testing policy.[57] It remains difficult to predict how this issue will eventually be resolved.

Ironically, according to a National Institute of Justice AIDS Bulletin, "Most inmate suits regarding testing seek *increased* testing, either on a voluntary basis or, much more commonly, as a systemwide mandatory policy."[58] Inmates are asserting a right to test in order to assure their own safety, although the courts have not always been receptive. A 1992 decision rejected inmate demands for mandatory testing and segregation of HIV-positive inmates in Maryland. The state argued that mandatory testing was too expensive and that mandatory testing was not the correct approach to minimizing in-prison transmission of the disease.[59] The courts have not yet fully resolved this issue, and it can be expected that suits will continue to appear as the number of infected inmates grows.

A second legal issue concerns confidentiality. The results of AIDS tests may form the basis for policy decisions that ultimately threaten privacy rights. A ruling in a New York case invalidated a separate housing policy because it labeled inmates as infected, and thus violated inmate privacy rights.[60] A New Jersey court ruled that unauthorized disclosure by police of a citizen's AIDS status was a violation of Fourteenth Amendment privacy rights.[61] Such revelations in a prison environment by correctional officers could well result in similar decisions.

Of course, the primary purpose of testing is to obtain information useful in formulating management policy. One important management option is segregation of HIV-positive inmates. Mandatory segregation is thus our third legal issue, and court challenges have been filed asserting that segregation practices are discriminatory and violate both privacy and medical care rights. The previously noted Alabama ruling upheld the segregation policy of that state, even though most states have not adopted mass segregation policies.[62] Alabama justifies its policy by claiming that failure to segregate increases fear and anxiety among inmates and staff, increases violence, and helps hasten the rate of transmission within the institutional environment. Critics of this view point out that the vast majority of states have not adopted such a policy, and there is no evidence that these fears are justified.[63]

In the case of Lewis v. Prison Health Services, the plaintiff objected that his segregation subsequent to testing positive for AIDS resulted in limitations placed on his being able to eat, exercise, or go to religious services with other inmates. The courts ruled in favor of the state and upheld the segregation policy.[64]

A fourth issue concerns the right to a safe institutional environment. Because of the high level of sexual assault in prisons, estimated to be as high as 28 percent in some systems, inmates have reasonable concerns about infection resulting from such assaults. In Florida, an infected inmate has filed suit alleging that he was infected when gang-raped while in prison.[65] The plaintiffs in an Indiana case argued that the state correctional system was negligent in its failure to segregate an infected inmate who bit another prisoner.[66] An Eighth Amendment federal case filed by an inmate who had been forced to share a cell with an infected inmate was dismissed by a judge who noted that the plaintiff failed to prove that the system's cell-sharing policy placed him in any serious jeopardy.[67] Although current cases have not resulted in decisions forcing states to assume responsibility for assaults by infected inmates, such decisions may not be long in arriving. Even without such a ruling, however, cases such as those in Florida and Indiana will probably motivate correctional officials to devote more attention to protecting inmates from assaults.

Another important issue concerns inmate rights to adequate medical care within prison. Several suits have been filed against correctional systems alleging various rights to medical care. To date, conflicting decisions have been handed down by the courts. For instance, although some courts have ruled that the state is not responsible for providing AZT to infected inmates, other rulings seem to affirm the right to this potentially life-prolonging drug.[68] A consent agreement reached in a Connecticut case has resulted in significant enhancements to the state's care system for infected inmates. The decision requires

> provision of infectious disease service specialists at all institutions; designation of a coordinator of AIDS-related medical services at all institutions; systematic intake screening and followup monitoring for persons with, or at risk for, HIV infection; individual treatment plans and followup schedules; referrals to infectious disease specialists; access to experimental drugs on a "compassionate use" and/or treatment IND basis; access to counseling and psychosocial services; careful maintenance of medical records; extensive discharge planning; and thorough quality assurance for all services.[69]

Connecticut's plan may well represent the most comprehensive health care program to date and provide a model for other states.

A number of cases in other states are still pending,[70] and these and other cases will be decided over the next several years. Nonetheless, U.S. Supreme Court decisions seem to suggest that "mere inadvertent failure to provide adequate medical care, however, does not reach constitutional limits. Prison officials must exhibit deliberate indifference to serious medical needs, through systemic deficiencies, such that unnecessary suffering is inevitable. In order to implicate constitutional rights, medical care must be grossly inadequate."[71]

There is evidence that in some cases such care **is grossly** inadequate. In a report to then-President George Bush, the National Commission on AIDS found that U.S. prisons were not providing adequate health care to AIDS-infected prisoners. Commission Vice Chair Dr. David E. Rogers noted that

> Health and medical care of prisoners has always been low priority, and nothing highlights this more than the large amounts of HIV infection and resulting illness in our prisoners . . . . I think all of us on the Commission were moved by the level of human misery this has created within our prison systems. Most of those incarcerated

will rapidly return to society. It is an ideal time to arm them with the knowledge and protection necessary to protect themselves and others.[72]

Inmate rights are not the only rights to come before the courts in recent years. Staff rights were at stake when a New Jersey court convicted an infected inmate of attempted murder for biting a correctional officer, presumably with the intent of transmitting AIDS. The defendant claimed that the "guard cut his hands on the prisoner's handcuffs while administering a racially motivated beating."[73] The prisoner was given a 25-year prison sentence. A similar decision was handed down in Texas for an inmate who spit in a guard's face.[74]

The rights of citizens outside of the prison environment have also been taken up in the courts. Consider the following scenario.

> David, tested HIV-seropositive, is paroled after counseling, in which he is told to inform his wife, Bronwyn, and to ensure that he practices "safe sex." He does not do so, and David's parole officer does not respond truthfully or helpfully when Bronwyn phones him to inquire whether David has AIDS. Subsequently, but still within the parole period, she becomes pregnant and gives birth to a child showing AIDS symptoms.[75]

What are the rights of spouses to be informed that their partner is HIV-positive? Does the state have an obligation to provide this information or must it permit the inmate to relay such information to his or her family? Should Bronwyn have been informed when David was released from custody, or at least when she called and explicitly asked whether David was infected? This issue is of substantial significance when one considers that more than 400,000 inmates are released from the adult correctional system annually.[76] Although the Federal system does require releasees to notify spouse prior to discharge, only a few states have adopted such policies.

Other legal issues, such as the right of infected inmates to participate in work and education programs, the right of staff to current information regarding AIDS, and the rights of inmates to sophisticated and expensive treatment regimens have been, and will continue to be, taken up in the courts. In the current overcrowded environment within which the correctional system must operate, it will not be easy to find ways to satisfy the AIDS-related demands of all the parties involved in the correctional process.

Summary

AIDS has created enormous difficulties both inside and outside correctional institutions. We have merely touched on some of the more serious problems. For several reasons, it should not be surprising if these problems prove to be extremely difficult to resolve.

First, efforts to address the AIDS epidemic in general have been slowed by the perception that the disease is an affliction of the wicked. Its association with homosexuality and drug use distinguishes it from other lethal conditions that have received more immediate and sympathetic attention.

Second, AIDS in prison involves a special group of stigmatized individuals. Not only are they likely to have used illegal drugs or engaged in homosexual conduct, but they have also broken criminal laws serious enough to result in their being sent to prison.

Third, the kinds of citizens in prison typically are not those associated with political power. As we have already seen, prison inmates tend to be disproportionately poor, minority, uneducated, and lacking in vocational skills. It is unlikely that such a group will be able to acquire sufficient political influence to assure that adequate effort is invested in addressing AIDS-related problems.

It should therefore come as little shock if citizens do not rise up in a public outcry for quick attention to the problems of AIDS in prisons. This is especially true in view of the fact that many of the remedies proposed to deal with the problems of AIDS in prisons will cost significant amounts of money. Citizens are thoroughly disgruntled about having to spend what is already being committed to crime and criminals. That they should resist spending additional resources for special medical facilities, education programs, or psychological counseling programs is understandable, if perhaps unfortunate.

Nonetheless, new ideas are beginning to appear that address the various problems associated with AIDS-infected inmates. In New York, for instance, a program has been started to make it possible for infected inmates to spend their final days at home. The program prohibits release of murderers and other violent offenders and is designed to allow only non-dangerous inmates out of prison. Despite promising beginnings, to date very few inmates have been able to take advantage of the program. According to Assemblyman Daniel L. Feldman of Brooklyn, "These people pose no danger to society. . . . But the program is moving incredibly slowly. The problem so far is that people die by the time you process the paper."[77] In fact, by the beginning of 1993 more applicants had died while awaiting processing than had been released to die at home.

Innovations such as the New York program do, however, offer some hope that eventually it will be possible to address the many pressing AIDS-related issues confronting the correctional system. Moreover, a variety of advocacy groups, such as the Alliance for Inmates with AIDS, have begun to appear across the country.[78] These groups are committed to increasing awareness of the problems of AIDS in prison as well as acting to develop strategies to create solutions to such problems.

Tuberculosis and the Modern Prison

The Return of a Menace

In the days before modern drug therapy and sanitation methods, tuberculosis was regarded as a major public health threat. The galloping consumption, as it was called, claimed many a famous victim, and even afflicted major figures in fiction, such as Raskolnikov in Dostoyevski's **Crime and Punishment**. About 25 percent of deaths in the United States were the result of tuberculosis at the outset of the twentieth-century.[79] Until recently, however, tuberculosis (TB) was no longer was regarded as a major health hazard. This situation has changed.

 TB is a communicable disease that attacks the lungs and can result in death. Only a subset of infected persons have active cases of the disease, and even these persons can be treated with drugs if diagnosed early enough.

In some respects TB is even more frightening than AIDS. For instance, it can be transmitted far more easily. The germ is usually transmitted through the air and does not require the kind of close interpersonal contact necessary to transfer the AIDS virus. It is possible for a healthy individual in a closed room with a coughing infected individual to catch the disease.

In the initial phase of infection the body's defenses attempt to destroy or confine the bacteria. This may be successful, and the progress of the disease may be terminated. In some cases the body's unaided efforts are not adequate, and a second stage, commonly referred to as "consumption," sets in. Lung damage increases, and lung function becomes impaired. This stage is characterized by coughing, shortness of breath, fever, night sweats, and weight loss. Ultimately death may occur.

Despite popular perceptions to the contrary, TB has never completely disappeared in the United States. In fact, more than 20,000 active cases of TB were reported in 1985, the lowest number in the post-World War II period. That number increased to 26,000 cases in 1991.[80] The Centers for Disease Control estimate that as many as 10 million Americans are infected with the disease. Equally troubling is the fact that several strains of the disease seem to be energetically resistant to the drugs that are typically used to treat the affliction. This is no minor matter because "[t]he average death rate from strains of TB resistant to two or more drugs is 50 percent, according to the American Lung Association."[81]

Some health officials do not foresee an encouraging immediate prognosis. "The outbreaks of the disease 'will be devastating,' said Dr. Michael Iseman of the National Jewish Center for Immunology and Infectious diseases, one of the country's leading experts on TB. 'We'll see lethal outcomes and massive epidemics—particularly in shelters, hospitals, AIDS hospices, and prisons. It has all the makings of a tragedy.'[82]

TB in Prisons

Although national data are still limited, there is growing evidence that TB represents a serious hazard in penal institutions. A study of New York State inmates revealed that the incidence of infected individuals rose from 15.4 per 100,000 in 1976-1978 to 105.5 in 1986.[83] This represents an enormous 700 percent increase in the rate of infected inmates in the New York system. A more recent 1991 report asserted that "25 percent of the state's new inmates test positive for tuberculosis."[84] Moreover, 12 inmates and one guard died of the disease during the first ten months of 1991.[85]

Although data on other states are still relatively sparse, and New York may be exceptional, it is likely that at least some other states will begin to experience worrisome difficulties with TB. In addition, jails are not immune to the hazard. Crowded conditions in the Cook County, Illinois jail, for example, led to a serious outbreak of the disease.[86] Dr. Alan Bloch of the Centers for Disease Control points out that "corrections facilities are sitting on a powder keg. . . . If TB gets in those systems, you have the potential for a very large number of cases to develop in a very short period of time."[87]

▦ TB-related Issues in Prisons

Many of the issues raised with regard to AIDS apply in the case of TB as well. Concerns have already been articulated regarding testing, segregation, education, staff training, and legal liability. The presence of TB in prison raises similar issues, but there also are some additional concerns.

First, the ease with which TB may be transmitted creates special difficulties for prison administrators. Unlike AIDS, TB can be transmitted through the air by infected individuals who cough in the presence of other persons. The germ is airborne, and close physical contact is not required for infection. Crowded conditions without adequate ventilation, similar to conditions found in many prison environments, increase the opportunities for contagion. "Studies have even shown that spending time in prison or jail can be an independent risk factor in itself for the contraction of tuberculosis."[88]

Second, there is growing evidence that TB and drug use are related. A study conducted in Fort Worth, Texas found that 25 percent of TB patients admitted to having used crack cocaine. The behavior of many crack addicts appears to lend itself to both contagion and disease progression. Such addicts may spend a considerable amount of time in closed rooms breathing the air of other addicts who may be infected. They may neglect their diet and general health, thereby reducing their ability to fight the infection. The Fort Worth study appears to confirm the findings of a smaller study conducted in Contra Costa, California.[89]

The relationship between drug use and TB is of special significance because, as we have already seen, substantial numbers of prison inmates have histories of drug abuse. As with AIDS, it should come as no surprise that increasing numbers of inmates are testing positive for TB.

Third, TB and AIDS also appear to be related. The New York study noted above found the increase in TB infection was accompanied by similar increases in AIDS infection. Research reveals that "extrapulmonary TB has been shown repeatedly to be increased in patients with AIDS and in HIV-infected patients."[90] Moreover, all 12 of the inmates who died of TB in New York tested positive for HIV. They may, therefore, have had immune systems that had been compromised by the virus, rendering them more vulnerable to TB.[91] "People who carry HIV have proven unusually susceptible to tuberculosis and, like any patient with tuberculosis, they can spread the germ if they are coughing."[92]

Naturally, inmates are worried about the threat of TB. But correctional staff and officials are also concerned. Thomas Kennedy, president of a local union representing correctional officials, noted that

> I have to tell you that in my 11 years as a correctional officer, I have never seen my people more scared. They're asking "Are my kids in danger? Is my family threatened?" This disease is killing people and I'm not confident that the state is going to act quickly and appropriately to protect our people.[93]

In recognition of this hazard, New York State instituted a mandatory TB testing program in its prisons in November 1991. In addition, inmates with TB will not be transferred between facilities. Drug therapy will be used to counter the disease, but drug resistant strains are making this difficult. Moreover, the treatments for resistant strains may take considerably longer and involve extraordinary costs. Dr. Iseman estimates that treatment may cost as much as $200,000 per patient, as compared to $150 for standard treatment.[94]

It can be expected that the problem will continue to grow worse, at least in the near future. About the deaths in New York, Dr. Iseman noted that

> These germs represents a new strain that is very frightening. . . .
> One case is chilling, but a dozen or 13 is nearly overwhelming because the prospects for treatment are so dreary.[95]

A judge has now ordered New York City to open an isolation unit on Rikers Island. The facility will eventually have space for 140 TB-infected inmates and will provide special care for such prisoners.[96] It is likely that other jurisdictions may eventually have to follow New York City's lead if they are to prevent large-scale outbreaks of TB within their correctional systems.

Focus 4-2
Disease in Prisons:
A Brief Historical Look

Concern with disease in prison extends back to the early days of the modern prison. In fact, some analysts argue that prisons are really an extension of the quarantine notion that was first applied to victims of leprosy and the plague. Fourteenth-century "hospitals"

> were institutions designed primarily to isolate, rather than to cure, the sick — to remove them from the mainstream of society so they would not infect or offend the healthy. When a sick person entered the hospital he was treated as if he were dead.[97]

Johnson thus refers to the modern prison as a form of "enlightened quarantine."[98]

From the point of view of corrections, therefore, the problem of disease in prison is potentially the problem of establishing an operational quarantine within a quarantine. Prisoners are isolated from the outside world, and again isolated from their fellow inmates within the prison.

A wide range of afflictions bedeviled prisoners in the eighteenth and nineteenth centuries, including scurvy, general malnutrition, jail-fever, smallpox, and a host of other diseases. Disease in European prisons was a continuing problem, as John Howard's report in the 1770s revealed. Only when a crisis occurred, however, was serious attention focused on prison health problems. In 1750, for instance, two diseased prisoners infected more than 50 individuals in the London courtroom where they were standing trial. The event motivated the authorities to do something about the disease-facilitating conditions within Newgate Prison, and the facility was rebuilt with more careful attention to hygiene.[99] Nonetheless, in the absence of such calamities resources were seldom committed to prison health issues.

A quarter-century after the London contagion, John Howard's famous tour of the prisons of Europe revealed that many prison health problems had still not been solved. In The State of the Prisons he wrote that prisoners could be seen pining under diseases, "sick, and in prison"; expiring on the floors, in loathsome cells, of pestilential fevers, and the confluent smallpox; victims, I must not say to the cruelty, but I will say to the inattention, of sheriffs, and gentlemen in the commission of the peace.[100]

I am ready to think, that none who give credit to what is contained in the foregoing pages, will wonder at the havoc made by the goal-fever. From my own observations in 1773, 1774, and 1775, I was fully convinced that many more prisoners were destroyed by it, than were put to death by all the public executions in the kingdom.[101]

Howard proposed a number of solutions to the health hazards of the prison environment. For instance, he argued that every institution ought to have an experienced medical officer. This physician should "constantly inculcate the necessity of cleanliness, and fresh air; and the danger of crowding prisoners together."[102] Howard saw the health risks of crowded penal conditions and submitted sensible recommendations that were only occasionally adopted.

Prisoners who were employed outside of prison walls by contractors experienced similar problems. An 1881 report in Alabama disclosed that convicts were ". . . poorly clothed and fed. . . . The sick were neglected, insomuch that no hospital had been provided, they being confined to their cells with the well convicts."[103] At two work sites in South Carolina the death rate was 52 percent. "An investigation showed the prisoners to be suffering from malnutrition, vermin, and beatings, and from living in indescribable filth."[104]

It is obvious that significant strides have been made in addressing the health-related issues associated with inmates. Diseases such as scurvy have been eliminated, although other maladies, such as AIDS, have taken their place. Moreover, although AIDS did not exist in the early period of imprisonment in America, tuberculosis was a serious problem. One study of 12 prisons in the latter decade of the nineteenth-century revealed that 45 percent of prison deaths were the result of this disease.[105] It is extraordinary that this disease has returned to claim modern inmate victims and to pose new challenges for correctional administrators.

Prisons and Older Offenders

Concerns about the costs of health care and the future of the Social Security system have focused popular attention on the fact that the American population is aging. Life expectancy in the United States has steadily increased, and the percentage of the population over age 65 has doubled during the course of the twentieth century.[106] Although persons aged 65 or over represented 8.5 percent of the population in 1950, 30 years later that percentage had increased to approximately 12 percent.[107] Moreover, some estimates indicate that the percentage of citizens 65 and over will increase to more than 15 percent by the year 2020.[108]

Increasing numbers of inmates in prisons and jails are also older citizens, although reliable national data on older inmates are not yet available. In part, the absence of such data reflects uncertainty regarding the age limit that ought to be used to classify offenders as older inmates. A publication of the U.S. Department of Justice used 50 as a possible age of demarcation. Although 50 may not sound old, there is some evidence that the physical age of prison inmates may be older than the chronological age. According to Steve Dann, chief of operations, Health Service Division, Bureau of Prisons,

> there is a 10-year differential between the overall health of Bureau of Prisons inmates and that of the general population. Because of the previous lifestyles of the inmates (a large number of them having used drugs and alcohol to excess, poor eating habits, stress in life) they have aged faster than the normal population, and a 50-year old will typically have the health problems of a 60-year old person on the outside."[109]

Using an age standard below the conventional standard of 65 for older age may well make sense in the context of the correctional system because concerns with older inmates generally do have to do with their health, rather than with the mere fact of their chronological age. A 1988 study conducted by the American Correctional Association found that there were almost 20,000 offenders older than 55 in prison. This represents a 50 percent increase over the figure for 1984.[110] Estimates in the **Corrections Yearbook—1991** indicate that approximately 50,000 offenders aged 50 or more were admitted to adult correctional institutions in 1990, representing slightly more than 5 percent of the total inmate population.[111] The Federal system appears to confine an even higher percentage of such inmates (12 percent in 1989).[112]

Other analysts argue that 50 is not a meaningful cutoff for categorizing offenders as elderly. Ruth Cavan notes, "Age 65 often signifies a break in life style and is more appropriate in identifying the beginning of old age than some arbitrarily selected younger age."[113] Sol Chaneles estimates that by the turn of the century between 40,000 and 50,000 inmates will be over 65.[114]

Whether defined as over 50 or over 65, the number of inmates requiring special care in the American prison system will increase substantially in the next decade. Both increased willingness to send offenders to prison and the increasing length of prison sentences assure that the proportion of older inmates will continue to grow.

Profile of the Older Inmate

As is the case for younger prisoners, older inmates are generally male. Ninety-six percent of inmates in the federal system are male,[115] while figures in the state penal systems range from 85 to 98 percent.[116] The literature provides contradictory evidence regarding the kinds of crimes for which these inmates are incarcerated. Ann Goetting notes that "available information strongly links elderly offenders, especially first offenders, with crimes of violence."[117] An analysis of elderly inmates in a southwestern prison found that "60 percent of the elderly had violent crime convictions."[118] Other evidence fails to confirm this violent profile. A study of more than 5,500 inmates over 50 in the federal system, for instance, found that only 13 percent had been committed to prison for crimes of violence.[119]

Part of the uncertainty regarding involvement in violence may stem from treating older inmates as a homogenous body. In fact, there are several ways to classify inmates that may be relevant to the issue of violence. Some older inmates are first-time offenders who might normally have been spared imprisonment save for the seriousness of their crime. Other inmates are long-time multiple offenders who have spent significant portions of their lives in prison for a variety of crimes, most often non-violent offenses. It is important to realize that violent offenders represent only a minority subset of even repeat older offenders. Carl Brahoe and Donald Bachand found that only slightly more than one-third of arrests of habitual older offenders were for violent crimes.[120] There is evidence that most older offenders do have prior convictions for crime, and many have already served prison terms.[121]

Irrespective of the crime of current commitment, it appears that most older inmates are not classified as dangerous. This may well have to do with their relatively advanced age and lack of apparent aggression. Of more than 5,000 older inmates classified in the federal system, only 46 were classified as highest risk (Level 6). About 80 percent of all older federal inmates were classified in the three lowest levels of the six-tier federal classification system.[122]

In terms of their physical well-being, older inmates are less healthy than their younger peers. An assessment of the federal system projected that by the year 2005 "more than 30 percent of the inmate population aged 50 or above will have some form of cardiac and hypertensive disorder which will require substantial medical attention."[123] A study of all 179 older inmates in a southwestern state institution found that only three had no medical alerts on their records. Approximately three-quarters had two to four alerts.[124]

Special Problems and Needs

In light of the increase in the number of older inmates projected for the American penal system, there are several special problems and needs that will have to be addressed by correctional administrators in the years to come. We will briefly touch on four of these issues: protection, physical and mental health care, management of inmates without special needs, and release of older inmates.

Protection

As is the case on the outside, older individuals are at greater potential risk for a wide variety of victimizations. Diminished physical strength, agility, and sharpness of senses make such individuals easy targets for assailants. It can be argued that the prison environment is especially dangerous, and that older inmates stand a greater risk of assault, including sexual assault, than do their younger counterparts.[125] A New Jersey study found that older inmates expressed a greater need for protection against the aggression of other inmates than did more youthful inmates.[126]

The full extent to which the concern with safety is legitimate is not fully understood at this point. Some analysts point out that elderly inmates are accorded a level of status and deference not available to younger inmates.[127] Their social status may thus insulate them from victimization. Of course, even if this has been the case traditionally, the increase in the numbers of elderly inmates may transform the dynamics of the status hierarchy within the prison and diminish the protections often accorded to the heretofore small number of older inmates. It is also possible that, like on the outside, older inmates may recognize their vulnerability and successfully take precautions to reduce their risk of victimization.

Physical and Mental Health Care

It is not controversial that with the increase in the number of older inmates will come an increase in the demands for medical services. It is likely that older inmates will not, however, require the kinds of trauma care associated with younger inmates. Injuries typically associated with aggressive younger inmates, such as stab wounds, may be less problematic. Older inmates will require more long-term care for problems resulting from normal physical and mental deterioration. A study of inmates aged 63 to 80 found that 80 percent of these prisoners claimed to have one or more medical problems, and 60 percent indicated that they had three or more medical problems.[128] The demand for care designed to handle emphysema, cancer, heart disease, and many other conditions associated with aging will increase. Alzheimer's patients will presumably become more numerous. As in the free population, nursing care will become increasingly important as medical advances make prolongation of life possible. Many of those who live longer will be unable to get around without assistance, if at all. Their basic needs, including those associated with feeding and bathing, will have to be met by staff. Environmental changes, such as those needed to accommodate wheelchair bound inmates, will have to be incorporated into facility design.

None of these adjustments will be possible without a serious rethinking of traditional resource utilization. "All evidence suggests that correctional systems will need to increase the resources allocated for the geriatric care of long-term inmates."[129] One study of elderly inmates found that "the elderly convict suffers from an average of three chronic illnesses, tripling the cost of his care from a yearly average of $23,000 to over $70,000." [130]

A number of approaches will have to be considered. Existing facilities can be modified to handle increasing numbers of older inmates. New facilities can be constructed with specially designed wings for elderly inmates. Specially-designed facilities to provide effective health care to high-demand inmates can be built. This would essentially copy the nursing home model in free society. Typically, in such nursing home-type environments inmates would live in a world essentially isolated from younger residents.

As matters currently stand, little national effort has been expended to address the special needs of older inmates. California has been at the forefront of a number of correctional innovations. According to California Board of Corrections spokeswoman Cristine May, however, if older inmates "have a specific need, that's handled. But we don't have any one person who is in charge of them. From our perspective, they're just part of day-to-day business."[131] A few states, such as South Carolina, have designed special programs and staff training seminars to address the special needs of older inmates.[132] Nonetheless, California's approach is far more typical.

Elderly Inmates without Special Needs

Another issue which mirrors conditions in free society is the problem of how older inmates who do not have special problems or limitations ought to be treated. In the free world older citizens are often forced into retirement before they elect to abandon working life. They are excluded, intentionally or not, from personal, family, and social planning activities. Older citizens are often made to feel useless despite the fact that they possess significant experience and abilities and could continue to make valuable contributions.

Similar to the free world, many older inmates are not physically or mentally incapacitated. Correctional administrators will have to grapple with the question of whether, on the basis of age alone, older inmates should be excused from the obligations that must be shouldered by other inmates. Should older inmates not be asked to discharge cleaning and maintenance duties which are typically the responsibility of inmates? Should they be freed from workshop assignments? Should they be denied the opportunity to participate in income-producing activities, such as those in prison factories? In fact, denying inmates opportunities to participate in such activities on the sole basis of age may raise legal questions akin to those currently being litigated on behalf of older free citizens. (One issue currently receiving increasing attention involves the right of the elderly to continue to drive and to be free from frequent special examinations to assess driving competence.)

Release of the Elderly

Finally, the question of the conditions under which the elderly ought to be released from prison will have to be addressed. Is it fair to refuse to release an inmate who is not a threat to society, and who has served a term as long as those served by similar but younger offenders, simply because they are aged? Is this a form of age discrimination? Presumably the grounds for trying to retain custody would be that such inmates are not able to look after themselves. But is the assessment of the ability to look after oneself a determination the state should be making? In one sense the issue is similar to that confronted by the mental health system. Should the state have the right perpetually to confine a non-dangerous mental patient in an institution? The deinstitutionalization movement in the 1960s and 1970s resulted in the release of thousands of individuals from institutions. Defenders of this shift argue that these releases were justified because most could look after themselves, and that mentally troubled or not, they had a right to their freedom. Critics insist that the problem of the homeless mentally ill is a product of this policy, and that these releases merely guaranteed such citizens higher risks of poverty, disease, and criminal victimization. The issue has never been satisfactorily resolved in the mental health system, and it is perhaps unreasonably optimistic to anticipate that the problem of the release of the elderly will be handled any more easily by the criminal justice system.

Conclusions

This chapter has examined three inmate groups that will become of increasing importance to correctional administrators: AIDS-infected inmates, tuberculosis-infected prisoners, and elderly inmates. These groups pose special challenges that will require potentially extraordinary infusions of human and economic resources. In one sense, they provide a dramatic representation of the increasing complexity of the correctional mission. The doubling of the incarceration rate from 1980 to 1990[133] has produced not only more inmates but also a wider variety of inmates. Correctional systems strained by overwhelming numbers of inmates also find themselves beset by problems associated with the special needs of inmate groups such as those that have been the subject of our discussion in this chapter. Because of the quantitative and qualitative aspects of current and near-future correctional conditions, a good case can be made that the correctional mission has never been more difficult.

Notes

[1] Dillingham, Steven D. and Greenfeld, Lawrence A. (1991) "An overview of correctional statistics," *Corrections Today*, 55(2), p. 29; Gilliard, Darrell K., Bureau of Justice Statistics, (1993) *Prisoners in 1992*, Washington, D.C.: U.S. Department of Justice, 1993.

[2] Altman, Lawrence K. (1992) "Researchers report much grimmer AIDS outlook," *New York Times* June 4, p. A1.

[3] See Dillingham and Greenfeld, note 1 above at 5.

[4] Hammett, Theodore M. (1989) *AIDS in Correctional Facilities: Issues and Options*, Washington, D.C.: National Institute of Justice, p. 3.

[5] See Altman, note 2 above.

[6] *New York Times* (1993) "The Unyielding AIDS Epidemic," June 17, p. A14. *New York Times* (1993) "U.S. says spread of AIDS to slow," Jan. 15, p. A8.

[7] Leary, Warren (1993) "Spread of AIDS is spurred by racism, U.S. panel says," *New York Times*, Jan. 12, p. A10.

[8] See *New York Times*, note 6 above.

[9] Id. at 6.

[10] Id. at 5.

[11] See *New York Times*, Jan. 15, 1993, note 6 above.

[12] See Altman, note 2 above at A1.

[13] Id. at 7.

[14] Jarlais, Don Des, and Hunt, Diana E. (1988) "AIDS and intravenous drug use," National Institute of Justice Research Bulletin, Washington, D.C.: Bureau of Justice Statistics, p. 1.

[15] Beck, Allen, et al (1993) "Survey of State Prison Inmates, 1991" Washington, D.C.: Bureau of Justice Statistics, p. 22.

[16] Moiri, Saira and Hammett, Theodore M. (1990) "1989 Update: AIDS in Correctional Facilities," Washington D.C.: National Institute of Justice, p. 16.

[17] Nacci, Peter L. and Kane, Thomas R. (1983) "The incidence of sex and sexual aggression in federal prisons," *Federal Probation*, 47(4); Wooden, Wayne S. and Parker, Jay (1982) *Men Behind Bars: Sexual Exploitation in Prison*, New York: Plenum Press.

[18] Hammett, Theodore M. and Daugherty, Andrea L. (1991) "1990 Update: AIDS in Correctional Facilities," Washington, D.C.: National Institute of Justice, p. 11.

[19] See Moiri and Hammett, note 16 above at 16.

[20] See Hammett and Daugherty, note 18 above at 13.

[21] Associated Press (1989) "One in 24 inmates infected with AIDS," *Corrections Today*, 51 (December), p. 165.

[22] Smith, Perry F. (1991) "HIV infection among women entering the New York State correctional system," *The American Journal of Public Health*, 81 (supplement), May, p. 35.

[23] Id. at 12-13. Some state studies, especially those that have not screened all incoming inmates, have found higher percentages, up to more than 30 percent. See Dugdale, David and Peterson, Ken (1989) *The Prison Journal*, 69(1), p. 36.

[24] See Smith, note 22 above at 12-13.

[25] Camp, George M. and Camp, Camille Graham (1991) *The Corrections Yearbook*, South Salem, NY: Criminal Justice Institute, p. 28.

[26] Gido, Rosemary (1989) "A demographic and epidemiological study of New York State inmate AIDS mortalities, 1981-1987," *The Prison Journal*, 69(1).

[27] See Hammett and Daugherty, note 18 above at 13.

[28] Id. at 15.

[29] Id.

[30] See, e.g., Newman v. Alabama 349 F. Supp. 278 (M.D. Ala. 1972); Estelle v. Gamble, 429 U.S. 97, 97 S. Ct. 285, 50 L. Ed. 2d 251 (1976).

[31] See Moiri and Hammett, note 16 above at 50.

[32] See Hammett and Daugherty, note 18 above at 43.

[33] Blumberg, Mark and Langston, Denny (1991) "Mandatory testing in criminal justice settings," *Crime and Delinquency*, 37(1).

[34] Hammett, Theodore M. (1986) "AIDS in prisons and jails: Issues and options," *Research in Brief*, Washington, D.C.: National Institute of Justice.

[35] See Hammett and Daugherty, note 18 above at 51.

[36] Id.

[37] Id. at 54.

[38] Derived from Hammett and Daugherty, see note 18 above at 54.

[39] Branham, Lynn S. (1990) "out of sight, out of danger?: Procedural due process and the segregation of HIV-positive inmates," *Hastings Constitutional Law Quarterly*, 17.

[40] Belbot, Barbara A. and del Carmen, Rolando V. (1991) "AIDS in Prison: Legal Issues," *Crime and Delinquency*, 37 (1), p. 146.

[41] Id. at 147.

[42] See Hammett, note 34 above at 3.

[43] See Hammett and Daugherty, note 18 above at 29.

[44] Id. at 30-31.

[45] Id. at 34.

[46] See Beck, note 15 at 4.

[47] Criminal Justice Newsletter (1990) "Correctional systems struggle with ever-increasing AIDS cases," Aug. 15, 21(16), p. 5.

[48] Greenspan, Judy (1991) "Women develop effective AIDS education programs," *National Prison Project Journal*, 6(4), p. 18.

[49] Olivero, Michael (1990) "Intravenous Drug Use and AIDS: A review and analysis of evolving correctional policy," *Criminal Justice Policy Review*, 3(4), p. 368.

[50] See Hammett and Daugherty, note 18 above at 31-32.

[51] Id.

[52] Id. at 32.

[53] Id. at 40.

[54] Id.

[55] Quoted in Hammett and Daugherty, note 18 above at 57.

[56] See Hammett and Daugherty, note 18 above at 65.

[57] Criminal Justice Newsletter (1991) "Court upholds Alabama policy of segregating inmates with HIV," Oct. 1, 1991, 2(19), p. 6.

[58] Takas, Marianne and Hammett, Theodore M. (1989) "Legal issues affecting offenders and staff," *National Institute of Justice AIDS Bulletin*, Washington, D.C.: National Institute of Justice, p. 2.

[59] "Inmates' request for mandatory testing denied." (1992) *On the Line*, 15(2), p. 2.

[60] See Takas and Hammett, note 58 above at 3.

[61] See Hammett and Daugherty, note 18 above at 66.

[62] Criminal Justice Newsletter (1991) "Court upholds Alabama policy of segregating inmates with HIV," Oct. 1, 1991, 2(19), p. 6.

[63] Carroll, Leo "AIDS and human rights in the prison: A comment on the ethics of screening and segregation," in Hartjen and Rhine (eds.) *Correctional Theory and Practice* Chicago: Nelson Hall Pub., pp. 162-177.

[64] Olivero, Michael (1990) "The treatment of AIDS behind walls of correctional facilities," *Social Justice*, 17(1), p. 116.

[65] Id. at 121.

[66] Id.

[67] See Hammett and Daugherty, note 18 above at 67.

[68] Id. at 66.

[69] Id. at 66.

[70] Id. at 67.

[71] Lambrou, Irene (1989) "AIDS behind bars: Prison responses and judicial deference," *Temple Law Review*, 62(1), p. 338.

[72] Corrections Compendium (1991) "AIDS Commission reports prisons fail to provide adequate care for HIV-infected inmates," 16(4), pp. 13-14.

[73] See Hammett and Daugherty, note 18 above at 67.

[74] Id.

[75] Klenig, John and Lindner, Charles (1989) "AIDS on parole: Dilemmas in decision making," *Criminal Justice Policy Review*, 3(1), p. 9.

[76] See Camp and Camp, note 25 above at 15-16.

[77] Clines, Francis X. (1993) "Inmates with AIDS long for death at home," *New York Times*, Jan. 5, p. A7.

[78] Walker, Jackie (1992) "Dynamic N.Y. alliance convenes on behalf of inmates with AIDS," *The National Prison Project Journal*, 7(2), p. 18.

[79] Elvin, Jan (1992) "TB comes back, poses special threat to jails, prisons, *The National Prison Project Journal*, 7(1), p. 1.

[80] Chapman, Lou (1992) "TB lurks among crack users, study says," *Fort Worth Star-Telegram*, May 16, p. A8.

[81] Chapman, Lou (1992) "At the front—Tarrant wages new drug war on TB with unique program," *Fort Worth Star-Telegram*, May 17, p. 34.

[82] See Beck, note 15 at 10; Rosenthal, Elisabeth (1991) "Doctors warn of a looming TB threat," *New York Times*, Nov. 16, p. 22.

[83] Braun, Mile M, Truman, Benedict I., Maguire, Barbara, DiFerdinando, George T., Wormser, Gary, Broaddus, Raymond, and Morse, Dale (1989) "Increasing incidence of tuberculosis in a prison inmate population," *Journal of the American Medical Association*, 261(3), p. 393.

[84] McFadden, Robert C. (1991) "Mandatory testing for TB in prisons starts with guards," *New York Times*, May, 19, p. B3.

[85] McFadden, Robert D. (1991) "A drug-resistant TB results in 13 deaths in New York prisons," *New York Times*, Nov. 16, p. 1.

[86] See Elvin, note 79 above at 3.

[87] Id. at 4.

[88] Id. at 3.

[89] See Chapman, note 80 above at 1.

[90] See Braun, Truman, Maguire, DiFerdinando, Wormser, Broaddus, and Morse, note 83 above at 396.

[91] See McFadden, note 84 above at 1.

[92] See Rosenthal, note 82 above at 22.

[93] See McFadden, note 84 above at B3.

[94] See McFadden, note 85 above at 22.

[95] Id. at 22.

[96] See Elvin, note 79 above at 21.

[97] Gottfried (1983), quoted in Johnson, Robert (1987) *Hard Time—Understanding and Reforming the Prison*, Monterey, CA: Brooks-Cole, p. 10.

[98] Id. at 17.

[99] Ignatieff, Michael (1978) *A Just Measure of Pain*, New York: Columbia University Press, pp. 44-45.

[100] Howard, John (1929) *The State of the Prisons* (orig. 1777), London: J.M. Dent & Sons, p. 1.

[101] Id. at 6.

[102] Id. at 29.

[103] Quoted in Sellin, J. Thorsten (1976) *Slavery and the Penal System*, New York: Elsevier, p. 151.

[104] Id. at 158.

[105] McKelvey, Blake (1977) *American Prisons: A History of Good Intentions*, Montclair, NJ: Patterson Smith, p. 191.

[106] Coleman, James W. and Cressey, Donald R. (1990) *Social Problems*, 4th ed. New York: Harper and Row, p. 258.

[107] Id.; Cavan, Ruth S. (1987) "Is special treatment needed for elderly offenders?" *Criminal Justice Policy Review*, 2(3), p. 213.

[108] See Cavan, note 107 above at 213.

[109] Kratcoski, Peter C. and Pownall, George A. (1989) "Federal Bureau of Prisons programming for older inmates," *Federal Probation*, 53(2), p. 30.

[110] *Corrections Today* (1990) "The aging prison population—Inmates in gray," 52(5), p. 138; Sullivan, Larry E. (1990) *The Prison Reform Movement—Forlorn Hope*, Boston, Twayne Publishers, p. 135.

[111] See Camp and Camp, note 25 above at 12-13.

[112] See Kratcoski and Pownall, note 109 above at 30.

[113] See Cavan, note 107 above at 214.

[114] Chaneles, Sol (1991) "Growing old behind bars." in Haas and Alpert (eds.) *The Dilemmas of Corrections*, Prospect Heights, IL: Waveland Press, pp. 490-491.

[115] See Kratcoski and Pownall, note 109 above at 31.

[116] Goetting, Ann (1983) "The elderly in prison: Issues and Perspectives." *Journal of Research in Crime and Delinquency*, 20(2), p. 292.

[117] Id. at 292.

[118] McShane, Marilyn and Frank P. Williams III (1990) "Old and ornery: The disciplinary experiences of elderly prisoners," *International Journal of Offender Therapy and Comparative Criminology*, 34(3), p. 209.

[119] See Kratcoski and Pownall, note 109 above at 31.

[120] Brahoe, Carl I. and Bachand, Donald J. (1985) "Criminal activity and characteristics of habitual vs. nonhabitual elderly offenders," Paper presented at 38th Annual Meeting of the Gerontological Society of America, Nov. 22-26.

[121] See Goetting, note 116 above at 292; see Kratcoski and Pownall, note 109 above at 31.

[122] See Kratcoski and Pownall, note 109 above.

[123] Id. at 30.

[124] See McShane and Williams III, note 118 above at 208.

[125] Aday, R.H. and Webster, E.L. (1979) "Aging in prison: The development of a preliminary model," *Offender Rehabilitation*, 3(3).

[126] Walsh, C. Eamon (1992) "Aging inmate offenders: Another perspective," in Hartjen and Rhine (eds.) *Correctional Theory and Practice*, Chicago: Newson Hall Pub., pp. 206-208.

[127] See Goetting, note 116 above at 294.

[128] Vega, Manuel and Silverman, Mitchell (1988) "Stress and the Elderly Convict," *International Journal of Offender Therapy and Comparative Criminology*, 32(2), p. 159.

[129] See Kratcoski and Pownall, note 109 above at 34.

[130] See Sullivan, note 110 above at 135.

[131] *Corrections Today* (1990) "The aging prison population—Inmates in gray," 52(5), p. 139.

[132] Morton, Joann B. (1993) "Training staff to work with elderly and disabled inmates," *Corrections Today*, 55(1).

[133] Greenfeld, Lawrence A. (1992) "Prisons and prisoners in the United States," Washington, D.C.: U.S. Dept. of Justice, p. ii.

5

Women in Prison

As has been well-documented in previous chapters, prison and jail populations in the United States have soared. Although our focus has been upon prisons for men, the same phenomenon has been experienced in prisons for women. The number of women in state and federal prisons at the beginning of 1992 approached 50,000 inmates, a historic high water mark.

The increase in women sentenced to serve prison terms has created a number of problems that resemble difficulties we have already encountered in our discussion of males. Prison crowding, increasing costs, inadequate services, and a host of gender-neutral problems have exacerbated existing circumstances and created new difficulties. Beyond these, however, special problems associated with the incarceration of women have emerged or have become more serious as a result of the increasing use of imprisonment for female offenders.

In this chapter we will accomplish several objectives. First, in an effort to place the current situation in context we will recount the major events in the history of imprisonment of women offenders in the United States. Second, we will detail the current status of the incarceration of women in the nation's prisons. Third, we will examine three of the special problems posed by the imprisonment of women that must be addressed in the coming years. Finally, we will consider some of the lessons that might be learned from these problems which can help us better understand the advantages and disadvantages of the imprisonment of both females and males as a response to crime.

Women in Prison: A Historical Perspective

As was true for men in the early colonial period, incarceration was not a punishment of regular resort for women offenders. Although some early jails did exist, most convicted criminals were subjected to banishment, execution, corporal punishment, fines, or public humiliation. Women whose behavior put them beyond the boundaries of acceptable standards found themselves isolated, and sometimes excluded, from the larger society. "Officials warned out widows with children and unwed mothers with bastards; the one would drain relief funds, the other would imperil morality."[1]

It was not until the end of the eighteenth century that incarceration became an important aspect of the American response to crime. In the 1880s both men and women were confined in the Walnut Street Jail, and there was no physical segregation by gender.[2] Prisons, such as Newgate of New York, held both sexes but made an effort to separate them in different rooms.[3] This became the standard pattern in the early part of the century.[4]

Although women could be incarcerated for serious crimes, most were sentenced to confinement for relatively minor offenses, such as begging, larceny, vagrancy, and prostitution.[5] Because women were regarded as more pure than men, these relatively minor offenses were regarded in a more serious light. They were seen as indicative of a deeper depravity and therefore merited more serious sanctions.[6]

With the emergence of penitentiaries, women were separated from men but were not initially provided with separate buildings or institutions.[7] In the 1820s, women administrators were put in charge of units holding female inmates for the first time.[8] In Baltimore, for example, segregated housing was provided and a female matron placed in charge of operations.[9] By the 1830s another step was taken. Under the technical supervision of New York's Sing Sing prison, a separate building was erected to confine women, and in 1837 a woman was given administrative responsibility for the unit.[10] New York's Mount Pleasant Prison "was the first and only penal institution for women established before the great era of prison construction that commenced in the late nineteenth-century."[11]

Although it is difficult to obtain adequate data to conduct careful comparisons of men's and women's prisons in this period of penal history, some analysts have concluded that women were sometimes, though not always, forced to endure harsher conditions than those experienced by their male counterparts. Women, for instance, typically were not provided with single cells in the early penitentiaries. Instead, they were confined in large rooms with a number of other inmates.[12] Whether this is a liability or an advantage depends on a number of variables. One of the common criticisms of the early penitentiary system, for instance, was that single-celling imposed levels of isolation on inmates that proved psychologically tortuous. The human need for contact might thus have been better met in the congregate living arrangements characteristic of units holding women. On the other hand, there is evidence that some of these congregate units were disorderly places where some inmates would have experienced discomforts that single-celling would have eliminated.[13]

Whatever the relative experience of male and female prisoners, the experience could not have been particularly pleasant for either group. Endemic crowding during the early part of the second half of the nineteenth century made it increasingly difficult to maintain adequate segregation between the sexes. By 1872 even Mount Pleasant was jammed with inmates.[14] When Mary Carpenter toured American prisons in 1873 she found that

> The existing jails are insufficient both in size and number, and the overcrowding of the prisoners necessarily causes great demoralization among them . . . The female prisoners are not properly separated from the males, nor are they under proper supervision. . . . I saw in the cells two or three prisoners together, without anything to prevent them from spending the whole day in idleness and injurious conversation.[15]

During this period Zebulon Brockway converted a house of shelter for women into a women's prison to which "the better behaved women could be removed and detained under a more liberal and homelike discipline until the expiration of their sentences."[16] Penal historian Blake McKelvey regards the facility as the "first women's reformatory in America."[17]

The use of reformatories was not at first extended to the handling of female convicts. McKelvey notes that this omission was "possibly because their number in most states seemed too insignificant to demand special care and they fitted into the household economy of both jails and prisons."[18] In 1881, however, the Hudson House of Refuge was opened primarily to handle female misdemeanants, chiefly minor sexual morality offenders. A full-scale reformatory was established around the turn of the century at Bedford Hills.[19] "The inmates here were the first women to receive the complete reformatory treatment—indeterminate sentences, grades and marks, literary and trade instruction, and wholesome farm labor—and the provision of separate cottages for the accommodation of those of the top grade added a significant feature to the environment of adult reformatories. . . . It not only heralded a new day for female prisoners but led the next generation in its attempts to improve on the Elmira technique."[20] Other states emulated the New York example, and the federal system built its first reformatory at Alderson, West Virginia in 1927, using the cottage plan that had been developed in New York. This facility in turn provided the model for states such as California, which opened its first separate prison for women in 1929.[21] Nonetheless, not all regions of the nation were equally affected by the reformatory movement, and southern and western states demonstrated little inclination to apply the plan to the handling of women inmates.[22]

Rafter divides the early period of women's imprisonment into two periods: the custodial (1790-1870) and reformatory (1870-1935). The former period was characterized by significant concerns with cost-management, emphasis on the incarceration of felony offenders, primarily property offenders, relatively powerless female prison administrators, an emphasis on discipline, and only limited interest in institutional programs beyond work (for example, clothing and manufacturing furniture). Reformatory institutions, on the other hand, were generally physically separate institutions situated in rural areas. They used the cottage model of architectural design. Inmates tended to be misdemeanants committed for prostitution, petty theft, vagrancy, public intoxication, and waywardness. Women ran these institutions, and had more control than did their predecessors in custodial institutions. Discipline in these institutions was milder than had been typical for custodial prisons. Finally, reformatory institutions featured a variety of programs for inmates. These programs differed from reformatory programs in men's reformatories in that they prepared women to assume the typical female responsibilities of the historical period. Programs were available in domestic arts such as sewing, cooking, and cleaning and were designed to make it possible for women to step into typical feminine social roles.

After 1935, women's institutions resembled both custodial and reformatory prisons to various extents. There were substantial regional differences, and no new model emerged to overwhelm the influences of the earlier traditions. "It is difficult to discern a distinctive correctional model for women among the correctional approaches that have been tried since the 1930s. This situation may be due to the fact that recent theories about the causes and treatment of criminal behavior do not discriminate between the sexes."[23] A number of women's prisons opened in the period beginning in the mid-1930s,[24] but they received relatively little attention from penologists or reformers. There were few truly significant innovations in women's corrections although, as we will see, a number of innovations have changed some of the ways in which these prisons now operate.

Current Status of Women in Prison

Women have never represented a substantial portion of citizens incarcerated in American prisons and jails. Even with the incredible rise in the general use of incarceration during the past decade, the 44,010 women imprisoned in state facilities and the 6,399 held in federal prisons at the beginning of 1993 represented only 5.7 percent of all inmates held in state and federal prisons.[25] This is essentially identical to the rate at the beginning of the 1970s. However, it represents a percentage increase of about 40 from 1980 (4.1 to 5.7 percent).[26] Nonetheless, with but a single exception, in all states with more than 500 female inmates the proportion of females is less than 7 percent.

It is important to note that the "rate of growth for female inmates exceeded that for males in each year since 1981."[27] The percentage increase for females in 1992 was 5.9 as compared with 7.3 for males.[28] Nonetheless, "percentage increases are drastically influenced by the size of the base number. The number of women in prison has been, until recently, extremely small; therefore, large percentage increases have not represented huge numerical increases."[29] In 1992, the number of male prisoners per 100,000 population was 636 compared to only 35 per 100,000 for females, an 18-fold difference.[30] The growth rate for females has actually declined from 1991 to 1992, dropping from 8.4 percent to 5.9 percent.[31]

For this same period, of states with at least 500 female inmates, eight had increases of 10 percent or more in female prisoners, while four states actually showed small decreases. During this period the number of female inmates in the federal system grew 13.2 percent.[32]

Females held in single-sex prisons are about as likely as their male counterparts to be held in medium or minimum security facilities. About 65 percent of women were held in such institutions while 62 percent of males were similarly situated.[33]

Although the focus of this chapter is on women in prison, a brief word about jails is in order. The picture for jails is very similar to that for prisons. The average daily jail population of females in 1991 was 38,818, about 9 percent of the total jail population. The percentage of women is about 11 if the annual number of jail admissions is examined for 1991. About 10 percent of convicted jail inmates are women, while 8.7 percent of inmates awaiting trial are women.[34] Data from the National Jail Census reveal that the percentage of women in jail has increased from 6.3 in 1978 to 8.4 in 1988.[35] By the beginning of 1990 9.5 percent of jail inmates were women.[36] Again, the proportion of women held in custody has increased, although women still represent a small fraction of all inmates.

Not surprisingly, the increase in women inmates has been accompanied by an increase in facilities to house them. During the 1980s, 34 states created either new facilities or additional space to house female prisoners. Currently half of the states have plans in the works for even more construction.[37]

Why are more women being confined in American prisons and jails? Several explanations have been put forth to explain the increase. First, it is possible that women have become more heavily involved in the kinds of crimes that lead to imprisonment. Indeed there has been an increase in the number of offenses perpetrated by women in some crime categories, such as embezzlement, aggravated assault, and forgery.[38] There has also been a sharp increase in arrests of women for drug-related offenses, and women are being sentenced to prison in historically unprecedented numbers for such crimes.[39] Nonetheless, a fair amount of evidence indicates that there has not been enough of a female crime wave during the past decade to account for the rise in women in prisons and jails.[40]

Another explanation is the general interest in tougher sanctions for criminals of either gender. At least with regard to drug offenses, this seems to be a reasonable explanation. Studies of the relationship between female drug addiction and crime indicate that increasing numbers of women are struggling with addiction problems and engaged in crime to support their addictions.[41] The War on Drugs has resulted in decreased tolerance of drug-related crime, and many states as well as the federal government have increased the penalties for such offenses.

The emergence of determinate sentencing may also play a role. In states where judges have been stripped of their traditional sentencing discretion, both women and men who might have received community-based sanctions in the past may be finding themselves serving time in penal institutions.

Finally, it may be that women who had previously been the beneficiary of more lenient sentencing, the so-called chivalry effect, are now being treated like their male counterparts, or even more harshly. The evidence is mixed regarding whether this effect has ever existed, or if it has, where and how it has operated.[42] Still, "most statistics indicate that some type of chivalry did operate to divert women from prison."[43] The increase in women in prison may reflect, in part, a reduction in the willingness to practice such diversion.

An American Correctional Association survey conducted in the late 1980s provides insight into the characteristics of women sentenced to terms in the state and federal prison systems. More than 2,000 inmates were surveyed at over 400 different facilities. Three-quarters of these women had prior arrest records. Similar to males, a subset had extensive arrest records. About one out of every six inmates had records of ten or more arrests. Slightly less than half of the inmates were serving their first prison term, while the remainder had been previously incarcerated. About 15 percent had served at least five terms of incarceration.[44]

According to official police statistics, women are involved in 18 percent of all arrests. Despite percentage increases in the involvement of women in violent crime, the numbers remain relatively limited when compared to males. About 12 percent of homicide arrests are of women, 1 percent of forcible rape arrests, 8 percent of robbery arrests, and 14 percent of aggravated assault arrests.[45] Naturally, these serious offenses are the kinds most likely to result in a term of incarceration subsequent to conviction. Current data on women inmates reveal that they are about as likely to be serving a sentence for a violent (32 percent) as for a property (29 percent) or a drug (33 percent) offense. Public order offenses (5.1 percent) lagged behind violent and property crimes. It is important to point out that the percentages for violent crimes declined from the late 1970s through the early 1990s, while the other three categories showed increases.[46] This is consistent with what has been observed for males: A higher proportion of nonviolent offenders are being incarcerated now than in the past.

Like their male counterparts, the use of drugs by women who are eventually sentenced to terms of incarceration is quite high. A National

111

Institute of Justice study found that in 21 major American cities the percentage of females arrestees testing positive (urinalysis) for drugs (for example, cocaine, marijuana, heroin, ice, PCP) was as high as 76 percent (Philadelphia). The lowest percentage was 39 in Indianapolis, and the average for the 21 cities was 63 percent. This was higher than the average for male arrestees (58.3 percent), and a greater percentage of women than men tested positive in 13 of the 21 cities where comparison data were available. In almost all the cities (18 of 21) a majority of females arrested tested positive.

A survey that asked female state prison inmates to indicate whether they had used illegal drugs prior to entering prison revealed that more than 70 percent had used such drugs. More than half (56.5 percent) had been regular users, and one-third were under the influence of drugs when they committed the crime for which they were incarcerated.[47]

In light of these findings it might be expected that the percentage of women in prison confined for drug-related offenses has climbed substantially during the past decade. While in 1979 10.5 percent of females in state prisons were serving time for drug convictions,[48] by 1991 the figure had risen to 33 percent, an enormous increase.[49]

In sum, although 3 out of 10 incarcerated women are in prison for violent crimes, the majority serve time for non-violent crimes. The vast majority (three-quarters) are not new to the criminal justice system, having accumulated arrests prior to the arrest that resulted in their incarceration. On average, female state prison inmates are sentenced to 66 months, but serve only 16 months of the sentence (24 percent). As might be expected, the longest sentences imposed and served are for crimes of violence, with murder heading the list at 200 months imposed and 42 months served.[50]

In many respects, the women who are confined in prison mirror their male counterparts. Only 39 percent are high school graduates, minorities are disproportionately represented (57 percent), and they tend to be young (a majority between the ages of 25 and 34). Less than one-quarter are currently married, and about 80 percent have at least one child.[51] About 40 percent report that they had been "physically or sexually abused at some time in their lives before their current imprisonment."[52] Unlike many male prisoners, however, significant numbers of women inmates are the primary or sole provider for children. As we will see, this creates special challenges in handling and providing for female inmates.

Problems in Women's Prisons

We now turn to consideration of several of the problems posed by the increasing incarceration of women. Our focus will not be on problems that also bedevil the male system but rather on those difficulties that are of special concern to the incarceration of women. Although there are a number of such problems, we will focus on three in particular. Some of these have been addressed through various initiatives, while others remain essentially neglected. We begin with brief discussions of economies of scale and prison conditions, and then turn to a more detailed consideration of motherhood in prison.

Economies of Scale

One of the traditional justifications for not building separate and adequate facilities for women in the nineteenth century was that there simply were not enough women to justify the expenditures required to create such institutions. It did not make economic sense to build prisons to hold the very few women who needed to be imprisoned. During the early period of female incarceration women were confined within prisons that also held men.[53] Although that began to change as the century wore on, the problem has not altogether disappeared. States such as Washington, South Carolina, and Oklahoma did not open state prisons for women until the 1970s.[54] Even so, the increasing numbers of women in these and other states has precipitated a crowding crisis in many respects similar to that which troubles the male component of the correctional system.

Denial of resources on the basis of the small scale of women's confinement has assumed a variety of forms. For instance, Jane Chapman reports that a review of the implementation of the Manpower Development and Training Act found that 45 correctional programs were evaluated, none of which were women's programs. "The rationale for such exclusion has been that no programs could be found for women that would meet the requirements of the act and also be feasible on a cost-benefit basis."[55] A Michigan class-action lawsuit revealed that "women inmates had access to only five 'job-training opportunities,' while men had some twenty vocational programs."[56] Other aspects of differential treatment based on economies of scale include poorly equipped women's prison law libraries and inadequate recreational facilities.[57]

113

It is ironic that in many states women inmates have been denied access to resources because as a group they simply are not numerous enough. Had women been more inclined towards participation in serious crime, and more likely therefore to have ended up in prison, perhaps adequate resources would have been provided to attend to their needs as prisoners. For instance, because states generally have only one or two facilities to hold women, it is not possible to provide single tier security level institutions. The expense of building maximum security facilities for the relatively small number of maximum security risk female inmates has been deemed too great to justify. Although men typically find themselves assigned to minimum, medium, or maximum security institutions, women may find themselves imprisoned in facilities that handle the full range of offender types. Women who are minimum security inmates may find themselves forced to endure medium or even maximum security restrictions and to interact with maximum security risk inmates.

Now that greater numbers of women are entering the correctional system an opportunity has emerged to commit adequate resources to their confinement. As a matter of equity, it seems increasingly difficult to justify withholding resources from those components of the correctional system that serve women. Joycelyn Pollock-Byrne argues, however, that women respond better to community-based sanctions, and resources ought to be invested in alternatives to incarceration.[58] From yet another perspective, it can be argued that the historic reluctance to send women to prison can provide the basis for a reconsideration of the value of imprisonment as a response toward crime for both women *and* men.

Focus 5-1
Vocational Programs in Women's Prisons

Women in prison have been provided with a variety of different kinds of vocational programs. A number of criticisms have been raised, however, about both the character and quantity of such programs. For instance, Clarice Feinman notes that programs for women reflect the social stereotypes regarding what women's roles ought to entail. Programs to train women to be clerks, seamstresses, domestic servants, secretaries, and housewives have typified women's programs.[59] At the federal prison for women at Alderson, West Virginia, only 200 of the 700 inmates are able to work in the kinds of prison industries that are available to provide real vocational training. The majority of the female inmates are consigned to sewing in the garment shop.[60] Conditions are changing, and more institutions are beginning to offer nontraditional vocational programs for women. "On the whole, one can say that vocational programs for women are improving, but programs are still far too few, and too many programs do not prepare a woman to support herself upon release."[61]

Are women discriminated against in the vocational offerings made available to them? It is true that women have been provided with programs that mirror traditional roles (such as those related to domestic obligations). The same can be said for men, however. And it is also true that some available vocational programs are not being utilized by female inmates, and that the rehabilitative programs in greatest demand by women seem to be those associated with parenting skills.[62] Women in prison may have preferences based, in part, upon the traditional roles to which they have been exposed in the socialization process.

Whether this is a problem depends in part on whether women will be leaving prisons to assume household responsibilities or whether they will find it necessary to compete in the market for employment. Although the answer may have been more ambiguous in the past, it is quite clear today. Women inmates, who are often the sole support of their children, will have to enter the workforce to provide for themselves and their families. The lack of programs that prepare women to enter the workplace in financially productive occupations may create serious obstacles for women attempting to responsibly discharge familial financial obligations subsequent to release.

Of course, men's programs have also long been criticized for failing to provide adequate training to enable them to secure and retain employment subsequent to release. The wider range of vocational opportunities for men have not produced the kinds of recidivism rates that would provide confidence that the system is working for them. It may well be that women might be more responsive to serious vocational training, and money spent in women's, rather than in men's, facilities might reap greater long-term benefits. Alternatively, it may be that vocational training programs in

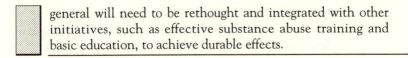

general will need to be rethought and integrated with other initiatives, such as effective substance abuse training and basic education, to achieve durable effects.

Prison Conditions

Most prisons for women do not appear to resemble the typical male maximum security institutions.

> Unlike prisons for men, many women's prisons resemble college campuses, rather than fortress penitentiaries. Often there are no gun towers, no armed guards and no stone walls strung on top with concertina wire. Neatly pruned hedges, well-kept flower gardens, attractive brick buildings and wide-paved walkways greet the visitor's eye at women's prisons in many states. Often these institutions are located in rural, pastoral settings which may suggest tranquility and well-being to the casual observer.[63]
>
> Often, there are rooms for inmates rather than open cells or dormitories. Typically, women are allowed to have curtains and bedspreads. Decorated with pictures and handiwork, their rooms take on a personal appearance. Women are more likely to be allowed to wear their own clothing, at least in the living units.[64]

Despite such outward appearances, many of the restrictions that characterize male prisons are far from absent within women's facilities. Although most authorities agree that prisons for women are not as harsh as those for men, prison is intended as punishment, and life is regimented and routinized in ways that significantly restrict freedom of movement and association. Security measures, such as those associated with receiving mail and visitors, regularly remind inmates of their "lack of autonomy, powerlessness, and loss of identity."[65] "Rules govern everything from the number of minutes one may shower, to gumchewing, to touching. Women report that prison staff control is perhaps more extreme in prisons for women: for instance, women may be held to higher standards of grooming than male inmates."[66]

Some analysts have argued that irrespective of the objective features of male and female prisons, prison is *experienced* as more harsh by women inmates. D. Ward and G. Kassebaum argue, "The impact of imprisonment is, we believe, more severe for females than for males because it is more unusual."[67] The argument is that relative to what men typically experience *subjectively*, what women must endure is far more severe, in large part due to their pre-prison experience. This is an interesting argument and, upon reflection, makes some sense. The point is not that women are inherently less able to cope with imprisonment because of some constitutional attribute or characteristic, but rather that because of conventional gender socialization, penal conditions have more impact on women. We see the same general argument applied in discussions of the impact of incarceration on juveniles versus adults, and on first-timers versus hardened offenders. If it also applies to women, then the reality of the increasing numbers of women in prison raises some important questions.

For instance, as new facilities are built to handle the swelling female population, decisions must be made regarding what kinds of facilities will be most useful in accomplishing the goals we have for incarcerating these women. The goals of sentencing of women are not, at least in theory, different from those for men: retribution, deterrence, incapacitation, and rehabilitation. The question is whether these goals can be accomplished simply by following the model established for males, or whether they can be more effectively achieved through the use of approaches that depart from the practices established to handle male offenders. It is already apparent, for example, that few women are confined in maximum security-type facilities. Such security measures have not proven necessary to accomplish the goal of incapacitation for women. In terms of escape potential or dangerousness to the community women have not been regarded as representing the same threat as males.

There may be other measures, including deinstitutionalization, that may make good sense in trying to achieve the same objectives with women that we are trying to secure with men. Pollock-Byrne notes that

> Every evaluation indicates that prison, while it may serve to punish, does little or nothing to rehabilitate. Indeed, the prison stay may make it harder for the individual to salvage any part of his/her life as it was before incarceration once the individual is released from prison. It is at least possible that part of the reason women have not seemed to participate in crime to the same extent or to the same degree as males might be that we have, until recently, been less likely to place women in prisons where their criminality can be solidified.[68]

She argues that ties to the community are more important for women than for men because of their role as primary caregivers for children and family. It is such ties that insulate women from involvement in crime; thus, removing women from the community context merely increases the potential for future criminal activity. Community-based punishments therefore may prove far more effective with women than with men.[69]

Modifications of conditions within women's prisons alone cannot solve all the problems associated with the imprisonment of women. Even though such conditions may be less harsh than those which characterize men's prisons, the nature of the isolating experience of incarceration may operate to prevent the achievement of the objectives of punishment.

Motherhood in Prison

Current estimates suggest that more than 75 percent of female inmates have at least one child. Moreover, the vast majority are the legal custodian of their children, and 80 percent were living with their children before their commitment to prison.[70] Although male partners do assume responsibility for some of these children, about half are cared for by mothers or grandmothers of the inmate.[71] While it is true that many male prisoners are fathers, and are deeply troubled by being isolated from their children, American gender role expectations place the primary burden for child care on women. Although there are clear benefits for women associated with this expectation, when women find themselves in a position within which they are unable to satisfy the requirements of the role, they may experience enormous guilt.

> They overwhelmingly experience or relate feelings of despair, frustration, and depression related to their imprisonment, and to their separation from and inability to care for their children. This is true even though many women were not good mothers before they were in prison. Drugs or lifestyle often resulted in mother/offender abdicating her role as mother or other caregivers. Once in prison, however, she has time to think about her children and her failings. No research indicates that children create the same emotions for men in prison or constitute the same feelings of deprivation.[72]

Phyllis Baunach's study of the impact of separation on mothers revealed that "regardless of race or age, women expressed guilt and shame that they committed crimes that separated them from their children."[73]

Despite the guilt and shame expressed by some women in prison, some will still choose to neglect their parental responsibilities upon release. For others, the experience of imprisonment may act as an inducement to consider more carefully the well-being of their children when deciding upon courses of action. For still others, the prison experience may reduce the capacity of an inmate to fulfill her parental responsibility upon release, despite the inmate's good intentions.

Some children are placed in foster care while the mother is in prison, even when the child can be cared for by relatives. "In the long run, this separation may severely damage the family relationship."[74] Nonetheless, the long-term effects on children of imprisoned mothers is not yet clearly understood. One study found that about half of mothers who had been imprisoned reported problems of various kinds (for example, aggression, withdrawal, school difficulties).[75] Mothers' reports, however, may be far less reliable than clinical evaluation. As a result of their experience as prisoners, some mothers may be less than objective. For instance, they may harbor resentment at having been separated from their children, and thus be more ready to interpret conventional forms of child misbehavior as indicators of problems resulting from their separation from their children. Moreover, many of these children are forced to endure neighborhoods and environments that may produce problems irrespective of the presence of the mother. Tracing such problems to the absence of the mother is thus difficult. Other research suggests that it may not be the fact of separation so much as the disruption separation creates in the lives of children that is responsible for the disciplinary and academic problems experienced by children of imprisoned mothers.[76]

Of course, it should come as little surprise that removal of a parent from the household, especially if the parent is the primary caregiver, might create problems for children. It has long been recognized that other kinds of separation, such as those associated with divorce or death, may have significant impact on children. What is less evident is what ought to be done to address the difficulty.

One obvious remedy is to ensure that women inmates have regular contact with their children. This is not always easy to accomplish. First, because there are fewer institutions for women than for men, the chances that a mother confined in prison will be located near the residence of the children is less than that for males. In addition, although many inmates come from urban environments, many women's prisons are located in rural areas. The practical matter of physically transporting children to the prisons to visit their mothers is thus often quite difficult. Moreover, because these children are often cared for by relatives who may not have the resources to pay the cost of travel to the prisons, visits will be made less often than might otherwise be desired.

When visits are undertaken they are usually for limited periods of time, and must take place within regularly scheduled visiting hours. These hours, typically during the daytime, create problems for children who must travel long distances to visit their mothers. For many, it means taking a bus the day or night before, and sometimes paying for lodging near the penal facility in order to be able to get to the facility within the visiting hours.

These problems have not made it impossible for most mothers to have contact with their children. A study of one women's institution found that two-thirds of mothers had visits from their children during their incarceration. Moreover, 70 percent managed to maintain weekly contact through phone calls and letters.[77] Nonetheless, there is serious concern regarding whether the frequency and quality of visits with children make it possible for women to maximize what they might be able to accomplish in maintaining the stability of the family unit.

Some prisons have made efforts to respond to such difficulties. A survey of women's prisons found that more than one-third of prisons had special visiting hours for visitors who found it impossible to visit during regular hours.[78] A few institutions have made it possible for women to have two or three-day visits with their children and/or husbands in residential quarters specially outfitted for such purposes.[79] Nebraska makes it possible for children to live with their mothers for up to five days a month.[80] Many institutions now provide play areas for children, and child care is available in some facilities to make it possible for adults to visit privately.[81]

Pregnant inmates and inmates with infants represent another aspect of this general problem area. Some women become pregnant while in prison, either as a result of spousal visitation or as a consequence of sexual assault by staff. Other women are pregnant when they are admitted. A recent survey revealed that 6 percent of female state prison inmates entered prison while pregnant. States vary widely regarding how pregnant inmates are treated in prison. Some women are prevented from terminating a pregnancy even if the mother chooses to have an abortion.[82] On the other hand, "the American Civil Liberties Union reports that pregnant prisoners are sometimes pressured to abort. In Morales v. Turman (1974), a pregnant woman testified that prison officials instructed her to take 10 unidentified pills and exercise. Other prisoners told her it would lead to a miscarriage and, indeed, she later aborted."[83]

Social awareness of the importance of prenatal care has been increasing in the past decade. Yet medical care for imprisoned pregnant women is often quite inadequate.[84] Prison mothers may also find it difficult to satisfy basic nutritional needs during the period of pregnancy.[85] At this point in time, nationally recognized standards for the care of such prisoners have yet to be adopted.

Various accommodations have been made in some states to assist new mothers. In Massachusetts inmates may actually be discharged from prison if a judge or parole board decides release is appropriate and in the best interest of the child. In Illinois a newborn may be left in the care of the mother until the age of one.[86] New York's Bedford Hills has a prison nursery. Inmates can live with their newborn children for a year after birth.[87] California permits mothers to live with their infants for up to two full years.[88] Such arrangements are, however, relatively unusual. Typically a custody hearing is held, and if the child cannot be placed with relatives he or she is placed in foster care. In fact, mothers may run the risk of losing custody of their children, in part as a result of the fact of their incarceration.[89] See Focus 5-2 for a description of what a California county has been able to accomplish in providing for the needs of pregnant inmates.

Focus 5-2

Addressing the Needs of Pregnant Inmates: The Santa Rita County Jail[90]

Through the first half of the 1980s, the Santa Rita County Jail in northern California made few provisions to accommodate for the special needs of incarcerated pregnant women. For instance, despite their condition, pregnant inmates were not provided with an appropriate diet or with adequate medical examinations. Such treatment led to the filing of a lawsuit on their behalf in 1986. The suit was settled in 1989, and the county agreed to make significant changes in the treatment of pregnant inmates.

A new facility was built, with modern features that permitted administrators to address the concerns articulated in the suit. A special obstetrical/gynecological unit was outfitted in the new jail and was staffed by a medical team which included a prenatal coordinator, physician, nurse practitioner, and other support staff.

Upon admission to the institution female inmates are given a general health screening, including a pregnancy test if the inmate is of childbearing age. Pregnant women are housed in a special unit and share a cell with an older non-pregnant inmate who can provide support for the pregnant resident. If the inmate is drug-addicted, she is transferred to the county hospital to receive treatment for her addiction.

Pregnant inmates are provided with a special diet suitable to their condition, as well as with thorough and ongoing medical monitoring. Counseling services are available in the facility, and women who have concerns about their pregnancy can discuss these with trained professionals. Women who decide to terminate their pregnancy may elect to have an abortion. Educational materials on various aspects of pregnancy and motherhood are provided to inmates.

A variety of tests are performed during the pregnancy, including ultrasound and screening for gestational diabetes. In addition, social workers are available to provide information on relevant services available to mothers. After delivery, which takes place in the county hospital, postpartum exams are conducted, and family planning services are provided.

The Santa Rita program for pregnant inmates represents a dramatic turnaround from the jail's previous practices. An assessment of the program by the court-appointed monitor concluded that the county was successfully meeting the stipulations agreed upon in the settlement of the lawsuit.

In light of the increasing number of women in American prisons, issues associated with motherhood pose significant and growing challenges. This may be especially true in light of the overrepresentation of minorities in prison, and the fact that two-thirds of black births now occur out of wedlock. Such women are statistically more likely to end up in prison than non-minority women, and more likely not to have spousal support to help maintain the family unit in the mother's absence.

Several approaches to addressing these difficulties have been proposed. Of course, one approach is simply to commit more resources to the kinds of programs that already exist in various states. With regard to pregnant inmates and new mothers, and in recognition of the importance of early bonding, it might include expanding the correctional system's capacity to make it possible for mothers and newborns to spend the first year together. It also could include more resources for prenatal care and pre-parental counseling and training.

Mothers who have children on the outside could benefit from creation of programs and facilities to make possible overnight visits. As has already been tried in a few places, mobile homes or cottages could be erected on site to enable inmates and families to experience family relations away from the multiple distractions of normal prison life. This would be especially valuable for poor families who must come great distances to visit the inmate. In some European countries cottages are made available to mothers with children. Mother and children are then permitted to live together on a permanent basis.

In light of the fact that virtually all imprisoned women are eventually released, society has a significant stake in maintaining the family units to which women typically return upon release. There are sufficient difficulties of readjustment, such as finding employment, without the hindrance of family problems. Families that are allowed to deteriorate will not be available as an integrating or support mechanism when these women return to society.

Of course, in many families the woman is the main provider. The significance of this is that even women who are permitted close and regular contact with children will not necessarily be prepared to discharge their responsibilities as providers upon release. Part of a comprehensive approach to preparing women for successful adjustment is providing them with education and training that will give them marketable skills. If they cannot earn a living they will find themselves confronting obstacles that may actually undo some of the good work (in terms of family relations) that may have been accomplished through effective institutional programs during the period of imprisonment.

This leads to one final aspect of the problem. It is possible to argue that preparing women with children for productive life beyond prison requires adjustment to community life, including supervised exposure to the circumstances and temptations that may have resulted in incarceration in the first place (such as drug abuse). It may well be that imprisonment for many women, while seeming appropriate when considering only the retributive aspects of punishment, may prove counterproductive if long-term desistance from crime is to be an important objective of punishment. It makes sense, therefore, to give some hard thought to expanding the use of community-based residential facilities that permit the women to retain contact with family, while at the same time undergoing punitive restrictions, close supervision, parenting skills training, basic education, and vocational education. Although significant numbers of male inmates probably do not represent a serious danger to public safety, this may be even more true for women. Various kinds of "half-way house" placements might prove far more effective than imprisonment in achieving society's multiple goals in its efforts to deal with female offenders.

This could have the additional potential benefit of increasing the participation of the men involved in the family unit. Arrangements could be structured to motivate men to assume more responsibility for the discharge of family functions and to play a more significant role in the reintegration of the offender. As in other areas of family relations, such as economic support of children, men have often been permitted to avoid responsibilities that should be shared. Of course, some men will not be suitable for involvement in such strategies, but others may find that it offers a means to accomplish some personal objectives that permit them to assume responsibilities that they might have wanted to shoulder, but felt unable to handle in the past. Because a sizable number of such men may themselves be economically marginal, a comprehensive approach would involve initiatives that provide males with the economic, parental, and social skills to become an effective participant in family life.

There should be no illusions about the ease with which such a comprehensive approach might be implemented, and both practical and philosophical issues must first be addressed. However, if society desires to increase its complement of effectively functioning families, it must recognize that at least some female and male involvement in criminality is an expression of family disfunction. At the same time, such criminal involvement is a signal and an opportunity for the state to become involved in meaningful ways to try and secure the future for families in trouble. Although some analysts may regard such an approach as an overreach of the state's power and authority, the reality is that the state **is** going to be involved. The question is whether the state will be involved merely as a prison custodian or as an agent for enduring changes that will reduce the likelihood that female offenders will return to crime. The choice that is made will affect not only the women involved but their children, significant males, and ultimately the rest of us as well.

Thinking about Women in Prison... Thinking about Men in Prison

As we have already noted in earlier chapters, the judiciary essentially maintained a "hands off" posture with regard to prison operation until the 1960s. In part as a result of the civil rights movement, prisoners began to file lawsuits contesting the conditions of their confinement, and the courts began to listen and respond. By and large, however, the flurry of suits was the result of the initiative of male inmates. Most of the significant cases decided by the courts in the 1960s, 1970s, and 1980s were cases involving male prisoners. A. Aylward and J. Thomas found that although females represented 13 percent of the total inmate population, only 6 percent of cases filed were brought by women prisoners.[91]

Although this is still the case, largely due to the enormous disparity in the numbers of male and female offenders confined, women have begun to file lawsuits, and the courts have handed down favorable rulings in a number of areas. Women have won, for instance, the right to retain possession of newborn infants,[92] the right of women to have equal access to vocational programs,[93] and the right to adequate medical services.[94] In Lett v. Withworth a woman won the right to an abortion that had been denied because prison officials did not want to pay the guard expense required to move her to a hospital.[95] In a Pennsylvania case a woman successfully contested her commitment to state prison on the grounds that a man convicted of the same offense would have been sentenced to county jail.[96] Of course, women's suits have not always been successful. In Los Angeles County Department of Adoptions v. Hutchinson, for instance, a woman lost in her efforts to retain custody of her daughter.[97] Nonetheless, as their awareness of legal options has increased, women have become more energetic in their pursuit of legal remedies.

Some of the cases brought by women have argued for relief on the basis of the equal protection clause of the Fourteenth Amendment. In short, such cases have argued that inequities in access to resources (for example, recreational facilities, vocational programs) violate the equal protection clause. Although the United States Supreme Court has yet to issue a ruling affirming unqualified equity in access to resources, numerous lower courts have ruled that particular inequities serve no reasonable purpose, and thus do violate the Fourteenth Amendment (for example, Barefield v. Leach, Glover v. Johnson).

Although it is not difficult to identify circumstances in which equal access to resources seems fair and proper, in other areas strict equality may make little sense. Should the state be obligated to provide women with weight-training equipment of equal quantity and quality as that it purchases for male inmates? What if women are simply less interested in making use of such equipment? Could not that money be better spent in other areas (purchasing toys to outfit child care facilities, for instance, or funding aerobics instructors)? What about medical services? It is obvious that the kinds of medical services required by women do differ from those needed by men.

Adherence to strict equality may also mean loss of some privileges women currently enjoy. As noted above, women may experience living conditions superior to those found in male institutions (for example, single rooms rather than cells, more privacy). It may be argued that the loss of some advantages is both reasonable and overdue. Some of the justifications for differential treatment of women were based upon notions of women as the fragile sex, notions which are gradually eroding as gender distinctions continue to undergo modification in society at large.

At a fundamental level, the issues being raised with regard to the relative treatment of men and women are issues that perhaps ought be raised for *all* inmates. Do we want to place inmates of whatever gender in group settings characterized by noise and chaos? Do we want to allow the "worst of the worst" to have essentially unrestricted access to each other within our prisons and thus facilitate the preservation of deviant values? Is it in society's interest to deny adequate substance abuse programming or vocational training to any of America's inmates? The ongoing debate about how women prisoners ought to be treated relative to their male counterparts will be in part a failure if it does not lead us to reconsider the predicates of the largely ineffective correctional system now in operation. As in other areas of social life, working through the problems of gender in the correctional system represents a terrific opportunity to rethink global correctional objectives, assess the utility of the approaches that have been tried, and refresh our thinking about what is likely to prove useful in the future.

Notes

[1] Rothman, David (1971) *The Discovery of the Asylum*, Boston: Little, Brown and Company.

[2] Rafter, Nicole H. (1983) "Prison for Women, 1790-1980." in Tonry and Zimring (eds.) *Punishment and Reform: Essays on Criminal Sentencing*, Chicago: University of Chicago Press.

[3] Id.

[4] Dobash, R., Dobash, R., and Gutteridge, S. (1986) *The Imprisonment of Women*, New York: Basil Blackwell, p. 1.

[5] Pollock-Byrne, Joycelyn (1990) *Women, Prison, and Crime*, Pacific Grove, CA: Brooks Cole, pp. 38-39.

[6] Freedman, E. "Their sister's keepers: A historical perspective of female correctional institutions in the U.S.," *Feminist Studies*, 2.

[7] Rafter, Nicole H. (1985) *Partial Justice: Women in State Prisons: 1800-1935*, Boston: Northeastern University Press.

[8] See Freedman, note 6 above at 80.

[9] McKelvey, Blake (1977) *American Prisons: A History of Good Intentions*, Montclair, NJ: Patterson Smith, p. 16.

[10] Id. at 39.

[11] See Rafter, note 2 above at 138.

[12] Id. at 134.

[13] Id. at 135.

[14] See McKelvey, note 9 above at 100.

[15] Quoted in McKelvey, note 9 above at 105.

[16] See McKelvey, note 9 above at 84.

[17] Id.

[18] Id. at 165.

[19] See Freedman, note 6 above at 57.

[20] See McKelvey, note 9 above at 166.

[21] See Rafter, note 2 above at 164.

[22] Id. at 164.

[23] Clear, Todd R. and Cole, George F. (1990) *American Corrections*, 2nd ed., Pacific Grove, CA: Brooks Cole, pp. 507-508.

[24] See Freedman, note 6 above at 144-145.

[25] Gilliard, Darrell K., Bureau of Justice Statistics, (1993) *Prisoners in 1992*, Washington D.C.: U.S. Department of Justice, 1993.

[26] Id.; Greenfeld, Lawrence A. and Minor-Harper, Stephanie (1991) "Women in Prison," Washington, D.C.: U.S. Dept. of Justice, Bureau of Justice Statistics, p. 7.

[27] See Greenfeld and Minor-Harper, note 26 above at 1; see Gilliard, note 25 above at 5.

[28] See Gilliard, note 25 above at 4.

[29] Pollock-Byrne, Joycelyn M. (1992) "Women in prison: Why are their numbers increasing?" in Benekos and Merlo (eds.) *Corrections: Dilemmas and Directions*, Cincinnati: Anderson Pub., pp. 79-80.

[30] See Gilliard, note 25 above.

[31] Id. at 5.

[32] Id.

[33] Stephan, James (1992) "Census of state and federal correctional facilities, 1990," Washington, D.C.: Bureau of Justice Statistics, p. 8.

[34] Jankowski, Louis W. (1992) "Jail inmates 1991," Washington, D.C.: U.S. Dept. of Justice, Bureau of Justice Statistics, p. 2.

[35] Id. at 5.

[36] Snell, Tracy L. (1992) "Women in jail," Washington, D.C.: U.S. Dept. of Justice, Bureau of Justice Statistics, p. 2.

[37] See Pollock-Byrne, note 29 above at 80.

[38] Federal Bureau of Investigation (1990) *Uniform Crime Reports*, Washington, D.C.: U.S. Dept. of Justice.

[39] Chesney-Lind, Meda (1991) "Patriarchy, prisons, and jails: A critical look at trends in women's incarceration," *The Prison Journal*, 71(1).

[40] See Pollock-Byrne, note 5 above at 29-30.

[41] Id. at 31.

[42] See, e.g., Wilbanks, William (1986) "Are female felons treated more leniently by the criminal justice system?" *Justice Quarterly*, 3(4); Steffensmeier, D. (1980) "Sex differences in patterns of adult crimes, 1965-1977: A review and assessment," *Social Forces*, 58; Kruttschnitt, C. and Green, D. (1984) "The sex-sanctioning issue: Is it history?" *American Sociological Review*, 49; Chesney-Lind, Meda (1982) "Guilty by reason of sex: Young women and the juvenile justice system," in Price and Sokoloff (eds.), *The Criminal Justice System and Women*, New York: Clark Boardman.

[43] See Pollock-Byrne, note 29 above at 92.

[44] Crawford, J. (1990) *The Female Offender: What Does the Future Hold?* Washington, D.C.: American Correctional Association, pp. 66-70.

[45] Maguire, Kathleen and Flanagan, Timothy J. (1991) *Sourcebook of Criminal Justice Statistics—1990*, Washington, D.C.: U.S. Department of Justice, Bureau of Justice Statistics, p. 422.

[46] Beck, Allen, et al (1993) "Survey of State Prison Inmates, 1991" Washington D.C.: Bureau of Justice Statistics, p. 4.

[47] See Greenfeld and Minor-Harper, note 26 above at 5.

[48] See Maguire and Flanagan, note 45 above at 616.

[49] See Beck, note 46 above.

[50] Id. at 649.

[51] See Crawford, note 44 above.

[52] See Greenfeld and Minor-Harper, note 47 above at 6.

[53] See Rafter, note 7 above.

[54] See Pollock-Byrne, note 29 above at 80.

[55] Chapman, Jane R. (1980) *Economic Realities and the Female Offender*, Lexington, MA: Lexington Books.

[56] Hawkins, Richard and Alpert, Geoffrey P. (1989) *American Prisons Systems—Punishment and Justice*, Englewood Cliffs, NJ: Prentice Hall, p. 304.

[57] See Pollock-Byrne, note 5 above at 170-171.

[58] See Pollock-Byrne, note 29 above at 92.

[59] Feinman, Clarice (1983) "An historical overview of the treatment of incarcerated women: Myths and realities of rehabilitation," *Prison Journal*, 63.

[60] Weisheit, Ralph and Mahan, Sue (1988) *Women, Crime and Criminal Justice*, Cincinnati: Anderson, pp. 66-67.

[61] See Pollock-Byrne, note 5 above at 94.

[62] Id. at 91-94.

[63] Baunach, Phyllis Jo (1985) "Critical problems of women in prison," in Moyer (ed.) *The Changing Roles of Women in the Criminal Justice System*, Prospect Heights, Ill.: Waveland Press, p. 96.

[64] See Pollock-Byrne, note 5 above at 86.

[65] See Baunach, note 63 above at 96.

[66] See Pollock-Byrne, note 29 above at 85.

[67] Ward, D. and Kassebaum, G. (1964) "Homosexuality: A mode of adaptation in a prison for women," *Social Problems*, 12, p. 161.

[68] See Pollock-Byrne, note 29 above at 92.

[69] Id. at 92-93.

[70] Greenfeld, Lawrence A. and Minor-Harper, Stephanie (1991) "Women in prison," Washington, D.C.: Dept. of Justice, Bureau of Justice Statistics, p. 6.

[71] See Crawford, note 44 above.

[72] See Pollock-Byrne, note 29 above at 87.

[73] See Baunach, note 63 above at 98.

[74] Id. at 98.

[75] Cited in Pollock-Byrne, note 5 above at 65.

[76] Stanton, A. (1980) *When Mothers go to Jail*, Lexington, MA: Lexington Books.

[77] Datesman, Susan K. and Cales, Gloria L. (1983) "'I'm still the same mommy': Maintaining the mother/child relationship in prison," *The Prison Journal*, 63—Autumn.

[78] Neto, V. and Ranier, L. (1983) "Mother and wife locked up: A day with the family," *The Prison Journal*, 63(2).

[79] Id.; Baunach, Phyllis Jo (1984) *Mothers in Prison*, New Brunswick, NJ: Transaction.

[80] See Chapman, note 55 above.

[81] See Neto and Ranier, note 78 above; Haley, K. (1977) "Mothers behind bars: A look at the parental rights of incarcerated women," *New England Journal of Prison Law*, 4(1).

[82] Holt, K. E. (1981-1982) "From nine months to life—The law and the pregnant inmate," *Journal of Family Law*, 20.

[83] See Pollock-Byrne, note 29 above at 88; see also Holt, note 82 above.

[84] Leonard, E. (1983) "Judicial decisions and prison reform: The impact of litigation on women prisoners," *Social Problems*, 31(1).

[85] Mann, C. (1984) *Female Crime and Delinquency*, Birmingham: University of Alabama Press.

[86] See Holt, note 82 above.

[87] See Baunach, note 63 above at 75.

[88] Bartollas, Clemens, and Conrad, John P. (1992) *Introduction to Corrections*, 2nd ed., New York: Harper Collins, p. 488.

[89] See Clear and Cole, note 23 above at 520; see Pollock-Byrne, note 5 above at 66-67.

[90] Based upon Ryan, T.A. and Grassano, James B. (1992) "Taking a progressive approach to treating pregnant offenders," *Corrections Today*, 54(6), pp. 184-186.

[91] Aylward, A. and Thomas, J. (1984) "Quiescence in women's prisons litigation: Some exploratory issues," *Justice Quarterly*, 1(2).

[92] See Mann, note 85 above.

[93] See Pollock-Byrne, note 29 above at 89.

[94] Id. at 90.

[95] See Pollock-Byrne, note 5 above at 172.

[96] Id. at 174.

[97] See Pollock-Byrne, note 29 above at 185.

6

Changing the Offender

According to the F.B.I., more than two million adults are arrested annually for serious crimes.[1] Significant numbers of these arrestees ultimately are convicted. Some are first-time criminals who will never commit another offense, while others are hardened career offenders who will continue to commit crimes as long as they are allowed to remain in the community. In between these two extremes can be found a substantial number of offenders whose commitment to criminality is not immutable. This is of enormous importance in light of the fact that approximately one-quarter million adults are sentenced to state prisons every year.[2] More than 95 percent of these individuals will eventually be returned to society, thus how the state handles these individuals while they are in our prisons is of crucial importance.

As we have already noted, the criminal justice system has a number of objectives in punishing the guilty. One important objective is to secure the cessation of criminal activity. This is sought through the imposition of painful experiences, such as incarceration, on the convicted. If specific deterrent effects are achieved, it is because the individual desires to avoid re-experiencing the torments of punishment and thus opts to obey the law. A somewhat different approach to producing law-abiding behavior seeks to expose the offender to experiences, not necessarily painful, that help motivate the individual to avoid further involvement in crime. In general terms, this approach is referred to as rehabilitation. It is sometimes difficult to determine whether an individual's abandonment of a life of crime is the result of deterrent or rehabilitative processes.

This chapter considers both approaches to changing the behavior of convicted offenders, with a primary focus on rehabilitation. We begin with deterrence, then take up the hotly debated issue of rehabilitation, and conclude with a discussion of the extent to which the two approaches may be related.

Deterring the Offender

There are two primary forms of deterrence. *General Deterrence* refers to the instillation of fear in those who are not the immediate subject of punishment. In theory, the application of punishment to offenders becomes known to others, who learn of the consequences of criminal involvement and decide not to risk subjecting themselves to such punishment. *Specific Deterrence* refers to the deterring of offenders who are being punished for committing a crime. Presumably, the offender decides to obey the law after having experienced directly the pains of punishment, and deciding that the risk of being subjected to more punishment is not worth the chance of getting away with new crimes.

Deterrence has a special kind of appeal for many of us because it is easy enough to recall personal experiences in which it seems that we were deterred. Everyone can remember how the threat of parental punishment seemingly motivated us to refrain from committing some breach of household rules. Recollections of threats of sanctions in school and in the workplace, as well as remembrances of their influence on our behavior, are also relatively easy to summon from memory.

What are perhaps less often recalled, however, are those many occasions when the threat of sanctions did not prevent us from violating various rules. Careful and thorough recollection of our teenage years will probably supply most of us with enough evidence to indicate that the threat of punishment was not always effective as a deterrent. In many cases peer pressure or the belief that we would not be caught encouraged us to violate the rules.

When citizens are asked about the purposes of punishment, specific deterrence is often listed as an important objective. In Maryland, a survey was conducted to determine citizen attitudes toward the correctional goals of deterrence, incapacitation, punishment, and rehabilitation. In spite of the popular attention accorded to incapacitation and punishment in the press, the survey found that deterrence and rehabilitation were at the top of the ranking.[3]

This study was not an aberration. An Illinois study found that 40 percent of respondents identified specific deterrence as the "reason for punishing criminals," about the same percentage that identified general deterrence.[4]

A Canadian study of public sentiment found that deterrence was the most often selected objective for punishment, with about one-third of respondents choosing deterrence as the *most* important objective.[5] With particular regard to specific deterrence, Anthony Doob and Julian Roberts report that more than 60 percent of Canadian respondents to a Gallup Poll rate identified "deterring the offender" as a very important reason why sentences should be more severe.[6]

It seems clear, therefore, that both general and specific deterrence are regarded as important objectives of corrections. What does the research on the effectiveness of correctional strategies designed to achieve specific deterrence tell us? Hundreds of studies on various aspects of deterrence have been conducted over the last several decades, using a wide range of methodological approaches. Scholars continue to debate both the findings of the research as well as the adequacy of the research methodologies used to identify deterrent effects.

Although studying deterrence is a methodologically challenging enterprise, examination of recidivism rates indicates quite clearly that significant numbers of prison inmates are not deterred from at least some subsequent involvement in crime. A six-year follow-up study of inmates released from prisons in 11 states found that within three years of release almost two-thirds had been re-arrested for new crimes, and 41 percent had been convicted and returned to prison.[7] Moreover, the problem may be getting worse. A Texas study found that the percentage of paroled inmates returning to prison increased from about 33 in the 1980s to 43 in 1991.[8] Because only a subset of all those who commit crimes is detected, these figures likely represent underestimates of the true level of reinvolvement in crime.

Of course, the worst of the worst tend to end up in state prison. That these offenders are least susceptible to deterrent influences is not altogether surprising. Research on probationers, offenders at the other end of the sanction severity scale, has produced mixed results. Dean Champion summarizes this research by noting that "Experts disagree about the deterrent effect that probation serves . . . studies of convicted felons on probation in Kentucky, Missouri, and specific sites in cities such as Cincinnati and Dayton show reconvictions within a three-year follow-up ranging from 12 to 29 percent."[9] Of course, because probation often handles the offender group least inclined toward continued criminality to begin with, it is difficult to determine whether such offenders would have desisted from criminal involvement even without serving a probationary sentence.

However, a recent study of felony offenders sentenced to probation suggests that probation does not create significant specific deterrent effects for serious offenders. Forty-three percent of felony probationers

135

were rearrested within a three-year follow-up period. More than a third were reincarcerated and another 10 percent absconded.[10] There is thus evidence that, at least for felons, neither prison nor probation provides an adequate specific deterrent.

Focus 6-1

The Failure of a "Can't Miss" Program
SCARED STRAIGHT

In thinking about the kinds of offenders that might be most easily dissuaded from involvement in lawbreaking, many analysts believe that young people are the best candidates. Presumably, their youthful character is still not fully formed and has not developed an enduring commitment to crime.

With this idea in mind, a program operated at New Jersey's Rahway State Prison opened in the mid-1970s. The Juvenile Awareness Program, more popularly known as the Scared Straight program, was based upon the idea that youth could be influenced by the terrifying experience of being in a prison environment with hard-core inmates, even for a short period of time.

Juveniles were taken on a tour of the prison and then brought before a group of inmates in an intensive confrontation session.

> At the end of the brief tour, juveniles in groups of about 15 were taken to a room for an intensive confrontation session with adult inmates serving long or life sentences. During these sessions inmates attempted to "cover the full spectrum of crime and its nonrewards . . . explain . . . about prison, crime and its ramification . . . show . . . young people that the stories about the big house . . . being the place of bad men is in all reality the place of sad men . . . prove the fact of what crime and its involvement is all about."
>
> Explaining about crime and the reality of prison

life involved shouting, swearing, and threats of physical abuse. What follows are some of the statements directed at the juveniles by the adult inmates:

I'm gonna hurt you.
You take something from me and I'll kill you.
You see them pretty blue eyes of yours? I'll take one out of
    your face and squish it in front of you. . . .
Who do you think we get? Young, tough motherfuckers
    like you. Get a pretty fat buck like you and stick a prick
    in your ass.[11]

The program consisted primarily of intimidation, threats, and providing youth with frightening information about what awaited them if they maintained their law-violating behavior. The program was described in a documentary film which aired on television in 1979, and which stimulated a tremendous national response. In states as different as California, New York, and Alabama programs were established that emulated the New Jersey program.[12]

The program possessed substantial common sense appeal. It only seemed reasonable that young people would be frightened by what they experienced in the program. The comments of program participants confirmed this, as many of them swore off any future involvement in lawbreaking. It seemed obvious to all that the program had to work.

Unfortunately, the empirical research conducted on the program in Rahway failed to find evidence that the program was effective in deterring young people from involvement in trouble. A comparison of program youth with a control group of similar youth who did not go through the program found that the program not only "failed to control delinquency, but it apparently made things worse as well."[13] The control group had less involvement in delinquency than the Scared Straight group. Subsequent evaluations of programs in Michigan and Virginia provided mixed results on the effectiveness of scared straight programs.[14]

The Scared Straight experience is thus an excellent example of an approach to creating specific deterrent effects that is based upon a solid common sense foundation, which created enormous popular and political interest, and yet which was not proven effective when subjected to careful scientific evaluation.

The absence of compelling evidence of specific deterrent effects for serious offenders may be a reflection of what is required for specific deterrence to operate. Potential offenders must have some capacity for free choice. They must be able to think rationally in weighing the potential risks and benefits of various courses of action. They must perceive that the probability of being detected, arrested, convicted, and punished is significant. (This would be, of course, an erroneous perception.) They must fear the punishments that might be imposed, and such fear should be based, at least in part, on their previous involvement with the criminal justice system. Of course, an individual who does not believe he or she will be caught will not be energetically motivated to avoid future involvement in crime, even if they do fear the punishment that might be imposed. This last process is similar to that which leads many citizens to continue to resist wearing seat belts when they drive. Such drivers refuse to wear belts not because they believe that seat belts fail to protect those who get into auto accidents, but rather because they believe that *other* people get into accidents. Their behavior is predicated on the belief that the painful consequences of not wearing a seat belt are real, but do not apply to them. Similarly, potential offenders may believe that punishment exists, but that it does not apply to them because they will not be caught.

Meeting all of these conditions may be extremely difficult, although failure to meet them may destroy whatever opportunities might otherwise exist for creating specific deterrent effects. Studies have been conducted which reflect the influence of such factors, such as the perceived certainty of arrest. A study of driving while under the influence of alcohol, for instance, found that the threat of formal punishment had less influence on subsequent driving behavior than did the threat of informal sanctions, such as social disapproval.[15] In another research project, the deterrent impact of legal sanctions on drug use and property offenses was measured for approximately 300 individuals. The drug use careers of these individuals were examined for evidence of a deterrent effect. The researchers found that

> no such suppression, or deterrence effect, is demonstrable as originating from legal sanctions as represented by the percentage of time under legal supervision. . . . The complete absence of any longitudi-

nal suppressive effects signifies the failure of legal sanctions represented by probation and/or parole supervision to generate specific deterrence.[16]

In sum, although there are exceptions,[17] deterrence research has yet to reveal significant and consistent specific deterrent effects. As we will consider at the conclusion of this chapter, the creation of specific deterrent effects ultimately may depend upon the efficacy of rehabilitation. We turn now to detailed consideration of the rehabilitation of criminal offenders.

Rehabilitation

The term *rehabilitation* encompasses a wide range of responses to criminal involvement and often means different things to different people. Some regard rehabilitation as an intervention into the lives of criminals that provides an opportunity for offenders to materially better themselves, such as through education or job training. Others view rehabilitation as focused upon transformation of the offender's psychological adjustment or personality. Still others perceive rehabilitation as a matter of influencing the offender's social integration. In all of these approaches, the emphasis is not so much on punitive, painful experiences, although such experiences may play a role, but rather upon finding ways to reach offenders that in some measure change their character or social capability.

In what follows we consider the history of rehabilitation, fall from grace of the rehabilitative ideal, impact of the correctional reforms of the 1970s and 1980s, problems with rehabilitation, public support for rehabilitation, and new evidence on rehabilitation.

Early Forms of Rehabilitation

In Amsterdam in 1596, the Rasphuis opened in an abandoned convent. Its primary purpose was to confine "young and dissolute incorrigible petty offenders, beggars, vagrants, and thieves, who might be turned into the path of civic virtue,"[18] and to commit such individuals to a regime of labor, discipline, and routine. It was thought that the wayward were often unregulated in their habits, and that exposure to a well-ordered environment in which proper habits could be developed would help to address such personal shortcomings.[19]

Eventually, some form of the Rasphuis model was adopted in many other countries. The proliferation of workhouses that sprang up in Europe and the American colonies represented expressions of the Rasphuis concept. The focus was not upon the most severe offenders, but on the wayward. Prostitutes, minor thieves, wayward juveniles, and drunkards were generally found in such houses. Their transgressions were, in the larger scheme, viewed as relatively minor, and they were thought to be souls who could be reclaimed.[20] Colonies such as Connecticut opened workhouses long before the American revolution, and the idea spread throughout the new world.[21]

The rise of the penitentiary movement in the late eighteenth and early nineteenth centuries created new interest in reformation of the offender. Although a number of other factors, such as economic variables, have been identified as instrumental in the rise of the modern prison system,[22] significant numbers of penal reformers were interested in devising methods to change the offender through means other than those traditionally associated with specific deterrence. It is important to remember that at the time the penitentiary system was first initiated, capital and corporal sanctions were the primary means of dealing with serious offenders. Penal reformers were looking for ways other than mere terror to change the behavior of offenders.

Early efforts to reform the character of the offender were largely based upon the notion of discipline, order, routine, and labor. In institutions such as Auburn Prison in New York State, inmates were required to observe the rule of total silence, compelled to march in lockstep to work and meals, and expected to obey commands and rules unwaveringly. Inmate work programs within Auburn and many similar nineteenth-century prisons consisted of congregate manufacturing enterprises which produced products such as "footwear, barrels, carpets, cotton ticking, carpenter's tools, steam engines and boilers, combs, harnesses, furniture, and clothing."[23] In the Eastern State Penitentiary system in Pennsylvania, inmates endured solitary confinement, often for years on end. In their solitary cells inmates were expected to work at their workbenches and contemplate the error of their ways.

One important aspect of early efforts at the reform of offenders is that there was little interest in the individualization of treatment. Inmates were essentially treated as clones of each other and forced to experience identical kinds of attention. This undifferentiated treatment regime was based upon the theories of the day. Lack of disciplined upbringing, greed, personal disorder, and inadequate moral training were regarded as largely responsible for criminal involvement. There was little knowledge of, or interest in, the ways in which individuals differed from one another. This reflected general social values which placed far less emphasis on the individual than is common in twentieth-century American society. Moreover, techniques for distinguishing individuals from one another did not begin to become well-established until the latter portion of the nineteenth century. In institutions committed to inmate reform, regimes were established that essentially treated all convicts similarly. This practice reflected the perception that citizens became involved with legal troubles for essentially the same reasons.

This perception began to change during the course of the nineteenth century. In mid-nineteenth-century Europe, Walter Crofton developed the Irish system that divided the period of incarceration into stages that convicts would move through at their own pace.[24] Movement to higher stages was based upon the inmates' behavior and performance, and would be accompanied by increasing numbers of liberties. In theory, this provided inmates with incentive to reform at least their behavior, if not their hearts, to the requirements of convention. Inmates could accelerate their release, as well as increase the comforts of life, if they reformed their conduct while in prison.

This idea spread throughout Europe and the Western world. At the first National Prison Congress, held in Cincinnati in 1870, the notion of release on parole was introduced and affirmed, along with a number of other rehabilitatively-oriented proposals.[25] The immediate product of the declaration of principles articulated at the Congress was the opening of the Elmira Reformatory in 1876 in New York State. Under the guidance of warden Zebulon Brockway, the institution featured various stages that inmates would move through as a result of their own efforts. Activities, such as those associated with general education, vocational instruction, work on prison industries, and religious training, were designed to accomplish the reform of the inmate. The stage system represented explicit recognition that convicts were not clones, and different aspects of the reformative regime would have different kinds of impact on various offenders.

An important part of this system was the indeterminate sentence. Such sentences permitted the state to keep inmates until they had demonstrated that they were cured or rehabilitated. An inmate's release date was not specified at the time the sentence was delivered by the judge, but would be determined later by correctional officials. This practice continued into the twentieth century, and many states still use parole boards to determine the release dates of inmates.

In the very same year that Elmira opened, Cesare Lombroso published Criminal Man, an analysis of the causes of crime. This book reported the findings of Lombroso's anthropomorphic measurement of groups of offenders.[26] Detailed physical measurements of convicts were made, and on the basis of this information Lombroso concluded that there were various criminal types. Best known is his notion of the born criminal. This offender is naturally inclined toward criminal activity by virtue of his or her biological inheritance. Other kinds of criminals in Lombroso's typology included the occasional criminal, criminaloid, and the insane criminal.[27]

Although Lombroso's book was highly publicized, it was also severely criticized during the first several decades subsequent to its publication. Nonetheless, Lombroso applied systematic, scientific measurement to the study of criminals. He observed criminals, made measurements, analyzed the data, and derived conclusions. While critics have raised serious questions about his actual methods, Lombroso recognized that criminals were not identical, that differences between them could be identified through appropriate scrutiny and measurement, that they could be classified into various groupings, and that rational strategies to deal with the different kinds of criminals could be based upon understanding of the characteristics of the respective criminal types.

Although Lombroso's views regarding the biological basis of some criminality generally have not been well regarded during most of the twentieth century, his notions that criminals were not all cut of a single piece, that they could be studied and differentiated, and that the proper response to crime ought to depend in part upon the attributes of the offender, have all become important aspects of the modern response to criminals. Measurement techniques for measuring non-physical individual characteristics, such as the Stanford-Binet Intelligence test, began to appear around the turn of the century, and have been followed by a wide range of measures designed to distinguish individuals, identify their salient characteristics, and make possible classification for purposes of correctional treatment. During the course of the twentieth century, an extraordinary range of rehabilitation programs emerged to address the specific problems and needs of various kinds of criminal offenders (for example, individual and group counseling, psychotherapy, vocational training, basic education, anger management).

There is some disagreement regarding when the modern rehabilitation period began. In two studies of California, for instance, the origins of modern rehabilitation is traced to either the second decade of the twentieth century or after the conclusion of World War II.[28] Nonetheless, at the end of the 1960s rehabilitation continued to be an important aspect of correctional intervention. Public poll data indicated that about three-quarters of Americans thought that rehabilitation should be the "emphasis" of American prisons, while about half believed that rehabilitation was in fact the primary purpose of correctional institutions.[29] But this reality was soon to change.

Hard Times for Rehabilitation

In the 1960s and early 1970s crime increased significantly. The President appointed a special commission to study crime and the criminal justice system, and a second commission was convened to study violence. American cities experienced riots, political rhetoric was filled with discussions of "law and order," civil rights was a highly visible issue that was discussed in the context of crime and the criminal justice process, and the courts began to establish various legal rights to protect citizens from a number of kinds of state intrusion (for example, search and seizure, wiretapping). The concern with crime led many analysts to wonder what had gone wrong during the presumably enlightened age of sophisticated rehabilitative techniques designed to assist offenders in abandoning lives of crime. Recidivism statistics suggested that significant numbers of criminals were becoming re-involved in crime subsequent to release from the supervision of the criminal justice system. A number of careful studies were conducted to measure the effectiveness of various kinds of rehabilitative programs.[30] In 1974 the so-called "Martinson Report" appeared and stimulated enormous controversy over the correctional system's efforts to rehabilitate offenders.

In short, Martinson's article described an assessment of 231 research studies that had been conducted to assess the effectiveness of various kinds of correctional programs. All kinds of programs were examined, including those providing counseling (individual and group), vocational training, work release, parole supervision, and even cosmetic plastic surgery. Although there were some programs that appeared to offer promise, Martinson's general conclusion was that "[w]ith few and isolated experiences, the rehabilitative efforts that have been reported so far have had no appreciable effect on recidivism."[31] Because the study had examined only those program evaluations that were rigorously conducted, Martinson's report was hailed by some as the final word on rehabilitation. Rehabilitation had not worked, would not work, and could not work.

Of course, Martinson's article was not the last word. Critics of Martinson responded to the research on a variety of grounds, and the National Science Foundation commissioned its own study to assess the fairness of the Martinson study. In general, the NSF report found that "Lipton, Martinson, and Wilks were reasonably accurate and fair in their appraisal of the rehabilitation literature."[32] A National Science Foundation follow-up to this study was published in 1981, and found that "[t]he search for rehabilitative techniques and programs has borne little fruit."[33]

Several other related developments occurred during the 1970s. In 1971 the American Friends Service Committee published **Struggle for Justice**, an analysis of the use of imprisonment in America.[34] The book argued persuasively that the indeterminate sentence that had been a crucial part of efforts to rehabilitate offenders since the opening of Elmira was being used as an instrument of repression. According to this line of thought, denying inmates the opportunity to know when they would be released and holding out the promise of release for compliant behavior was an intrusion on inmate rights. The volume concluded that the indeterminate sentence ought to be abandoned on human rights grounds. This argument was well received in many circles, perhaps in part due to the general interest in civil rights that had emerged in the 1960s.

A third consideration was the high level of concern with crime. The civil disturbances of the 1960s and the escalating crime rates nationwide motivated many individuals inside and outside of the criminal justice system to look for new approaches. Crime was not being addressed by what had been done in the past, thus changes were in order. The liberal crime control strategies that were perceived to have dominated in the past were attacked as inadequate in terms of public protection.

The combination of rising crime, evidence questioning the value of rehabilitative programs, and concerns about the use of the indeterminate sentence as a pretext for practices that violated inmate rights led influential penal analysts to seek other alternatives. Andrew von Hirsch, for instance, presented a compelling argument that punishment should be based primarily upon the seriousness of the crime and prior criminal record, not upon the perceived amenability of the offender to rehabilitation.[35] He argued that moral considerations related to the individual's exercise of free will and power of choice provided a more than adequate basis for sentencing. Retribution, not rehabilitation or other forward-looking utilitarian concerns, should be the main interest of the penal system.

This essentially conservative argument, and other similar arguments, attracted considerable attention from both liberals and conservatives. The argument appealed to conservatives because they had always possessed reservations about rehabilitation and the implicit assumption that society, rather than the individual, was responsible for an individual's actions. Liberals, who had concerns about the civil rights of inmates incarcerated under the pretext of rehabilitation, were attracted to the position because it meant being able to specify at the time of sentencing how long the state would retain custody of an inmate. And of course, both liberals and conservatives were concerned about the rise in crime.

By the end of the 1970s many states had already begun to rewrite their penal codes. Determinate sentencing systems of one type or another began to replace the old indeterminate systems. By 1987 a majority of the states had adopted such systems.[36] Although different states have accomplished this in a variety of ways, in general sentences in determinate systems are distributed such that the offender knows his release date at the time of sentencing. Special provisions, such as good time discounts, may modify this date, but the level of certainty is significantly higher than under the old indeterminate systems. In addition, many states have now either abandoned rehabilitation programs or have made participation voluntary where once it was required. Due to both philosophic orientation and overcrowding, many states now seem satisfied with the mere warehousing of offenders.

Having briefly described the history of interest in rehabilitatively-oriented correctional initiatives, it is important to point out that the reality of rehabilitation during most of twentieth-century American history is that relatively few resources have been committed to rehabilitation. Todd Clear and George Cole estimate that even during the 1950s, when rehabilitation was energetically pursued as a correctional policy, only 5 percent of correctional budgets were allocated to rehabilitation.[37] In some jurisdictions serious efforts have been made to implement innovative rehabilitation approaches, while in others lip service has been the primary product of correctional initiatives. In correctional systems offering various kinds of programming, it has been estimated that of those offenders in need of help in the areas of education, vocational training, and drug/alcohol rehabilitation, "frequently less than half actually participate in available programs."[38]

The Impact of Correctional Reform

As might be expected, it is exceedingly difficult to determine the full impact of the abandonment of the rehabilitative ideal. However, we do know several things. First, after a brief decline in the beginning of the 1980s, official data reveal that national crime rates have resumed their upward climb. Second, public concern with crime remains high. Third, as we have already learned, our correctional institutions are jammed with inmates. This reflects several elements, including the fact that the war on drugs has had a dramatic impact on the flow of offenders into prisons and jails.[39] Of perhaps equal importance is the fact that, as already noted above, significant numbers of released offenders recidivate and return to prison.[40] This high return rate continues to be a problem despite increases in some jurisdictions in the length of sentences. The average time served in federal prison for robbery under the old indeterminate sentencing system was about 45 months, compared to the current figure of about 78 months, a 73 percent increase in sentence length.[41]

The new determinate sentencing systems have thus not had the anticipated impact on crime. It is, of course, possible that without the initiatives spawned in the late 1970s matters would be even worse. Nonetheless, strategies such as the abandonment of correctional rehabilitation have not led us out of the wilderness. It is therefore worth reconsidering whether this abandonment may have been premature. In the remainder of this chapter we will examine problems associated with rehabilitative initiatives, public support for rehabilitation, new evidence on the effectiveness of rehabilitation, and the interrelationship between deterrence and rehabilitation.

Focus 6-2
A Right to Treatment?

Even before the collapse of the rehabilitative ideal many analysts began to express concern over the realities of the correctional system. They noted that even in systems ostensibly committed to rehabilitation, inmates often were denied access to rehabilitative services.

Although most of the adult cases to come before the courts regarding rights to treatment have concerned fundamental medical rights or the rights of inmates of mental institutions, there have been a few cases which dealt with the question of whether inmates in prisons were entitled to rehabilitation. In general, these cases have addressed issues associated with the totality of conditions within prisons, and rehabilitation has been considered as only a portion of that totality. However, "grounds for requiring rehabilitation programs in their own right have not been constitutionally established to date."[42]

There have been some cases in the juvenile justice system supporting the right to treatment. In the case of Martarella v. Kelley the district court found that "detention of a child for thirty days or longer without treatment constituted a deprivation of constitutional proportions."[43] The court further ruled that although institutions did not have to prove that their efforts to rehabilitate were successful, "the effort must be to provide treatment adequate in light of present knowledge."[44] This was followed by a similar decision in Texas[45] in which "the United States District Court for the Eastern District of Texas ruled that confined juveniles have a right to treatment."[46] The court went even further by specifying criteria that would have to be met by institutions in satisfying the treatment obligation. However, the notion of a constitutionally based right to treatment was rejected by the appellate court in overturning the lower court decision. Nonetheless, "the decision achieved improvements for many delinquent youths in Texas. The Superintendent resigned, two of the worst facilities were closed, and Texas embarked on the development of community facilities for delinquents."[47]

Although many jurisdictions have since mounted efforts to provide treatment options for juveniles, the courts have still failed to issue a ruling establishing a constitutionally based right to treatment. The reluctance to guarantee a right to treatment to juveniles, who presumably are under state control for treatment rather than punishment, suggests that a right to treatment for adults is unlikely to emerge anytime in the near future.

▨ *Problems with Rehabilitation*

Although the rehabilitation research reported in the 1970s led some critics to argue that the notion of rehabilitation itself is a fundamentally flawed concept, its defenders have argued that rehabilitation has not been successful because it has been bedeviled by a number of problems. They further suggest that if these difficulties could be resolved it would become apparent that rehabilitation can be effective. Because of the significance of the consequences for crime control if these defenders are correct, it is important to look briefly at a few of these difficulties. In this section we consider three of these important problems: problems of theory, implementation, and outcome assessment.

Problems of Theory

These difficulties involve the theoretical predicates upon which a correctional intervention is based. The earlier discussed concept of deterrence, for instance, assumes that human beings are essentially rational creatures possessed of free will and able to make choices based upon assessment of costs and benefits. If such an assumption about human nature is flawed, and humans are both irrational and lacking the ability to assess and choose, then it should come as no surprise if efforts to deter future crime are ineffective. Similarly, if rehabilitative efforts are based upon misconceptions about human character and capability, then programs designed around such misconceptions are unlikely to be effective.

For instance, an anger management program designed around the assumption that offenders want to change their ability to handle frustration, but simply lack the know-how, will founder if in fact offenders have no interest in managing such anger. On the other hand, a program designed around the assumption that offenders want to be successful in the initiatives in which they engage, even if they have no particular interest in managing their anger, may stand a better chance of influencing the offender. Such a program might, for example, offer counseling sessions which focus on identification of meaningful goals for the offender, as well as specification of both the conditions that will help the offender achieve those goals and the personal issues that must be addressed to secure such conditions. Counseling can show the offender that uncontrolled anger in a cooperative work environment can have a debilitating effect on an individual's chance of being successful within that environment. Because anger management is tied directly to the offender's *own* goals, this revelation may strike a responsive chord. Thus a program that seeks to sensitize the offender to this reality may have a better chance of motivating an offender to seek to develop the ability to manage anger than would a program that assumes the existence of such motivation. The particular strategies that will be used to reach the offender will depend, therefore, on the theoretical assumptions that are made about the recipient of the services, the offender.

Problems of Implementation

These dilemmas are related to how rehabilitation programs are actually put into action. There are many issues of implementation, but we will look briefly at three: program integrity, duration, and offender amenability.[48]

Program integrity refers to the extent to which a program is operationalized as originally designed. The National Science Foundation report on rehabilitation describes the example of an experiment designed to test the effectiveness of group counseling. Offenders were randomly assigned to groups that received counseling or that did not. Parole performance at 12, 24, and 36 months was examined, and it appeared that offenders who had received counseling did not do any better than those who had not received counseling. However, upon closer scrutiny it was found that the individuals providing counseling were not trained counselors. In addition, for many counselors there appeared to be little personal commitment to or involvement in the counseling. The counseling experiment thus cannot be used as strong evidence regarding the effectiveness of counseling. In reality, the program did not provide the kind and quality of counseling that was ostensibly the object of the research.[49]

Program duration refers to the length of time a program is in operation. Although a program may be implemented properly, it may not be given enough time to fully demonstrate what it is capable of accomplishing. For instance, some correctional programs are funded by federal money intended as incentives to local government. Under such an ar-rangement the local government accepts the federal dollars, initiates a program, and is then expected to take over funding after a trial period of a year or two. Unfortunately, when the time comes for the local government to assume responsibility for funding the program, it sometimes balks, funds are cut off, and the program closes down. This is especially unfortunate because such funding cut-offs may occur just as the program is ready to begin making solid contributions. The initial bugs in program administration and operation may have been worked out, and program staff may have acquired the experience necessary to assure effective performance.

Finally, *offender amenability* issues may compromise the ability of a program to achieve intended effects. Amenability refers to the extent to which an offender is suited to a particular form of correctional treatment. For instance, rehabilitation programs designed to build self-esteem, and which use written exercises to help inmates develop self- confidence, will be unsuccessful if inmates lacking adequate reading and writing skills are permitted into the program. Similarly, programs attempting to build self-confidence through difficult physical challenges may be less effective for physically weak and uncoordinated offenders than for offenders possessed of significant physical skills. The success rate of a program will thus depend in part on the care exercised in selecting inmates for program admission. A program that might be very successful for certain kinds of inmates may be a spectacular failure with others.

Recognition of the amenability problem naturally leads to awareness of the importance of proper classification of inmates for treatment purposes. Although many methods for classification have been developed over the course of the twentieth century, getting the right kinds of inmates into the proper programs is still an issue that has yet to be adequately resolved.

Implementation issues are beginning to be addressed with more energy and enthusiasm in the literature. Works such as Mark Hamm and Jeffrey Schrink's "The Conditions of Effective Implementation—A Guide to Accomplishing Rehabilitative Objectives in Corrections"[50] are providing guidance on how correctional administrators can avoid the hazards that have kept some rehabilitative initiatives from reaching their objectives.

Outcome Assessment

The final problem category, outcome assessment, is related to the first two difficulties. The ultimate value of a rehabilitation program is in its ability to reform the conduct, if not always the nature, of the offender. On the surface it may appear that assessment of a program's effectiveness is relatively simple and straightforward. Inmates are admitted into the program, exposed to the treatment regime, then monitored subsequent to release to determine whether they desist from further involvement in crime.

The reality is significantly more complicated. For instance, the standard measure of program failure is recidivism. Offenders who are exposed to a rehabilitative initiative are followed after release from supervision, and their record of subsequent involvement with the law is noted. As the committee which examined rehabilitation for the National Science Foundation pointed out, "The use of recidivism as an outcome variable is replete with problems."[51] For instance, what level of involvement in lawbreaking indicates program failure? More specifically, what constitutes recidivism? Is it rearrest? If so, it can be argued that former offenders are at greater risk of rearrest simply because they are being watched more closely than are citizens without prior records. Is it reimprisonment? The reimprisonment standard fails to address the fact that only a subset of those arrested actually are imprisoned. One study of arrests, convictions, and imprisonments found that even when felony arrests are involved, only 32 percent result in imprisonment.[52] Thus significant numbers of "failures" will be missed by using the imprisonment standard.

Moreover, even if adequate measures of lawbreaking could be devised, it can be argued that rearrest, conviction, or imprisonment alone do not adequately capture program effectiveness. What about the *frequency* of involvement in lawbreaking? What about changes in the *seriousness* of the new crimes that are committed? What about the other kinds of new and positive social contributions that offenders may make even while continuing to violate the law (for example, caring for parents and children, holding gainful employment, paying taxes)?

Finally, meaningful outcome measurement depends heavily upon having essentially equivalent control groups to compare with the group receiving the correctional treatment. A finding that a group of offenders had only a 5 percent recidivism rate after undergoing a particular kind of treatment is only meaningful if these offenders can be compared with a group of offenders who differ from the rehabilitation group only in the receipt of treatment. This can be an important issue because often the lowest risk offenders are assigned to rehabilitative programs, while the most incorrigible inmates are denied access to program services. That recidivism rates should be low for the program group should therefore come as no surprise because they were low risk offenders to begin with.

The three major kinds of problems with rehabilitation discussed above are not insurmountable. Nonetheless, in practice these difficulties have not been met with the measure of resolve required to handle them adequately. Practical considerations, such as local program funding, continue to complicate rehabilitative initiatives. As we will see, however, the public continues to maintain a strong interest in rehabilitation as a legitimate correctional objective. There is good reason, therefore, to consider investing resources into addressing these problems.

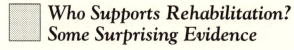

Who Supports Rehabilitation?
Some Surprising Evidence

Despite the abundant political rhetoric about getting tough, locking up offenders and "throwing away the key," the fact is that significant numbers of citizens, correctional officials, and politicians are supportive of reha-bilitation as an important goal of punishment. Although levels of sup-port may be less than what they have been in the past, most citizens view rehabilitation as an appropriate and valuable correctional objective.

In a 1967 Harris Poll, citizens were asked what the main purpose of prison should be: punishment, rehabilitation, or incapacitation. Almost three-quarters of respondents (73 percent) indicated that rehabilitation should be the main emphasis. Although this figure fell to 44 percent in 1982, it is significant that such a large percentage of citizens still value rehabilitation.[53] More recently, a 1989 Gallup Poll asked a sample of citi-zens, "In dealing with those who are in prison, do you think it is more important to punish them for their crimes, or more important to get them started 'on the right road'?" Only slightly more than a third of respondents chose punishment (38 percent), while 48 percent wanted to start them on the right road. This viewpoint varied little by political party, with Democrats and Republicans being equally likely to support rehabilitation.[54]

Several other recent studies affirm that the public continues to have a high level of interest in rehabilitation. When asked if rehabilita-tion was just as important as making criminals pay for their crimes, a majority of Illinois respondents agreed.[55] Another sample of approxi-mately 600 midwesterners was asked to indicate whether punishment, rehabilitation, or incapacitation should be the main emphasis of prisons. Approximately 55 percent of respondents selected rehabilitation, while only about 6 percent chose punishment, and about 32 percent selected incapacitation.[56] A study of Texas residents revealed that although they supported punishment as an important purpose of prisons, support for rehabilitation was also very high. Approximately 70 percent of respon-dents supported rehabilitation.[57]

Some analysts have been critical of the use of paper and pencil and telephone surveys such as those discussed above. They fear that surveys provide at best a superficial understanding of public sentiment. In an effort to address this concern, focus group methods have been employed in studies of public views of punishment. Focus groups provide opportu-nities for citizens to obtain information about issues as well as to express their own views. These generally involve small groups of respondents who participate in a discussion of issues led by a group leader. The leader provides information to participants, who are then able to articulate their views on various subjects. A 10-city focus group study was conducted to examine a number of crime and justice issues, including those associated with punishment. In accord with some of the conventional survey research, this study found that "Americans feel that a primary goal of the prison system should be to rehabilitate offenders, especially young or first offenders."[58]

A study of victims of burglary provides additional evidence of the concern with rehabilitation. Face-to-face interviews were conducted with 50 victims of burglary. One major focus of the study was the issue of fairness as it pertained to the victims of the burglaries. The author of this research found that "[t]he most frequent and intense concern about fairness expressed by victims of burglary by juveniles was related to rehabilitation services for their offenders."[59] More than 90 percent of the victims possessed this concern. Some victims remarked that

> [t]hey need counseling and therapy rather than just the punishment of putting them away for awhile.[60]
> We've got to look at these people and see what we can do . . . we're responsible for what our kids do, how they turn out . . . we owe it to them to try and correct some of their problems.[61]

Although citizens did not support reduced sentences, they did want inmates given opportunities for rehabilitation while they served their time.

There is some evidence that correctional officials also support rehabilitation as an important correctional objective. A study of correctional officials in Walla Walla Prison in Washington found that corrections line staff "seem to support the rehabilitative purpose of the prison, and the long-term goals it attempts to accomplish."[62] (Somewhat surprisingly, prison counselors and administrators at Walla Walla were less enthusiastic about rehabilitation.) A study of Illinois correctional officers found that 70 percent of officials agreed with the statement "Rehabilitating a criminal is just as important as making a criminal pay for his or her crime."[63] Only 21.9 percent agreed that "[t]he rehabilitation of adult criminals just does not work."[64] A recent national survey of 512 state and federal prisons found that although wardens are most concerned with maintaining order and preventing escapes, they also regarded "rehabilitation as a secondary but fundamental goal of corrections."[65]

A survey of citizens, politicians, and decisionmaking elites asked "What do you think should be the main purpose of the prison system for persons sent to prison for the first time." Three-quarters of citizens, 70 percent of legislators, and 80 percent of decisionmaking elites selected "change their behavior." "Punish them" was only selected by about 10 percent of respondents, while "Keep them away" (incapacitate) was chosen by 5 percent. This represents a solid mandate for rehabilitation for first-time inmates. Support for rehabilitation dropped to about 19 percent when repeat offenders were considered. Another striking finding of this research is that legislators mistakenly estimated that 59 percent of the public supported "Punish them" while public support for "Change their behavior" was estimated by legislators at only 23 percent. This is a significant finding for it suggests that politicians severely underestimate public interest in rehabilitation.[66]

This research accords with the findings of a Maryland research project. The study found that policymakers seriously misunderstood public sentiment regarding correctional goals.

> While policymakers likewise feel that the general public strongly supports the goal of retributive punishment (also, in this case, by a wide margin in the original metric), this goal is actually assigned the lowest priority by our sample of the public. It is therefore not surprising that while policy makers feel that the goal of rehabilitation would be lowest in the public esteem (and by a very wide margin indeed), this goal is in fact tied with that of deterrence for the public's highest priority. Quite clearly, then, there is considerable misperception of the public viewpoint on the part of the correctional policy makers.[67]

It is thus apparent that rehabilitation continues to be an important correctional objective for the public, at least some correctional officials, and even for politicians. In light of this support, it is important to begin asking why so few resources are being committed to developing the rehabilitative potential of the correctional system.

The Current Debate over Rehabilitation: Some Promising Evidence

If what has been tried during the last 15 years has not moved us any closer to addressing the crime problem, then perhaps it makes good sense to take another look at rehabilitation. Five years after the publication of his "nothing works" article, Robert Martinson published the results of a new survey of correctional programs. In this new research report he modified his original conclusion.

> . . . contrary to my previous position, some treatment programs do have an appreciable effect on recidivism. Some programs are indeed beneficial; of equal or greater significance, some programs are harmful.[68]
> . . . new evidence from our current study leads me to reject my original conclusion and suggest an alternative more adequate to the facts at hand. I have hesitated up to now but the evidence in our survey is too overwhelming to ignore.[69]
> More precisely, treatments will be found to be "impotent" under certain conditions, beneficial under others, and detrimental under still others.[70]

Although some analysts have read this as a rejection of the position that correctional treatment is ineffective, other analysts have argued that Martinson's 1979 position merely represented a modification of his earlier view. Anthony Doob and Jean-Paul Brodeur note that Martinson was pointing out that under the proper circumstances (treatment given to appropriate clients in appropriate settings) some treatments do seem to work, but that only a very small percentage of correctional clients seem to be positively influenced by treatment.[71]

In any event, the debate over rehabilitation has shifted from whether anything works to the circumstances under which it works. In the mid-1980s Thomas Orsagh and Mary Ellen Marsden argued for greater attention to matching treatments with offender types.

> Thus, one reason for the apparent ineffectiveness of treatment programs may be their application to all offenders rather than to those for whom such training might be more effective. . . .We suggest that some treatments have been found to be ineffective because practitioners misconceive or disregard the underlying causal theory that specifies how the treatment is most effectively applied.[72]

This issue has been taken up in an important recent exchange of views on the effectiveness of correctional treatment which appeared in a 1990 issue of **Criminology,** the official journal of the American Society of Criminology. In the lead article Professor D.A. Andrews and his colleagues presented the findings of a detailed analysis of 80 studies of the effectiveness of correctional treatment. The authors of this analysis found considerable evidence that rehabilitative correctional services can be effective when three conditions are met:

1. Rehabilitative services are delivered to high risk offenders.
2. The criminogenic needs of offenders are identified.
3. Treatment matched to client needs and styles of learning is provided.[73]

Andrews and his colleagues examined research on programs conducted within correctional institutions, as well as those operated as part of probation and parole. It included both juvenile and adult offenders but excluded programs which dealt with substance abusers. When offenders were exposed to the right kinds of programs, the authors found that rehabilitation could be effective. They concluded that

> This review has convinced us that the positive trends that we and others detected in the literature of the 1960s and early 1970s were indeed worthy of serious application and evaluation. There is a reasonably solid clinical and research basis for the political reaffirmation of rehabilitation.[74]

Because the Andrews study had focused in part on research conducted by S.P. Lab and J.T. Whitehead[75]—research that had failed to arrive at such optimistic conclusions—Lab and Whitehead published a response to the Andrews research.[76] They pointed to a number of difficulties in the methods used in the Andrews study and affirmed their view that most of the evidence on correctional programs did not suggest widespread success. Lab and Whitehead did, however, acknowledge that their own work reveals that "the majority [of interventions] were not effective, but some interventions were effective."[77]

Other research also suggests that the effectiveness of rehabilitative initiatives may depend as much on how it is applied as on the theoretical soundness of the approach employed. An analysis of juvenile programs, for instance, examined 46 evaluations of juvenile intervention programs and found considerable variation in levels of effectiveness. The authors conclude that "Whether a program works depends on who does what to whom, why, and where."[78]

Despite the continuing appearance of some research that fails to uncover evidence of rehabilitative effectiveness,[79] the best current sense of the effectiveness of rehabilitation is now somewhat more positive than during the immediate post-Martinson period. Peter Greenwood of the Rand Corporation notes that

> ... two developments during the past decade have encouraged some researchers to conclude that progress in identifying effective treatment methods is finally being made. One of these is the development of the procedure called meta-analysis ... which allows one to measure the magnitude of treatment effects observed in individual evaluations on a standardized scale, so that treatment effects can be combined across individual studies. ... The second development has been the observation of strong and consistent positive effects for some new forms of programming that appear to combine many of the most promising approaches of the past two decades—social learning, family therapy, and life skills training.[80]

A recent assessment of the meta-analysis literature concluded that there was good reason to be optimistic about rehabilitation for at least some kinds of offenders. Ted Palmer, long a defender of rehabilitation, notes, "The large number of positive outcomes that have been found in the last three decades with studies whose designs and analyses were at least adequate leaves little doubt that many programs work, and not just with one or two types of offenders and programs."[81]

It appears, therefore, that the debate over rehabilitation has shifted away from whether rehabilitation does, or can ever, work to the circumstances under which it will work. There still remain substantial differences of opinion regarding both the likelihood of being able to identify such circumstances and the practical and political realities which influence the adoption of new information about effective correctional treatment. Nonetheless, it appears that the "nothing works" viewpoint adopted by many analysts and policymakers during the 1970s has been displaced with a more optimistic, yet cautious, assessment of the prospects of rehabilitation.

Focus 6-3
Rehabilitating Drug Offenders
The Cornerstone Program

As has been noted in several places in this volume, the recent influx of drug offenders into the criminal justice system has been extraordinary. Both the state and federal correctional systems are reeling under the weight of these offenders. A profile of state prison inmates revealed that two-thirds of inmates had at one time used drugs on a regular basis, and about 40 percent had used drugs on a daily basis during the month prior to their offense.[82]

It is obvious to many analysts that if drug-related crime is to be reduced, significant progress must be made in weaning offenders away from drug use. The Cornerstone Program is an example of a program committed to such an objective.

Cornerstone is based on the therapeutic community idea and is situated in the Oregon State Hospital in Salem, Oregon.[83] It is devoted to drug-addicted offenders with long histories of drug use (the average age of first substance abuse was 12½). These offenders averaged more than 13 prior arrests and had spent an average of more than seven years in incarceration at the time they entered the program. Clearly, the program was not designed to handle only low-risk inexperienced first offenders.

The program was based on several major principles:

1. Segregation of participants from the general institutional population
2. Rules that are unambiguous and clear regarding actions and consequences
3. Incentives for privileges that can motivate inmates
4. Inmate participation in operation of the program
5. Exposure to intensive treatment interventions, generally with-in a highly structured environment
6. Simultaneous focus on drug abuse and criminal involvement
7. Provision of transition and aftercare services to assure successful community re-entry

The program environment isolated participants from the influences of inmates who were not in the program, and they were required to engage in a variety of highly structured activities. Inmates were, however, provided with opportunities to take responsibility for their own affairs, as well as for the more general operation of the program.

How effective is the Cornerstone Program? An evaluation of the program followed approximately 200 participants for three years subsequent to their release from prison. They were divided into groups based upon whether they had graduated from the program, and how long they had participated in the program. Data were obtained on arrests, convictions, and incarceration for each of the groups.

The results show that the longer the time spent in the program, the lower the level of re-involvement in arrest, conviction, or incarceration. For example, 74 percent of graduates avoided subsequent incarceration, while the figure for non-graduates who had been in the program for at least six months was 37 percent. The figure for offenders who left Cornerstone in less than 60 days was only 15 percent. Examination of the rates of offending (number of involvements in lawbreaking) revealed essentially the same pattern: those spending the most time in treatment had the lowest rates of re-offending.

Of course, this study does have limitations. The offenders staying longest in the program may well have been those most motivated to desist in their criminal involvement. The treatment features of the program may have had little to do with their post-release success. On the other hand, it may be that the program itself is effective for a wide range of drug-addicted offenders, and the key is to find ways to keep offenders in the program.

Changing Behavior: A Partnership of Deterrence and Rehabilitation?

In this chapter we have considered the possibilities of changing the behavior of offenders. Our focus has been on deterrence and rehabilitation. As noted at the outset of this discussion, it is sometimes difficult to determine when an individual's desistence from crime is the result of the simple fear of future punishment or of a more fundamental transformation in the nature of the offender's character. For most citizens, of course, it matters little whether the desired behavioral change is the consequence of fear, newly acquired religion, enhanced job skills, a recrafted sense of morality, or any of a score of other changes which might lead to a law-abiding existence. Citizens are much more interested in living in a safe world than in possessing a full understanding of the causes of criminal involvement.

In a more analytic sense, there is reason to wonder whether the distinction between deterrence and rehabilitation continues to be useful. Although fear of punishment is a primary characteristic of specific deterrence, such fear is not unrelated to rehabilitation. For instance, the capacity to feel concern for future punishment may well be related to the belief in a meaningful personal future. Some juveniles appear indifferent to the consequences of their actions because they do not believe they have viable future prospects. The fear that most of us would feel at the thought of being killed in a gang fight or a drug transaction, or of being locked away in a state prison simply is not relevant to some youths because they believe they have little future to live for anyway. In analyzing the causes of a juvenile "thrill killing," Preston Elrod argues, "They don't have the ability to look at the consequences of their actions. A person's life isn't that important because they don't see their own life as being very important."[84] A rehabilitatively-oriented program that persuades these young people that they do have prospects, and that provides them with the education and vocational training to succeed, thereby also provides them with the capacity to care about their future. Youths who truly believe that the future might indeed hold good things for them are youths who are then capable of caring about preserving such future prospects. Thus, rehabilitation may help them to develop both future prospects and the ability to experience fear and concern about loss of such prospects. Because the capacity to fear is an indispensable element of deterrence, rehabilitation may enhance the potential for deterrent effects.

This relationship between rehabilitation and specific deterrence has not escaped at least some crime analysts. James Q. Wilson, for instance, argues that "the study of deterrence and the study of rehabilitation must be merged—that, at least for a given individual, they are the same thing."[85]

In their analysis of the legal supervision and community treatment of chronic offenders, George Speckart, Douglas Anglin, and Elizabeth Deschenes point out that

> [i]t has long been known, for example, that more prolonged retention in treatment programs is correlated with favorable outcomes. To the extent that both treatment and legal supervision improve retention of clients in a complimentary fashion, the use of both interventions in conjunction with each other should improve client outcomes and increase the potential for rehabilitation.[86]

Speckart and his colleagues argue that the imposition of restrictive legal conditions, typically thought of as purely punitive, may prove useful in accomplishing rehabilitative objectives.

Whatever the theoretical promise of a marriage between rehabilitation and deterrence, there are practical realities that must be addressed before there can be any realistic hope of success. For instance, identification of effective methods to deter and rehabilitate depend on energetic research efforts to sort out the weak from the strong approaches. This requires money. In writing about what works in corrections, Joan Petersilia notes that

> [t]he Federal Government is, by order of magnitude, the largest funder of criminal justice research, and it had never chosen to spend more than a small fraction of 1 percent on such research. For every U.S. citizen, the National Science Foundation reports that Federal funders spend about $32 on health research, $4 on environmental research, $1.20 on education research, but only 13 cents on criminal justice research. And, dollars allocated to research have steadily decreased since 1980, as a proportion of all money spent on criminal justice. This allocation hardly accords with priorities of the American public, for which crime has nearly always ranked first among domestic policy concerns.[87]

From a pragmatic point of view, it thus may make excellent sense to begin to reconceptualize deterrence and rehabilitation as aspects of each other, at least in a limited sense. The realities of modern politics and public funding suggest that the probability of obtaining meaningful changes in public policy supportive of securing rehabilitative initiatives may well depend upon the extent to which they are linked to "tougher" sanctions and responses to crime. A publicly visible marriage of deterrence and rehabilitation may go far in creating the best possible opportunities to achieve maximal rehabilitative and deterrent effects.

Notes

[1] Boland, Barbara, Mahanna, Paul, and Sones, Ronald (1992) "The prosecution of felony arrests," Washington, D.C.: U.S. Dept. of Justice, p. 3.

[2] Id.

[3] Gottfredson, Stephen D., Warner, Barbara D., and Taylor, Ralph B. (1988) "Conflict and consensus about criminal justice in Maryland," in Walker and Hough, eds. *Public Attitudes to Sentencing*, Brookfield: Gower, pp. 38-40.

[4] Thomson, Douglas R. and Ragona, Anthony J. (1987) "Popular moderation versus governmental authoritarianism: An interactionist view of public sentiments toward criminal sanctions," *Crime and Delinquency*, 33(2), p. 348.

[5] Brillon, Yves (1988) "Punitiveness, status, and ideology in three Canadian provinces." in Walker and Hough, eds. *Public Attitudes to Sentencing*, Brookfield: Gower, p. 86.

[6] Doob, Anthony N. and Roberts, Julian (1988) "Public punitiveness and public knowledge of the facts: some Canadian surveys," in Walker and Hough, (eds.) *Public Attitudes to Sentencing*, Brookfield: Gower, p. 119.

[7] Beck, Allen and Shipley, Bernard (1989) "Recidivism of prisoners released in 1983," Washington, D.C.: U.S. *Department of Justice—Bureau of Justice Statistics*.

[8] "Parolees' recidivism rate higher, study says," (1992) *Fort Worth Star-Telegram*, May 22, Sec. A., p. 23.

[9] Champion, Dean J. (1990) *Corrections in the United States—A Contemporary Perspective*, Englewood Cliffs, NJ: Prentice Hall, p. 126.

[10] Bureau of Justice Statistics (1992) "National Update," 1(4), p. 10.; Langan, Patrick A. and Cuniff, Mark A. (1992) "Recidivism of felons on probation, 1986-1989," Washington, D.C.: Dept. of Justice, Bureau of Justice Statistics, p. 1.

[11] Lundman, Richard (1984) *Prevention and Control of Juvenile Delinquency*, New York: Oxford University Press, pp. 140-141.

[12] Id. at 138.

[13] Id. at 143.

[14] Id. at 143-150.

[15] Green, Donald E. (1989) "Measures of illegal behavior in individual-level deterrence research," *Journal of Research in Crime and Justice*, 26(3).

[16] Speckart, George, Anglin, M. Douglas, Deschenes, Elizabeth Piper (1989) "Modeling the longitudinal impact of legal sanctions on narcotics use

and property crime," *Journal of Quantitative Criminology*, 5(1), pp. 48, 50.

[17] See, e.g., Smith, Douglas and Gartin, Patrick (1989) "Specifying specific deterrence: The influence of arrest on future criminal activities," *American Sociological Review* 54; Sherman, Lawrence and Berk, Richard (1984) "The specific deterrent effects of arrest for domestic assault," *American Sociological Review* ,49.

[18] Sellin, J. Thorsten (1944) *Pioneering in Penology*, Philadelphia: University of Pennsylvania Press, p. 41.

[19] Id.

[20] Rothman, David (1971) *The Discovery of the Asylum*, Boston: Little, Brown and Company.

[21] Durham, Alexis M. III (1989) "Newgate of Connecticut: Origins and early days of an early American prison," *Justice Quarterly*, 6(1), p. 95.

[22] Melossi, D. and Pavarini, M. (1981) *The Prison and the Factory*, Totowa, NJ: Barnes and Noble.

[23] Lewis, W. David (1965) *From Newgate to Dannemora—The Rise of the Penitentiary in New York, 1796-1848*. Ithaca, NY: Cornell University Press, p. 182.

[24] Johnson, Herbert A. (1988) *History of Criminal Justice*, Cincinnati: Anderson Pub. Co., p. 159.

[25] Id. at 217.

[26] Lombroso-Ferrero, Gina (1972) *Lombroso's Criminal Man*, Montclair, NJ: Patterson Smith.

[27] Vold, George B. and Bernard, Thomas J. (1986) *Theoretical Criminology*, New York: Oxford University Press, p. 38.

[28] Messinger, Sheldon L., Berecochea, John E., Ruma, David, and Berk, Richard (1985) "The foundations of parole in California," *Law and Society Review*, 19, pp. 69-106; Irwin, John (1970) *The Felon*, Englewood Cliffs, NJ: Prentice Hall.

[29] In Cullen, Francis T. and Gilbert, K. (1982) *Reaffirming Rehabilitation*, Cincinnati: Anderson, p. 8.

[30] See e.g., Bailey, Walter C. (1966) "Correctional outcome: An evaluation of 100 reports," *Journal of Criminal Law, Criminology and Police Science*, 57(2).

[31] Martinson, Robert (1974) "What works?—questions and answers about prison reform," *Public Interest*, Spring, p. 25.

[32] Sechrest, Lee, White, Susan, and Brown, Elizabeth (1979) *The Rehabilitation of Criminal Offenders*, Washington, D.C.: National Academy of Sciences.

33 Martin, Susan E., Sechrest, Lee B., and Redner, Robin (1981) *New*

Directions in the Rehabilitation of Criminal Offenders, Washington, D.C.: National Academy Press, p. 22.

[34] American Friends Service Committee (1971) *Struggle for Justice*, New York: Hill and Wang.

[35] von Hirsch, Andrew (1976) *Doing Justice—The Choice of Punishments*, New York: Hill and Wang.

[36] Allen, Harry E. and Simonsen, Clifford E. (1989) *Corrections in America—An Introduction*, New York: Macmillan Pub. Co., p. 76.

[37] Clear, Todd R. and Cole, George F. (1986) *American Corrections*, Monterrey, CA: Brooks-Cole Pub. Co., p. 88.

[38] Clear, Todd R. and Cole, George F. (1990) *American Corrections*, 2nd ed., Pacific Grove, CA: Brooks-Cole, p. 357.

[39] In the federal prison system, for instance, 79 percent of new admissions between the years 1986 and 1988 were for drug-related offenses. Government Accounting Office (1989) "Federal prisons—Trends in offender characteristics," Washington, D.C., pp. 1-2.

[40] Beck, Allen and Shipley, Bernard (1989) "Recidivism of prisoners released in 1983," Washington, D.C.: U.S. Department of Justice—Bureau of Justice Statistics.

[41] Luttrell, Mark H. (1991) "The impact of the Sentencing Reform Act on prison management," *Federal Probation*, 55(4), p. 56.

[42] Hawkins, Richard and Alpert, Geoffrey P. (1989) *American Prison Systems—Punishment and Justice*, Englewood Cliffs, NJ: Prentice Hall, Inc., p. 424.

[43] Volenik, Adrienne (1980) "Right to treatment: Case developments in juvenile law," in Rubin, H.T. (ed.) *Juveniles in Justice*, Santa Monica, CA: Goodyear Pub. Co., p. 281.

[44] Id.

[45] Morales v. Turman, 364 F. Supp. 166 (E.D. Tex. 1973).

[46] See Volenik, note 43 above at 282.

[47] Polier, Justine Wise (1989) *Juvenile Justice in Jeopardy: The Distanced Community and Vengeful Retribution*, Hillsdale, NJ: Lawrence Erlbaum Associates, Pub., p. 114.

[48] See Sechrest, White, and Brown, note 32 above at ch. 3.

[49] Id. at 40-41.

[50] Hamm, Mark S. and Schrink, Jeffrey L. (1989) "The conditions of effective implementation—A guide to accomplishing rehabilitative objectives in corrections," *Criminal Justice and Behavior*, 16(2).

[51] See Sechrest, White, and Brown, note 32 above at 71.

[52] See Boland, Mahanna, and Sones, note 1 above at 3.

[53] Flanagan, Timothy, J. and Caulfield, Susan L. (1984) "Public opinion and prison policy: A Review," *The Prison Journal*, 64, p. 42.

[54] Maguire, Kathleen and Flanagan, Timothy J. (1991) *Sourcebook of Criminal Justice Statistics—1990*, Washington D.C.: U.S. Dept. of Justice, Bureau of Justice Statistics, p. 198.

[55] Cullen, F., Cullen, J. and Wozniak, J. (1988) "Is rehabilitation dead? The myth of the punitive public," *Journal of Criminal Justice*, 16.

[56] Cullen, Francis T., Skovron, Sandra E., Scott, Joseph E., and Burton, Velmar S., Jr. (1990) "Public support for correctional treatment: The tenacity of rehabilitative ideology," *Criminal Justice and Behavior*, 17(1).

[57] Penley, Victoria (1991) "Public opinion, punishment, and rehabilitation: A convergence of ideologies," presented the American Society of Criminology national conference, San Francisco, November.

[58] Doble, John (1987) "Crime and punishment: The public's view," The Public Agenda Foundation, p. 27.

[59] Umbreit, Mark S. (1989) "Crime victims seeking fairness, not revenge: Toward restorative justice," *Federal Probation*, 53(3), p. 53.

[60] Id.

[61] Id.

[62] Blayney, Marianne H. (1991) "Rehabilitation in the prison: An Organizational goal? A study of staff attitudes," presented at the American Society of Criminology national conference, San Francisco, November.

[63] Cullen, Francis T., Lutze, Faith E., Link, Bruce G., and Wolfe, Nancy Travis (1989) *Federal Probation*, 53(1), p. 38.

[64] Id.

[65] Cullen, Francis T., Latessa, Edward J., Burton, Velmer S., and Lombardo, Lucien X. (1993) "The correctional orientation of prison wardens: Is the rehabilitative ideal supported?" *Criminology*, 31(1), p. 85.

[66] Johnson, Bruce and Huff, C. Ronald (1987) "Public opinion and criminal justice policy formulation," *Criminal Justice Policy Review*, 2(2), pp. 124-125.

[67] Gottfredson, Stephen D., Warner, Barbara D., and Taylor, Ralph B. (1988) "Conflict and consensus about criminal justice in Maryland," in Walker and Hough, eds. *Public Attitudes to Sentencing*, Brookfield: Gower, p. 40.

[68] Martinson, Robert (1979) "New findings, new views: A note of caution regarding sentencing reform," *Hofstra Law Review*,7(2), p. 244.

[69] Id. at 252.

[70] Id. at 254.

[71] Doob, Anthony and Brodeur, Jean-Paul (1989) "Rehabilitating the debate on rehabilitation," *Canadian Journal of Criminology*, 31(2), p. 186.

[72] Orsagh, Thomas and Marsden, Mary Ellen (1985) "What works when: Rational-choice theory and offender rehabilitation," *Journal of Criminal Justice*, 13, pp. 270-271.

[73] Andrews, D.A., Zinger, Ivan, Hoge, Robert D., Bonta, James, Gendreau, Paul, and Cullen, Francis T. (1990) "Does correctional treatment work? A clinically relevant and psychologically informed meta-analysis," *Criminology*, 28(3).

[74] Id. at 384.

[75] Lab, S.P. and Whitehead, J.T. (1988) "An analysis of juvenile correctional treatment," *Crime and Delinquency*, 34.

[76] Lab, S.P. and Whitehead, J.T. (1990) "From "nothing works" to "the appropriate" works: The latest stop on the search for the secular grail," *Criminology*, 28(3).

[77] Id. at 414.

[78] Izzo, Rhene L. and Ross, Robert R. (1990) "Meta-analysis of rehabilitation programs for juvenile delinquents," *Criminal Justice and Behavior*, 17(1), p. 141.

[79] A 1991 report released on the Patuxent Institution in Maryland, for example, failed to provide evidence of rehabilitative effectiveness, despite the institution's energetic use of rehabilitative approaches. See *Criminal Justice Newsletter*, 22(4), p. 3.

[80] Greenwood, Peter (1988) "The role of planned interventions in studying the desistance of criminal behavior in a longitudinal study," Santa Monica, CA: The Rand Corporation, pp. 3-4.

[81] Palmer, Ted (1992) *The Re-Emergence of Correctional Intervention*, Newbury Park, CA: Sage, p. 76.

[82] Innes, Christopher (1988) "Profile of State Prison Inmates," Washington, D.C.: Bureau of Justice Statistics, p. 6.

[83] Description in this FOCUS based upon Field, Gary (1989) "The effects of intensive treatment on reducing the criminal recidivism of addicted offenders," *Federal Probation*, 53(4), pp. 51-56.

[84] Elrod, H. Preston (1992) quoted in Steckner, Susie and Moewe, M.C. "Teen-ager killed for the thrills, police say," *Fort Worth Star-Telegram*, 9 April 1992, p. A6.

[85] Wilson, James Q. (1991) ""What works?" revisited—New findings on criminal rehabilitation." in Haas and Alpert (eds.) *The Dilemmas of Corrections*, 2nd edition, Prospect Heights, IL: Waveland Press, p. 343.

[86] Speckart, George, Anglin, M. Douglas, and Deschenes, Elizabeth Piper (1989) "Modeling the longitudinal impact of legal sanctions on narcotics use and property crime." *Journal of Quantitative Criminology*, 5(1), p. 52.

[87] Petersilia, Joan (1991) "The value of correctional research: Learning what works," *Federal Probation*, 55(2), p. 24.

7

Alternatives to Incarceration: Intensive Supervision, Home Confinement, and Electronic Monitoring

In his address to the National Association of Pretrial Service Agencies Chief Justice Douglas Lay of the Eighth Circuit Court of Appeals noted that

> In an effort to fight crime we aimlessly set goals of putting more people into jails and prisons, regardless of consequential costs or the complete denigration of dignity and resulting human sacrifice. . . . The kneejerk reactions by angry executives, politically conscious legislatures and vindictive judicial officers is taking us down a primrose path with little success in combatting crime. The resulting approach is accomplishing nothing more than exorbitantly wasting tax dollars, creating a warehouse of human degradation and in the long run breeding societal resentment that causes more crime.[1]

In light of the many difficulties we have considered in our examination of the correctional system, it should come as no surprise that Judge Lay's view is far from rare. The Rand Corporation's report on felony probation puts the issue this way. "Without alternative sanctions for serious offenders, prison populations will continue to grow and courts will be forced to consider probation for more and more serious offenders. . . alternative "intermediate" sanctions must be developed and imple mented."[2] Alabama's Public Affairs Research Council articulated similar sentiments in a Fall 1990 report on incarceration in Alabama.

> Alabama law provides for alternatives to imprisonment in criminal cases that do not endanger public safety. . . . These alternatives cost less than imprisonment, require the offender to pay part of the cost, and create a potential for rehabilitating some offenders before they become career criminals. However, the state has not invested enough to make such programs available and adequate to accomplish their aims.[3]

Federal leadership in the drug war now reflects a similar understanding.

> If state and local officials wish to expand their capacity to prosecute and sentence drug offenders, they must broaden their notion of punishment. This recommendation from the President's National Drug Control Strategy has focused attention on intermediate punishments—penalties that fall between traditional probation and incarceration.[4]

Even at the height of the drug war then-Attorney General Richard Thornburgh acknowledged that

> [o]ur systems are on overload. In too many places there are simply not enough investigators, prosecutors, judges or prison cells. We also know that there are many for whom imprisonment is not appropriate. But is simple probation sufficient, particularly when probation officers are carrying caseloads far beyond what is manageable? We need to fill the gap between simple probation and prison. We need intermediate steps—intermediate punishments.[5]

These sentiments are a direct reflection of the magnitude of the kinds of problems currently confronting the correctional system. Massive institutional overcrowding, at both the state and federal levels, has crippled the ability of the penal system to fully pursue its objectives. Dramatically rising correctional costs have placed extraordinary restrictions on both the practical and political realities of addressing the crime problem. Public concern and frustration is further exacerbated by the endless upward spiral of resource commitment and the apparent failure of such commitment to provide an adequate solution to crime. A growing number of citizens in public, academic, and private sectors now display significant interest in development of correctional approaches that do not rely primarily upon incarceration. The increasing urgency of this situation prompted the National Institute of Justice to convene an invitation-only conference in 1990 to study the problem.[6]

In the next two chapters we will discuss the variety of sanctions that are available as alternatives to incarceration. It is important to understand at the outset that non-incarcerative sentences, often referred to as intermediate sanctions, assume a wide range of forms. Failure to recognize this diversity will result in a distorted sense of the kinds of objectives that might be pursued effectively through such sentences. All of the objectives of punishment can be addressed by alternatives to incarceration although certain alternatives are better suited to some objectives than to others. We will discuss a number of the most promising forms of intermediate sentences and show how they might be used to best effect. Before turning to examination of these alternatives, we will examine the history of non-incarcerative sanctions, look at ideological considerations in the modern context, discuss the political context within which sentencing reforms occur, and describe public opinion regarding the value of alternatives to incarceration. The remainder of the chapter will discuss probation, intensive supervision programs, home confinement, and electronic monitoring.

Historical Background

As noted in a previous chapter, the earliest known substantially complete legal codification is the Code of Hammurabi (2000 B.C.). The remedies specified in the Code for acts that we would regard as criminal did not include imprisonment. Rather, Hammurabic sanctions included capital punishment, restitution, and corporal punishment.[7] The Mosaic Code specifies very similar kinds of punishments, but again, imprisonment is not included as a punishment for violations of God's law.[8] In accord with the tradition established in the Hammurabic and Mosaic codes, the severity of Greek punishment depended heavily upon social class. Although a slave might be executed for crimes, even property crimes, a member of the upper class might receive a fine for a violent act, including homicide. Other punishments included flogging, public shaming, and enslavement. Imprisonment, despite claims made by Plato in The Laws, appears not to have been utilized as a sanction.[9]

Thus, virtually all punishments in the ancient world were non-incarcerative. Unlike the modern context, however, the use of such punishments was not as an alternative to imprisonment. Imprisonment was simply not part of the array of sanctions used to punish law-violators.

The Roman tradition was similar to that in Greece. However, incarceration was used to punish slaves on private estates. Nonetheless, imprisonment was used only for slaves and only by private estateholders. It was not a government sanction.[10]

During the 1,000 years after the fall of the Roman Empire (429 A.D.) imprisonment remained a neglected punitive option. Corporal punishments, blood feuds, and elaborate restitutionary schemes were relied upon to punish violators of law or custom. Imprisonment did not begin to achieve significance until the late fifteenth and early sixteenth centuries with the opening of the Rasphuis in Amsterdam and the Bridewell in England.[11] Even so, these institutions were not designed to handle the kinds of serious offenders that are the objects of modern incarcerative approaches. They generally handled petty offenders, while serious offenders were accorded traditional corporal sanctions.

Imprisonment as a punishment for serious crime did not become an important punishment until the latter stages of the eighteenth century. Some American institutions were at the forefront of the movement to use incarceration as a punishment of regular resort for serious offenders. Newgate Prison of Connecticut, Castle Island of Massachusetts, and the Walnut Street Jail of Philadelphia were the institutions that led to the explosive interest in incarceration which developed during the nineteenth century in America and Europe.[12]

As David Rothman and others have documented, imprisonment quickly became the default punishment for a wide range of offenders. By the middle of the nineteenth century American prisons were packed with prisoners.[13] Imprisonment did not eliminate the use of all non-incarcerative punishments, but some sanctions, such as public shaming and corporal punishment, were largely abandoned.

The increasing emphasis on imprisonment continued into the twentieth century and has remained a mainstay of the modern justice system. It is interesting to note, however, that even in the nation's initial period of frenetic prison construction the seeds of an elaborate system of alternative sanctions were being sown. In 1841 a Massachusetts shoemaker named John Augustus offered to assume legal responsibility for a convicted drunkard. He promised the court that he would keep the offender from indulgence in alcohol and risked forfeiting a personal monetary bond if he could not keep his promise. Augustus was successful, and upon returning to the court three weeks later the judge changed the offender's sentence from imprisonment to a nominal fine. This was the first of nearly 5,000 cases in which Augustus would eventually become involved. He worked with men and women, adults and children, and risked thousands of dollars of his personal resources in efforts to bail out offenders who would otherwise have been institutionalized. Although earlier practices of benefit of clergy and judicial reprieve antedated the work of Augustus, modern probation dates most directly from the tradition initiated by Augustus.[14]

Augustus worked as a volunteer, not a state employee. However, in 1878 Massachusetts passed legislation establishing probation as a state function, with provision for a paid probation officer. State after state adopted similar legislation, and by the mid-twentieth century probation was being used for juveniles and adults nationwide. Probation appealed to legislators and judges on several grounds. It was clearly less costly than incarceration, it helped keep institutional populations at a manageable level, and it offered at least theoretical opportunities for rehabilitation. In 1917 Massachusetts was able to boast that

> [p]robation became universal in (Massachusetts) courts in 1898, and in the period that has elapsed, while the population of the state has increased by nearly a million, no additions have been built to its penal institutions, either state or county, and practically half the cells are vacant today. The great causative factor in such a result is conceded to be the use of probation.[15]

We will return to consideration of probation, but for now it is sufficient to note that the origins of the major device by which many kinds of alternative sanctions are applied, probation, began in the middle of the explosion of interest in incarceration in America. As we shall see, there are many kinds of alternative sentences which do not involve probation, but the underlying rationales for their use, as well as the benefits claimed for such sanctions, generally resemble those responsible for the origination of probation in the nineteenth century. By the close of the nineteenth century incarceration was a well entrenched punishment for a wide range of offenders. Many of the problems associated with incarceration had, however, also become evident by this time. The need for a wider range of punishments was clear to penal reformers then, and this need continues to exist to the present day.

Ideology

The diversity of alternative sentences makes it difficult to summarily characterize the ideological attractions of such sanctions. Although it is typically assumed that conservatives tend to regard non-incarcerative sanctions with suspicion while liberals embrace them enthusiastically, the matter is somewhat more complicated.

It is generally correct that conservatives seem comfortable with incarcerative sanctions. The conservative emphasis on personal responsibility fits nicely with the just deserts model of punishment, which stipulates that offenders be punished to the extent of the seriousness of the crime. Serious crimes deserve serious punishment, and in modern terms this means imprisonment. The belief in the rationality of human nature accords with the ideology of deterrence, wherein individuals weigh the costs and benefits of alternative courses of action, comparing potential pains and pleasures. Imprisonment, as the most serious punishment in use today, save for the death penalty, thus has value in helping to influence such calculations in favor of decisions not to violate the law.

It would appear, therefore, that conservative ideology naturally favors incarceration. However, in discussing conservative priorities, Charles Colson and Daniel Van Ness note that

> . . . it's clear that many see alternatives to incarceration for non-violent offenders as a natural extension of conservative political philosophy. Legislators cite the following principles: Punishment is appropriate, it should serve victims' needs, public safety is essential, local is better, and wise use of government resources is needed.[16]

They argue that community-based sanctions, such as restitution centers, house arrest, and intensive probation supervision, can be effective instruments in pursuing the conservative agenda. Such sanctions are relatively inexpensive, can provide effective public protection through intensive offender monitorship, are typically operated at the local rather than state level, and can help to address the concerns of crime victims. It can also be argued that the use of such sanctions can reduce the size of government because private entrepreneurs have traditionally operated many community-based programs.

With regard to liberals, it might be assumed that interest in alternative sanctions would flow naturally from their traditional concern with rehabilitation, and their relative lack of interest in harsh punish-ment applied merely to achieve purely retributive objectives. Although this is generally true, liberals also express concern about the expansion of government sanctions into places where government has traditionally been excluded. The emergence of electronically monitored house arrest, for instance, raises liberal concerns about government intrusions on the civil rights of citizens. Thus although liberals may be less enthusiastic about incarceration than many of their conservative counterparts, they may nonetheless have significant reservations about at least some kinds of alternative sanctions.

In thinking about the main goals of punishment (deterrence, retri-bution, incapacitation, and rehabilitation) as they relate to alternative sentences, it is important to consider the entire range of interests that typify ideological positions. As we have seen, when the full spectrum of interests associated with conventional ideological positions is taken into consideration, and not merely those most directly related to punishment, there are aspects of such ideologies which are fully consistent with adop-tion of various alternatives to incarceration. The attractiveness of pun-ishments for crime will be the result of numerous factors, including historical tradition and the fit with ideological content. There is support from both conservative and liberal traditions for alternatives to incarcer-ation.

Political Context

As anyone who has watched recent political campaigns can attest, politi-cal rhetoric regularly focuses on crime and punishment. Candidates often duel over who is the toughest on crime. The presidential campaign of 1988 featured the famous Willie Horton case. Horton was released from a penal institution in the Democratic candidate's home state, and subsequent to his release he committed another heinous crime. The Republican candidate used this episode to demonstrate the soft crime position of his opponent. In the 1990 Texas Democratic gubernatorial primary campaign, candidates believing in the value of the death penalty engaged in energetic efforts to prove to the electorate that they were more vigorous in their support for the use of capital punishment than were their opponents. In state after state, candidates for office lobby for

175

increasing penal capacity in order to "get tough" on crime. There are exceptions to this pattern. The sheriff of Genessee County, New York was elected to office despite arguing for alternative programs that would reduce reliance on incarceration.[17] But such cases are often few and far between.

In light of the many polls revealing public concern with crime, it is not surprising that political leaders choose to adopt an aggressive approach to crime control. Moreover, the decision to address the problem through so-called "tough" measures doubtless reflects the perception of political leaders that the public wants tougher penalties for crime. It is relatively simple to communicate the potential value of putting someone behind bars. At the very least, incarcerated offenders can do little damage while they are incapacitated in prison. That the economic costs of such incarceration may reduce opportunities to adopt more effective measures, or that offenders who have been institutionalized may represent an even greater threat when they are released, is far more difficult to demonstrate. Some political advertisements have featured the loud slamming of a prison cell door as a dramatic punctuation to the "get tough on crime" message. There is no comparable way to create such drama in a sound bite on restitution or work release programs.

Thus the development of alternative sentences often confronts political conditions that are not particularly favorable. Despite this, economic realities have forced the states and federal government to develop an increasing number of alternatives to incarceration.[18] Although headline-grabbing political rhetoric suggests that efforts in this area are not likely to be received with enthusiasm by the public, in fact some of the survey data suggest quite the opposite.

The Public's View

As we have noted previously, the public identifies crime as lagging behind only economic problems and drug abuse as the most important problem facing the community.[19] In a 1989 poll conducted by Roper, more than 70 percent of citizens indicated that too little money was being spent on the crime problem.[20] It is also true that evidence exists suggesting that citizens welcome use of imprisonment as a response to crime. The National Punishment Survey found that the vast majority of survey respondents thought incarceration should be the punishment of choice for virtually all serious common crimes (robbery, assault, burglary, forcible rape, drugs, for example).[21] Norval Morris and Michael Tonry express what is typically regarded as the public view of punishment. "Americans tend to equate criminal punishment with prison. To the public, to the public official, even to the judge, sentencing is often seen as a choice between prison and nearly nothing."[22]

Despite these sentiments, the impression that citizens are not interested in alternative sentences is simply erroneous. A California survey asked 1,000 citizens to suggest punishments for offenders in 25 hypothetical crime cases. When given the choice of prison or probation, 60 percent of offenders in these cases were given imprisonment. However, when respondents were also provided with the options of community service, restitution, strict probation, boot camps, drug treatment, and house arrest, only 27 percent of the hypothetical offenders were assigned prison sentences.[23]

Data from Texas reveal similar sentiments. Although only about 20 percent of surveyed Texans indicated that the solution to prison overcrowding was to "build as many prisons as are needed," about two-thirds of respondents favored developing community-based correctional programs either with or without new prison construction.[24]

In an investigation conducted in cities across the country John Doble found that citizens "strongly favored increasing the use of alternatives to incarceration. Alternatives included restitution, community service, fines, mandatory treatment for drug and alcohol abuse, intensive or enriched probation, the use of halfway houses, and mandatory attendance at a job, school or job training facility."[25]

Finally, a national survey of 1,000 Americans found that 80 percent of citizens are either "somewhat in favor" or "strongly in favor" of "non-prison programs in which non-dangerous criminal offenders are required to hold a job, perform community service, repay their victims and receive counseling."[26]

There is also evidence that when the public is made aware of the consequences of incarceration their enthusiasm for alternative sanctions is even more substantial. Douglas Thomson and Anthony Ragona found that citizens assigning punishments to a hypothetical burglar were more likely to assign alternative sanctions when they were made aware of the economic costs of incarceration.[27] A study of a mid-Atlantic state which provided respondents with information on such costs revealed, "Over three-fourths of those interviewed favored using community-based programs for non-dangerous offenders."[28] In Delaware, an analysis of more than 400 citizens revealed that when respondents were given information about prison crowding and about alternatives to prison the majority of respondents selected non-prison sentences for most crimes.[29] Such findings are important, of course, because in the real world decisions to incarcerate have significant consequences. When citizens are given an opportunity to consider such consequences they are not insensitive to the value of alternative sentences.

Nonetheless, the evident public interest in alternatives to incarceration has been poorly publicized and inadequately represented by political leaders. Many political leaders apparently fail to understand public attitudes toward punishment in general, and attitudes toward alternatives to incarceration in particular. A study of American citizens and policymakers found that policymakers perceived that the American public was more punitive than was actually the case. Policymakers failed to understand the extent to which the public possesses interest in correctional goals such as rehabilitation. The study also found that policymakers failed to fully appreciate the extent to which the public supported the establishment of community rehabilitation centers for adults.[30]

In sum, despite widespread popular impressions and energetic political rhetoric to the contrary, there is substantial public support for alternatives to incarceration. The level of support varies with the kinds of offenders under consideration, as well as with the kinds of alternatives at issue. In light of the enormous difficulties confronting the American prison system, it is somewhat remarkable that more attention has not been committed to public discussion of alternative sentences.

What Are Alternative Sentences?

Before turning to examination of the major kinds of alternative sentences it is important to consider the general features of such sanctions. As we learned from our brief historical examination, there have always been non-incarcerative sentences used to respond to crime. Because imprisonment was not historically a common punishment, however, these sanctions were not regarded as alternatives to imprisonment. While earlier use of such punishments was based upon considerations that generally had nothing to do with imprisonment, the modern interest in punishments such as restitution and community service in part reflects concern with the shortcomings of imprisonment as an effective response to crime. The failure of typical incarcerative approaches to provide restitution to victims is an excellent example of such shortcomings.

Alternative sanctions such as house arrest, restitution, mandatory counseling, work release, and community service have usually been applied to relatively minor offenders. Misdemeanants and minor felons are rarely sent to prison for a first offense. Most of the discussion of expanding the use of alternative sentences still revolves around consideration of such minor criminals. As we will see, however, more serious kinds of offenders have been handled through alternative sanctions, sometimes with positive results.

Alternative sanctions are often administered in conjunction with probation. This has the advantage of providing a ready-made enforcement mechanism, the probation officer, to monitor the progress of the offender in completing his or her sentence. Although probation officers have traditionally been regarded as therapeutic agents, this mission is changing. Probation officers now find themselves engaged in a heavy preponderance of enforcement-oriented activities. Many of the new community-based alternatives require high levels of monitorship but little effort devoted to traditional rehabilitative activities.

Along this same line of thought, non-incarcerative sanctions have traditionally been viewed as rehabilitative in nature and mission. This is no longer always the case. A wide range of alternative sentences now have incapacitation and deterrence as their main objectives. Moreover, analysts who were at the forefront of the movement toward desert-based sanctions in the 1970s and 1980s, such as Andrew von Hirsch, have proposed sentencing models that make energetic use of alternatives to incarceration in pursuit of desert.[31] Such sentences are sometimes regarded as hard time by offenders who, when confronted with the choice of conventional imprisonment or strict community-based sanctions, have sometimes chosen imprisonment. In Oregon, for instance, about one-third of a group of convicted non-violent felons elected to serve a prison term rather than return to the community in an intensive supervision program.[32]

The remainder of this chapter will be devoted to consideration of some of the major kinds of non-financial alternative sanctions currently in use or being considered for adoption. We have focused on those non-financial alternatives associated with either the highest levels of current interest or the greatest promise of being successful. We begin with a brief discussion of conventional probation, then consider intensive supervision programs, home confinement, and electronic monitoring.

Probation

As noted earlier, probation has an extensive history extending back into the mid-nineteenth century. The personal initiative of John Augustus has led to the nationwide adoption of probation services in all 50 states and the District of Columbia.

In a technical sense it is important to understand that only a few states have enacted legislation establishing probation as a formal sen-tence.[33] This follows the original tradition established by Augustus. In most states formal sentencing is suspended pending the results of the probationary period. If the offender is successful in meeting the condi-tions of probation, the court may elect to take no further action.

The primary rationale for probation has traditionally been rehabili-tative. Augustus sought to wean his first client from involvement in alcohol, and his enthusiasm for rehabilitative efforts was continued by other nineteenth-century public welfare groups. Advocates of probation have argued that it provides the offender with a variety of opportunities to come to grips with his or her criminality, develop marketable job skills, pay restitution, perform community service, or overcome personal liabilities which prevent successful independent functioning in society.

However, probation eventually became associated with a number of other objectives including community protection, reintegration of offenders, and justice. This diverse array of objectives characterizes mod-ern probation initiatives. A glance at current probation caseloads, how-ever, calls into question the extent to which probation is likely to be successful in pursuing any of these objectives. The average caseload for American probation officers at the outset of the 1990s exceeds 100 clients.[34] Such high caseloads obviously limit the capacity of probation officers to achieve the objectives now associated with probation.

Adult probation is administered by state departments of correc-tions in 30 of the 50 states. In other states, counties either share or split responsibility for probation administration with the state.[35] At the begin-ning of 1990, 2.5 million individuals were under probation supervision in the 50 states, District of Columbia, and federal system. This represents an increase from 1980 of 126 percent.[36] Contrary to public impression, the majority of convicted offenders are under probation supervision, not in prison or on parole. Only 457,000 individuals were completing their sentences as parolees at the beginning of 1990. This represents 11.3 per-cent of convicted offenders held under the care or custody of a correctional agency. The figure for probation is 62 percent, while about 27 percent of offenders were incarcerated.[37]

Although advocates of probation sympathetic to the model established by John Augustus are still plentiful, changes in probation indicate that its rehabilitative function has been and continues to be further subordinated to other pursuits. Enormous probation caseloads represent one significant constraint, but are not the only factor. The advent of intensive supervision is perhaps the most important recent modification of the original probation ideal.

Intensive Supervision Programs

An assessment of the effectiveness of conventional probation for felons in California revealed that two-thirds of felony probationers were rearrested for new crimes within a 40-month follow-up period. Fifty-one percent of these felons were convicted of new crimes. Moreover, about three-quarters of the original charges filed against this group involved serious crimes such as burglary, robbery, and theft. The authors of the research report examining the California data concluded that "felons granted probation present a serious threat to public safety."[38] The authors recommended intensive surveillance programs as a possible alternative to conventional probation.

In fact, intensive probation supervision programs have attracted significant attention during the last few years. Although they first appeared in the 1950s and 1960s, in recent years there has been renewed interest in such programs,[39] and 44 states now have intensive supervision programs in their probation or parole systems.[40] Preliminary research indicates that, despite apparent interest in tougher sanctions for offenders, the public is not unreceptive to intensive community supervision. In one opinion survey intensive supervision was identified by a third or more of respondents as the appropriate sanction for minor and major theft, burglary, driving under the influence of alcohol, and drug use.[41]

There are actually two major variations of intensive supervision. The first is intensive *probation* supervision, which provides intensive supervision in the community in lieu of incarceration. The second variety is intensive *parole* supervision, which permits community-based monitorship of offenders only after they have served some time in an incarcerative facility. This period of incarceration may be lengthy or, under the new shock probation arrangements, relatively brief. Most of the current interest in intensive supervision has centered around probationary supervision because of its obvious potential immediate impact on institutionalized population size. In this discussion we will refer to both kinds of programs as intensive supervision programs (ISPs).

Focus 7-1
New Jersey's Intensive Supervision Program

In 1983 New Jersey began operation of one of the nation's first intensive supervision programs. The program was designed to achieve four objectives. First, the program was intended to shorten incarcerative terms to only three to four months for some offenders. This would relieve precious prison space for use with more serious offenders. Second, the program would provide intermediate-level punishment in the community. Third, deviant behavior would be controlled through a high level of monitorship. Finally, the project would operate at a cost-savings to the state.

Homicide, robbery, and some sex offenders are not eligible for participation in the program. Most other kinds of offenders are eligible, although admission to the program is formally determined by a screening board and an ISP Resentencing Panel comprised of three judges. In an effort to assure that participants would actually have otherwise been sentenced to incarceration, all participants must first have been sentenced to incarceration.

Program participants are required to have a minimum of 20 contacts with probation officers, 12 of which must be face-to-face during each of the initial six months of participation. The number of contacts required diminishes to eight per month for 120 days, then to six for the remainder of program involvement. Late-night visits are used to assure that offenders are complying with curfew regulations. In addition, random drug testing can be imposed when deemed appropriate.

Participants must be employed, and it is the participant's responsibility to provide officers with evidence of employment. Participants in school must provide continuing documentation of school attendance. All participants must also supply a minimum of 16 hours per month of community service. Community service is also used as a punishment for first-time violations of the conditions of probation.

Unlike some other programs, New Jersey requires that each participant have a community sponsor to assume custody of the offender during the first 180 days of the program. The sponsor monitors the client's progress and assists the client in utilizing community resources, such as drug treatment resources.

The program provides group counseling sessions which focus on a variety of concerns such as drug abuse, family difficulties, psychological problems, and financial difficulties. The extent of participation in such sessions is contingent upon the needs of the offender.

New Jersey's program has provided a model that has been emulated by other states. Although evidence on the impact of the New Jersey program does not provide unambiguous guidance regarding promising future directions, it does appear that under the proper circumstances programs such as New Jersey's may ultimately prove valuable in addressing some of the numerous problems associated with incarceration.

The recent interest in intensive community supervision has been the result of several concerns. First, incarcerative facilities have become increasingly overcrowded. In an effort to relieve the pressure on institutions, probation has been examined as a possible solution. Although probation had long been an important part of the American correctional apparatus, it began to be rethought as a sanction for more serious kinds of offenders. In addition, for many penal analysts it was reconceptualized as a sanction designed to be punitive, rather than therapeutic. Probation conditions were designed to impose discomfort and suffering on the convicted offender. As evidenced by the willingness of some offenders to select conventional imprisonment over ISP when given the choice, it is evident that some offenders do find ISP painful. Finally, the costs of routine incarceration have simply become unmanageable, and probation represents a way of reducing penal expenses.

An early example of the ISP idea is represented by Georgia's program. In 1983 Georgia created an intensive probation supervision program to combat the state's endemic prison crowding problem. Georgia's program is designed for offenders who would otherwise be sentenced to prison and primarily handles white males convicted of property offenses. Participants move through several stages while serving their sentence. In the initial phase five face-to-face contacts between the probation official and offender are required weekly. The number of required contacts decreases in the final two stages. Offenders in the program must be employed, perform community service, and pay a fee toward the cost of the program. Other conditions may be imposed by the judge if deemed warranted.

According to an analysis of Georgia's program, ISP probationers had fewer rearrests, reconvictions, and imprisonments than parolees. Comparison of the ISP group with those serving terms of regular probation revealed little difference.[42] However, critics of the Georgia evaluation have pointed out that these comparisons are not meaningful because the groups examined were not comparable with respect to variables traditionally associated with recidivism.[43] Judges decided who went into intensive supervision and who went into regular supervision. The groups were not randomly selected, the best procedure for obtaining meaningful comparisons.

A number of other states with large numbers of ISP clients have also permitted judges to sentence offenders directly into the supervision program. As Todd Clear and Patricia Hardyman point out in their discussion of Arizona's program:

> Arizona claims a diversion rate of about 90 percent, but this is based on an internal study that reviewed a sample of ISP cases and found that 90 percent could have gone to prison under Arizona law. Of course could and would are very different. Because there is so much of an overlap between probation and prison case profiles, there is a large probability that the direct-sentence cases would have gone to regular probation without the ISP alternative.[44]

Critics of intermediate sanctions of whichever strain raise several important concerns. First, they argue that probation represents a lenient sanction that fails to adequately punish offenders. Second, the leniency of the sentence interferes with the creation of either specific or general deterrent effects. Third, the presence of offenders in the community creates risks of additional citizen victimization. Fourth, they argue that the research on intensive supervision does not demonstrate that rehabilitation is a likely product of the probationary process. Finally, they suggest that the move to alternative sanctions such as intensive supervision may widen the legal net. Relatively minor offenders who would otherwise have received traditional probation may find themselves in unnecessary high-surveillance, high-punishment programs.

Although each of these potential difficulties represents a significant concern, defenders of modern intermediate sanctions argue that current techniques are capable of addressing the problems. With regard to the punishment issue they note that intermediate sentences can be distributed that are far longer in duration than the incarcerative sentences they replace. Furthermore, the rationale for intensive community supervision is in part based on punishment. "The most compelling reason for continued development of ISP programs is the objective of just deserts, i.e., making the punishment fit the crime. . . . Routine probation clearly does not constitute just punishment for felons with serious prior records."[45] A recent study of the parole ISP in Texas concluded that it did provide intermediate punishment, more severe than regular parole, but less severe than incarceration.[46]

Regarding costs, the national average cost of probation is about $2.00 per day.[47] The national average cost of incarceration is more than 20 times higher, at $46.00 per day.[48] The cost of ISPs falls in between, but closer to standard probation. Georgia's intensive program cost $4.36 per day, compared to $30.43 for incarceration and $.76 for conventional probation.[49] Cost savings have also been achieved in New Jersey and Kentucky.[50] Obviously, the fiscal ability of the state to keep an inmate under government control for a significant amount of time is far greater with probation or parole. However, as research discovered in the above-noted Texas study, program failures who ultimately must be placed in an incarcerative environment can drive up total costs.[51]

With regard to incapacitation, Georgia's ISP program requires five face-to-face contacts with a probation officer every week, regular and unannounced drug tests, and weekly arrest record checks.[52] Although the level of incapacitation is therefore significant, it does not rival that which is possible while an offender is under lock and key. However, the proper question to be considered is whether, given the constraints of crowding and economic costs, offenders are likely to spend the amount of time under in jail or prison that they might be forced to endure under rigorous community supervision. Despite the hardened resolve of states across the country, increased sentences have led to severe crowding which has in turn led to releases of many inmates before the full expiration of their sentences.[53] When such offenders are released it is generally not under the kinds of close monitorship characteristic of ISPs.

The fourth issue, rehabilitation, is typically assessed through a comparison of recidivism rates. Although such rates often do not com-

185

municate information about the level of seriousness of new offenses, nor information about offenders that may indicate positive change in other areas of behavior, they do provide some sense of the effectiveness of probation. The probation research conducted before 1980 provided mixed results. Failure rates ranged from only about 16 percent to more than 50 percent.[54] A more recent federal study found that about 80 percent of probationers successfully completed their probationary sentences.[55] A study of high-risk probationers in California's Intensive Probation Supervision Program revealed that about two-thirds of high-risk probationers, offenders with serious felony records, committed no new crimes during a one-year follow-up period. Furthermore, only 10 percent of these offenders committed new violent crimes. However, these rearrest rates were about the same as those for offenders given conventional probation, thus casting doubt on the relative effectiveness of intensive supervision programs.

A recent national assessment of evaluation research on ISP programs conducted by the Government Accounting Office found that recidivism rates for ISPs were generally somewhat higher than for regular probationers, but lower than those for parolees. The report points out, however, that methodological difficulties with the evaluation research make it impossible to draw firm conclusions at this point in the development of such programs.[56] Nonetheless, these results mirror the results of long-term follow-ups on offenders in Georgia's path-breaking program. After five years, 36 percent of ISP offenders had been sent to prison for new offenses, while the figure for those originally sent to prison was 42 percent.[57]

Somewhat less optimistically, a recently reported study that is unusual in its use of randomized assignment of offenders to ISP or routine parole found that "[t]he ISP program was no more effective than routine parole in reducing recidivism, as measured by arrests and convictions."[58] The contrast between these results and those for some probation programs may indicate that the ISP concept may be of more value in dealing with probationers rather than parolees.

Of course, recidivism rates are not the only measure of rehabilitative effectiveness. One assessment of intensive versus conventional probation revealed that although those in the intensive program did not have lower recidivism rates than their counterparts in conventional probation, they were more successful in all measures of social adjustment (for example, alcohol abuse, drug abuse, emotional stability, family relations).[59]

A related concern involves the potential reduction of probation officer interest in the traditional mission of community supervision officers, rehabilitation and reintegration. Some critics argue that new high surveillance and control programs have resulted in new probation officer attitudes toward their responsibilities. A recent study comparing attitudes of probation and parole officer attitudes in 1970 with those in 1983 found that "[c]oncern for authority has become a more meaningful philosophy than either assistance or treatment."[60] Other critics have suggested that the heavy emphasis on surveillance and control ignores the community and offender-related difficulties that produce criminal activity.[61]

Finally, net-widening is a potential hazard that merits careful attention. Without random assignment of offenders to prison, traditional community control programs (probation or parole), and intensive programs it will be difficult to assess the extent to which net-widening is occurring. As we will continue to learn in our discussion of other alternatives to incarceration, few research evaluations incorporate random assignment into their design. This problem must be overcome if we are to gain an adequate understanding of the relative effectiveness of imprisonment and various community-based sanctions.

Home Confinement

The idea of restricting offenders to their homes is not without historical tradition. Such diverse individuals as Galileo and Czar Nicholas II were compelled to live under house arrest.[62] Nonetheless, modern American use of house arrest as a sanction of regular resort is a relatively recent innovation. A number of jurisdictions adopted various forms of house arrest during the 1970s, and it has become even more widespread in the last decade. House arrest, an alternative name for home confinement, has been implemented in conjunction with parole and as part of probationary sentences. It has been adopted at the state and county levels and is becoming an increasingly attractive alternative in light of crowded institutional conditions.

In the early 1980s Florida became the first state to adopt home confinement as a standard punishment for criminals convicted in courts throughout the state.[63] The Florida Community Control Program (FCCP) is designed to accomplish several objectives. First, the program "is aimed at diverting non-violent offenders from prison by providing round-the-clock surveillance of these offenders."[64] As is true for many states, Florida was and is confronting serious institutional crowding difficulties. Thus diversion of some offenders from incarcerative sanctions represents an attractive option. Eligible offenders include probation or parole violators charged with technical violations and felons or misdemeanants whose offense or prior criminal history would not lead to placement in regular probation programs.[65] Second, it provides regular intensive monitorship of offenders while in the community. A minimum of 28 contacts between the offender and probation officer are required each month. Third, the offender is permitted to leave home only to go to work or to run essential errands like obtaining medical treatment. This provides a punitive aspect that comports with the view expressed in Florida's legal code.

> The primary purpose of sentencing is to punish the offender. Rehabilitation and other traditional considerations continue to be desired goals of the criminal justice system but must assume a subordinate role.[66]

Fourth, important community relationships can be maintained while serving a community control sentence. The reintegration process that is often so difficult for incarcerated inmates is eased, thus hopefully enhancing the chances of success in the community after the sentence is served. Finally, offenders may be expected to pay some of the cost of their program participation.

Other states have also turned to home confinement programs. Oklahoma, which actually passed enacting legislation before Florida initiated its community control program, began to process offenders in 1984. During the 1980s a steady stream of states adopted various kinds of home confinement programs, and as of 1990 27 states had such programs for probationers or parolees.[67]

Research findings on the effectiveness of home confinement is at best preliminary due to the relatively recent adoption of such programs. During its first few years of operation, Florida's program experienced a 16 percent failure rate. This includes probationers committing new crimes or technical violations.[68] The failure rate in the ground-breaking Oklahoma program was higher, standing at about 33 percent when new offenses and technical violations are included.[69]

A number of concerns have been expressed regarding home confinement. First, critics question whether home confinement is really an alternative to incarceration. They suggest that offenders sentenced to home confinement typically would have received conventional probation if home confinement were not available. This phenomenon, known as net-widening, suggests that instead of removing offenders from over-crowded institutions, home confinement actually increases the number of convicts held under restrictive sanctions. Impressive success rates, such as the 84 percent rate in Florida, are not surprising in the view of these critics because the offenders serving home confinement sentences are low-risk offenders who would not recidivate under the conditions of conventional probation.

This concern has implications for the alleged cost-effectiveness of home confinement. If those sentenced to home confinement would otherwise have received standard probation, an even less costly sanction, then the costs to the state will actually be greater than they would have been without home confinement.

At this early stage in the evaluation of home confinement programs we do not possess a clear understanding of the extent to which net-widening is a problem. Oklahoma has tried to address this issue by requiring that home confinement participants serve at least 15 percent of a maximum incarcerative sentence before being placed in a home confinement program. In addition, inmates serving terms for violent crimes must be six months or less from final discharge.[70] Oklahoma has thus attempted to enroll participants from its institutional population. A home incarceration program in Kenton County, Kentucky permitted only offenders who legally could have been institutionalized to enter the program. Based on an analysis of the characteristics of program participants, chiefly prior record of incarceration and conviction, the authors of an analysis of the Kentucky program concluded that net-widening had not occurred.[71] However, as is typical for most studies of alternatives to incarceration, this assessment did not involve use of random or mandatory assignment to home incarceration. Although the prior record of the offenders suggests that these convicts would have received incarcerative sentences, the study's authors point out that it is not possible to be sure of this. Palm Beach County, Florida's home confinement program permits the county sheriff to select participants from volunteers who wish to enter the program after having served some time in the county jail. Again, this selection procedure does not lend itself to firm conclusions about the extent to which home confinement actually functions as an alternative to incarceration. It is possible that the procedure did result in the removal of inmates from the jail earlier than would otherwise have been the case, but it is not possible to reach confident conclusions with this selection procedure. A recent assessment of Florida's state-wide community control program (FCCP) did, however, find that "over 50 percent of FCCP placements were diversions from prison. Given the rather grim record of alternative programs, a diversion rate that exceeds 50 percent could well be viewed as an unqualified success."[72]

Critics of home confinement also raise questions about public safety. If advocates of home confinement are correct in their claim that offenders who would otherwise be sent into institutions will be handled in home confinement programs, serious offenders will now be placed into the community where they have opportunities for further involvement in crime.

Although it is still too soon to offer confident assessments of this potential difficulty, we do know that the vast majority of those participating in home confinement programs do not become involved in law violation. An initial assessment of the first 9,000 offenders in Florida's program revealed that only 619 had committed new crimes, a rate of less than 7 percent. In addition, the majority of these offenses were not the serious violent crimes with which the public is most concerned.[73] The rate of re-offending in Oklahoma's program was a similar 5 percent.[74] In an Ohio home confinement program for juveniles more than 90 percent of participants successfully completed the program without either new crimes or technical violations.[75] Like Florida and Oklahoma, the majority of failures in Ohio were due to technical violations (such as failure to notify a probation officer of an address change) rather than new offenses. Thus preliminary assessments suggest that public safety is not being compromised by controlling offenders in home confinement programs.

Despite such data, critics point out that there is substantial public opposition to the use of home confinement. This opposition may be based upon the perception that home confinement represents either an unacceptably lenient sentence or a threat to neighborhood safety. Whether such opposition is well-grounded, as a political fact of life public opposition may reduce the political viability of home confinement programs. The 1990 Texas gubernatorial campaign provides an excellent case in point. Although crime was indeed among the issues discussed by the candidates, remedies discussed included imprisonment, capital punishment, and boot camps. The neglect of sanctions such as home confinement represents the view of politicians that the public simply wants the toughest measures possible.

In fact, as noted earlier, the views politicians possess of public preferences are often mistaken. Studies both in the United States and abroad indicate that citizens are less punitive than politicians believe.[76] This misperception may lead political leaders to ignore sanctions which may have significant public attraction. In addition, even minimal efforts to educate citizens about the consequences of various punitive approaches may result in heightened interest in non-incarcerative sanctions.[77]

Finally, critics of home confinement suggest that the important distinction between private and public spheres may be blurred by home confinement. Prisons are generally viewed as unambiguously non-private. Inmate expectations of personal privacy are virtually nonexistent. The home, on the other hand, is an essentially private environment. Although the level of personal deprivation may be far less for offenders serving sentences at home rather than in institutional confinement, extension of the state into the home may well serve to break down the sharp barrier between the personal and the public, ultimately laying the groundwork for an even greater expansion of state authority.[78]

Despite the potential hazards of home confinement, it appears likely that burgeoning prison populations will continue to encourage states to adopt home confinement as an alternative to incarceration. Crowded jails will also provide incentive to counties and municipalities to move minor offenders and persons awaiting trial back into the community. In addition, emerging cost data suggest that home confinement can be extremely inexpensive. An assessment of Ohio's home confinement program found that house arrest cost less than $15.00 per day compared to more than $42.00 daily for secure detention.[79] Such cost differentials are not lost on policymakers and will likely inspire increasing enthusiasm for home confinement in the future.

Electronic Monitoring

The advent of electronic means to track the whereabouts of convicted offenders serving sentences in the community has added a new dimension to the potential for community-based alternatives to incarceration. In the past decade electronic devices have been developed that are capable of transmitting data on the presence of an offender at work or at home and that provide a heretofore unknown form of state supervision.

There are two major kinds of electronic monitoring technology: telephone-based and nontelephone-based systems. Telephone-based systems assume a number of forms, but the basic system includes a computerized receiver-dialer that accepts transmission from a wrist or ankle transmitter worn by the offender. Information is then relayed over telephone lines to a central monitoring location. A variation on this approach requires that the offender insert his or her wristlet into a verifier box, which then confirms through the telephone system that the offender is home. Nontelephone-based systems also involve use of electronic wristlets or anklets, but their transmissions are sent via radio waves to a centrally situated control center.[80]

Palm Beach, Florida initiated the nation's first electronic monitoring program in late 1984. The decision to adopt electronic monitoring was based primarily upon the need to control crowding in the county jail (see Focus 7-2). Program participation was limited to certain classes of inmates, and participants were expected to pay a daily fee to cover the costs of operating the program.[81] By 1988, 33 states had put electronic monitoring programs into operation.[82] This represents dramatic growth over an extremely short period of time. Programs have been established in all regions of the nation, and at the beginning of 1990 more than 4,400 offenders were serving sentences that included electronic monitoring.[83] In 1988 the federal government initiated a home confinement program using electronic monitoring for federal parolees.[84] Considerable variation still exists in the extent to which such programs have been embraced by the states. Although at the beginning of 1990 North Carolina had more than 1,300 offenders under electronic monitorship, Virginia had only two.[85] The majority of program participants were serving sentences for traffic, property, or drug offenses. Offenders convicted of crimes against persons represent about 10 percent of those being monitored electronically.[86]

Focus 7-2
Palm Beach County—Pioneering in Electronic Monitoring

Although an initial experiment was conducted in 1966 to track human movements with electronic tracking equipment, the technology was not applied to monitoring convicted criminals until the early 1980s. Palm Beach County, Florida was one of the earliest jurisdictions to adopt electronic monitoring as part of a house arrest program. Beginning in late 1984, the approach was used both for probationers and for work release inmates released from the county stockade. The program was operated by Pride, Inc., a private non-profit company.

Electronic monitoring was first used for drunken driving offenders who were given the choice of a 10-day jail sentence or house arrest for 30 to 40 days. The judge selected all program participants with the agreement of the prosecutor and defense attorney. Conditions of the electronically monitored probationary required that participants:

pay a $5 daily fee for monitoring equipment costs
have a telephone (for transmission of monitoring data)
obey curfew regulations
make weekly appearances at Pride, Inc. offices for
   equipment check, fee payment, and discussion of
   other issues

This early program did encounter some implementation difficulties. The electronic anklet was uncomfortable to wear for some offenders, and its ability to transmit data to the telephone receiver-dialer (which would then send data to Pride offices) was compromised by certain environments. Trans-mission from kitchens and areas outside of mobile homes was especially problematic. Finally, some program participants had concerns about the visibility of the anklet and feared the questions they would have to answer about its presence. All of these difficulties were eventually resolved.

This pioneering program was initially used for a very small number of offenders. Six months after its inception only 13 offenders were in the program. However, it has been succeeded by the state-operated Community Control program which now serves hundreds of offenders.[87]

The rationale for use of electronic monitoring consists of five main elements. It provides enhanced control of inmates serving sentences in the community, thus increasing public safety. The costs of such programs are small compared to incarceration, and are often borne at least in part by those under electronic surveillance. It permits the offender to remain in the community, making it possible for employment and family relationships to be maintained. It is a real punishment in that the offender is generally not permitted to be anywhere except home and work. Finally, the stigma associated with imprisonment is reduced.[88]

A typical sentence to electronic monitorship may include a variety of other conditions. These conditions may include abstinence from drugs

Stipulations:

and alcohol, satisfactory work performance, random work and home checks by a probation officer, and a host of other stipulations. For instance, a Beverly Hills neurosurgeon was convicted of health, building, and safety codes as a result of his failure to properly maintain rental apartments he owned. His sentence included a $1,000 fine and $1,000 in inspection costs incurred by the state for inspecting his apartment complex. In addition, he served 15 days in jail followed by a period of confinement in his own run-down apartment building. To assure that he would remain in the building he was forced to wear an electronic anklet that would inform the authorities if he left the property.[89] Obviously this is not a typical situation, but it does convey the kinds of creative sentences that are possible in conjunction with electronic monitoring.

Assessments of the effectiveness of electronic monitoring remain preliminary at best, and many of the assessments that do exist are troubled by poorly designed evaluation methodology. Among the better studies are two recent assessments conducted in California and Indiana. These projects compared electronic and non-electronic monitoring and used randomized participant assignment. Neither study found that electronic monitoring was more successful with regard to technical violations or arrest rates.[90] A study of pretrial releasees found that although electronically monitored releasees had higher rates of technical violations (for example, failure to meet conditions such as curfew violations or neglecting to notify probation of address change), they had lower rates of new offenses and failures to appear for trial. Although the comparison groups in this study were not randomly selected, and there were differences between the groups in terms of the seriousness of the charges pending, this preliminary study suggests that electronic monitoring may have promise for those awaiting trial.[91]

One highly touted advantage of electronic monitoring is that it provides a surveillance method that presumably results in enhanced public safety. Recent preliminary evidence from Georgia, however, suggests that electronic monitoring does not enhance such safety. Probation officers in Georgia's model ISP program did not feel that the level of surveillance afforded by electronic monitoring exceeded what could be achieved through the normal ISP program use of home visits. They did indicate that electronic monitoring may be effective for use with special offender population such as burglars.[92]

Thus there is currently little clear evidence that intensive supervision programs using electronic monitoring are likely to enjoy higher success rates than similar programs using conventional monitoring. Nonetheless, research on the impact of electronic monitoring is in its infancy, and it is often difficult to disentangle the impact of a program's electronic monitoring component from the effects of its other supervision components.

Beyond issues associated with effectiveness in protecting the public, reducing correctional costs, and enhancing the probability that offenders will successfully distance themselves from involvement in crime, critics of electronic monitoring have raised several other concerns that ultimately will have to be confronted. First, despite the use of sophisticated technology, electronic monitoring systems are not foolproof. New Jersey State Senator Louis Kosko lead an initiative to restrict the kinds of inmates who are eligible for electronic monitoring. His efforts were the result of two incidents in which program participants left their homes without being detected and perpetrated crimes of violence, one resulting in a death.[93] Such incidents are relatively rare, but nonetheless raise public concern about their effectiveness.

Early advocates of home confinement anticipated that home arrest would be administered, at least partially, by volunteers. This would help in the process of reintegrating the offender into the conventional normative system. Electronic monitoring has, however, reduced the need for such volunteer participation, thus the anticipated reintegrative effects may not materialize.[94] A further extension of this concern is that the time of professional probation officers may be heavily devoted to maintaining and monitoring the electronic technology, rather than being spent on conventional rehabilitatively-oriented activities. Of course, this allocation of effort may be deemed appropriate as probation assumes increasing surveillance and monitorship functions.[95]

Correctional analysts have also raised questions about the political risks of electronically monitored house arrest. They suggest that the exposure of the community to those released from confinement under conditions of electronic monitorship creates special kinds of political hazards. In his study of Montgomery County, Ohio Walker notes that

> [e]ach of those at risk in the local political system is an elected official, with the exception of the aforementioned federal judge. Each has to answer to his or her relevant public for fair treatment of prisoners, good husbanding of available resources, and the safety of the community.[96]

In this instance, locally elected judges, who might be enthusiastic in principle about electronic monitoring, must be cautious in its actual use. Because of the publicity typically associated with new offenses commit-

195

ted by defendants or convicted offenders released into the community, such judges are wary of using the sanction too readily. "In this situation it is clear that there is no incentive for any one of the actors to take a lead in the increased use of house arrest."[97]

One final particularly troubling issue concerns the possibility that electronic monitoring represents an extension of state power that threatens the privacy interests of citizens in their homes.

> In a democracy, the concept of "home" is a near national icon; home represents a refuge, a sanctuary, the last bastion of privacy. . . with e.m. the home becomes deprivatized. The intrusion is telemetric and nearly invisible. . . . Figuratively, prisons have been dismantled and each individual cell has been reassembled in private homes.[98]

The concern is that the emergence of electronic monitoring devices has created the opportunity for the Big Brother scenario of Huxley's Brave New World to finally become a reality. Is use of such technology an appropriate invasion of private domains, and is its application to convicted offenders merely the first step in a process that will lead to monitorship of other citizens? It is worth noting that electronic monitoring has already been used to keep track of defendants awaiting trial, some of whom will be found to be innocent.[99] The issue clearly merits watching.

Conclusion

Intensive surveillance, home confinement, and electronic monitoring all represent potentially valuable approaches to addressing the nation's increasingly difficult correctional problems. In contrast to the historically earlier focus of non-incarcerative sanctions, these innovations offer the potential to achieve deterrent, incapacitative, and retributive objectives. Although the existing evaluation evidence is still fairly rudimentary and at this point provides little conclusive evidence that these sanctions are effective, in light of the relatively limited resources that have been committed to such penalties there is good reason to be guardedly optimistic about their future prospects. Program design and implementation, as well as program evaluation, will continue to improve during the next decade, and we will be in a much better position to pass judgment by century's end. The debilitating correctional conditions now in existence do not, however, provide the luxury of a leisurely period of implementation and evaluation. It is imperative that rigorous and energetic efforts be initiated immediately.

Notes

[1] Lay, Douglas P., Fort Worth Star-Telegram, section 2, p. 3, 12 Oct. 1990.

[2] Petersilia, J., Turner, J., Kahan, J. and Peterson, J., *Granting Felons Probation*, Rand, R-3186-NIJ, 1985.

[3] "Deciding the future direction of criminal punishment in Alabama."— *The PARCA Report*, number 11, Fall 1990, Public Affairs Research Council of Alabama.

[4] DeWitt, Charles B. (1991) "Director's Notes," National Institute of Justice Bulletin Board, Feb., Washington, D.C.: National Criminal Justice Reference Service Bulletin Board.

[5] *Corrections Today* (1990) "U.S. Attorney General Thornburgh Urges Incarceration Alternatives," 52(5), p. 132.

[6] *Criminal Justice Newsletter* (1990) "Officials aim to 'fill the gap' between probation and prison," 21(18).

[7] Code of Hammurabi (1903) trans. by C.H.W. Johns, Edinburgh: T. and T. Clark.

[8] Mosaic Code, Old Testament, Deuteronomy.

[9] Sellin, J. Thorsten (1976) *Slavery and the Penal System*, New York: Elsevier.

[10] Id.

[11] Sellin, J. Thorsten (1944) *Pioneering in Penology*, Philadelphia, PA: University of Pennsylvania Press.

[12] Durham, Alexis M. III (1988) "Newgate of Connecticut: Origins and early days of an early American prison," *Justice Quarterly*, 6(1).

[13] Rothman, David (1971) *The Discovery of the Asylum*, Boston: Little, Brown and Company.

[14] Killenger, George, Kerper, Hazel, and Cromwell, Paul (1976) *Probation and Parole in the Criminal Justice System*, St. Paul: West Pub. Co.

[15] Quoted in Klein, Andrew R. (1988) *Alternative Sentencing—A Practitioner's Guide*, Cincinnati: Anderson, p. 61.

[16] Colson, Charles and Van Ness, Daniel (1990) "Alternatives to Incarceration," in *Criminal Justice—Annual Editions—90/91*. Guilford, CT: Dushkin Pub. Group: 214.

[17] See Klein, note 15 above at 284.

[18] Florida is a good case in point. After years of new prison construction,

the Governor and other political officials are now calling for serious consideration of expanding alternatives to incarceration. See Lavelle, Louis (1993) "Criminal sentencing reform urged to help solve prison overcrowding," *Tampa Tribune*, Feb. 2, Florida/Metro, p. 6.

[19] Jamieson, Katherine M. and Flanagan, Timothy J. (eds.) (1989) *Sourcebook of Criminal Justice Statistics—1988*, Washington, D.C.: U.S. Government Printing Office, p. 183.

[20] Flanagan, Timothy J. and Maguire, Kathleen (eds.) (1990) *Sourcebook of Criminal Justice Statistics—1988*, Washington, D.C.: U.S. Government Printing Office, pp. 146-147.

[21] See Jamieson and Flanagan, note 19 above at 219.

[22] Morris, Norval and Tonry, Michael (1990) *Between Prison and Probation—Intermediate Punishments in a Rational Sentencing System*, New York: Oxford University Press, p. 39.

[23] Bennett, Lawrence (1989) "Californians accepting of community punishments for criminal offenders," presented at the American Society of criminology national conference, Reno, Nevada, 1988.

[24] Cullen, Frank T., Clark, Gregory A., and Wozniak, John F. (1985) "Explaining the get tough movement: Can the public be blamed?" *Federal Probation*, 49(16-24).

[25] Doble, John (1987) *Crime and Punishment: The Public's View*, The Public Agenda Foundation.

[26] *News Release* (1991) "Survey shows overwhelming support for community corrections programs," International Association of Residential and Community Alternatives, Sept. 30, 1991, p. 1.

[27] Thomson, Douglas R. and Anthony Ragona (1987) "Popular moderation versus governmental authoritarianism: An interactionist view of public sentiments toward criminal sanctions," *Crime and Delinquency*, 33: 337-357.

[28] Williams, J. Sherwood, Johnson, Daniel M., and McGrath, John H. (1991) "Is the public committed to the imprisonment of convicted felons? Citizen preferences for reducing prison crowding," *Journal of Contemporary Criminal Justice*, 7(2), p. 90.

[29] Doble, John and Immerwahr, Stephen (1991) "Delawareans favor prison alternatives," *Overcrowded Times*, 2(5).

[30] Gottfredson, Stephen D., Warner, Barbara D., and Taylor, Ralph, B. (1988) "Conflict and consensus about criminal justice in Maryland," in Walker, N. and Hough, M., *Public Attitudes to Sentencing*, Brookfield: Gower.

[31] von Hirsch, Andrew, Wasik, Martin, and Greene, Judith (1989) "Punishments in the community and the principles of desert," *Rutgers Law Review*, 20(3).

[32] Petersilia, Joan "When probation becomes more dreaded than prison," *Federal Probation*, 54(1).

[33] See Klein, note 15 above at 65.

[34] Camp and Camp, (1990), The Corrections Yearbook—1990, *Probation and Parole*, Salem, NY: Criminal Justice Institute, p. 14.

[35] Id. at 3.

[36] Jankowski, Louis (1990) "Probation and Parole 1989." *Bureau of Justice Statistics Bulletin*—Nov., Washington, D.C.: U.S. Dept. of Justice.

[37] Id.

[38] Petersilia, Joan, Turner, Susan, Kahan, James, and Peterson, Joyce (1985) "Executive Summary of Rand's study: "Granting Felons Probation: Public Risks and Alternatives," *Crime and Delinquency*, 31(3).

[39] Clear, Todd, R. and Hardyman, Patricia L. (1990) "The new intensive supervision movement," *Crime and Delinquency*, 36(1); Senese, Jeffrey D. "Intensive supervision probation and public opinion: Who cares one way or the other?" paper presented at the American Society of Criminology Annual Conference, Baltimore, MD, Nov. 1990.

[40] GAO (September 1990) "Intermediate Sanctions—Their Impacts on Prison Crowding, Costs and Recidivism Are Still Unclear," Report to the Chairman, Select Committee on Narcotics Abuse and Control, House of Representatives, GAO/PEMD-90-21: 14-15 Washington, D.C.: Government Accounting Office.

[41] Senese, Jeffrey D., "Intensive supervision probation and public opinion: Who cares one way or the other?" paper presented at the American Society of Criminology Annual Conference, Baltimore, MD.

[42] Erwin, Billie S. (1987) "Evaluation of intensive probation supervision in Georgia: Final Report," Georgia Department of Corrections, Atlanta, GA.

[43] Petersilia, Joan and Turner, Susan (1990) "Intensive Supervision for high-risk probationers—Findings from three California experiments," Santa Monica, CA: Rand Corporation, pp. 13-16.

[44] Clear, Todd and Hardyman, Patricia L. (1990) "The new intensive supervision movement," *Crime and Delinquency*, 36(1): 42-60.

[45] See Petersilia, Turner, note 43 above at xiii.

[46] Turner, Susan and Petersilia, Joan (1992) "Focusing on high-risk parolees: An experiment to reduce commitments to the Texas Department of Corrections," *Journal of Research in Crime and Delinquency*, 29(1).

[47] See Camp and Camp, note 34 above at 12.

[48] Camp and Camp, (1990) *The Corrections Yearbook—Adult Prisons and Jails*, Salem, NY: Criminal Justice Institute, p. 38.

[49] See Erwin, note 42 above at 5.

[50] Latessa, Edward J. (1986) "The cost effectiveness of intensive supervision," *Federal Probation*, 50(2).

[51] See Turner and Petersilia, note 46 above.

[52] See Erwin, note 42 above.

[53] Austin, James (1986) "Using early release to relieve prison crowding: A dilemma in public policy," *Crime and Delinquency*, 32(4): 404-502.

[54] McCarthy, Belinda R. and McCarthy, Bernard J., Jr. (1984) *Community-Based Corrections*, Monterey, CA: Brooks-Cole Pub. Co., table 4-5, p. 119.

[55] Greenfield, L. "Probation and Parole—1987" 1988–Washington: D.C.: Bureau of Justice Statistics.

[56] GAO (September 1990) "Intermediate Sanctions—Their Impacts on Prison Crowding, Costs and Recidivism are Still Unclear," Report to the Chairman, Select Committee on Narcotics Abuse and Control, House of Representatives, GAO/PEMD-90-21: 14-15 Washington, D.C.: Government Accounting Office.

[57] Erwin, Billie (1990) "Old and new tools for the modern probation officer," *Crime and Delinquency*, 36(1).

[58] See Turner and Petersilia, note 46 above at 57.

[59] Bennett, Lawrence A. (1987) "A reassessment of intensive service probation," in McCarthy (ed.) *Intermediate Punishments: Intensive Supervision, Home Confinement, and Electronic Surveillance*, Monsey, NY: Criminal Justice Press.

[60] Harris, Patricia M. Harris, Clear, Todd R., and Baird, S. Christopher (1989) "Have community service officers changed their attitudes toward their work?" *Justice Quarterly*, 6(2).

[61] Byrne, James M. (1990) "The future of intensive probation supervision and the new intermediate sanctions," *Crime and Delinquency*, 36(1).

[62] Meachum, Larry R. (1986) "House arrest: The Oklahoma experience," *Corrections Today*, 48: 102-110.

[63] Blomberg, Thomas G., Waldo, Gordon P., and Burcoff, Lisa C. (1987) "Home confinement and electronic surveillance," in McCarthy, B.R. (ed.) *Intermediate Punishments: Intensive Supervision, Home Confinement and Electronic Surveillance*, Monsey, NY: Willow Tree Press.

[64] Id. at 170.

[65] Florida Statutes, FS 948.10.

[66] Fla. Stat. Ann. & 648 (West 1986).

[67] GAO (September 1990) "Intermediate Sanctions—Their Impacts on Prison Crowding, Costs and Recidivism Are Still Unclear," Report to the

Chairman, Select Committee on Narcotics Abuse and Control, House of Representatives, GAO/PEMD-90-21: 14-15 Washington, D.C.: Government Accounting Office.

[68] Flynn, Leonard E. (1986) "House arrest—Florida's alternative eases crowding and tight budgets," *Corrections Today*, July.

[69] See Meachum, note 62 above.

[70] Id.

[71] Lilly, J. Robert, Ball, Richard A., and Wright, Jennifer (1987) "Home incarceration with electronic monitoring in Kenton County, Kentucky: An evaluation," in McCarthy, B.R. (ed.) *Intermediate Punishments: Intensive Supervision, Home Confinement and Electronic Surveillance*, Monsey, NY: Willow Tree Press.

[72] Baird, S. Christopher and Wagner, Dennis (1990) "Measuring diversion: The Florida Community Control Program," *Crime and Delinquency*, 36(1).

[73] See Flynn, note 68 above.

[74] See Meachum, note 62 above.

[75] Ball, Richard A., Huff, C. Ronald, and Lilly, J. Robert (1988) *House Arrest and Correctional Policy—Doing Time at Home*, Newbury Park, CA: Sage Publications, p. 50.

[76] Gottfredson, Stephen D., Warner, Barbara D., and Taylor, Ralph B. (1988) "Conflict and consensus about criminal justice in Maryland," in Walker, N. and Hough, M. *Public Attitudes to Sentencing—Surveys from Five Countries*, Brookfield: Gower; Doob, Anthony N. and Roberts, Julian (1988) "Public punitiveness and public knowledge of the facts: some Canadian surveys," in Walker, N. and Hough, M. *Public Attitudes to Sentencing—Surveys from Five Countries*, Brookfield: Gower; Cullen, Francis T., Clark, Gregory A., and Wozniak, John F. (1985) "Explaining the get tough movement: Can the public be blamed?" *Federal Probation*, 49; Doble, John (1991) "Survey shows Alabamians support alternatives," *Overcrowded Times*, 2(1).

[77] Doble, John (1987) "Crime and punishment: The public's view," The Public Agenda Foundation.

[78] Ball, Richard A., Huff, C. Ronald, and Lilly, J. Robert (1988) *House Arrest and Correctional Policy—Doing Time at Home*, Newbury Park, CA: Sage Publications.

[79] Id. at 51.

[80] Schmidt, Annesley K. and Curtis, Christine E. (1987) "Electronic monitors," in McCarthy, B. *Intermediate Punishments: Intensive Supervision, Home Confinement, and Electronic Surveillance*, Monsey, NY: Criminal Justice Press.

[81] Palm Beach County, Florida Sheriff's Department (1987) "Palm Beach County's in-house arrest work release program," McCarthy, B. *Intermediate*

Punishments: Intensive Supervision, Home Confinement, and Electronic Surveillance, Monsey, NY: Criminal Justice Press.

[82] Schmidt, Annesley K. (1989) "Electronic monitoring of offenders increases." National Institute of Justice Reports, No. 212 Washington, D.C.: U.S. Department of Justice.

[83] See Camp and Camp, note 34 above at 19.

[84] Klein-Saffran, Jody and Beck, James L. (1990) "Expanding electronic monitoring: Practices and policy implications." presented at the American Society of criminology Annual Meeting, Baltimore, MD, Nov. 1990.

[85] See Camp and Camp, note 34 above at 20.

[86] Renzema, Marc and Skelton, David T. (1990) "Use of electronic monitoring in the United States: 1989 update," *NIJ Reports,* No. 222.

[87] Based upon Ford, Daniel and Schmidt, Annesley (1985) "Electronically monitored home confinement," *National Institute of Justice Research in Brief—* Washington, D.C.: National Institute of Justice.

[88] Ball, Richard A. and Lilly, J. Robert (1983) "Home incarceration: An alternative to total incarceration," paper presented at the Ninth International Meeting of the Society of Criminology, Vienna, Austria.

[89] See Klein, note 15 above at 120.

[90] Petersilia, Joan and Turner, Susan, Dec. 1990; Baumer, Terry L. and Mendelsohn, Robert I. (1990) *The Electronic Monitoring of Non-violent Convicted Felons: An Experiment in Home Detention,* Final Report, Washington, D.C.: U.S. Department of Justice.

[91] Cooprider, Kenneth W. and Kirby, Judith (1990) "A practical application of electronic monitoring at the pretrial stage," *Federal Probation,* 54(1).

[92] Erwin, Billie S. (1990) "Old and new tools for the modern probation officer," *Crime and Delinquency,* 36(1).

[93] *Law Enforcement News* (1992) "New Jersey senator wants to limit use of ankle bracelets," 30 Jun. 1992, p. 3.

[94] Lilly, J. Robert and Richard A. Ball (1990) "The development of home confinement and electronic monitoring in the United States." in Dufee, David E. and McGarrell, Edmund F. (eds.) *Community Corrections—A Field Approach,* Cincinnati: Anderson Pub. Co., pp. 73-92.

[95] See Erwin, note 92 above.

[96] Walker, James L. (1990) "Sharing the credit, sharing the blame: Managing the political risks in electronically monitored house arrest." *Federal Probation,* 54(2).

[97] Id. at 18.

[98] Corbett, Ronald P., Jr. and Marx, Gary T. (1990) "No soul in the new

machine: Technofallacies in the electronic monitoring movement," Presented at the Annual Meeting of the American Society of Criminology, Baltimore, MD: 18-19.

[99] Cadigan, Timothy P. (1991) "Electronic monitoring in Federal pretrial release," *Federal Probation*, 55(1); Baumer, Terry L., Maxfield, Michael G., and Mendelsohn, Robert I. (1990) "A comparative analysis of three electronically monitored home detention programs," presented at the Annual Meeting of the American Society of Criminology, Baltimore, MD.

8

Alternatives to Incarceration: Fines, Restitution, Community Service, and Day-Reporting Centers

Our examination of alternatives to incarceration now turns to sentences that focus upon material returns to individual victims or to society. The sanctions we discussed in the preceding chapter were largely concerned with punishments served in the community under various conditions of control and monitorship. Intensive supervision, home confinement, and electronic monitoring are sanction forms that are primarily concerned with the manner in which offenders are to be released into and regulated within the community. Such sanctions have multiple goals, but they are tied together by a serious concern with incapacitation through surveillance and control, as well as with imposition of punitive conditions to satisfy the retributive and deterrent objectives of sentencing. The sanctions under consideration in this chapter are also designed to address multiple objectives, but the emphasis is shifted toward securing material or labor-related benefits for individual victims and society.

Fines, victim restitution, and community service represent important variations on this theme. Each of these sanctions provides the opportunity for offenders to do more than merely experience the pains of punishment, or serve as examples to discourage others from involvement in crime. They make it possible for offenders to right moral wrongs, as well as to restore the material conditions affected by their offending acts.

These sanctions also create opportunities for offenders to participate in activities which may have therapeutic psychological effects for both the offender and victim. We begin our discussion with fines, then consider restitution and community service. The chapter concludes with a description of day reporting centers, a new institutional device possessing the potential to link together the kinds of activities and objectives discussed in the two chapters on alternatives to incarceration.

Fines

Financial penalties have long been a standard sanction for dealing with socially unacceptable behavior. In the ancient Code of Hammurabi (1750 B.C.), for instance, it is provided that "If a man has stolen ox or sheep or ass, or pig, or ship, whether from the temple or the palace, he shall pay thirtyfold."[1] Some acts of violence were also punished with financial sanctions. "If a man of gentle birth has struck the strength of a man of gentle birth who is like himself, he shall pay one mina of silver."[2] The Law of Moses also made provision for financial penalties. In a passage very similar to the Code of Hammurabi it is provided that "If a man steals an ox or a sheep and slaughters it or sells it, he shall pay five oxen for the ox and four sheep for the sheep."[3] In ancient Greece fines were also used, but only to punish free citizens. Although slaves could be subject to severe corporal punishments and death, citizens were generally fined for even serious violent offenses.[4] Roman law was also class-based, but provided a somewhat wider range of punishments for citizens. Sanctions included death, deportation, hard labor, corporal punishment, and fines. The offender's class standing was often more significant in the sentence-determination process than his or her offense. Financial penalties tended to be reserved for upper-class offenders.[5]

The use of financial penalties continued into the Middle Ages. Victim compensation for acts that are today regarded as crimes was essential as a method of minimizing blood feuds. Families or kinship groups would resolve disputes through payment of restitutionary fees. Again, factors other than the seriousness of the offense were determinants of the amount of compensation. "The amount of compensation varied according to the nature of the crime and the age, rank, sex, and prestige of the injured party. . . . Thus the 'value' of human beings and their social positions were involved in determining compensation. . . ."[6] The payments went directly to the families, not to the state. The eventual division of such traditions into civil and criminal law modified this practice. After a period during which payments were split between the state and the victim, payments for violations of criminal law were generally collected and retained by the state.

Although the distinction between fines and restitution may seem insignificant to the offender who must pay them, in theory as well as in practice the distinction is quite important. Fines are generally regarded as payments to the state for crimes committed against society. They resemble imprisonment in this respect. The penalty does not offer any direct compensation to the victim, although knowledge that an offender is being punished may make a victim feel better. Restitution, on the other hand, represents recognition that the state and society are not the only victims of crimes. Compensation to victims both acknowledges the suffering of individual victims and attempts to restore the individual to a state of being resembling that existing before victimization.

The rationale for the use of fines is essentially punitive. Fines are primarily designed to impose pain and suffering on the convicted offender. Not incidentally, such sanctions may also have deterrent effects, such as is commonly intended for certain traffic offenses. Additionally, they may be used to recover at least some of the costs of court proceedings, although such costs may be assessed separately in addition to fines. Finally the cost of imposing fines is much less than that associated with sanctions such as incarceration.

Fines are currently in use in every state, although there is variation in the offenses for which they are used. All states use fines heavily for traffic offenses. Beyond traffic offenses, they may be used for crimes as diverse as public order offenses, such as public intoxication, and serious white collar violations, such as embezzlement. Other offenses commonly punished with fines include prostitution, minor drug offenses, shoplifting, minor assaults, and disturbing the peace.[7] Fines tend to be most heavily used in courts of limited jurisdiction handling misdemeanor cases. However, a survey of 24 felony-only courts found that about 40 percent of these courts used fines as sentences in at least half of the cases. Moreover, in only 2 of the 24 courts were fines never used.[8]

According to a National Institute of Justice analysis, "Fines are most often imposed on first offenders with a known ability to pay."[9] In this respect modern practices follow the ancient traditions noted earlier wherein the financial status of the offender determined whether financial or other sanctions would be imposed. The fine amounts typically

207

How much?

imposed vary significantly by jurisdiction, and legislatively established maximums tend to be well in excess of amounts actually imposed by judges.

The upper and lower limits of fines are typically established by statute. Such limits have resulted in some extraordinary outcomes. For instance, former public officials in Massachusetts are not permitted to work as lobbyists after leaving public service for one year. But as Andrew Klein points out, "The maximum fine for violating this conflict of interest law is only $1,000. The last person convicted for this violation has made over $30,000 in commissions during the forbidden period of work."[10] To accommodate for such statutory inequities, fines are often imposed in conjunction with other penalties, such as community service.

Fines are thus an important part of the array of sanctions used in the American justice system. As two of the more important commentators on modern punishment point out, however, "The heart of the matter is that for a variety of reasons the fine is widely disregarded as a punishment for all but traffic offenses, minor misdemeanors, and ordinance violations."[11] They further note that

> [i]t is paradoxical that a society that relies so heavily on the financial incentive in its social philosophy and economic practice should be so reluctant to use the financial disincentive as a punishment for crime. . . . One need only recall the overheated economy in December 1986—when consumers bought cars at record rates, in order to be able for the last time to take a full tax deduction for their sales tax payments. . . to recognize how powerfully financial incentives drive our behavior. . . . Yet for some reason our sentencing practices seem premised on the belief that financial disincentives will not have comparable effects on offenders.[12]

A survey of judges revealed that although judges acknowledged the potential value of fines, they were reluctant to impose them as punishment because they were seen as insufficiently punitive for the wealthy and beyond what could be paid by the poor. These judges were also reluctant to use fines as punishment for the more serious kinds of offenses.[13] Even if they were inclined to use fines, they often did not have access to the kinds of information on offender economic circumstances to make effective use of fines as sanctions.[14]

Fines are generally not regarded as substitutes for incarceration. Because they have not usually been imposed for the kinds of offenses the public is most concerned with, conventional street crimes such as robbery, burglary, rape, and assault, there has been relatively little effort expended to assess their effectiveness in reducing recidivism. In addition, the imposition of fines in conjunction with other sentences makes it difficult to sort out the independent effects of fines on subsequent behavior. It is worth noting, however, that many European nations do use fines as an alternative to incarceration. West Germany, for example, modified its penal code to encourage use of fines in lieu of short terms of incarceration. This modification resulted in a significant decline in short incarcerative sentences.[15] (See Focus 8-1.) The practice of using financial penalties for common street crimes is, in fact, an extension of an ancient tradition. In the Code of Hammurabi certain thieves could avoid the death penalty by making a monetary payment. The amount to be paid was based upon the offender's wealth, although those without the means to make such payments were put to death.[16]

Focus 8-1
Fines: The German Experience

In 1969 the First Law Reforming the Penal Code was enacted to replace provisions of the existing code of 1871. The initiative embodied interest in decriminalizing many offenses and in moving from pursuit of retribution to resocialization of offenders. The revision contained many changes, including elimination of incarcerative sentences of six months or less. Offenses punished under the old code with such short terms of incarceration were to be sanctioned with fines and probation.

There were two primary rationales for this shift. First, some analysts believed that imprisonment provided too many opportunities for offenders to attend "crime school," where they would be exposed to the values of the criminal lifestyle. Offenders might return to society more, rather than less, inclined to continue their involvement in crime. Second, many critics were skeptical about the feasibility of resocializing offenders within the prison environment. They argued that prison conditions simply worked at cross purposes to the resocialization process. Community-based sanctions would be more effective in helping offenders to adopt law-abiding values and practices.

The effects of the shift to use of fines in Germany were immediate. The new law went into effect in the fall of 1969. In 1968, 113,273 prison terms of six months or less were given to convicted offenders. That number plummeted to 22,664 in 1970. The percentage of total sentences represented by prison terms of six months or less declined from 20 percent to 4 percent. Conversely, fines increased from 361,074 in 1968 to 464,818 in 1970. The percentage of all sentences represented by fines increased from 63 percent to 84 percent.

In 1975 the German law was again modified, this time to add the day-fine system. This system administered fines based upon the amount of work-time an offender would typically require to pay off his or her debt to society. The judge first decides how many days the offender ought to receive based upon the seriousness of the crime. The value of the day-fine is then determined. This requires examination of the economic status of the offender. The law requires that daily wages, standard of living, assets, maintenance costs, and family situation be taken into consideration. Thus two offenders may receive different fine amounts in dollars for the same offense. The intent, however, is that the penalty have the same impact on offenders of differing economic means.

Day-fines in Germany are used for property offenses, but are also heavily employed for crimes against the person. The most serious kinds of violent offenses are still handled with incarceration. Only 5 percent of robbers, for instance, received fines as penalties. Nonetheless, almost 80 percent of assault-related crimes were dealt with through fines.

In light of crowded conditions in American incarcerative institutions, and the fact that significant portions of the American prison population are in prison for non-violent offenses, it may be worth considering the value of emulating the German day-fine system to respond to some forms of non-violent criminal involvement.[17]

Critics of fines argue that they do not provide adequate punishment for serious offenders. In addition, they question whether fines provide sufficient incapacitative effect and wonder about the resultant threat to public safety associated with not incarcerating such offenders.

Critics are also concerned about the fairness of fines because their use may favor the wealthy. Finally, they raise questions about the difficulties of collecting fines.

Advocates of fines argue that fine amounts have traditionally been minimal because they have been applied to relatively minor kinds of offenses. There is no reason why new statutes cannot be passed authorizing much heavier fines for more serious kinds of crimes, such as crimes against the person. The German day-fine system noted above was used to punish two of every three offenders convicted of crimes against the person.[18] In England about half of offenders convicted of sex crimes and assault were punished with fines.[19] There appears to be some movement in the United States to follow this practice. The federal system has now increased the maximum fine for a felony to $250,000, making it possible to use fines for more serious kinds of offenses.

Supporters of fines also suggest that with proper precautions certain serious offenders, those not representing a threat to society, can be selected for fines. In addition, they point out that the kinds of felons who would receive fines are not going to be incapacitated in a jail or prison for long terms anyway, thus the extent to which the public is protected by incarceration is at best limited.

The fairness issue can be addressed by tailoring the severity of the fine to the means of the offender. As noted in Focus 8-1, day-fine systems have been utilized in Europe with apparent success. Such systems do not impose an absolute dollar amount fine, but rather require an amount equivalent to a specified number of work days. Two offenders of different economic means who committed the same offense would be required to pay fine amounts associated with an equal number of days of salary. An offender earning $100 a day might pay five days worth of wages, or $500, while an offender earning $1,000 a day would pay $5,000, again five days worth of salary.

With regard to the fine collection issue, there is evidence that even the poorest offenders are able to pay properly proportioned fines. A Staten Island day-fine project found that the payment records of unemployed or student offenders was indistinguishable from the payment records of those holding jobs.[20] Examination of the effects of this project also revealed that more than $71,000 of the $93,000 in fines levied during the project's first year of operation had been collected within 11 months. According to Staten Island Criminal Court Judge Michael Brennan, "Very, very few can't handle any fine. If an offender has the $10 to spend on crack cocaine, even if she gets it from welfare, that's her discretionary income and I'm going to take it."[21]

It is true, however, that a number of studies have revealed that there are difficulties in assuring that fines will be collected. A federal study conducted in the mid-1980s found significant collection failure rates.[22] In addition, the results of a survey of trial court judges indicate that half or more of courts responsible for collecting fines have collection difficulties.[23] Practices in European countries have produced results, and many of the problems in fine collection can be resolved through emulation of the administrative methods used in such countries.[24] Sweden punishes thousands of offenders annually with fines, and less than 50 persons per year are incarcerated because of failure to make their fine payments.[25]

A variety of new methods have been adopted to address the fine collection issue. Several jurisdictions have permitted offenders to use credit cards to pay fines, thus transferring collection responsibility to banks. Installment payments, modeled after those used in department stores, have been used in Phoenix. The offender signs a contract, and missed payments initiate other kinds of enforcement activity.[26]

Norval Morris and Michael Tonry have proposed turning over responsibility for collecting fines to self-interested private companies. Companies that have been successful in collecting debts for conventional obligations, they argue, would be even more effective with the authority of the criminal court to back them up.[27] In fact, the private sector has begun to become involved in fine collection. Tacoma, Washington uses a private telemarketing company to enhance fine collection. The company uses computerized dialing, recorded and live telephone contact reminders, and recordings of offender remarks about fine payment delays. The cost of employing this firm has only amounted to about 7 percent of the fine revenue collected.[28]

In 1987 the state of Washington authorized the use of private collection agencies to collect fine revenue. An assessment comparing the effectiveness of collection agencies versus court-generated billing and private billing agencies found that collection agencies collected almost four times the percent of total fines owed than the amount collected through the court. Having noted this, it must however be pointed out that only about 20 percent of total fines owed had been collected during the period of the assessment.[29] Nonetheless, with the advent of these new approaches there is reason to believe that if the effort that has gone into developing the system of incarceration is invested in refining and implementing these approaches, it will be possible to devise effective systems of fine collection.

Although fines have not been given serious consideration as an alternative to incarceration in America, the German experience suggests that offenders now serving short incarcerative sentences might be handled effectively with fines at significantly less cost. Such evidence also indicates that adoption of a system of fines for serious offenders may help reduce prison populations.[30]

Restitution

Restitution typically involves offender efforts to compensate victims for lost or damaged property or for physical harms sustained. Many states now have special programs to facilitate the payment of restitution.[31] Such programs are to be distinguished from state victim compensation programs, which provide payments to victims out of a general government fund.[32]

There are several additional objectives associated with restitution beyond restoration of victim losses. Perhaps the most visible is the retributive function, best captured in the biblical "eye for an eye, tooth for a tooth." This rationale emphasizes the justice of restitution, the obligation of the offender to restore the victim to their pre-offense condition. The restitution process is also thought by some to have a rehabilitative function in that it may force the offender to confront guilt about his or her victim, as well as to come to grips with the fact that victims are human beings rather than mere victimizable objects. In addition, restitution may contribute to the psychological well-being of the victim if the victim is permitted to participate in the process by which restitution is accomplished. Furthermore, when restitutionary programs are implemented in lieu of incarceration, they may be significantly less expensive to operate than imprisonment. The cost of restitution is also less expensive than some other kinds of community-based sanctions, such as intensive probation supervision.

Until recently, modern twentieth-century initiatives to establish restitution as an important component in criminal justice have not been particularly effective. Although by the 1930s about one-fifth of the states had victim restitution as a sentencing option in conjunction with probation, use and enforcement of restitution has been inconsistent.[33] The Model Penal Code framed by the American Law Institute in 1962 suggested the use of restitution in conjunction with probation. Restitution has been supported by various professional associations, such as the American Bar Association.

In 1982 the Victim and Witness Protection Act was passed by the United States Congress.[34] This legislation emphasized the use of restitution outside of the traditional probationary context and permitted restitution as a response to violent, as well as property, offenses. The federal penal code now makes provision for restitution orders as part of the array of available sentences for federal crimes. Such restitution may entail repayment for stolen or destroyed property, or it may involve substitution of labor or services in place of direct economic compensation.[35]

States also devoted some efforts to developing restitution programs. There are now several hundred state restitution programs currently in operation,[36] although the provisions of such programs vary substantially. For instance, some states permit restitution to direct victims and third parties, such as insurance companies, while other states permit restitution to direct victims only.

Focus 8-2
Restitution Centers—The Texas Approach

Crowded penal conditions and the declining tax revenues associated with an economic slump in the early 1980s forced the Texas legislature to seek cost-effective ways of handling its convict population. Texas was also operating under court restrictions imposed on its prison system subsequent to a suit filed against the state. These pressures led the legislature to provide $26 million to fund intensive probation and restitution centers. Locally operated restitution centers were authorized with the hope that pressure on the prison system would be relieved while offenders would repay their victims and the community. Rehabilitation was not mentioned in the enacting legislation. Sixteen restitution centers have been opened statewide since 1983.

Based largely upon the seriousness of the offense and the probation pre-sentence investigation, district judges decide which offenders will be sentenced to a restitution center. Although Texas restitution centers do have a residential component, offenders residing in the centers are evaluated for release every three months. Most inmates spend six to twelve months in the restitution centers. Thus, although the Texas restitution centers do not eliminate institutionalization, they do restructure and presumably reduce it. Ironically, crowding in state prisons has resulted in the early release of state prison inmates after increasingly shorter periods of confinement. Although the centers may be diverting offenders from state prisons, they may not be reducing the total amount of person-days of custodial supervision being funded by the state.

The centers themselves are relatively small, generally holding only 30 to 60 offenders. They are situated in industrial rather than residential areas, and unlike prisons they are not locked down. Residents leave the centers in the daytime to report to job sites. Regular employment, as well as community service work, comprise daytime activities for program participants. Wages go to the center's director, who then allocates amounts to cover room and board, court costs, fees, transportation expenses, restitution, and support for family.

There is reason to be optimistic about the restitutionary mission of the centers. A study of seven Texas restitution centers found that hundreds of thousands of dollars have been paid by participants. Data indicate that about half had paid their restitution by the time of their discharge, and the majority of the remainder continued to make payments after discharge.

With regard to recidivism, although restitution center clients had higher overall failure rates than a comparison group of parolees, only 6.5 percent of those studied in a three-year follow-up were arrested for a new offense. Most of the failures for the restitution group were due to technical violations rather than new crimes.

Finally, there is evidence that the centers did divert hundreds of inmates from the crowded state prison system. Unfortunately, other factors, such as changes in sentencing practices, have kept the state's prisons packed.[37]

In formulating a restitution order, judges generally take into consideration the seriousness of the offense, impact of the offense on the victim, and capacity of the offender to pay. Probation staff are usually responsible for enforcing restitution orders, and installment payment programs are often designed to assist offenders in meeting their obligations. As discussed above in reference to fines, new methods for enforcing restitution orders have shown promise. In Philadelphia, for instance, a well-structured computer-supported system has greatly enhanced the criminal justice system's ability to motivate offenders to pay their restitution amounts.[38]

Not surprisingly, most restitution orders are issued for property offenses.[39] As was the case for fines, the ability of the offender to make restitutionary payments is considered when various sentencing options are being evaluated.

The evidence regarding the effectiveness of restitutionary programs is mixed. With regard to recidivism, although some studies suggest that recidivism rates are positively influenced by restitution, other analyses do not find such evidence.[40] A study of six experimental restitution programs found that offenders randomly assigned to the restitution group had lower recidivism rates than those given conventional sanctions such as probation or short terms of incarceration.[41] An analysis of four juvenile restitution programs found significantly lower recidivism rates for participants in two of the programs when compared to offenders serving traditional sentences, such as incarceration.[42] Other evidence finds that a properly operated program can produce relatively high levels of program completion. In Wisconsin, for example, about 80 percent of offenders assigned restitution orders paid them in full.[43] Data from a juvenile restitution program suggests that offenders committing rape, robbery, and aggravated assault may do as well as property offenders in terms of successfully completing restitution programs.[44] A national assessment of restitution for juvenile offenders found relatively impressive completion rates.[45]

Data on the impact of restitution as an alternative to incarceration are sparse, in part because restitution has traditionally not been utilized as an incarcerative alternative. Evidence is, however, beginning to appear pertaining to this issue. An analysis of Texas's system of restitution centers concluded that ". . . the restitution program is a success. In the sample used for this study, 717 offenders were diverted from prison in just seven centers in fiscal 1987. More than 3,000 offenders have been diverted to the restitution centers statewide since the beginning of the program in 1983."[46] The author of this study does point out that the Texas prison population has continued to rise, despite these diversions.

There seems to be fairly clear evidence that restitution costs less than many other kinds of sanctions. At the most expensive end of the scale, the per offender cost for Texas's residential restitution centers was $27 per day. This compares favorably with the daily per inmate cost for state prison inmates of $33. The difference is even greater because these figures do not include the $50,000 per cell land purchase and building construction costs for prisons. The restitution facilities are leased and leasing costs are included in the $27.[47] Nor does it include the money earned by offenders as part of their restitution obligation. At the other end of the spectrum, a comparison of a pre-adjudication juvenile restitution program found that per case costs were only $216 as compared to $750 for standard juvenile probation case costs.[48]

One recent variation on the restitution theme is the victim offender reconciliation program (VORP). VORPs are intended to place the offender and victim in direct contact in meetings which are often designed to work out the details of restitution plans. The face-to-face meeting between the victim and offender may accomplish a number of objectives. Some analysts suggest that this kind of arrangement may increase the likelihood of restitution orders being fully satisfied.[49] Others suggest that when victims are permitted to participate in the process, they feel better about their treatment at the hands of the justice system, and about the ultimate resolution of their case.[50] Offenders may also develop a better understanding of the victims' point of view, and this may eventually have an influence on the offenders' subsequent behavior.

The first American VORP began operations in Indiana in 1978. Although the idea has spread quickly across the nation, it is too soon to have a solid understanding of the impact of such programs on recidivism. In addition, significant variations in administration will make it difficult to develop a clear perception of the effects of VORPs. In some jurisdictions they have been used as an alternative not only to incarceration but also to formal justice system processing.[51] In other locales VORPs have been used in conjunction with other sanctions. Oklahoma uses the VORP in association with its shock incarceration program.[52]

Community Service

Although we have been considering restitution in the context of financial payments, community service is another common restitutionary mechanism. Community service can assume a number of forms. A 15-state survey found that community service projects included such diverse activities as litter collection, landscaping, park maintenance, and growing vegetables for food banks. Most offenders serving such sentences are males, and some receive wages ranging from $1 to $2.50 per hour. In an effort to assure that such work projects do not threaten private sector enterprises, some states have restrictions on the kinds of work that can be done by offenders.[53]

Largely as a result of manpower needs, community service orders were imposed on criminals during World War II in the United States.[54] However, the first significant modern community service program was initiated in California in 1966. It targeted traffic violators who were unable to pay the cost of the normal traffic fine.[55] Many states have well-established community service programs that permit the offender to make restitution to the victim, the community, or both. Currently, about one-third of states now authorize community service sentences as alternatives to incarceration.[56] In New York, for instance, a community service program operated by the Vera Institute was implemented in part to alleviate crowding in the city's jail system. Most of the offenders in the program would typically have received jail sentences of up to six months for their crimes. The program puts offenders to work on public labor projects such as painting buildings, hauling construction materials, and cleaning up garbage. The focus of this program is obviously repayment to the community rather than to individual victims.[57] Such sentences have become especially popular for offenders convicted of drunk driving.

Other uses of community service do not, however, focus on restitution. "Community service, when used as an alternative to imprisonment, is also a deterrent. It punishes, provides for reparation, and assists in resocializing the offender. . . . Community service orders should focus on the offender's need for resocialization and on the protection of the community."[58] A recent study of offenders sentenced to community service reveals that almost 70 percent of these offenders felt that their punishment was effective as a resocialization instrument.

> Community service gave me an opportunity to give back something
> to the society that I had wronged. When I was finished, I felt better.
> I felt that I had corrected something that needed to be corrected.[59]

In addition to punishment, deterrence, and rehabilitation, community service sentences are attractive because they may be extremely cost-effective.

Like restitution, community service may be one component of a sentence that includes several parts. Intensive probation supervision, victim restitution, and community service may be combined in a single sentence. In Georgia, concern with community protection has made it necessary to use community service within the confines of intensive probation supervision. The Georgia Intensive Probation program, for instance, was designed to act as an alternative to incarceration. The kinds of offenders participating in the program were, therefore, higher risk offenders than those typically sentenced to conventional probation or community service. Thus the 132 hours of community service required in the Georgia program are part of a high-monitorship program designed to accomplish both incapacitative and punitive goals.[60]

Community service sentences do not appear to have particularly dramatic effects on recidivism. An analysis of the New York project noted above found that within three months of completing all the requirements of the program, 44 percent of offenders were rearrested.[61] Other studies have found similarly discouraging results.[62] Nonetheless, the high recidivism rates associated with conventional incarceration and the relatively inexpensive costs of administering community service will continue to make it an important alternative to imprisonment. Moreover, not all studies have failed to find evidence of positive impact on recidivism. An analysis of federal probationers in Illinois found that 90 percent completed their community service sentences successfully.[63] A study of California's Community Service Order program revealed that "Sentencing offenders to community service does not increase the likelihood that they will recidivate by comparison with sentencing them to straight probation or to incarceration."[64] The discovery that recidivism rates are no worse with community service than with incarceration is heartening because of the enormous cost savings associated with community service.

To date, community service has not been employed as a primary sanction for serious offenders. When serious offenders are given community service, it is generally in the context of a sentence containing other punishments and restrictions. In light of the increasing problems in the American prison system, community service stipulations may represent a method for enhancing the punitiveness of other community sentences in order that the current interests in deterrence and just deserts may be satisfied.

Day-Reporting Centers

Our coverage of alternatives to incarceration has included a variety of different sanctions. Many of these sanctions can be used in concert with other penalties to achieve desired effects. Intensive probation supervision, for example, can be used with community service to assure high levels of surveillance and control over the offender while at the same time compelling the offender to return something to the community. In fact, all of the alternative sanctions discussed in this and the previous chapter can be enhanced through combination with other alternatives. Day-reporting centers (DRCs) provide an administrative mechanism to assure smooth integration of these non-incarcerative sanctions.

Although DRCs vary in their features, in general they are non-residential facilities that provide surveillance, drug testing, and programming services (education, counseling, employment preparedness, for example). Offenders are required to report regularly and frequently to these facilities as part of a sentence or as a condition of release. Contact levels with authorities are higher than those typical of traditional control and surveillance methods (such as probation). Services are offered directly or brokered, and these services generally exceed those that would be available through other means.[65]

DRCs originated in Great Britain in the early 1970s. Four Day Treatment Centers were opened in 1972 for judges to use as a condition of probation release.[66] Probationers could be required to attend these centers for up to two months. The spread of such centers across Britain during the 1970s and 1980s occurred without strong central control, and the centers thus varied significantly in terms of their structure, program content, and even size. Current facilities in Britain, however, appear to be concerned with a single objective—reducing institutional populations.[67] A survey of American DRC practitioners suggests that the objectives of American DRCs are threefold: increasing supervision in the community, providing treatment, and reducing institutional crowding.[68]

The first American DRC, Genesis II, opened in Minneapolis in 1976. It was designed to handle women referred from both the criminal justice system and child protection agencies. New Jersey followed suit in 1977, and Massachusetts and Connecticut opened DRCs in 1986. By the fall of 1989 there were 14 DRCs in operation, with 6 additional facilities about to open.[69] Three-quarters of the DRCs are situated in Massachusetts, Connecticut, and Minnesota. Clearly DCRs have not yet become well established nationwide.

Although the objectives of American DRCs are multiple, reducing institutional crowding is an extremely important objective. Connecticut and Massachusetts, the states most active in opening DRCs in the last five years, adopted DCRs primarily as a method of reducing institutional populations. It must be noted, however, that the small size of current DRCs can result in at best a modest contribution to reducing crowding. The largest of the 14 DRCs had a maximum client capacity of 150 clients daily, while 9 of the programs had maximums of 50 or fewer clients.[70] In light of the fact that representatives of 11 of the 14 DRCs have identified reducing institutional crowding as a major goal,[71] it is perhaps surprising that larger centers or a greater number of centers have not yet materialized.

Focus 8-3

Hartford's Alternative Incarceration Center

In an effort to reduce jail and prison populations, the Connecticut Department of Correction opened its first day-reporting center in 1985. Operated by the Connecticut Prison Association, the Alternative Incarceration Center (AIC) is designed to divert offenders from Connecticut's incarcerative institutions. To assure that the AIC was truly diverting offenders, and not merely widening the net, sentencing research was conducted to identify and target offenders likely to receive terms of incarceration. In addition, the AIC is used for probation violators, who would typically be sent to jail or prison for probation violations. Finally, the AIC handles some inmates who would be released from custody on home confinement except that they lack a suitable residence.

The AIC does house a few offenders who are in the process of seeking housing, but the majority of clients live at home. Program participants must report in at least four times weekly. Some offenders are required to participate in AIC-operated programs, such as employment counseling. Community service is also required of participants. Daily monitoring of participant schedules provides for the kind of surveillance typical of intensive probation supervision. Recreational resources, such as cards, board games, and tele-

vision, are available to clients. The amount of time participants spend in the program depends on their status.
Probationers may be in the program for six months, while
parolees generally stay for about three months.

In 1989 about 120 clients were handled daily by the
AIC. The Connecticut Department of Correction is enthusiastic about the future of the program, and plans have been
made to increase the number of AICs in the state. It is possible that in the near future significant numbers of
Connecticut offenders may serve at least part of their sentences in a day-reporting center.[72]

With regard to the programs that are now in operation, we do not
yet know whether offenders sentenced to these DRCs would actually
have been sent to jail or prison had the DRC option not been available.
Until we have a better sense of whether net-widening or actual diversion
from incarceration is taking place, it will not be possible to determine
the extent to which DRCs actually affect the institution-bound offender
population.

As noted above, providing treatment programs is also an important
element in the DRC concept. All of the 14 DRCs surveyed in a
National Institute of Justice (NIJ) survey provided job-seeking skills
training and job placement. All but one provided counseling and drug
use testing, and 11 of the DRCs provided educational programs.[73] In
addition, DRCs offer high levels of surveillance, in some cases comparable to the surveillance typical of the intensive probation supervision programs discussed in the previous chapter. Participants in Hartford,
Connecticut's Alternative Incarceration Center must report to the center *at least* four to five times each week. Clients submit daily itineraries,
which are monitored by staff through random telephone calls. On average, clients will spend 8 to 12 hours per week at the center itself.[74] This
level of face-to-face contact exceeds that of many ISP programs.

Beyond reducing institutional crowding, maintaining surveillance,
and providing treatment, advocates of DRCs argue that they are cost-
effective. All but one of the 14 DRCs had daily per offender costs of less
than $19.[75] This compares favorably with the costs of residential confine-
ment. Minnesota's least expensive prison, Stillwater, costs the state
about $45 per day for each inmate.[76] As the NIJ report points out, how-
ever, much of these costs are fixed costs that will not be significantly

affected by the kinds of small population reductions now characteristic of current DRCs. In addition, the British experience does not provide clear evidence that DRCs are necessarily cheaper than custodial institutions.[77] Nonetheless, a serious commitment to sending significant numbers of inmates to DRC programs could result in substantial savings. At this point in the development of the DRC movement it is still too early to offer an assessment of the extent to which DRCs will be cost-effective.

Much the same can be said about DRC effectiveness regarding recidivism. Well-designed evaluation studies have not yet appeared in the research literature, although states such as Connecticut have earmarked funds for independent impact and effectiveness evaluation.[78] No studies of recidivism exist that compare DRC offenders with similar offenders not sentenced to DRCs. We do know that program completion rates, the percentage of offenders successfully completing their DRC sentence, vary enormously. The success rate ranges from more than 90 percent to only about 40 percent. The vast majority of offenders failing to complete their sentence failed not because they committed new crimes, but because they did not follow the conditions of their sentence. Failure to pass drug tests and failure to report to the DRC were the most frequent reasons.[79] There is thus no evidence at this point, with the kinds of offenders now being sentenced to DRCs, that public safety is being seriously compromised by the use of DRCs. It appears that less than 5 percent of failures were the result of new crimes by DRC participants.[80]

In sum, DRCs offer the prospect of a relatively inexpensive alternative to incarceration that may reduce institutional populations, provide surveillance of offenders in the community, and offer rehabilitative opportunities that may reduce recidivism rates. In addition, because most participants do not live at the DRC, DRCs are not troubled by the community resistance that often emerges when residential facilities for criminals, such as halfway houses, are planned for neighborhoods. Furthermore, there appears to exist real opportunity for the private sector to become involved in this aspect of corrections. Many of the more troubling elements of private involvement in custodial institutional management, such as issues associated with the use of force in resolving residential disciplinary problems, are not present with DRCs. In fact, 13 of the 14 DRCs surveyed by the NIJ were operated by private firms.

Currently ongoing evaluations of present DRCs will provide insight into the extent to which they will be able to fulfill the potential foreseen by its advocates. In view of our severely strained custodial institutions, it seems important to make an effort to fully develop the DRC concept, and apply rigorous evaluation technology to monitor the impact of the innovation.

Conclusion

The alternatives to incarceration discussed in this and the previous chapter represent some of the more significant approaches to addressing problems associated with current correctional difficulties. In the aggregate, they possess at least the potential to provide punishments for crime that appropriately reflect the seriousness of the crime, are associated with manageable economic costs, make possible effective supervision of offenders, and perhaps offer opportunities to modify offender behavior. The approaches vary in terms of their value in addressing each of these objectives. Their ultimate value, therefore, may depend heavily upon the sentencing mechanisms that are used to selectively impose and combine alternative sanctions.

Of course, it is not altogether clear that these sanctions will prove to be as effective as anticipated by their advocates. For instance, current evidence on intensive supervision programs does not indicate that such programs will be the panacea many enthusiasts had anticipated. Other alternatives have yet to be subjected to rigorous evaluation, and predictions of success at this point are little more than speculation. Even "enlightened" programs that attempt to combine various non-incarcerative penalties may founder if not carefully conceptualized and administered. An analysis of a Florida program, for example, found that the availability of multiple sanctions may result in a "'piling up of sanctions' that can predispose offenders to failure in program compliance, thereby resulting in a return to court, often followed by jail and upon jail release return to the same multitude of community program requirements with the potential for additional program violations and court returns."[81] The authors of this analysis caution that "'more is not always better' when attempting to successfully implement and operate intermediate punishment systems."[82]

In light of the magnitude of current correctional difficulties, however, it is imperative that energetic efforts be mobilized to test the full potential of these alternatives. In addition, it must be remembered that shortcomings in alternative sanctions must be measured against shortcomings associated with current incarcerative practices. The quest for punishments that will satisfy all of our social objectives is worth sustaining. However sanctions that fall short of this ideal, but which nonetheless represent enhancements over our current situation, merit serious consideration.

Perhaps the most formidable obstacle to a full and energetic commitment to such pursuits is political ideology. As noted earlier in this book, American political traditions at both ends of the ideological spectrum provide little evidence of a willingness to assume leadership roles in moving away from traditional incarcerative responses to crime. The desperate fear of being branded "soft on crime" propels politicians into rhetoric and action that both shields them from perceived political risk and destroys their capacity to provide the kind of leadership required to effectively address crime and justice dilemmas. This is especially troubling in light of the fact that data exist indicating significant public interest in alternatives to incarceration. Unhappily, it is not likely that public policy will undergo serious change until the lack of correspondence between this public interest and political orthodoxy is addressed.

Notes

[1] Code of Hammurabi (1903) trans. by C.H.W. Johns, Edinburgh: T. & T. Clark.

[2] Id.

[3] Old Testament, Exodus 22:1.

[4] Sellin, J. Thorsten (1976) *Slavery and the Penal System*, New York: Elsevier.

[5] Id.

[6] Schafer, Stephen (1977) *Victimology: The Victim and His Criminal*, Reston, VA: Reston Pub. Co., p. 12.

[7] Hillsman, S.T., Mahoney, B., Cole, George, and Auchter, Bernard (1987) "Fines as Criminal Sanctions," National Institute of Justice—Research in Brief, Sept. Washington, D.C.: U.S. Dept. of Justice, p. 2.

[8] Id.

[9] Id.

[10] Klein, Andrew R. (1988) *Alternative Sentences—A Practitioner's Guide*, Cincinnati, OH: Anderson Pub. Co., p. 196.

[11] Morris, Norval and Tonry, Michael (1990) *Between Prison and Probation—Intermediate Punishments in a Rational Sentencing System*, New York: Oxford University Press, p. 128.

[12] Id. at 111-112.

[13] See Hillsman et al, note 7 above at 4.

[14] Cole, George F., Mahoney, Barry, Thornton, Marlene, and Hanson, Roger A. (1988) "The use of fines by trial court judges," *Judicature*, 71(6), p. 333.

[15] Gillespie, Robert W. (1980) "Fines as an alternative to incarceration: The German experience," *Federal Probation*, 44(4).

[16] See Hammurabi, note 1 above at 3, #8.

[17] See Gillespie, note 15 above.

[18] Id. at 24.

[19] See Morris and Tonry, note 11 above at 116.

[20] Id. at 113.

[21] *Criminal Justice Newsletter* (1990) "Successes cited in Staten Island 'day fine' project," 21(18), p. 3.

[22] Id. at 131.

[23] Cole, George F. (1989) "Innovations in collecting and enforcing fines," Washington, D.C.: National Institute of Justice Research in Action.

[24] Hillsman, Sally T., Mahoney, Barry, Cole, George F., and Bernard Auchter (1987) "Fines as criminal sanctions," National Institute of Justice—Research in Brief: 5, Washington: D.C.

[25] See Morris and Tonry, note 11 above at 144.

[26] Id.

[27] Id. at 137-138.

[28] See Cole, note 23 above at 5.

[29] Id.

[30] See Gillespie, note 15 above.

[31] Elias, Robert (1986) *The Politics of Victimization—Victims, Victimology, and Human Rights*, New York: Oxford University Press, p. 175.

[32] See Schafer, note 6 above at 112-113.

[33] See Klein, note 10 above at 144-145.

[34] Id. at 146.

[35] Id. at 147.

[36] McDonald, Douglas C. (1988) "Restitution and community service," Washington, D.C.: U. S. Government Printing Office.

[37] Based on Lawrence, Richard (1990) "Restitution as a cost-effective alternative to incarceration," in Galaway, B. and Galaway, J (eds.) *Criminal Justice, Restitution, and Reconciliation*, Monsey, NY: Criminal Justice Press.

[38] Maiolino, Francis W., O'Brien, Jack, and Fitzpatrick, James J. (1990) "Computer-supported restitution programming in county probation and parole," in B. Galaway and J. Hudson (eds.) *Criminal Justice, Restitution, and Reconciliation*, Monsey, NY: Criminal Justice Press.

[39] Martin, Susan (1981) "Restitution and community service sentences: Promising sentencing alternative or passing fad?" in S. E. Martin, et al (eds.) *New Directions in the Rehabilitation of Criminal Offenders*, Washington, D.C.: National Academy Press.

[40] Schneider, Anne L. and Schneider, Peter R. (1985) "The impact of restitution on recidivism of juvenile offenders: An experiment in Clayton County, Georgia," *Criminal Justice Review* 10(1); Schneider, Anne L. (1986) "Restitution and recidivism rates of juvenile offenders: Four Experimental studies," *Criminology*, 24; Krajiick, Kevin (1982) "This is work, but it's freedom," *Corrections Magazine* 8(5), pp. 17-19.

[41] Ervin, Laurie and Schneider, Anne (1990) "Explaining the effects of restitution on offenders: results from a national experiment in juvenile courts,"

in B. Galaway and J. Hudson (eds.) *Criminal Justice, Restitution, and Reconciliation*, Monsey, NY: Criminal Justice Press, p. 224.

[42] Schneider, Anne L. (1986) "Restitution and recidivism rates of juvenile offenders: Results from four experimental studies," *Criminology*, 24(3).

[43] Legislative Audit Bureau—Wisconsin (1985) "An evaluation of restitution by adult probationers, Madison, WI: Audit Bureau.

[44] Schneider, Anne L. (ed.) (1988) *Guide to Juvenile Restitution*, Washington, D.C.: U.S. Government Printing Office.

[45] Schneider, Peter, Schneider, Anne, and Griffith, William (1982) *Two Year Report on the National Evaluation of the Juvenile Restitution Initiative: An Overview of Program Performance*, Eugene, OR: Institute of Policy Analysis.

[46] See Lawrence, note 37 above at 214.

[47] Id. at 215.

[48] Rowley, M.S. (1990) "Recidivism of juvenile offenders in a diversion restitution program (compared to a matched group of offenders processed through court)." in B. Galaway and J. Hudson (eds.) *Criminal Justice, Restitution, and Reconciliation*, Monsey, NY: Criminal Justice Press, p. 224.

[49] Zehr, Howard and Umbreit, Mark (1982) "Victim offender reconciliation: An incarceration substitute?" *Federal Probation*, 46(4).

[50] Launay, Giles (1985) "Bringing victims and offenders together: A comparison of two models," *The Howard Journal*, 24(3).

[51] See Elias, note 31 above at 184-185

[52] See Klein, note 10 above at 146.

[53] *Corrections Compendium* (1991) "Inmates' community projects range from collecting litter to growing food, " 16(8), p. 18.

[54] Davis, James R. (1991) "Community service as an alternative sentence," *Journal of Contemporary Criminal Justice*, 7(2).

[55] Krajick, Kevin (1982) "Community service: The work ethic approach to punishment," *Corrections Magazine*, 8(5): 6-19.

[56] Maher, Richard J. and Dufour, Henry E. (1987) "Experimenting with community service—An punitive alternative to imprisonment," *Federal Probation*, 51(3).

[57] McDonald, Douglas Cory (1989) *Punishment without Walls—Community Service Sentences in New York City*, New Brunswick, NJ: Rutgers University Press.

[58] See Maher and Dufour, note 56 above.

[59] Allen, G. Frederick and Treger, Harvey (1990) "Community service orders in federal probation: Perceptions of probationers and host agencies," *Federal Probation*, 55(3).

[60] Erwin, Billie S. and Bennett, Lawrence A. (1987) "New Dimensions in probation: Georgia's experience with intensive probation supervision (IPS)," Washington, D.C.: National Institute of Justice.

[61] See Krajick, note 55 above.

[62] Leibrich, Julie (1984) "Criminal history and reconviction of two sentence groups: Community service and nonresidential periodic detention," in Leibrich, J., Galaway, B., and Underhill, Y. (eds.) *Community Service Orders in New Zealand*, Wellington, NZ: Planning and Development Division, Department of Justice; Pease, K. et al (1985) "Community Service Orders," in Tonry, M. and Morris, N. (eds.) *Crime and Justice: An Annual Review of Research*, Chicago: University of Chicago Press.

[63] Allen, F. and Treger, H. (1990) "Community service orders in Federal Probation: Perceptions of probationers and host agencies," *Federal Probation*, 54.

[64] Quoted in *Criminal Justice Newsletter* (1991) "Community service sentencing in California found effective," 22(15), p. 5.

[65] Parent, Dale G. (1990) "Day reporting centers for criminal offenders—A descriptive analysis of existing programs," Washington, D.C.: U.S. Dept. of Justice.

[66] Vass, Anthony (1990) *Alternative to Prison—Punishment, Custody, and the Community*, London: Sage.

[67] See Parent, note 65 above at 9.

[68] Id. at 9.

[69] Id. at 3.

[70] Id. at 4.

[71] Id. at 5.

[72] Based on Parent, Dale G. (1990) "Day reporting centers for criminal offenders—A descriptive analysis of existing programs," Washington, D.C.: U.S. Dept. of Justice.

[73] Id. at 8.

[74] Id. at 10-12.

[75] Id. at 29.

[76] Id. at 30.

[77] See Vass, note 66 above at 161.

[78] See Parent, note 65 above at 12.

[79] Id. at 28.

[80] Id. at 28.

[81] Blomberg, Thomas, and Lucken, Karol (1991) "Stacking the deck by pil-

ing up sanctions: Is intermediate punishment destined to fail?" Presented at the American Society of Criminology national meeting, Nov., San Francisco, CA, p. 28.

[82] Id. at 30.

9

Shock Incarceration: The Prison Boot Camp

In the last few years a new term has slipped into the vocabulary of punishment and correction in the United States: prison boot camps. These
camps have attracted substantial amounts of recent attention and are
quickly being adopted in a growing number of states. In brief, prison
boot camps are modeled after military boot camps and expose inmates to
hard physical labor, rigorous discipline, and often spartan living conditions. As we saw in the previous two chapters, the search for solutions to
the crime and prison crowding problems has led to the adoption of a
range of novel sanctions. The prison boot camp represents yet another
effort to provide an alternative to conventional sanctions.

The rapid adoption of the boot camp results, in part, from the common sense appeal of the concept. Good hard physical work, rigorous discipline, and personal accountability are commonly regarded as important
values in American culture, even if in daily practice they appear somewhat less significant. Thus it should not be surprising that a sanction
that provides structure and activities expressive of those values naturally
possesses popular appeal. Perhaps the sentiments articulated in the
National Drug Strategy best sum up this appeal. "Military-style boot
camps, with their rigorous regimes and austere conditions, bring a sense
of order and discipline to the lives of youthful, non-violent first-time
offenders, and perhaps serves as a deterrent against future crimes."[1]

The potential value of boot camps is multifaceted. This fact has
not been lost on American political leaders. In announcing the opening
of Illinois' first boot camp, Governor James R. Thompson noted that

> Boot camps don't solve the prison overcrowding problem, but they
> certainly help. The inmates at boot camp have a choice. They can

231

behave, get away from a life of crime, and go free earlier. Or if they misbehave and fail boot camp, they go directly to the penitentiary.[2]

Thompson's remarks indicate an interest in reducing crowding, providing punishment, and deterring offenders from future involvement in crime.

This chapter is devoted to a detailed consideration of this new form of punishment. We will examine the apparent attractions that have led to the prison boot camp, their ideological appeal, historical precursors, goals of modern boot camps, and the boot camp's current status. New York's boot camp system will be described, and the chapter concludes with an examination of the effectiveness of boot camps and some thoughts on their future prospects.

Why Prison Boot Camps?

As we have already seen, the correctional system has recently spawned a variety of innovations to handle the growing problems it faces. The growth of restitution, intensive supervision, and day-reporting centers are examples of the general interest in expanding the correctional tool kit. The emergence of prison boot camps can thus be seen as simply another expression of the general popular concern with crime, the apparent ineffectiveness of the correctional system, and the logjammed conditions in the penal system. Boot camps fit into a diverse correctional strategy designed to address these concerns.

More particularly, however, boot camps have a number of features which make them especially attractive. First, boot camps offer a sanction that retains the punitive orientation that became popular with the rise of the justice model of punishment in the late seventies. Inmates are not merely confined in an institutional environment, they are confined under austere conditions and made to work hard at physically demanding tasks. In a sense, boot camps are the antithesis of the "country club" prisons the public often believes are characteristic of the correctional system.

Second, the punitive character of the boot camp experience has at least the potential to achieve deterrent effects. The experience is intended to be painful and difficult. Those who have completed prison boot camp will presumably do what they must to avoid being re-incarcerated. This means going straight. There is also the possibility that word of the harsh conditions will become commonplace on the streets and act as a general deterrent to those contemplating future involvement in crime.

Third, boot camps are generally designed for first offenders, typically youthful convicts. This squares with the notion that it is important to reach budding criminals at the outset of their criminal careers, while they are young enough to learn to behave responsibly. This idea appeals because it is an extension of the popular notion that since old dogs cannot be taught new tricks, effort must be expended with those still able to learn.

Fourth, the highly disciplined environment is intended to develop sefl-control among the inmates, which hopefully will carry over in post-release activities.

Fifth, because inmates serve short sentences, typically 90 to 180 days, the cost of punishing each inmate is relatively inexpensive. This assumes, of course, that these short sentences do not increase the likelihood that an offender will re-offend and eventually end up in conventional state prison.

Finally, the short sentences are welcome in a time when regular prisons are becoming increasingly overcrowded. They syphon off some inmates from the conventional incarcerative system. Actually, some analysts argue that, in practice, reduction of crowding is the primary attraction of the boot camp.[3] This assumes, of course, that boot camp inmates would otherwise have been sent to state prison. We will return to this issue later.

The various attractions of the boot camp concept possess greater or lesser importance in different states. Some boot camp programs focus heavily upon more punitive kinds of activities (for example, hard physical labor) while others provide counseling and other traditional rehabilitative programs.[4] Although the term "boot camp" typically conjures up only the most punitive rendition of the shock incarceration concept, it is important to note that, despite numerous commonalities, boot camp programs do have significant differences and orientations.

Furthermore, different advocacy groups are attracted by different aspects of the boot camp ideal. Politicians generally focus on the punitive and economic aspects of shock incarceration. Texas gubernatorial candidate Clayton Williams, for instance, made it a regular part of his campaign to talk about sending convicts off to west Texas to break rocks. Political candidates such as Williams tend to refer to the toughness of the sanction, how it represents a no-nonsense strategy designed to instill the work ethic, and how the painfulness of the experience will deter future criminal activity. Public information on boot camps, being as new as they are, is still relatively sparse. It is likely that public sentiment about boot camps mirrors that expressed by political leaders.

Boot camps also have attractions for convicts. Many current boot camp programs are voluntary, and in some states there is no shortage of volunteers. Despite the harsh conditions and difficult work, inmates have the opportunity to significantly shorten their time in state custody if they successfully complete the program. As we will see, some inmates see it as a second chance and are motivated to take full advantage of the opportunity.

Ideology and Boot Camps

As should be evident by this point in our discussion of correctional dilemmas and solutions, ideology influences the attractiveness of the boot camp concept. Conservatives are comfortable with the punitive orientation of boot camps, the emphasis on discipline, and the value attached to personal responsibility. They regard the boot camp not so much as a shorter sentence but as a serious punitive experience, unlike the casual, chaotic, and undisciplined punitive experience they believe is typical of the conventional state prison. The potential for cost savings is also an attraction for conservatives. The weaknesses of the boot camp, from the conservative perspective, include the minor incapacitative effect and the potential for a weak general deterrent effect due to the shortness of the sentence.

Liberals may be less excited about the punitive aspects of the boot camp but can find solace in the fact that many programs, such as the IMPACT program in Louisiana, do offer traditional rehabilitative components. In addition, the volunteer nature of many programs means that such resources will be spent on highly motivated convicts. Moreover, the relatively short nature of boot camp sentences appeals to liberals who are more inclined to reserve long terms of incarceration for only the most serious offenders.

Both conservatives and liberals can be enthusiastic about the emphasis on youthful offenders. Conservatives have long argued that family failures in raising the young are at the heart of much criminal misbehavior. Although one can wonder about how much can be accomplished in a few short months, boot camps represent one effort to address some critical family failures. Liberals have been at the forefront in insisting that social conditions, rather than simple malevolence, lead the young into delinquency and ultimately criminal behavior. The exposure of young offenders to rehabilitative programs, even those that apply punitive strategies for achieving behavior modification, makes good sense to liberals who seek changes in the offender rather than merely holding the offender accountable.

The attraction of boot camps to both conservatives and liberals underscores an important point about corrections. On occasion, a single correctional intervention can make excellent sense to those holding opposing ideologies. With regard to boot camps, there is enough to appeal to both conservatives and liberals to generate political support. This is an important point if the political will necessary to carry the boot camp through the first experimental years of operation is to be sustained. Without such support, the very first sign of less than adequate performance provides the basis for political attacks that may result in the termination of what might actually be an excellent concept. (The current furor over privatization is a good example of this problem.) The apparent bipartisan appeal of boot camps suggests that any initial failures of boot camps may be less likely to provide a bloody platform for political opponents. The obvious advantage of this is that boot camps may be given enough of an opportunity to demonstrate what they are capable of accomplishing. On the negative side, however, the lack of ready opposition may mean that the clear and obvious failure of boot camps may not be sufficient to motivate the timely political and practical dismissal of the concept.

Historical Precursors

Boot camps are made up of a number of components, none of which are really unique to modern shock incarceration. In ancient Greece, for instance, hard labor was a punishment of regular resort for certain categories of citizens. At the bottom of the social structure were slaves, who were already condemned by virtue of their social status to a life of involuntary servitude. Metics (temporary visitors) convicted of crimes could be sentenced to penal slavery and the hard labor that went along with it. Classical Rome, which was also sharply partitioned into distinct social classes, reserved hard labor for certain subsets of offending citizens. Upper-class offenders during the Roman Empire could not be sentenced to hard labor. This sanction was available for lower-class offenders and might typically involve a life sentence to labor in the state mines. Other labor sentences set convicts to work on the public roads, in the sewers, and on other state operations.[5]

Although incarceration was not used, enslavement with hard labor was not uncommon during the Middle Ages. The Burgundian Code, for instance, extended not only to certain lower-class offenders but to their kin as well. Horse theft was often a capital offense, but "if a horse thief was executed, his wife and children over the age of fourteen years of age became the slaves of the horse's owner."[6]

By the late sixteenth century a new form of forced labor came into being. In 1596 the Rasphuis opened for youthful minor offenders in Amsterdam. The facility occupied the building and grounds of a former convent. Convicts were confined in a highly disciplined environment and, like the modern boot camp, served relatively short sentences. Most inmates were compelled to work at trades such as weaving. Although inmates were required to labor, the Rasphuis clearly had rehabilitative as well as punitive objectives.[7]

During the seventeenth century the restoration of Europe after the Thirty Years' War was made possible in part by the use of convicts sentenced to hard labor on reconstruction projects. In fact, by the middle of the eighteenth century, the longstanding sanction of banishment was replaced by labor on military fortifications.[8]

Sentences to labor in a military environment actually antedated the Thirty Years' War. Possibly as early as the first half of the fourteenth century, galley slavery was adopted as a sanction for certain criminals. Some of these offenders were set to work in private merchant fleets, while others served their sentences in state military vessels. It was a harsh sanction, and the mortality rate for convicts was staggeringly high.[9]

Hard labor was part of the American punitive tradition as well. What may well have been the first true prison, Connecticut's Newgate Prison, opened in 1773 and required that inmates labor in the copper mine that the prison occupied.[10] Although this idea foundered at Newgate, the use of labor in prison was adopted in subsequent American penal institutions such as Philadelphia's Walnut Street Jail. Both Eastern State Penitentiary and Auburn Prison, the two leading models in the developing nineteenth-century American prison system, required that inmates be engaged in labor. In the American South, backbreaking labor on road and chain gangs was a regular part of the nineteenth-century penal system.[11]

The military aspect of modern boot camps was also adopted in early American prisons. At Auburn Prison military routine was utilized instead of the solitary confinement characteristic of Eastern State Penitentiary. A former military officer developed a disciplinary regime which stipulated that inmates were not to converse with each other and required that they march in lock-step wherever they went.[12]

The nineteenth-century institution most closely resembling the modern boot camp was the Elmira Reformatory although the resemblance was the result of a retreat from the original reformatory plan. The Reformatory opened in 1876 and, following the innovations of Maconochie and Crofton in Australia and Europe, used a series of grades to motivate the inmates to improve themselves. Like the modern boot camp, the Reformatory's clients were youthful offenders. By performing well in work and academic classes inmates could move up the grade system and ultimately win their release from the institution. An industrial system was introduced into the prison, which provided work for the inmates as well as revenue to offset operating costs.[13]

The tough physical regime of the boot camp was also used at Elmira although at first only for a subset of especially intractable convicts. The use of physical exercise was extended to the general inmate population when the state legislature enacted restrictions on the kinds of income-producing industries that could be operated in prison. As Blake McKelvey notes, "The erection of a gymnasium in 1890 established the physical culture and military departments as year-round features and gave them, together with the evening school, a coordinate place with the trades department in the now completely evolved reformatory technique."[14] Trades instruction, military drill, and physical exercise kept the inmates well-occupied.

The emphasis on the military component is of special interest to us. Military training was initially introduced at Elmira in an effort to keep inmates from idleness when laws restricting inmate labor were passed. "The military organization permeated almost every aspect of the institution: schooling, manual training, sports teams, physical training, daily timetables, supervision of inmates, and even parole practices. In short, the training was used to discipline the inmates and organize the institution."[15]

By the turn of the twentieth century, however, overcrowding

placed severe restrictions on what could be accomplished in the Reformatory. Crowding in other New York institutions resulted in a steady stream of inmates to Elmira, some of whom were the kinds of older offenders originally deemed unsuitable for the rehabilitative agenda at the Reformatory. The crowding-related demise of Elmira is perhaps worth remembering in our current efforts to anticipate and avoid similar difficulties.

The words of J.C. Hite of the Ohio Boys' Industrial School in 1886 provide additional evidence that the theory underlying the modern boot camp was in full operation during the nineteenth century. He observed that the Industrial School

> is a place of discipline, which means to educate, to instruct, to correct, and in some cases to chastise . . . the principle that labor is honorable should be faithfully taught and upheld, but every wayward boy in a reformatory ought to be provided with such kinds of labor as will arouse his mind most and get him to thinking soonest. . . . Labor produces muscle, and muscle produces brain.[16]

Faith that discipline and muscle produce brain, and that brain eventually produces socially acceptable forms of behavior, is an important theme in the rationale for the modern boot camp.

One final and more recent bit of historical information merits mention before we move on to detailed consideration of modern boot camps. Shock probation programs were put into operation in the mid-1960s.[17] This sanction typically involves a short term of incarceration lasting from 30 days to six months, followed by a period of community supervision under conditions of probation. The objective of shock probation is essentially to scare the offender into law-abiding behavior and to provide a small taste of real punishment. Like shock incarceration, shock probation was designed for use with first offenders or offenders who have not been subjected to incarceration. The approaches differ in that shock probationers were generally neither required to participate in the physical activities typical of the new boot camps nor were they placed in specially designed institutions.[18]

Thus, most of the components of the modern boot camp have already been implemented either in America or in Europe. In addition, the rationale for the boot camp is not unique to the current period of correctional history. Work, discipline, and physical exertion have been imposed on offenders in one form or another since the earliest systems of punishment were designed and put into operation. The success of such early strategies to secure law-abiding behavior from convicted citizens has been mixed, thus there is reason to be cautious about what the modern implementation of this approach can achieve.

Major Goals of Modern Boot Camps

It is tempting to oversimplify current boot camp programs in terms of their goals. In reality, program goals do differ among the states, and the activities typically found in the boot camps of one state may vary significantly from those found elsewhere. A multi-site study of seven boot camps found four major types of goals for boot camps: system, individual, public relations, and prison/control management goals.[19] Public relations and prison control/management were, however, rarely cited as important goals by the study participants from each state. The most important were system goals, and the most significant among these goals were reduction of overcrowding, providing an alternative to long-term incarceration, and reducing the cost of punishment.

Most states also indicated individual level goals for their programs. These included reduction of criminal involvement and positive behavioral change. The nature of such change was not always clearly specified, but generally involved increased maturity and self-control, more positive attitudes toward authority, and enhanced personal responsibility.[20]

In addition to these general goals, some states have special goals for their programs. New York State is a good example because of its special interest in drug addiction.

> In contrast to other states, the Shock Incarceration Program run by DOCS [Department of Correctional Services] is designed to be a treatment-oriented program. For every 500 hours of physical training plus drill and ceremony that has led to the media calling it a "boot camp," Shock in New York also included 546 hours of the therapeutic approach to treating addiction, based on the Network and the A.S.A.T. [Alcohol and Substance Abuse Treatment] programs.[21]

As we will see, New York's goals and efforts resemble in many ways the kind of integrated effort Warden Brockway attempted to mount at the

Elmira Reformatory in the last quarter of the nineteenth century.

One of the great problems in corrections has been the lack of consensus regarding the proper goals for the correctional system. The tension between rehabilitation and punishment in particular has resulted in a tremendous amount of vacillation in the operationalization of modern correctional strategies and programs. As noted earlier, the wide-ranging theoretical appeal of the boot camp concept creates opportunities for significant disagreement regarding what the primary emphases of the boot camp ought to be. Those who view boot camps primarily as tough, relatively inexpensive, punitive experiences will have different ideas on how they ought to be run than will those who see boot camps as opportunities to motivate individuals to accept the challenge of changing themselves in positive, productive ways. A National Institute of Justice (NIJ) assessment of state shock incarceration programs found that "the programs differ in the amount of emphasis they place on rehabilitation, education, and vocational education."[22] Such variation reflects the differing goals of policymakers and program implementors in the individual states. It is likely that such goal variation will continue to be common in the early phase of the modern boot camp experience.

Current Status of Boot Camps

At the beginning of the new decade there were more than 9,000 inmates in shock incarceration programs across the nation.[23] Most inmates in such programs are confined in state-operated programs; a few are in local programs. A national survey of boot camp programs sponsored by the National Institute of Justice in 1988 revealed the existence of 14 programs located in 11 states. The earliest of these programs opened in 1984. A follow-up assessment published in 1990 found the number had grown to 21 programs in 14 states, a significant increase in a short two-year period.[24] By 1991, a Corrections Compendium survey revealed that 26 states and the federal system had boot camp programs in operation. More than 4,700 inmates can be handled in these programs, and an additional 14 states were seriously considering opening boot camps.[25] As this book is going to press a Government Accounting Office analysis reported that 26 states are now running a total of 57 boot camps holding more than 8,800 inmates.[26]

Georgia and New York have the greatest number of boot camps with 19 and 5 camps respectively. The number of program participants ranged from a low of about 20 in Wyoming to a high of 2,623 in Georgia.[27] Most of these camps are thus much smaller than typical incarcerative institutions. Although initially the majority of boot camps were actually located within a larger prison complex, now most are operated in separate camps or facilities.[28] (Some analysts argue that placing the camps in sight and sound proximity to state prison reinforces the scare message of the boot camp.)

The majority of states give judges the authority to send convicted offenders to boot camps. State corrections departments retain this power in other states. In most states offenders volunteer for boot camp. If accepted, they serve sentences ranging in length from 90 days to 180 days.[29] In a number of states inmates may voluntarily drop out of the program. Dropouts are sent to state prison to complete what are usually longer terms of confinement. Inmates who successfully complete the boot camp are typically placed under some form of community supervision. The rigor of this supervision varies significantly from state to state. In some states it is intensive while in others it resembles conventional probation supervision.

Although there are exceptions, most boot camps admit only youthful offenders convicted of nonviolent crimes. Most are confined subsequent to their initial conviction for a felony. Although boot camps were initially reserved for males, eight states now have boot camp programs for females.[30] In some states, women sent to boot camp may have more than a single felony conviction, and may be older, have more involvement in drug crimes, and have spent more time in jail than their male counterparts.[31]

Current boot camps vary significantly in the amount of resources they commit to rehabilitative activities. Programs examined in the updated NIJ national survey revealed that all provided at least some virtually rehabilitative programming, often more than would commonly be found in state prison. Three states exposed inmates to as much time in rehabilitation as in labor activities. Louisiana's daily schedule, for instance, mandates 4.5 hours each for rehabilitation, work, and military drill.[32] The more recent Corrections Compendium survey affirmed that rehabilitative programming is part of virtually all boot camp experiences.[33]

Thus the often communicated image of the boot camp as a purely punitive enterprise, singularly devoted to hard labor and rigid military-style discipline, is quite mistaken. Rehabilitative programming is an important part of most camps, especially when considered in the context of the paucity of programs available in many state prisons. Whether this reality represents a dilution of the original concept or an innovation that more adequately reflects the full range of offender needs depends on the goals one holds for boot camps, as well as on the effectiveness of such programs. We will return to the question of effectiveness, but first we turn to a more detailed examination of the boot camp experience of the state most energetic in operationalizing the concept, New York.

The New York Experience

With the exception of Georgia, New York State has more boot camps in operation, and more inmates in those boot camps, than anywhere else in the country. Because of this extensive commitment to shock incarceration it is worth looking more closely at what New York has done during the last few years.[34]

In the summer of 1987 the New York state legislature established shock incarceration.

> [T]he goals of the program were twofold. The first goal was to reduce the demand for bedspace. The second goal was to treat and release specifically selected state prisoners earlier than their court mandated minimum periods of incarceration without compromising the community protection rights of the citizenry.[35]

The New York program was designed "to enable the State to protect the public safety by combining the surety of imprisonment with opportunities for timely release of inmates who have demonstrated their readiness for return to society."[36] The bill further noted that "[a]n alternative form of incarceration stressing a highly structured and regimented routine, which will include extensive discipline, considerable physical work and exercise and intensive drug rehabilitation therapy, is needed to build character, instill a sense of maturity and responsibility, and promote a positive self image."[37]

The state's first boot camp began accepting inmates in the fall of 1987 at the Monterey Shock Incarceration Correctional facility. Female inmates were accepted for the first time in December. Monterey was designed to handle 250 inmates and is thus among the larger shock incarceration facilities in the country. New York now has five shock incarceration facilities in operation, the largest of which is the 750 bed Lakeview facility.

Clients

The originating legislation provided that convicts less than 24 years of age were eligible for boot camp consideration. On more than one occasion the legislature has modified this provision, and inmates are now accepted up to age 35.

To be considered for boot camp, convicts must be eligible for parole within three years. They must *not* have been convicted of a violent or A-1 felony, manslaughter, the most serious rape and sexual assault offenses, or escape. Program participants must have no record of having served a previous indeterminate sentence and they must undergo physical and psychological examination. Older inmates must have their case reviewed by their sentencing judge, must never have been previously convicted of a disqualifying offense (such as rape), and must spend at least one year in an incarcerative setting (including pretrial detention, reception, and shock). The State Department of Correctional Services imposes additional restrictions regarding previous disciplinary records, alien status, and outstanding warrants. Finally, convicts must volunteer to participate in the program.

Although these criteria are numerous, and obviously result in the exclusion of many potential participants, the intent is to assure that only offenders who do not seriously threaten public safety and whose records indicate a strong likelihood that they can benefit from the boot camp experience are placed in the program. As is exemplified by the Elmira experience in the late nineteenth century, an effectively designed program aimed at the wrong clients is doomed to failure. New York has made a concerted effort to address this potential hazard.

The Program

New York's program consists of much more than what is commonly conveyed by the boot camp notion. Although it does provide a disciplined, work-oriented environment, it also includes significant rehabilitative services, especially those aimed at drug problems. New York's Executive

Deputy Commissioner of the Department of Correctional Services emphasized this in a speech to the American Correctional Association soon after the first camp opened.

> First and foremost, it is not simply a boot camp. Governor Cuomo does not believe we can turn someone's life around simply by making them do pushups, march in formation, or take orders. The strict physical regimen is a pivotal tool for teaching discipline and respect about individuals as we are teaching them about teamwork and getting along with others. But of equal importance and weight in our programs are the components that deal with education, *professional and peer counseling plus drug and alcohol therapy.* It is the combination of programs that we believe offers young offenders the chance to get their heads on straight and their lives in order.[38]

New York thus provides a multifaceted approach to the correctional experience in its boot camps. Significant resources are committed to rehabilitation, and the approach utilized is based on the Therapeutic Community Model. The particular version of the model adopted in New York is the Network program. In this approach activities are designed to motivate offenders to "1) consider their own needs, 2) the effect which they have on others, and 3) the variables of the situations in which they find themselves."[39] Devices such as confrontation groups are used to help inmates to achieve these objectives.

The program component specifically oriented around drug-related problems is unusual because it is required of all inmates, those with and without histories of drug involvement. The program consists of education, behavior modification, and both individual and group counseling.

In sum, New York's boot camp program stipulates that "[f]or every 500 hours of physical training plus drill and ceremony . . . [it] also includes 546 hours of the therapeutic approach to treating addiction . . . [and] at least 260 mandatory hours of academic education, and 650 hours of hard labor."[40]

Inmate Perceptions

As might be expected, inmate perceptions of their experience in boot camp vary in accord with what they accomplish through the program. A few observations from inmates, as reported in the report to the Legislature by the Department of Correctional Services, convey a sense of both the nature of those experiences, as well as the amount of variation.

> Shock was a safe place to be. I wasn't worried about fights, or about my property or about any homosexual stuff. I felt safe going to bed at night, and it wasn't just the staff who protected us, it was the other inmates looking out for you. They treated us like people not just criminals.[41]

This inmate's remarks are interesting because, as prison assault data clearly indicate, personal safety is a significant issue in conventional prisons. Another inmate expressed his trust in his fellow boot camp inmates in a different way.

> We were family. I feel good just thinking about them. I have my platoon picture at home and I think I'm going to send for it.[42]

With regard to the impact of the program, a number of inmates felt that the boot camp experience had made a significant contribution to their future. In a letter to the superintendent of one of the facilities an inmate wrote:

> I would like to thank you for a second chance in life. The reason I say life is because if I had sat in prison I would have either wound up dead, or just rotted and my mind and body would have gone to waste worse than it was when I was abusing alcohol. I have gained a lot of knowledge from the staff here, some of which my parents tried to instill in me, and some of which was foreign. I now have self control, self discipline, I learned to think before I speak or act. I have also become responsible for myself, I have learned to look within myself and find my faults.[43]

Positive sentiments are even expressed by some inmates who do not succeed when they are released. A 21-year-old former inmate failed in his efforts to avoid further drug involvement. After having his parole revoked he noted that

> [p]robably the proudest day of my life was graduating from Shock (Camp) and getting my graduate equivalency diploma. . . . Then I came out and life came down on me like a ton of bricks. My best friend was stabbed to death and my dad died of cancer. . . . I'd gotten so attached to my instructors, and now there was nobody to look up to. Nobody knew how to help me. . . . When I first violated

(parole) last July, I thought, "if there was only some way they'd let me go back to shock (camp)" even though it was impossible."

Of course, most negative sentiments about the boot camp are not likely to make their way back to the authorities. The legislative report may therefore not offer an entirely representative account of inmate reactions to the boot camp experience. Nonetheless, it appears that a number of inmates do have positive experiences while in New York's shock incarceration system.

Irrespective of inmate sentiments about their boot camp experiences, does shock incarceration provide punishment and reduce recidivism, crowding, and economic cost? We now turn our attention to the research currently available on these important issues.

The Effectiveness of Boot Camps

As noted earlier, one of the great attractions of the boot camp is its common sense appeal. It just seems reasonable that rigorous discipline, hard labor, military drill, and spartan living conditions will motivate offenders to keep themselves on the right side of the law. Boot camp seems more punitive than the probationary sentences that most offenders receive. Moreover, holding an inmate for six months in boot camp must cost significantly less than confining them in state prison for longer terms.

As might be expected of such a relatively new sanction, research on the effectiveness of boot camps is only now beginning to appear in the literature. The following section examines this literature with regard to the major goals of boot camps.

Punishment

Advocates of boot camps argue that shock incarceration provides a truly punitive alternative to the typical probationary sentence given to first offenders. Such a sanction, they argue, distributes the proper measure of justice while accomplishing deterrent objectives as well. Of course, it is difficult to establish exactly how much punishment is the appropriate amount for which crimes. Nonetheless, we can look at the kinds of folks being sent to boot camps to determine if offenders who would have gotten off "light," rather than offenders who would otherwise have gone to state prison, are being sent to boot camp.

To establish whether boot camps are truly providing a punitive enhancement require data on the kinds of sentences previously administered for the types of offenders being sent to boot camp. If such inmates were previously receiving conventional probation, for instance, it could be argued that boot camps had indeed created increased capacity to punish first-time young, nonviolent offenders. The clearest situation would be that in which laws that absolutely required probation for a certain class of offenders were modified to now absolutely require that they be sent to boot camp. Unfortunately, none of the currently existing arrangements contain this provision. New York State's previously described procedure is typical. Although there are formal eligibility criteria, such as conviction of certain nonviolent offenses, both judges and corrections officials ultimately determine which of the legally eligible inmates are chosen for participation. In addition, convicts must volunteer for boot camp, and there exists the possibility that volunteers may not be typical.

In light of the fact that many legally eligible convicts are not chosen by the judge or Department of Correctional Services for the boot camp program, and end up doing longer sentences in state prison, it may be that some of the boot camp inmates are actually experiencing a lighter punishment than would have been the case before the opening of the boot camps. The same can be said for the claim that boot camps provide shorter, and thus less costly, sentences. Without data showing that boot camp-eligible inmates in the program would not have received probation but instead would have been sent to state prison, it is not possible to demonstrate that boot camps actually reduce total correctional costs.

Other states have placement processes that create similar evaluative difficulties. At least four states, in addition to New York, require that legally eligible inmates volunteer to enter the boot camp program. In addition, in states such as Louisiana, a judge may elect not to recommend boot camp although a convict may be legally eligible.[45] Thus whether an inmate goes to boot camp, state prison, or is freed under probation supervision depends on a number of factors beyond those associated with legal eligibility. Adequate comparisons with probation and prison populations of the exact kinds of inmates now being sent to boot camp do not currently exist, thus it is difficult to know whether the boot camp inmates are receiving more or less punishment than they might have without the boot camp option.

▨ *Recidivism*

Because of the punitive nature of the shock incarceration concept, many analysts anticipate that boot camp will reduce the subsequent involvement in crime of those who successfully complete the program. As noted earlier, some programs have more of a focus on rehabilitation than others, but whether an inmate desists as a result of specific deterrence or rehabilitation, there is an expectation that subsequent criminal involvement of boot camp graduates will be decreased.

Early studies of shock probation did not substantiate that rearrest rates were lower for shock probationers than for regular probationers. (Recall that shock probation was a predecessor of shock incarceration in that it provided a short stay in an incarcerative environment, but generally without the discipline, military format, or labor components found in modern shock incarceration.) A study in Ohio, for instance, found that "[w]hen the differences between the groups [shock and regular probationers] were held constant, regular probationers have a 42 percent lower probability of re-incarceration than shock probationers."[46] A 1985 study found that "[t]he policy implications seem clear and consistent with previous findings on shock probation. Persons on shock probation did not perform better than their counterparts on regular probation."[47]

Studies of these boot camp predecessors are important because they should have signaled caution in the expectations held for shock incarceration. To date there have been few studies of the impact of boot camps on recidivism. The work that has been done does not provide clear evidence that they are particularly effective in reducing recidivism.

Recidivism success rates can be very misleading. Initial claims of 80 percent success in Georgia, 95 percent in Mississippi, and 75 to 80 percent in Florida are based only on inmates who successfully complete the boot camp sentence. These figures obscure the fact that only about half of convicts sent to boot camp actually complete the program.[48] Using only graduates in follow-up assessments provides an inflated assessment of the effectiveness of the program. Furthermore, a National Institute of Justice assessment found that programs in Georgia and Oklahoma did not have lower recidivism rates than conventional incarceration.[49] An assessment of Florida's program revealed that there was no statistically significant difference in return-to-prison rates between boot camp and a matched group of convicts not sent to boot camp.[50] When other kinds of failure (absconding, new felony, new misdemeanor, technical violation) were considered, the boot camp did do better. But this difference was the result of a greater number of technical violations among the non-boot camp group. (Technical violations are breaches of the rules imposed for post-release supervision, not new crimes.) When technical violations were not included, there was no difference in the success rates of boot camp and matched control offenders.[51]

Data provided by the Georgia Department of Corrections indicate that shock inmates had slightly higher return-to-prison rates than a comparison group of regular parolees. This relationship held at one, two, and three-year follow-up points. Florida reported data showing an advantage to shock incarceration at the one-year follow-up point, but the difference had largely disappeared at two years. Louisiana showed slight differences between shock and parolee groups. Regular probationers in Louisiana, however, did better than either shock or regular parolees.[52] A detailed time series analysis of Louisiana shock inmates, regular prisoners, and probationers did not find that shock incarceration reduced recidivism.[53] A study of Louisiana's boot camp program published in the summer of 1993 found that "[t]here were no statistically significant differences between the groups [b]oot camp, parole, probation] in the first 6 months of community supervision." The analysis concluded that the effectiveness of Louisiana's program with regard to recidivism "remains questionable."[54] An examination of New York shock graduates and a comparison group revealed that "there was no statistically significant difference between the return rates of these two groups."[55] There *was* a statistically significant difference in returns for new sentences (versus for rule violations), although the actual percentage difference was only 3.4.[56] The New York follow-up analysis was based on a relatively short 12 month period. Data on return-to-prison rates in states with longer follow-up periods, such as Georgia and Florida,[57] seem to indicate that rates converge with the passage of additional time.

In some states boot camp programs have been designed to be responsive to special kinds of offender needs. Drug-related problems in particular have been a significant focus of attention. As already noted, states such as New York have programs intended to address drug-related illegal activity. To date there has been virtually no research on the impact of shock programs on this kind of criminal involvement. Research does exist on the Louisiana experience, however. Although Louisiana's boot camp program was not designed especially for drug offenders, many of its components are appropriate for treating such inmates.[58] An analysis of the data on boot camp drug-involved offenders revealed that post-release failure rates for boot camp, prison parolee, and regular probationers were essentially indistinguishable. One positive outcome uncovered by the study was that drug-involved offenders who did not require substance abuse treatment (that is, non-addicted drug distributors) did fare somewhat better than their drug-addicted counterparts.

In sum, there appears to be little current evidence confirming the kinds of dramatic impact on recidivism so often claimed for such programs by political leaders. There is some evidence that boot camp experiences may result in more pro-social attitudes,[59] but it is not clear that such changes are related to recidivism. Although it is early in the development of the modern boot camp technique, and it may ultimately be possible to enhance the effects of such programs, expectations for boot camps may have to be lowered. Such a revision in expectations is, of course, a common phenomenon in corrections.

Reducing Crowding

The current crowding crunch has provided ample incentive for legislative bodies to consider boot camps. Surprisingly, there has been little effort to estimate the impact of boot camps on penal crowding.[60] At least two factors are important in considering the impact of boot camps on prison crowding. First is the number of inmates held in boot camps. With the exception of Georgia and New York, states have at most a few hundred inmates in shock incarceration programs. Florida, for instance, handles 100 inmates at a time, each of whom serves a three-month term. This would mean 400 inmates are handled annually. When compared to the 50,000 inmates held in Florida's state prison system, it is obvious that boot camps in Florida simply hold too few inmates to have a significant impact on crowding. The previously noted study of Louisiana's program concluded that it did save prison bed space although again the number saved represented a small fraction of the state's prison population.[61] This phenomenon is typical of virtually all boot camp states. In states with small prison populations such as Idaho there appears to be some evidence that boot camps may have an impact on crowding.[62] But in most states the small number of boot camp inmates sharply limits the impact such camps can have on prison crowding.

The second factor that must be considered is whether boot camp inmates really would have served terms in state prison rather than in the community on probation. As we have already discussed, the discretion in the systems of most states makes it possible that some boot camp inmates would not have been sent to state prison at all, but would have remained in the community. In such states, more energetic research efforts are needed to determine whether boot camp inmates do, in fact, represent diversions from prison. The next few years should produce more evidence on this issue.

Practical problems also bedevil efforts to address prison crowding through boot camps. Focus 9-1 details Texas's problems in *filling* its boot camps, despite a serious prison overcrowding crisis.

Focus 9-1

Texas Boot Camps Facing Vacancy Problem (*Fort Worth Star-Telegram*) [63]

The state prison system is overcrowded, but the much-touted boot camp prisons have been running a high vacancy rate, officials said.

"We built the boot camp because the court ordered the agency to do so, but the courts have not proceeded since that time to fill up those beds," said Rep. Allen Hightower, D-Huntsville. He is chairman of the House Corrections Committee.

"We got two facilities sitting out there that we're not using?" asked Rep. Sam Johnson, R-Plano. "I can't believe that."

For the past year, the state prison system has operated two boot camps with a combined capacity of about 400 inmates.

But Andy Collins, a director in the Texas Department of Criminal Justice institutional division, said judges have not been sentencing people to the camps.

About two months ago, the camps had 250 vacancies, Collins said. He said that decreased to 127 vacancies after prison officials sent letters to judges informing them of the unused space.

He also said prison officials make a special effort at judicial conferences to tell judges about the program.

"Historically, they [the camps] have not been used. We just haven't seen a clamoring for it," Collins said.

Meanwhile, the overcrowded state prison system has about 46,600 inmates, with more than 7,000 inmates backlogged in county jails awaiting transfer.

Under state law, men who are 26 or younger and who

have been convicted on a first offense of a nonviolent crime can be sentenced to boot camps. There they undergo a military-style work and exercise schedule for 90 days.

The creation of the boot camps was touted by politicians as an alternative to more expensive incarceration in higher-security units. The vigorous regimen was seen as a way to deter first-time offenders and teach them good work habits.

Collins said one reason judges aren't sending people to boot camps is that in many instances, they now have more sentencing options, such as community-based corrections programs.

Reducing Correctional Costs

Associated with the crowding issue is the matter of correctional costs. Boot camps are attractive because they entail relatively short sentences when compared to conventional state prison sentences. New York is typical in its vigorous interest in reducing the cost of operating its correctional system.[64]

A study of the cost-effectiveness of New York's shock incarceration estimated that the state saves $1.6 million for every 100 shock graduates who would otherwise have been handled in state prison. According to this analysis, the first 1,158 graduates of the program saved the state almost $20 million.[65] These figures are based on estimates of the per diem costs of confining the inmates (which are actually higher in New York for shock inmates than regular inmates) and the length of time actually served in shock versus conventional prison. Moreover, the state estimates that because it was able to avoid having to create new bedspace, significant construction savings were realized. An assessment of the 698 inmates who graduated from boot camp in November 1989 revealed that more than $46 million in construction costs were avoided through adoption of boot camps in New York.[66] Research in Florida and Louisiana also reveals significant per inmate cost savings.[67]

Data reported by states such as Georgia and New York do seem to indicate that the inmate cost per day is greater for shock incarceration.[68] However, the shorter periods of time inmates spend in confinement appear to offset these costs, and shock programs seem to offer the potential for significant cost savings over conventional imprisonment. Of course, if boot camp inmates would otherwise have received straight probation, then boot camps are significantly more expensive. It is worth remembering that at least in some states (for example, Louisiana) research has failed to find lower recidivism rates for shock graduates than for probationers. In such states, therefore, it can be argued that the cost of achieving the *same* recidivism rates is much higher than it would be if straight probation were used instead of boot camp.

Concluding Observations

Boot camps will remain in the news during the next few years. Additional states are planning to open them, and states already having camps, such as Georgia, are planning to open new camps.[69] Boot camps will continue to be part of both the correctional and political landscape during the 1990s. Even in states where existing boot camps have high vacancy rates, political inertia is resulting in the opening of new camps.[70] It is important to realize, however, that many of the claims made on behalf of boot camps, such as those pertaining to recidivism and reduction of prison crowding, have yet to be substantiated. Eventually these claims may be validated, but political rhetoric to the contrary, they remain unproven at this point in time. While finding some positive evidence on boot camp performance, a 1993 Government Accounting Office report concluded that "[i]t is still too early to tell whether boot camps will reduce the overall costs of corrections, inmate recidivism and prison crowding in the long term."[71]

Apart from the as yet unproved status of the claimed major advantages of boot camps, there are other concerns that merit attention. First, some of the components of the traditional military boot camp have not been shown to be effective in their original military context. As Merry Morash and Lila Rucker point out, "The idea of boot camp as applied in correctional settings is often a simplification and exaggeration of an outdated system of military training that has been examined and rejected as unsatisfactory by many experts and scholars and the military establishment itself."[72] They note that the military no longer uses some of the techniques adopted in some boot camps because they were not shown to be useful.

Second, it can be wondered whether there is any reason to believe that inmates who are responsive to the military structure will be able to function when released into a world without the constraints and support provided by such structure. Mark Osler argues that without services to "bridge" transition from boot camp to community life it is unlikely that decreases in recidivism will occur.[73]

Third, because much of the labor demanded of inmates is physical labor that has no counterpart in the outside world, significant effort is being expended by inmates on tasks that have no real economic value after release when they are looking for a way to support themselves. Moreover, contrary to prevailing "common sense," much of the research on labor in other contexts does not support the contention that it has an effect on recidivism.[74] Of course, the argument justifying hard physical work includes providing punishment and teaching respect for authority and discipline. Even if these goals are achieved, however, it remains to be shown that gains foregone in recidivism are not more valuable than what is accomplished with regard to punishment and discipline.

Finally, Morash and Rucker raise the question of whether the male stereotypes amplified in the boot camp experience are those worth trying to instill in convicted offenders. "[T]he boot camp model, with its emphasis on unquestioned authority and aggressive interactions and its de-emphasis on group cooperation and empathy, promotes a limited image of the 'true man.' . . . The irony in emphasizing an aggressive model of masculinity in a correctional setting is that these very characteristics may explain criminality."[75] It does seem that current perceptions of the well-adjusted modern male do not merely emphasize the "macho" traits traditionally associated with males and the military.

Morash and Rucker's observations suggest that the concept of the boot camp probably has not received adequate theoretical consideration. States have hastened to open boot camps without full consideration of the wide range of implications such camps have for society at large and offenders in particular. The public and political focus has been on the punitive, deterrent, and cost potential of the concept. The interest in these conventional goals of corrections may be obscuring other important issues that need to be resolved if boot camps are to stand any significant chance of being successful.

Notes

[1] Quoted in MacKenzie, Doris, L. (1990) "Boot camp prisons: Components, evaluations, and empirical issues," *Federal Probation*, 54(3), p. 44.

[2] "First Illinois boot camp opens," (1990) *The Compiler*, 10(2), p. 2.

[3] Parent, D.G. (1988) "Shock incarceration programs," Address to the American Correctional Association winter conference, Phoenix, Arizona.

[4] MacKenzie, Doris L., Gould, Larry A., Reichers, Lisa M. and Shaw, James W. (1990) "Shock incarceration: Rehabilitation or retribution?" *Journal of Offender Counseling, Services, and Rehabilitation*, 14(2).

[5] Id. at 28.

[6] Id. at 34-35.

[7] Sellin, J. Thorsten (1944) *Pioneering in Penology*, Philadelphia, PA: University of Pennsylvania Press.

[8] Id. at 57.

[9] Id. at ch. 4.

[10] Durham, Alexis M. III (1989) "Newgate of Connecticut: Origins and early days of an early American prison," *Justice Quarterly*, 6(1).

[11] Sellin, J. Thorsten (1976) *Slavery and the Penal System*, New York: Elsevier, ch. 11.

[12] McKelvey, Blake (1977) *American Prisons—A History of Good Intentions*, Montclair, NJ: Patterson Smith, p. 14.

[13] Id.

[14] Id. at 136.

[15] Smith, Beverly (1988) "Military training at New York's Elmira reformatory 1888-1920," *Federal Probation*, vol. 52, March, p. 33.

[16] Quoted in Platt, Anthony M. (1977) *The Child Savers—The Invention of Delinquency*, Chicago: University of Chicago Press, p. 72.

[17] Vito, Gennaro (1985) "Development in shock probation: A review of research findings and policy implications," *Federal Probation*, 50, pp. 22-27.

[18] See MacKenzie, Gould, Reichers, and Shaw, note 4 above at 26.

[19] MacKenzie, Doris L. (1990) "Boot camp prisons: Components, evaluations, and empirical issues," *Federal Probation*, 54(3).

[20] Id. at 49.

[21] "Shock incarceration in New York State: The corrections experience,"

(1990) The Second Annual Report to the Legislature, New York State Division of Program Planning, Research and Evaluation, p. 15.

[22] MacKenzie, Doris L. and Ballow, Deanna B. (1989) "Shock incarceration programs in state correctional jurisdictions—An update." National Institute of Justice—Research in Action, Washington, D.C.: U.S. Department of Justice.

[23] Camp, George M. and Camp, Camille G. (1990) *The Corrections Yearbook*, Salem, NJ: Criminal Justice Institute, p. 41.

[24] See MacKenzie, note 1 above.

[25] Marlette, Marjorie (1991) "Boot camp prisons thrive," *Corrections Compendium* 16(1), p. 6.

[26] Prison Boot Camps: Short-term Prison Costs Reduced, But Long-term Impact Uncertain, 4/29/93, Govt. Acct. Off.: Washington, D.C.

[27] Id.

[28] See Marlette, note 25 above at 11-12.

[29] Id; see also note 26 above.

[30] See Marlette, note 25 above at 6.

[31] See note 21 above at 24.

[32] See MacKenzie, note 1 above at 45.

[33] See Marlette, note 25 above at 11-12.

[34] This is based primarily upon material contained in "Shock incarceration in New York State: The corrections experience." (1990) The Second Annual Report to the Legislature, New York State Division of Program Planning, Research and Evaluation.

[35] See note 21 above at 17.

[36] From enacting legislation, chapter 262 of the Laws of New York, 1987, quoted in id., p. 6.

[37] Id.

[38] Id. at 16.

[39] Id. at 12.

[40] Id. at 15.

[41] Id. at 54-55.

[42] Id. at 55.

[43] Id. at 55-56.

[44] Id. at 57.

[45] MacKenzie, Doris L. and Shaw, James W. (1990) "Inmate adjustment and change during shock incarceration: The impact of correctional boot camps," *Justice Quarterly*, 7(1), p. 128.

[46] Vito, Gennaro, F. and Allen, Harry E. (1981) "Shock probation in Ohio: A comparison of outcomes," *International Journal of Offender Therapy*, 25, p. 74.

[47] Vito, Gennaro, F., Holmes, Ronald M., Wilson, Deborah G. (1985) "The effect of shock and regular probation upon recidivism: A comparative analysis," *American Journal of Criminal Justice*, 9(2), p. 160.

[48] Sechrest, Dale (1989) "Prison 'boot camps' do not measure up," *Federal Probation*, 53(3), p. 16. According to MacKenzie (1990, supra, p. 49), there is significant variation between states in the dropout rate, ranging from less than 3 percent in Georgia and about 40 percent in New York, Louisiana, and Florida.

[49] Id.

[50] Id. at 16-17.

[51] Id. at 17.

[52] See MacKenzie, note 1 above at 51.

[53] MacKenzie, Doris L. (1989) "The parole performance of offenders released from shock incarceration (boot camp prisons): A survival time analysis," presented at the American Probation and Parole Association 14th Annual Training Institute, Milwaukee, Wis.—August.

[54] Mackenzie, Davis L., Shaw, James W., and Gowdy, Voncile B. (1993) An evaluation of shock incarceration in Louisiana, Washington, D.C.: Nat. Inst. of Justice, June, pp. 4 and 6.

[55] New York State Division of Program Planning, Research and Evaluation, (1990) "Shock incarceration in New York State: The corrections experience," (1990) The Second Annual Report to the Legislature, Albany, NY, p. 50.

[56] See note 21 above at 51.

[57] See MacKenzie, note 1 above at 51.

[58] MacKenzie, Doris L. (1990) "Boot camps: An initial assessment of the program and parole performance of drug-involved offenders," presented at the American Society of Criminology annual meeting, Baltimore, MD, November.

[59] See MacKenzie, and Shaw, note 44 above.

[60] See MacKenzie, note 1 above at 49.

[61] Mackenzie, Davis L., Shaw, James W., and Gowdy, Voncile B. (1993) An evaluation of shock incarceration in Louisiana, Washington, D.C.: Nat. Inst. of Justice, June.

[62] See Marlette, note 25 above at 10.

[63] News article reproduced from *Fort Worth Star-Telegram*, 17 Mar. 1991, p. B2.

[64] See note 53 above at 17.

[65] Id. at 33.

[66] Id. at 33-34.

[67] Florida Department of Corrections (1989) Boot camp evaluation and boot camp recommitment rate," Tallahassee, FL: Bureau of Planning, Research and Statistics; see MacKenzie, note 61 above.

[68] See Sechrest, note 47 above at 18.

[69] "Boot camps seen lowering recidivism," (1991) *Law Enforcement News*,. 15 May 1991, 17(336, 337), p. 3.

[70] "Boot camps facing vacancy problem," *Fort Worth Star-Telegram*, 17 Mar. 1991, p. B2; "Justice Council picks Mansfield for boot camp," *Fort Worth Star-Telegram*, 9 Feb. 1991, p. 1; "Leaders add funds to jail deal," *Fort Worth Star-Telegram*, p. B1.

[71] See Marlette, note 25 above at 33.

[72] Morash, Merry and Rucker, Lila (1990) "A critical look at the idea of boot camp as a correctional reform," *Crime and Delinquency*, 36(2), p. 210.

[73] Osler, Mark W. (1991) "Shock incarceration: Hard realities and real possibilities," *Federal Probation*, 55(1), pp. 40-41.

[74] See note 70 above at 209.

[75] Id. at 215, 216.

10

The Privatization
of Prisons

The period extending from 1980 through 1992 featured conservative leadership in the uppermost reaches of government. One priority of this conservative leadership was the reduction of reliance upon government for provision of a wide range of services. In 1984 the Grace Commission issued a report concluding that $424 billion could be saved within three years if private initiatives were adopted in place of traditional governmental processes.[1] As a result of both conservative ideological inclinations and the appearance of data such as appeared in the Grace Report, private enterprise has been encouraged to increase its role in areas typically reserved for government. For instance, cities have contracted with private companies for trash removal, security, fire protection, medical services, and educational services.[2]

The correctional system also has been affected by this general trend toward reducing the size and function of government. In the first half of the 1980s the National Institute of Corrections conducted a national study of private sector involvement in the correctional system. The study, published in 1984, revealed that almost 80 percent of the states use correctional services provided by the private sector.[3]

The interest in private corrections continued to grow during the 1980s, and by the end of the decade about 9,000 beds in adult correctional facilities were in private institutions.[4] Clearly the private sector is already heavily involved in correctional activities. In this chapter we examine the viability of correctional privatization as a solution to some of the major problems confronting the correctional system. Although community-based and juvenile facilities have attracted attention from the private sector, in addressing the current controversy over privatization our focus will be on adult institutional corrections. We begin with examinations of the major justifications for the transfer of correctional responsibilities to the private sector, current penetration of the private sector into corrections, and the primary forms such private involvement can assume. A brief account of the history of private sector participation in institutional corrections is presented, followed by analysis of the major concerns regarding privatization. We conclude with a discussion of the problems associated with the evaluation of correctional privatization.

Why Privatize?

In view of the multitude of difficulties confronting the correctional system it is not surprising that numerous justifications have been put forth in favor of privatization. Perhaps most visible is the claim that private initiatives can reduce the cost of corrections.[5] This is no minor claim given the anticipated correctional expenditures for the upcoming decade. The National Council on Crime and Delinquency has projected that it will require a minimum of $35 billion to build and operate state prisons over the five-year period from 1989 to 1994.[6] Even more pessimistically, John DiIulio estimates that by the year 2000 corrections expenditures may reach $40 billion annually.[7]

Advocates of private sector involvement argue that the profit-motive has operated as an effective mechanism for reducing costs in other spheres of enterprise and can accomplish the same objective in the correctional system. For instance, private companies interested in operating a jail will have to compete with other private contractors to obtain the right to operate the facility. In drafting their competitive proposals, forethought will thus necessarily be invested in identifying methods of jail operation that restrain costs. Presumably, contractors who are most successful in devising efficient operational plans will have the best chance of being awarded contracts. This layer of planning and forethought is absent under conventional government operation. In addition, because of the desire to maximize profits, incentives will exist for private entrepreneurs to continuously seek the most efficient methods for running institutions. Again, this incentive does not exist under conventional government operation. Private sector advocates claim that they can discharge correctional responsibilities at 10 to 25 percent less than the cost of traditional government operation.[8]

A related justification concerns the increase in the quality of service provision. In part as a result of enhancements in cost-efficiency, it is projected that private operations will be able to provide better quality services per dollar invested. In the words of a former official of the Corrections Corporation of America, enthusiasts of private prisons

> declare that private sector prisons will be operated according to higher standards and thereby improve the quality of service. Even if this were not so, they maintain, the introduction of competition into what is now a government monopoly will inevitably improve existing conditions.[9]

The provision of high-quality services, according to this line of reasoning, will be in the interest of private contractors because it will enhance the appeal of subsequent bids for contract renewal.

The third major justification concerns increased flexibility to meet changing needs. One of the main criticisms of traditional government-operated corrections is that it is heavily bureaucratized and thus extremely slow to implement change. The long-standing citizen gripe about government in general, that it is characterized by too much "red tape," can be applied to the correctional system. Ponderous slow-responding bureaucratic organization is simply not adequate to handle the stresses and strains associated with quickly changing penal conditions.

The rapid increase in the size of the correctional population during the 1980s and early 1990s, represents a perfect example of such change. The correctional system has not been able to keep pace with this increase, and as a result 38 states are currently under court order regarding overcrowding-related problems.[10] A system based more heavily on private initiatives might be far more responsive to changing conditions.[11]

Thus a fourth, and related, justification for privatization concerns handling dramatically increasing prison populations. With significant numbers of states currently under court-ordered prison population caps, many states are finding it necessary to release inmates early in order to make room for new admissions.[12] Not surprisingly, such release policies do not generate much popular enthusiasm. The private sector's capacity to create new prison space quickly represents a real attraction to states trying to remain in conformity with court orders while at the same time continuing to confine their dangerous offender population. In addition, leasing prison space from private companies makes it possible for government to handle prison populations in times of high demand while avoiding being saddled with expensive and empty facilities if and when prison populations decline.

Finally, as we have already discussed in a previous chapter, recent changes in penal law reflect an enhanced interest in retributive and incapacitative aspects of punishment and a decrease in the importance of rehabilitation. Nonetheless, there continues to exist a substantial amount of interest in rehabilitation.[13] Some advocates of privatization have suggested that the interest in rehabilitation can be served by the infusion of private energy into corrections. Joseph Fenton of Buckingham Security, one of the initial entrants into the field of private corrections, argues that "[c]orrections is not meeting its intended purpose. . . . Corrections is intended to positively modify criminal habit patterns, rather than reinforce them. Perhaps the private sector, which has a vested interest in the success of its program, can reestablish the intended purpose of corrections."[14] The general argument actually contains three important components. First, some of the evidence emerging on the effectiveness of rehabilitation during the last 20 years has called into question the ability of traditional government-operated rehabilitation programs.[15] Despite having the entire course of the twentieth century to develop effective rehabilitative programs, to some analysts this research suggests that government has failed to demonstrate an ability to rehabilitate significant numbers of offenders.

Second, the special interests of private entrepreneurs will create an environment that will be conducive to rehabilitation. The economic motives of contractors, for instance, will provide incentives for them to develop effective prison industry programs. These programs can generate revenue to further enhance contractor financial positions. Because of the economic interests involved, these programs will not resemble the "make-work" programs devised by government primarily to keep inmates busy. Nor will they involve "industries" that provide no useful skills-training for inmates such as the traditional government license plate industries. The industries that will prove most attractive to private entrepreneurs are those producing goods to meet real market demands. Thus prison industry programs will provide experience for inmates in industries that exist outside as well as inside the institution. Ultimately, this experience will help inmates obtain and maintain post-release employment.

Finally, if contract renewal is closely tied to recidivism rates, incentives will exist for entrepreneurs to invest resources in rehabilitative programs. This is an old idea that can be traced at least as far back as Jeremy Bentham. In his discussion of prison labor under the auspices of private contractors Bentham argued,

> Nor do I see why labour should be the less reforming for being profitable. On the contrary, among working men, especially among working men whom the discipline of the house would so effectually keep from all kinds of mischief, I must confess I know of no test of reformation so plain or so sure as the improved quality and value of their work.[16]

Although the motive for such investment is production of profit rather than general humanitarian concerns, these initiatives may nonetheless prove more effective than those mounted as humanitarian enterprises.

Thus cost efficiency, service quality, flexibility, reduction of penal crowding, and enhancement of rehabilitative capability represent some of the major justifications for involvement of the private sector in corrections. We will return to consider some of the concerns that have been raised regarding these justifications.

Current Penetration of Correctional Privatization

Correctional privatization assumes a wide variety of forms. Some forms involve assumption of substantial correctional responsibilities by the private sector, while in other forms the private sector acts in a relatively minor subsidiary role. A well-developed critical understanding of the potential of correctional privatization requires comprehension of these various forms. The unfortunate tendency of both critics and enthusiasts of privatization has been to focus on the shortcomings or advantages of those initiatives that support their own viewpoints without due consideration for other kinds of privatization approaches. This is unfortunate because a problem associated with one form of privatization may not occur with another form. Although the primary focus in this chapter is upon privatized facility ownership and management, in this section we consider the major forms that correctional privatization may assume, including facility financing, facility construction and management, prison industries, and provision of services.

According to a National Institute of Corrections survey, 32 kinds of correctional services are provided by the private sector. Most frequent are health-related services, followed by community treatment centers, facility construction, educational programs, drug treatment, staff training, college programs, counseling, vocational training, and a variety of other services.[17] The survey was done in the early 1980s. Since then, considerable energy has been committed to development of the private sector's role in facility ownership and management. Numerous facilities have been opened by or turned over to the private sector during the 1980s.[18] These facilities represent both juvenile and adult systems and now encompass institutional environments ranging from minimum to maximum security. In addition, institutions operated by local, state, and federal agencies can now be found under private management. Immigration and Naturalization Detention Centers, local jails, state prerelease centers, juvenile institutional facilities, and women's institutions were in operation in private hands at the beginning of the 1990s.[19]

Private ownership and management of correctional institutions is probably the most controversial aspect of correctional privatization. Although the correctional system has long contracted for various private services with good results, contracting for facility ownership and management is a significant departure from traditional reliance on private support services.

We turn now to consideration of some of the major forms correctional privatization has assumed in the past decade, beginning with facility financing.

Current Forms of Facility Financing

One of the most difficult stages in the planning and development of a new correctional facility is arranging the financing necessary to support construction. There are several methods that traditionally have been used to finance the building of new correctional institutions.

One common method involves issuing general obligation bonds. These bonds assure that investors will be repaid because they are backed by the taxing power of the state.[20] Revenue raised through these bonds is used to construct the facility, and the debt represented by these bonds is paid by government over time. Data from the National Institute of Justice indicate that about half of the states planned to finance new prison construction through bonds.[21] In many jurisdictions voter approval is required before such bonds can be issued. Not surprisingly, there have been numerous occasions when citizens refused to approve such bonds.[22]

When voters do reject bond issues, there are alternative methods to obtain the necessary resources. Lease arrangements permit government to lease a facility financed by a private investment firm. Such a lease may ultimately result in ownership being transferred to government or ownership may be retained by the private firm. In either case, voter approval is generally not required to enter into such an agreement, thus public officials unable to persuade the citizenry to approve a bond issue can still secure funding for new prison space.[23] This is exactly what transpired in Jefferson County, Colorado after voters refused on two occasions to approve a sales tax increase designed to generate revenue for prison construction. Funding was arranged through E.F. Hutton for a lease purchase agreement.[24]

Critics of such practices argue that they represent loopholes making it possible for public officials to ignore the public will. The requirement mandating public approval of funding through the bond process was designed to render visible government operations and to place limits on public expenditure processes. Lease purchase agreements make it possible to circumvent both objectives.

Facility Ownership and Management

A state may engage the private sector to finance and construct a penal facility while retaining government ownership of the facility. Under an alternative arrangement the private company would become the owner of the newly constructed facility and would either lease it to the state or operate the institution itself. New Mexico's recently opened (1989) prison for female felons is owned and operated by the Corrections Corporation of America (CCA). The state retains the right to purchase the facility if it decides to terminate the relationship with CCA. In Florida, CCA built an annex to the Bay County Jail, which it also manages. In a somewhat different arrangement, the Silverdale Detention Center in Hamilton County, Tennessee is leased by Hamilton County to CCA, which is then responsible for its operation.

As demonstrated by these examples, there are a number of ways in which government and private industry may work together in constructing, owning, and operating incarcerative facilities. Which methods are most sensible depend on a variety of contingencies, such as government's current fiscal position, anticipated needs in the near- and long-term future, and willingness of private companies to enter into arrangements with government. At the time of the National Institute of Justice survey published in 1984, there were no adult prisons being operated by the private sector. However, by the end of the 1980s more than 20 adult confinement facilities with approximately 9,000 beds were in operation.[25]

Focus 10-1
Venus Pre-Release Center[26]

The Venus Pre-Release Center is a minimum to medium security prison operated by the Corrections Corporation of America. It is situated in Venus, Texas, a suburb in the Dallas-Fort Worth metroplex. The facility was opened in 1989 and has a 500-bed capacity. In accordance with Texas regulations, the facility is accredited by the American Correctional Association.

Venus serves Texas Department of Corrections inmates who are transferred from state-operated penal facilities. Inmates must be within two years of their parole date to qualify for residence at Venus. Part of the mission of the prison is to provide such inmates with experiences that will enhance their probability of success once released back into the community. To accomplish this objective the prison offers a wide variety of services. Each inmate is subjected to a needs assessment upon arrival at the prison, and the results of this assessment determine the kinds of services that will be made available to the inmate. Such services include basic living skills training such as driver's education and pre-employment training. Conventional academic courses, such as the GED program, are offered, and inmates with advanced education may enroll in college-level courses. Special certificate programs are also offered in areas such as Culinary Food Service, Automated Warehousing, and Refrigeration and Air Conditioning. For inmates with drug or alcohol abuse histories, substance abuse counseling is provided, both in individual and group formats.

As is typical in many state-operated prisons, inmates who are not enrolled in academic classes are expected to spend part of their time working on institutional jobs. Such jobs involve activities in food service, maintenance, janitorial services and a variety of other areas.

Venus provides many recreational opportunities for

inmates. Weight equipment, basketball and handball courts, ping pong, softball, and volleyball are a few of the leisure activities available. In addition, library services are available for inmates, including law library access.

As a relatively new private institution, the Venus facility has not yet been subjected to rigorous impact evaluation. The initial contract award to CCA was for two years. CCA has now been awarded a renewal of this original agreement and plans to expand the scope of its programs during the next few years. Part of this expansion will include more attention to impact evaluation.

In states where the management of correctional facilities has been turned over to private enterprise, the state has retained various kinds of authority and monitorship functions. Such arrangements are typically contractually stipulated in an effort to insure that the private company is complying with the terms of the agreement. This is especially important in light of the fact that the transfer of correctional responsibilities to the private sector does not appear to release the state from responsibility for the consequences of institutional management.[27] If an inmate is assaulted by a private prison guard, for instance, the state nonetheless retains liability. The case of Medina v. O'Neill involved a prison guard in a privately operated Houston detention center who, during an escape attempt, shot and killed one inmate and wounded another. Although the state attempted to avoid liability by asserting that the victims were in the custody of the private agents, the District Court ruled that contractual delegation of state authority to private firms does not relieve the state of liability.[28] Although this is a new area in law, and the precise nature of governmental liability in contractual arrangements with the private sector is yet to be fully established, some correctional officials are concerned that lawsuits will become a regular and expensive cost to the state. Pennsylvania's Commissioner of Corrections suggests that jurisdictions electing to implement privatization in corrections will find it necessary to significantly increase legal staff to process the large number of lawsuits that will ultimately be filed.[29]

There has been a rapid spread of the privatization of institutional management during the past decade. However, a former Corrections Corporation of America official estimates that less than 2 percent of American inmates are housed in privately operated programs.[30] Although considerable heat has been generated over the privatization issue, even under the most facilitative circumstances one wonders whether a significant percentage of inmates will end up in privately operated facilities.

Prison Industries

More than half of the states now permit private companies to operate prison industries.[31] There are several arrangements under which the private sector is involved in prison industries. In the piece-price system the contractor provides raw materials and equipment and then purchases finished products for a fixed price per item. Leasing arrangements typically involve permitting inmates to work for a lessee outside of the facility often under the total supervision of the contractor. Some arrangements under the lease system have involved rental of entire prisons to private business. The company then assumes responsibility for the entire operation and may have the use of inmate labor to make products to generate revenue. Under the contract system the private entrepreneur generally provides raw materials and tools, pays a fee to the state, then markets the inmate-produced goods on the free market. Other systems of prison labor, such as the public works, public account, and the state use systems, do not involve private industry.

A current example of one form such arrangements assume is the computer disk drive assembly plant in the Minnesota State Prison at Stillwater. Inmates assemble computer equipment under the supervision of Control Data Corporation-trained employees of the Minnesota Correctional Industries.[32]

In an alternative arrangement, inmates of the Arizona Center for Women are permitted to leave the facility daily to work at the Best Western International, Inc. Reservation Center. All supervision is provided by Best Western employees, and wages begin at $4.50 per hour. Best Western has also hired some of its inmate workers subsequent to the worker's release from prison.[33]

Service Provision

Private companies have long been involved in providing special services to the correctional system. This is especially apparent in the juvenile system. According to a survey commissioned by the National Institute of Corrections, in the mid-1980s, 70 percent of all contracts with the private sector were with correctional agencies responsible for juveniles or for both juveniles and adults.[34] The survey revealed that more than 30 types of services were provided by private companies, including health care, education, drug treatment, vocational training, counseling, and construction.[35] Such services have been provided within the context of both state-operated and privately operated facilities.

Summary of Forms of Private Sector Involvement

There are thus a number of forms that may be assumed by correctional privatization. Although there are many potential benefits and hazards associated with correctional privatization, it is important that they be analyzed within the contexts of the specific forms assumed by privatization.

We have already discussed some of the anticipated advantages of privatization and will soon examine some of the hazards of the reform. In light of the lengthy American experience with privatization in the nineteenth-century, and in an effort to better inform the discussion of modern benefits and liabilities, we turn first to consideration of the early American experience with correctional privatization.

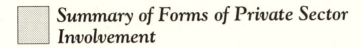

Punishment and Privatization in Early America

The history of private involvement in corrections in America extends back to the early colonial period. Unfortunately, this history is largely unknown to many of those expressing views on the value of private involvement in corrections. Possibly the first instance of private involvement in corrections occurred in 1634 in Massachusetts. Funds were raised through private subscriptions to fund the construction of a fort on Castle Island. This facility was originally intended to serve in the defense of the Massachusetts Bay Colony, but it also held troublesome convicts who could not be satisfactorily secured in Boston's common prison. The first offender of record was admitted in 1636.[36] In Maryland a private plantation was utilized as a private incarcerative facility in 1662.[37] In 1666 a private citizen entered into an agreement with the colony of Maryland to build a prison in exchange for 1,000 pounds of tobacco and a lifetime appointment as keeper of the facility.[38]

After the American Revolution there were increasing numbers of initiatives designed to allow the private sector greater involvement in corrections. The Walnut Street Jail in Pennsylvania operated its prison industries on what would now be referred to as the piece-price system.[39] In 1797 Newgate of New York opened, and within the first five years of operation attempted to utilize private contractors.[40] Inmate crowding led the New York state legislature to authorize the construction of Auburn Prison in 1816. Auburn ultimately served as the model for the congregate system that would be emulated throughout the country. From almost the very outset private contractors were permitted to operate various prison industries in the facility.[41]

The New York case is of special interest, and merits detailed discussion. Many of the difficulties encountered in New York, as well as the solutions adopted to handle these dilemmas, came to typify the experience of other states in both the North and South. In the first half of the nineteenth century New York struggled with several of the correctional problems currently being encountered.

To begin with, New York prisons were endemically overcrowded. Increasing prison populations forced the state legislature to construct new prisons to handle the growing number of inmates. Newgate opened in 1797, and was followed by Auburn in 1816, Sing Sing in 1825, and Dannemora in 1845.

In addition, the state was seriously concerned about both the costs of creating new facility capacity and maintaining the inmates confined in the prisons. Although this was the opening era of the American penitentiary movement, the citizenry and legislators were far less interested in inmate reformation than were the highly visible penal reformers of the age.[42] In addition, early nineteenth-century New York was not characterized by the kind of heavy state-level involvement that is typical of modern American society. As a result there was substantial resistance to taxing citizens to support the increasing number of prisons and prisoners in the state. Not surprisingly, therefore, the legislature applied substantial pressure on prison administrators to operate economically self-sufficient prisons. In 1833 the legislature criticized the management of Sing Sing and Auburn by noting that prisons in Connecticut and Massachusetts had managed to produce profits well in excess of what had been achieved in New York.[43] This pressure produced results. Under the administration of Robert Wiltse, Sing Sing produced substantial economic surpluses during the 1830s. Auburn also managed to create surpluses through most of the 1830s.[44]

In both Auburn and Sing Sing private entrepreneurs were permitted to bring materials and equipment into the prisons. Originally, the contractors themselves were not allowed into the shops where they might have contact with inmates. The reason for this was simple. In the words of warden Elam Lynds,

> When I was at the head of Auburn prison, I had made, with different contractors, contracts which even prevented them from entering the penitentiary. Their presence in the workshop cannot be but injurious to discipline.[45]

Despite the concern that contact with the inmate would have damaging effects on the discipline of the institution, the efficiency of industrial operations was seriously impeded by this restrictive policy. New York eventually abandoned the separation rule.[46]

What occurred in New York also took place across the country. Private entrepreneurs gained increasing access to the prison and the inmates. In southern states this access went beyond the operation of prison industry programs in the prisons. Inmates were leased out to entrepreneurs and were then removed from the prisons and transported wherever the entrepreneur chose to put them to work. The entrepreneur provided food, shelter, clothing, as well as supervision and security.[47] In other states, such as California, the prisons themselves were turned over to entrepreneurs who assumed responsibility for all aspects of operation.[48] During the second half of the nineteenth century the private sector was heavily involved in corrections in a significant number of states. In some states substantial amounts of revenue were generated to offset the cost of operating penitentiary systems.

The spread of private sector involvement in corrections had not, however, gone unchallenged. In the 1860s Enoch Wines and Timothy Dwight toured the American prison system in an effort to obtain an up-to-date view of current penal conditions. They were not pleased with much of what they observed. Among other problems they noted that

> [t]here is not a state prison in America in which reformation of the convicts is the one supreme object of the discipline[49] . . . one string is harped upon ad nauseam—money, money, money.[50]

The concern with producing revenue, and the utilization of private contractors to pursue this objective, had become a dominant theme within the first half-century of the initiation of the American prison system. Wardens unable to maintain economically productive facilities were soon replaced.[51] Both crowding and economics forced even the crown jewel of the solitary system, Eastern State Penitentiary, to compromise its reformative agenda. The cells once used to house single inmates began to hold two prisoners.[52] The fervor for revenue thus diminished the investment of effort in inmate reform.

There were other difficulties. In New York there were protests from both business and labor. Labor argued that permitting inmates to produce goods for sale in the market created unfair competition that resulted in a loss in the number of jobs available to law-abiding citizens. This was especially troublesome because inmate labor was very inexpensive, and thus products produced through such labor could be sold cheaply. Companies using inmates were therefore in a position to put other companies, and the free laborers that worked for them, out of work.[53]

Free labor also objected to the trades training being provided by entrepreneurs. Inmates in some institutions, such as New York, were receiving training to enable them to work while in prison. Upon release inmates were able to assume competitive positions in the employment market because of their prison-provided training. Free workers objected that once again they were being placed at a disadvantage.[54]

Businesses that had been unable to gain contracts for inexpensive inmate labor complained that they too were at a disadvantage. Moreover, they charged that contract bid systems were actually rigged, and that contracts were renewed without a fair competitive assessment of the proposals submitted.[55]

Such complaints created political pressure that resulted in a string of legislation restricting private enterprise in the correctional system. In 1842 the New York legislature placed limits on trades instruction in prison, the kinds of goods that could be produced, and the numbers of inmates that could be employed in various industries.[56]

Again, what took place in New York occurred other places as well. Numerous states passed legislation either outlawing or restricting privately operated prison industries. By the end of the nineteenth century private involvement in prison industries, as well as involvement in other aspects of corrections, had dwindled. The prisons that had been turned over to private companies were back in state hands. Prison shops were managed by state employees, and the products typically sold to state agencies.[57]

Thus, the first American experiment with correctional privatization was concluded by the end of the first quarter of the twentieth century. During the experiment, private entrepreneurs operated in-facility industrial programs, leased penal facilities from the state, and assumed supervision over convicts in their own privately constructed facilities. In some states during certain periods of time the engagement of the private sector did produce substantial economic surpluses. As we will see in our discussion of the potential hazards of correctional privatization, however, a number of undesired consequences also emerged during the experiment.

Major Concerns Regarding Modern Correctional Privatization

Although the crises confronting the correctional system have engendered substantial enthusiasm for privatization, the modern privatization reform movement has not been without its critics. In this section we consider the major criticisms articulated by skeptics and attempt to provide some sense of the extent to which each potential hazard is likely to represent difficulties. Naturally, any reform can be challenged by skeptics, and there are numerous potential difficulties associated with virtually any proposed alteration in correctional practice. The task of the policy analyst is to sort out the concerns meriting attention from those unlikely to represent legitimate difficulties. This section attempts to contribute to this sorting process. We will consider the right to punish, the profit motive, legal liability, cost efficiency, service quality, government dependency, expansion of the use of incarceration, and abuse of inmates.

The Right to Punish

Perhaps the most fundamental criticism of correctional privatization is the contention that the right and the power to punish is reserved for and limited to the state. The view expressed by the American Civil Liberties Union articulates this perspective.

We see the potential for serious abuse in the delegation of the control and custody of prisoners. No one but the state should possess the awesome responsibility or power to take away an individual's freedom; freedom should not be contracted to the lowest bidder.[58]

There are three basic kinds of responses to this criticism. First, it can be argued that in a representative democracy the government is empowered by the populace to conduct its business in whatever manner seems most effective, subject to the wishes of the electorate and the stipulations of the Constitution. Government regularly delegates power to the private sector for a variety of responsibilities. In the absence of any constitutional prohibition or the objection of the electorate, private sector engagement in handling correctional responsibilities seems quite permissible. Second, designating the private sector to carry out various aspects of the administration of punishment does not represent an abandonment of the proper role of government. Government has not transferred the power to punish, but merely employed citizens who are not government employees to administer the punishment.[59] Finally, as we have already seen, the state has an extensive historical tradition of turning over various functions of the correctional system to private entrepreneurs. The courts have never ruled that this practice represents an abrogation of the constitutionally specified responsibilities of government.

At the heart of this issue is probably not what is permissible under law or tradition, but rather what *ought* to be permitted. The question is thus a moral question, relying more upon ideology than upon law or tradition for an answer. This is not the place to elaborate on the philosophic basis of government, but in fact the issue is unlikely to represent a significant obstacle to the privatization process. Law and tradition both make quite clear that privatization has been, and continues to be, an acceptable alternative to conventional governmental discharge of public responsibilities.

▒ The Profit Motive in Corrections

A second concern expressed by critics of privatization involves the role of the profit motive in the administration of justice. Mark A. Cunniff, executive director of the National Association of Criminal Justice Planners, wonders whether the government wants

to undertake a public policy that makes the administration of punishment a money-making proposition? Does the government want to emphasize such a mercenary value as profit in its response to a social problem as opposed to values as fairness, equity, and personal accountability.[60]

More specifically, Anderson and his colleagues worry that

[w]hen the private corrections provider operates on a "for profit" basis, then the requirements of profitability can lead to programmatic and humanitarian shortfalls which have been part of the legacy of the past, such as inmate warehousing, labor subleasing, substandard food services, health, sanitation, and medical abuses, and the like.[61]

In sum, the fear is that the presence of the profit motive in corrections will result in a variety of practices that are antithetical to the objectives of punishment and to the maintenance of humanitarian conditions within prisons.

Defenders of privatization respond by noting that government has been less than successful in its pursuit of the objectives of punishment. Research on rehabilitative programs has failed to produce clear evidence that the state-operated system has achieved rehabilitative goals.[62] The evidence on deterrence is at best mixed, and it remains highly controversial whether incapacitative effects are of a magnitude to be of any real importance.[63] Moreover, it can be argued that retributive goals have fallen by the wayside as offenders are released prior to the full completion of their sentences. These early release policies have been adopted as states struggle to meet court-ordered population caps.[64] This dismal record, in the view of advocates of privatization, suggests that traditional government initiatives have both been unable to achieve correctional objectives in the past and are unlikely to have greater success in the future.

Beyond pointing out the failures of government, advocates of privatization note that the profit-motive has been successful in a variety of other spheres of traditional government operation, such as health care and trash collection, and that with proper government restraint and monitoring, there is no reason why the private sector cannot make a contribution in the field of corrections.

Defenders of the profit motive also argue that attacks on the pursuit of profit in corrections reflect an ideological bias against the profit motive in general. According to this argument, critics of the profit motive in corrections are often doing little more than expressing a general distrust of the profit motive as an incentive for action.

Although defenders of privatization may be correct in noting that there may be an ideological basis for some of the profit-motive-related criticisms levied at privatization, ultimately the criticisms of privatization must stand or fall on their merits rather than on the character of the motives of critics. Whether profit-motivated corrections will facilitate achievement of correctional objectives is ultimately an empirical question that will have to be answered over time and primarily through research, rather than through ideological struggle.

There is, however, a fair amount of evidence on nineteenth-century correctional privatization suggesting that the profit motive may lead to a variety of undesired consequences. For instance, the pursuit of profits on the part of both states and entrepreneurs resulted in numerous abuses of inmates in Auburn and Sing Sing during the first half of the nineteenth century. Inmates went without adequate food, clothing, and medical care. In addition, the pursuit of profits in privately operated prison industries resulted in various kinds of corruption, such as the payment of bribes.[65] In privately operated work camps in the South inmates were subjected to extreme hardship, and many of them died as a result of the severe conditions.[66] Lessees were often reluctant to invest anything beyond the bare minimum in the care and feeding of convicts. This neglect led to a series of investigations, some of which eventuated in the termination of contracts with private companies. In Mississippi, for instance, charges of abominable conditions led the state legislature to conduct an investigation of its privately operated penal camps. A grand jury investigation followed the legislative inquiry, and in the 1890s the system was abandoned.[67]

The historical record makes clear that in their pursuit of profits entrepreneurs have indeed engaged in practices resulting in abuses of inmates, compromises in correctional objectives, and violations of law. The significance of this historical reality is not that it proves that profit-motivated corrections cannot work. Rather, the record both renders visible the kinds of difficulties that may develop in a privatized correctional system and provides insight into the causes of such difficulties. The availability of historical information should be of value to policy analysts attempting to devise correctional strategies that will avoid the hazards encountered during the course of the nineteenth-century privatization experiment. It may, of course, eventually become evident that privatized corrections simply cannot avoid the major problems encountered in nineteenth-century initiatives. On the other hand, knowledge of earlier mistakes may make it possible to avoid a repetition.

Unfortunately, at this writing there has been relatively little interest in examining the history of the impact of the profit motive in American corrections. There exists a substantial amount of primary and secondary material on this history, yet adequate private or governmental funding has not been made available to support such historical investigations.

Legal Liability

A third objection to correctional privatization concerns the extent of the state's legal liability for the consequences of the acts of private providers. Suppose, for instance, that a private company is permitted to build, own, and operate a prison. Within the first year of operation the prison catches fire and burns to the ground. Several inmates are killed in the blaze, and it is demonstrated that the fire was the result of the private company's failure to observe the local fire code. Is the private company liable for damages or is the state, which authorized the company to confine the convicts, ultimately responsible? If the state retains its liability, then obviously the implications are significant. In this hypothetical example the state's failure to assure the private facility's conformity with fire codes would result in potentially expensive liability. To avoid such liability exposure the state would have to establish effective monitorship mechanisms.[68] Critics of privatization argue that the costs of establishing and maintaining such necessary mechanisms will offset cost advantages that might otherwise be obtained from employment of private companies.

In fact, the evidence does indicate that the state cannot avoid liability by contracting out correctional operations. In his legal analysis of privatization for the American Bar Association, Ira Robbins notes, "One argument in favor of private incarceration has been that it will eliminate, or at least reduce, government liability. This argument does not withstand examination."[69]

A case in point is the previously noted case of Medina v. O'Neill. The death of one inmate and the serious injury of another in an escape attempt led to a lawsuit against the Immigration and Naturalization Service. In the trial and the final appeal of the trial court decision, the courts held both the government and the private company liable for damages.[70]

Thus it seems clear that problems regarding state liability must be worked out before widespread engagement of private facility operation becomes a reality. In particular, attention needs to be committed to

277

specification of the extent and character of such liability and to the development of mechanisms to assure contractor compliance with contractual provisions.

Cost Savings

Critics of privatization argue that although the potential for saving substantial amounts of money is one of the major appeals of private sector involvement in corrections, much of the anticipated savings are merely illusory. The critics point out that many private businesses go bankrupt every year, that industry consolidation may actually reduce incentives for price competitiveness, and that in other areas such as trash collection, parking meter coin collections, and health care, there have been some conspicuous cost failures.[71]

At this point in the development of the debate there is relatively little evidence demonstrating the cost-superiority of the private sector in corrections. Both the National Institute of Justice and the states of Massachusetts and Pennsylvania examined the cost issues and concluded that current evidence is both anecdotal and unreliable.[72] A recent General Accounting Office analysis of private prisons concluded that

> [o]fficials of state governments that have recently used privatization say that it has demonstrated potential as a way to expand prison capacity quickly and economically. Further, they say it has generally provided the same level of service at lower cost. However, existing empirical studies on service and cost are inconclusive; thus more research and testing is needed.[73]

This evidence shortfall is in part due to the relatively brief period of time that adult prisons have been subjected to private management. A comparison of juvenile custodial centers, which have a longer history of private involvement, does provide some insight into the cost savings potential. An examination of approximately 3,000 juvenile custodial centers found virtually no difference between the cost per resident in private versus public facilities.[74] Data from adult facilities designed to handle adult illegal aliens for the Immigration and Naturalization Service also fail to reveal any clear cost savings in private facilities.[75]

An American Correctional Association report described one of the first relatively comprehensive cost analyses and reported the absence of evidence indicating that the privately managed Okeechobee School for

Boys decreased costs to the state.[76] A comparison of rates of cost increase between Okeechobee and the state-operated Dozier School for Boys found that, after a first year advantage in the rate of cost increase, the Okeechobee School showed virtually no advantage over Dozier.[77]

The struggle to provide cost-efficient services will not be without casualties. Even if it were the case that the majority of private facilities could provide at least some cost savings, both the fact that some will not be cost-effective and the threat of bankruptcy may cause public officials to temper their expectations. We have already seen private corporations lose significant amounts of money. Corrections Corporation of America, one of the most significant players in the private corrections industry, sustained a loss of $6.8 million between 1984 and 1986.[78] In addition, in 1986 a private prison in Pennsylvania, the 268 Center, declared bankruptcy under Chapter 11 and was placed under state supervision.[79]

Charles Logan's analysis of cost-effectiveness revealed mixed results. Although simple cost analyses indicated that some private facilities appear to be less expensive to run than public counterparts, in other cases public facilities were less expensive.[80] In summarizing his cost analysis Logan offers a cautious conclusion.

> Private prisons will not necessarily be less expensive than those owned and run directly by the government. . . . A very safe generalization from the broader literature on contracting for public services is that it often saves money, but sometimes it does not. It is too soon to say much more than that for prisons.[81]

This cautious assessment, offered by one of the more enthusiastic advocates of correctional privatization, suggests that the 10 to 25 percent savings suggested by privatization enthusiasts at the outset of the modern experiment represents an overly optimistic projection. Significant cost savings do not appear likely to provide a major basis for the shift to private corrections. Logan points out that the major economic benefit of private prisons may lie in their ability to render visible the actual costs of corrections.[82] One of the more difficult issues in assessing and comparing public and private costs is the lack of adequate data on public correctional costs. The focus on private alternatives to traditional government prisons may increase the interest in identifying the true costs of imprisonment.

One final point merits mention. The cost-efficiency argument is largely based on the idea that a competitive environment will motivate corrections service providers to find ways of providing services more efficiently, and thus at less cost. One of the major hazards to cost-efficiency under this rationale is a significant reduction in the number of competitors in the industry. The fewer the competitors, according to this line of thought, the easier it will be to informally eliminate significant competition. As a result, purchasers of services will have fewer real choices. A thriving competitive environment is generally, although not always, regarded as one with many energetic players working assiduously to attract business. Industry concentration is anathema to this ideal. There is evidence, however, that even at this early stage in the privatization industry concentration is already taking place. As of the fall of 1990, two-thirds of the beds in private adult correctional facilities were under the management of only two companies, Corrections Corporation of America and Wackenhut Corrections Corporation. The two firms generated about $70 million in revenue in 1989. This is an issue that bears watching during the coming decade.

Quality of Services

Another important concern of critics of privatization is that the quality of services provided by private firms will suffer as a result of the natural inclination to reduce costs to enhance profit margins. Beyond the difficult issue of defining quality, we again find that there is limited evidence on the extent to which this potential problem will become a significant issue.

The previously mentioned National Institute of Corrections survey of privately provided correctional services found that better service quality was the second most cited advantage of private sector contracting.[83] Although this survey dealt primarily with services rather than with facility ownership and management, it nonetheless provides some indication that correctional administrators are receptive to some kinds of private involvement in corrections. A more recent national survey of wardens conducted by Patrick Kinkade and Matthew Leone confirmed the continuing support of correctional administrators for certain kinds of private involvement in providing correctional services.[84]

With regard to facility ownership and management, the American Correctional Association (ACA) has established standards for correctional institutions. The ACA provides an accreditation process for institutions wishing to be considered for accreditation. Although most state public facilities are not accredited, a number of private facilities are required by contract to meet ACA standards. The Corrections

Corporation of America, for instance, has energetically pursued accreditation, and its Texas facilities are required by contract to be ACA certified. This stands in contrast to public facilities in the Texas penal system, which have not been required by law to be accredited.

Comprehensive comparative studies of service quality for the private versus public sector simply have not yet been done. Anecdotal evidence on institutions in Pennsylvania, Florida, and Tennessee is available but does not provide a consistent picture. Of this evidence shortfall Logan notes, "There has been almost no systematic empirical research comparing private and government-run prisons in terms of quality. Until such studies are available, we must rely upon . . . anecdotal evidence. . . . Evidence of this nature should be evaluated with caution."[85]

Governmental Dependency

The issue of governmental dependency reflects some of the ideological components of the general debate. The concern here is that if government turns over responsibility for correctional operations to the private sector and reduces its own capacity to meet those responsibilities, it leaves itself vulnerable. The state may elect to utilize private sector initiatives with growing frequency because such initiatives seem effective, yet ultimately this may result in a potentially debilitating over-reliance.

Assume, for purposes of illustration, that government comes to believe that the private sector can handle some of its responsibilities at less expense and with greater flexibility and efficiency. By indicating its willingness to use private services it essentially authorizes the creation of a new industry. This authorization may take the form of legislation removing restrictions on the involvement of private enterprise in the correctional sphere. (In recent years, for instance, more than 20 states have modified their laws to permit expansion of private sector involvement in prison-based industries.)[86] Companies respond to this new opportunity, the state obtains agreeable results, and the use of private sector initiatives expands. Before long, half of the institutionalized population is being held in private facilities owned and operated by a private company. Unfortunately, this company makes some poor management decisions and goes bankrupt. In response to the favorable initial results government has been able to sell off its own antiquated facilities, dismiss large numbers of staff, and dramatically trim the bureaucracy once required to run the state-operated institutions. Now what happens? Government has grown dependent on the private contractor's services and is unable to step in during a crisis and reassume responsibility for correctional functions.

Defenders of privatization respond to this scenario by arguing that if one company goes under another will be poised to step in and take its place. It is worth noting, however, that the more dependent government becomes on the private sector, the larger the companies will likely have to be to provide needed services. The larger the companies, the greater the capital investment required to enter the marketplace. The greater the required investment, the fewer the players that will be equipped to enter the market. As an example, consider the proposal submitted by the Corrections Corporation of America to take over the entire correctional system of Tennessee. The proposal was turned down, but assume for our discussion that it had been approved and implemented. Assume further that CCA then went bankrupt. The state apparatus would have been dismantled, and there would likely have been no other company with the enormous resources and expertise necessary to immediately step in and assume responsibility.

Nineteenth-century New York State provides an excellent case in point. The private entrepreneur operating Auburn's primary prison industry fell on hard times and was unable to make the contractually required payments for inmate labor. The state provided the contractor with additional time to pay, using his equipment as security. When the contractor remained unable to meet his obligations the state foreclosed on the equipment, intending to sell it off to recover lost payments. The state found, however, that there was no market for the equipment, and thus was essentially stuck with an uncollectible debt and unsalable equipment. No other contractor was available to fill the position occupied by the failed entrepreneur. The state was in a dilemma. If it terminated the contract it stood to lose all hope of recovering missed payments. In addition, terminating the contract would render idle 350 convicts, thus creating serious institutional management problems. Instead of being able to sell off the equipment, terminate the contract, and bring in a more successful entrepreneur, the state was forced to redraft the contract, providing more favorable terms to the contractor including several months free labor from all newly admitted inmates.[87] In practice, the dynamics of the marketplace did not prove capable of compensating for the business failure of the contractor, and the dependency of the state forced concessions that obviated the reasons for engaging the private sector in the first place.

The problem, therefore, is how to access the benefits of a competitive marketplace without eventually creating vulnerability that essentially places the state in a position of subordination to the companies it engages. This vulnerability may result in a forfeiture of whatever cost savings have been achieved and a loss of flexibility to respond to changing conditions. Again, it is unclear from the historical record whether the shackles of dependency can be avoided. What is clear is that efforts must be made to anticipate this difficulty before relations of dependency develop.

Encouragement of Excessive Use of Incarceration

One of the important arguments that can be adduced in support of privatization is that it will reduce substantially the cost of corrections. Nonetheless, skeptics suggest that the opposite effect may actually be achieved. States faced with increasing penal populations may be attracted by arrangements wherein they can reduce their per inmate/per day costs. It may be expected that because the cost of maintaining each inmate declines, the total cost of corrections will stabilize, perhaps even decline. As in any conventional supply and demand situation, however, the inexpensive product may induce the purchaser, in this case government, to purchase services to confine more inmates than it would have under more expensive supply circumstances. The concern is that the availability of relatively inexpensive correctional services will encourage policymakers and justice system operatives, such as judges, to place citizens under institutional confinement who might have otherwise been punished with noncustodial sanctions.[88]

Whether the increased willingness to use the custodial sanction is a positive development depends, of course, on one's view of whether the system currently confines too few or too many offenders. Conservatives may argue that if inexpensive corrections make it possible to remove greater numbers of offenders from society, then society is better off as a result. Liberals may point out that prisons already hold substantial numbers of non-dangerous property offenders, and that policy ought to be directed toward seeking alternatives to incarceration to address the crime problem.

In any event, at this early point in the development of the modern privatization initiative there is simply no evidence upon which to base a reasoned assessment of the inflationary impact of increasingly available prison space on prison populations. As the private corrections industry grows, and as the lobbying potential of the industry increases, critics will be watching closely for indications that the industry is stimulating the use of the incarcerative sanction for offenders previously punished with other means.

Abuses of Inmates

Social reform movements often create strange alliances. The privatization movement has led to such unlikely partners as the American Civil Liberties Union and the National Sheriff's Association. Both organizations have expressed concerns about the treatment of prisoners in private prisons. The ACLU has expressed concern that

> [p]risoners are likely to suffer deprivation because of placement in a private prison . . . private prisons are likely to have an adverse impact on various aspects of a prisoner's life . . . It is likely that a private prison will not comply with all the relevant health and safety standards.[89]

Although the modern privatization movement is so new that little evidence has emerged legitimizing this concern, scrutiny of the American experience with privatization in the nineteenth century provides serious cause for concern. It is a history laden with shocking abuses of inmates. Prisoners were forced by many private contractors to live in filthy, vermin-infested quarters, to endure merciless flogging, to work in, defecate in, and drink from the same water, to sleep in wet beds, and to suffer from inadequate nutrition.[90] In some states efforts to maximize profits led to unbelievable mortality rates—41 percent in Alabama for 1869.[91] Although conditions in public facilities were also often inadequate, the endless series of legislative investigations and actions to eliminate private involvement reflects, in part, recognition of the magnitude of abuses endured by inmates under private control.

Logan correctly points out that some of the abuses perpetrated in the nineteenth century took place under conditions that have no real modern analog.[92] Swamp-situated chain gangs, for instance, are unlikely to recur in the future. Many nineteenth-century contractors were also, however, given complete responsibility for running prisons that had been turned over to them by various state legislatures. The experience in these situations was no more heartening. The Louisiana experience, described in Focus 10-2, is an excellent example of the difficulties inmates faced in privately operated facilities.

Focus 10-2[93]
Post-Civil War Privatization in Louisiana

In 1869 the Louisiana legislature granted a lease of the state penitentiary to two private individuals, Huger and Jones. The governor, however, vetoed the lease, pointing out:

> There is too much power given to the lessees over the institution, and the Board of Control is ignored. The health, comfort, food, religious training, and discipline of the prisoners should be under the charge of disinterested officers of the government. . . . Where the lessees have absolute power over the prisoners the tendency is to work them too much and feed them too little and give no attention to their comforts and instruction.

The governor's action led the legislature to craft a new lease, giving the state more control over the issues of concern to the governor. This new lease was acceptable to the governor, and in the spring of 1869 it was signed.

The contractors promptly sold the lease to James, Buckner, and Company, clearing a profit of around $100,000. The lease did not provide for transfer to another firm, thus the legislature was forced to draft a second lease while the new contractor took control of the institution. The major figure in the company, Samuel James, then removed the inmates from the penitentiary to work them on farms, plantations and levees, despite having no legal authorization to do so. A lawsuit was filed against the company, challenging the removal of inmates. The threat of suit did not stop James from continuing to work inmates outside of the penitentiary, and for six consecutive years James failed to pay the rent stipulated in the lease. In addition, there was clear evidence that the company seriously mistreated convicts. According to one newspaper expose, they were brutally treated and everyone knows it. They are worked, mostly in swamps and plantations, from daylight to dark. Corporeal punishment is inflicted on the slightest provocation. . . . Anyone who has travelled along the lines of railroads that run through Louisiana's swamps . . . in which the levees are built, has seen these poor devils almost to their waists, delving in the black and noxious mud. . . . Theirs is a grievous lot a thousand times more grievous than the law ever contemplated they should endure in expiation of their sins.

Despite numerous clear violations of the law, James was well-connected politically and managed to retain control over state inmates until his death in 1894, the same year the legislature finally endorsed an anti-lease proposal.

Modern abuses of inmates will also be influenced by the involvement of the courts in correctional affairs. Many of the abuses perpetrated during the nineteenth century would be difficult to conceal under modern review policies. Developments in case law have accorded inmates judicial means of redress unavailable to nineteenth-century inmates. Nonetheless, private involvement raises issues of procedural visibility that need to be addressed. The relatively invisible internal environment of the penal institution makes it crucial that motivations to abuse inmates are minimized. If profitability is linked to cost savings, and cost savings are associated with treatment of inmates, then it becomes imperative that adequate monitoring mechanisms be implemented to assure that inmates will be able to take advantage of the rights granted to them by the courts. Jeremy Bentham was able to see the merit of this two hundred years ago. A proper prison design

enables the whole establishment to be inspected almost at a view . . . and not only on Sundays at the time of Divine service, but on ordinary days at meal times or times of work: providing therefore a system of inspection, universal, free, and gratuitous, the most effectual and permanent securities against abuse.[94]

Such visibility would ease the concerns that many critics have about private sector abuse of inmates hidden away from public view.

▨ *Summary of Major Concerns*

In this section we have considered some of the major difficulties that may impede the solution of correctional problems through privatization. One final observation merits comment before moving to discussion of the evaluation of privatization. The existence of potential hazards should neither be surprising nor be regarded as sufficient reason to abandon reform. There are few correctional reforms that do not entail the assumption of various kinds of risks. The real mission before us is to recognize these potential threats, design safeguards to protect against the harms represented by these hazards, and be willing to abandon ideology and make prudent choices when careful evaluation reveals that a concern is either well-founded or groundless.

Evaluating Privatization

Correctional reforms are generally proposed in an effort to solve difficulties confronting the correctional system. In view of this, it seems only reasonable that there would be considerable interest in determining whether such reforms actually accomplish the desired objectives. Correctional privatization is unexceptional in this regard. If the claims of privatization advocates are accurate there is much to be gained by deployment of the private sector. If they are mistaken, the losses associated with such deployment may be equally significant.

There are three basic types of evaluation that can be used in assessing correctional initiatives. First, process monitoring is useful to scrutinize the ongoing operations of private companies in their discharge of newly acquired responsibilities. Such monitoring can determine whether contractual stipulations are being met and can assure that violations of law are not occurring.

Second, operations research is intended to determine whether an institution's operations are producing the desired institutional outcomes. For instance, although a private institution may be following a contractually required security measure, the measure may not be achieving the security-related objectives for which the measure was designed. This kind of assessment can be valuable in determining whether intended

institutional activities are working in practice as intended in planning. When activities are not working as intended, mid-stream adjustments can be made to correct deficiencies.

The final general kind of evaluation is impact evaluation. The primary purpose of impact evaluation is to determine whether the anticipated objectives of the reform have been achieved. For instance, the decision to engage a private company to operate a local jail may be based upon the expectation that the company can operate the facility at 15 percent less cost than what would be possible under conventional government operation. Impact evaluation would be interested in determining whether that objective was achieved. Data on costs would be gathered over a trial period, then compared to cost data for previous government operation.

Despite the seeming simplicity that this brief description of the three kinds of evaluation may suggest, in practice evaluation is a tricky and often frustrating process. Evaluation of correctional reform in general, and correctional privatization in particular, is threatened by a number of hazards. Flaws in the initial evaluation design, political pressures associated with institutional overcrowding, breakdowns in necessary levels of cooperation between evaluators and private sector administrators, and restricted access to important data are but a few of the complications that may weaken evaluation efforts.[95]

In fact, as is too often true in other areas in criminal justice, there appears to have been very little interest in systematic, independent evaluation of privatization initiatives. In its study of American correctional privatization the Council of State Governments

> found few explicit, formalized monitoring procedures in existence either for regular or periodic reviews. . . . Some basic reporting was required in all cases, but there appeared to be little in the way of a formal system for aggregating and tabulating that data, analyzing it, and acting on the results obtained.[96]

In light of the alleged interest in solving correctional problems, it is peculiar that advocates of privatization would not have insisted on implementation of appropriate evaluation measures to assure that the new reforms were effectively addressing the target problems. That they have not been vigorously adopted may indicate the heavy ideological content of the reform movement. Although not all supporters of privatization are conservatives, the correctional privatization movement must be viewed in the larger conservative political context of the 1980s. As reflected by the Grace Commission report noted at the outset of this chapter, there has been significant interest in reducing the size of government and increasing the responsibilities of the private sector. The correctional privatization movement fits in nicely with these objectives, and comports well with the conservative emphasis on fiscal responsibility and tough crime measures. Privatization permits continued expansion of the use of imprisonment, but with enhanced cost-effectiveness.

In light of such ideological considerations, it is perhaps not surprising that there appears to be little interest in evaluation.

> The asserted advantages of private sector involvement are not mere hypotheses to be tested, they are predicates of a political philosophy that has already been validated. From this perspective it is obvious that the private sector will be more efficient, flexible, and cost-effective in its pursuit of correctional objectives. Therefore there is little interest in designing evaluation mechanisms to assess the truth of the obvious.[97]

From a purely ideological point of view, there is nothing to gain and much to lose by rigorous independent evaluation. Although there have been assessments of private program initiatives, independent ongoing assessments have not been typical. Assessments have often relied on company-provided data and on interpretation of such data by legislative investigations. In either case there are serious questions of self-interest and technical competence. Given the high stakes in the current correctional crisis it is somewhat astonishing that evaluation has not been accorded a higher priority in the reform movement.

Although one might have expected more initial effort to be devoted to evaluation, eventually properly designed evaluations will be conducted. An analysis conducted by the Urban Institute compared publicly and privately operated minimum security facilities in Kentucky and publicly and privately operated juvenile facilities in Massachusetts. In their assessment of service quality and effectiveness the study authors concluded that "[f]or a substantial majority of these performance indicators, the privately operated facilities had at least a small advantage."[98]

As this book is going to press, Charles Logan has just published an assessment of three women's prisons: one state operated, one privately operated, and one operated by the federal government. The analysis compared the three facilities in terms of various aspects of prison quality (security, safety, order, care, activity, justice, conditions, management). Although the "results varied, however, across different dimensions,"[99] "the weight of the evidence in this study supports the conclusion that by privately contracting for the operation of its women's prison, the State of New Mexico improved the overall quality of that prison while lowering its costs."[100]

Logan does note that broad generalizations based upon such research are premature.[101] The comparison time frame in the Kentucky and Massachusetts studies was little more than a year, and only six months in New Mexico. The Urban Institute study was limited to minimum security and juvenile institutions, while the New Mexico assessment involved only prisons for women. Many analysts are interested in how private facilities will do when handling male adult serious offenders. And of course, in deciding upon the potential value of private prisons it is important to examine carefully failures as well as successes. In Pennsylvania, for example, a number of problems developed over the private 268 Center in Cowansville, ultimately prompting a judge to prohibit new admissions to the prison in part because of "very minimal security provisions."[102] Pennsylvania ultimately adopted a statewide moratorium on private prisons, and the 268 Center declared bankruptcy.[103] (Focus 10-3 describes an example of a failed Texas project.) Nonetheless, the Urban Institute and Logan research efforts represent examples of the kind of work needed to provide useful information to assist policymakers in making well-reasoned decisions.

Focus 10-3
No Profits and No Inmates:
The Ron Carr Detention Center[104]

In Zavala County, Texas, public officials were looking for a way to energize the local economy. Following the course adopted by many poor rural counties across the nation, they decided to build an incarcerative facility. Revenue bonds were issued to support construction of the Ron Carr Detention Center, and it was hoped that the project would create jobs and generally enhance the economy.

In 1988 an arrangement was drawn up to rent the facility to the District of Columbia, which was seeking a location to hold the overflow from its own institutions. The facility was to be managed by Detention Services Inc., a private company. Naturally, the agreement was intended to benefit all the participants. Zavala County would get an economic boost, Detention Services would make a profit on its management of the facility, and Washington, D.C. would be able to relieve some of its institutional crowding.

It did not work. By the end of December 1989 the District of Columbia had withdrawn from the arrangement. Numerous problems had developed within the institution, including violence among inmates, escapees, and the inmates' clandestine manufacture of wine on the premises. A class-action suit was filed by inmates who claimed that their rights had been violated in the institution.

Matters could not have turned out worse. Zavala County blamed Detention Services while Detention Services blamed the county and, ultimately, the county and the company went to court in a series of lawsuits. Meanwhile, the institution sat without inmates, and without the income public officials had counted on. The District of Columbia removed its inmates, Detention Services left the county, and future operation of the Ron Carr Detention Center was turned over to the county.

Conclusions

It is clear that there exists considerable interest in correctional privatization as a solution to a number of the problems currently afflicting the correctional system. It is equally obvious that enthusiasm generated by contemplation of the potential advantages of privatization must be tempered by awareness of a number of significant potential hazards. Most reasonable defenders and critics of the privatization movement realize that evidence is only beginning to accumulate that will permit sensible assessment of the value of correctional privatization. It is imperative that energetic and careful efforts be made to collect and interpret this evidence, and to steer the discussion away from the kinds of ideology-driven disputes that have made short work of innumerable correctional initiatives. If the past is any guide, there is serious reason to suspect that this will be extremely difficult to accomplish.

Notes

[1] Grace Commission Recommendations—Hearing before the Committee on Finance United States Senate—98th Congress, second session, Feb. 8, 1984—published 1984, Washington, D.C.: Government Printing Office; President's Private Sector Survey on Cost Control (Grace Commission): hearing before the Committee on the Budget, United States Senate, 98th Congress, first session, Nov. 7, 1983—pub. 1984 Washington, D.C.: U.S. Government Printing Office.

[2] Mullen, Joan (1985) "Corrections and the private sector," *The Prison Journal*, 65(2).

[3] Camp, Camille G. and Camp, George M. (1984) "Private sector involvement in prison services and operations," Washington, D.C.: U.S. Dept. of Justice, p. 3.

[4] Logan, Charles H. (1990) *Private Prisons—Cons and Pros*, New York: Oxford University Press.

[5] Logan, Charles and Rausch, Sheila (1985) "Punish and profit: The emergence of private enterprise prisons," *Justice Quarterly*, 2.

[6] General Accounting Office (1991) "Private prisons—Cost savings and BOP's statutory authority need to be resolved," Washington, D.C.: U.S. General Accounting Office, p. 9.

[7] DiIulio, John J. (1991) *No Escape—The Future of American Corrections*, Basic Books, p. 4.

[8] Id. at 183.

[9] Hutto, T. Don (1990) "The privatization of prisons," in Murphy, J.W. and Dison, J.E. (eds.) *Are Prisons Any Better—Twenty Years of Correctional Reform*, Newbury Park, CA: Sage, p. 121.

[10] Camp, George M. and Camp, Camille G. (1990) *The Corrections Yearbook*, Salem, NY: Criminal Justice Yearbook, p. 6.

[11] Cikins, Warren I. (1986) "Privatization of the American prison system: An idea whose time has come?" *Journal of Law, Ethics, and Public Policy*, 2, p. 457.

[12] Austin, James (1986) "Using early release to relieve prison crowding: A dilemma in public policy," *Crime and Delinquency*, 32(4).

[13] Cullen, F.T., Cullen, J.B., and Wozniak, J.F. (1983) "Sanctioning ideology and the prospects for reform: Is rehabilitation really dead?" presented at annual meeting of Illinois Sociological Society; Cullen, F.T., Clark, G.A., and

292

Wozniak, J.F. (1985) "Explaining the get tough movement: Can the public be blamed?" *Federal Probation*, 49; Duffee, David and Ritti, R. Richard (1977) "Correctional policy and public values," *Criminology*, 14(4); Doble, John (1987) *Crime and Punishment: The Public's View*, Public Agenda Foundation.

[14] Fenton, Joseph (1985) "A private alternative to public prisons," *The Prison Journal*, 65(2), p. 46.

[15] Martinson, Robert (1974) "What works? Questions and answers about prison reform," *The Public Interest* 35; Lipton, D.R., Martinson, R., and Wilks, J. (1975) *The Effectiveness of Correctional Treatment: A Survey of Treatment Evaluation Studies*, New York: Praeger; Sechrest, Lee B., White, Susan O., and Brown, E.D. (1979) *The Rehabilitation of Criminal Offenders*, Washington, D.C.: National Academy of Sciences.

[16] Bentham, Jeremy (1962) *Panopticon—Letter* X, Bowring, John (ed.) *The Works of Jeremy Bentham*, (orig. 1797) NY: Russell and Russell, Inc., p. 50.

[17] See Camp, note 3 above at Appendix D.

[18] Calvert Hanson, Linda (1991) "The privatization of corrections movement: A decade of change," *Journal of Contemporary Criminal Justice*, 7(1).

[19] See Logan, note 4 above at ch. 2.

[20] DeWitt, Charles B. (1986) "Ohio's new approach to prison and jail financing," Washington, D.C.: National Institute of Justice, p. 2.

[21] Mullen, Joan, Chabotar, Kent John, and Carrow, Deborah M. (1985) *The Privatization of Corrections*, Washington, D.C.: National Institute of Justice.

[22] For instance, in 1981 New York voters defeated a bond referendum.

[23] See DeWitt, note 20 above at 9.

[24] Ryan, Mick and Ward, Tony (1989) *Privatization and the Penal System— The American Experience and the Debate in Britain*, New York: St. Martin's Press, pp. 10-11.

[25] See Logan, note 4 above at 20.

[26] Based upon information provided by the Corrections Corporation of America.

[27] Robbins, Ira P. (1988) *The Legal Dimensions of Private Incarceration*, Washington, D.C.: American Bar Association.

[28] Wiess, Robert P. (1989) "Private prisons and the state," in Matthews, R. (ed.) *Privatizing Criminal Justice*, London: Sage.

[29] Id. at 37.

[30] Hutto, T. Don (1990) "The privatization of prisons," in Murphy, J.W. and Dison, J.E. (eds.) *Are Prisons any Better? Twenty Years of Correctional Reform*, Newbury Park, CA: Sage, p. 124.

[31] Flanagan, Timothy J. (1989) "Prison industry and labor," in Goodstein, L. and MacKenzie, Doris L. (eds.) *The American Prison—Issues in Research and Policy*, New York: Plenum Press, p. 150.

[32] Sexton, George, Farrow, Franklin, Auerbach, Barbara (1985) "The private sector and prison industries,"—National Institute of Justice—Washington, D.C.: Government Printing Office.

[33] Auerbach, Barbara, Sexton, George, Farrow, Franklin, and Lawson, Robert (1988) "Work in American prisons, the private sector gets involved," National Institute of Justice—Washington, D.C.: Government Printing Office.

[34] See Camp, note 3 above at 4.

[35] Id. at 6.

[36] Powers, Edwin (1966) *Crime and Punishment in Early Massachusetts*, Boston: Beacon Press, pp. 219-220.

[37] Semmes, Raphel (1938) *Crime and Punishment in Early Maryland*, Baltimore: The Johns Hopkins University Press, p. 32.

[38] Id. at 33.

[39] Barnes, H.E. and Teeters, N.K. (1959) *New Horizons in Criminology*, Englewood Cliffs, NJ, p. 528.

[40] Pettigrove, Frederick G. (1910) "State prisons in the United States under separate and congregate systems," in Henderson (ed.), *Penal and Reformatory Institutions*, New York: Charities Publication Committee.

[41] Lewis, W. David (1965) *From Newgate to Dannemora: The Rise of the Penitentiary in New York, 1797-1848*, Ithaca, NY: Cornell University Press.

[42] Ayers, Edward L. (1984) *Vengeance and Justice-Crime and Punishment in the 19th-Century South*, New York: Oxford University Press.

[43] See Lewis, note 41 above at 178-179.

[44] Id. at 185-186.

[45] Quoted in Melossi, Dario and Pavarini, Massimo (1981) *The Prison and the Factory—Origins of the Penitentiary System*, Totowa, NJ: Barnes and Noble Books.

[46] See Lewis, note 41 above at 180-181.

[47] See Ayers, note 42 above.

[48] Lamott, K. (1961) *Chronicles of San Quentin*, New York: David McKay Company, Inc.

[49] Wines, Enoch C. and Dwight, Theodore (1976) *Report on the Prisons and Reformatories of the United States and Canada* (orig. 1867) reprinted Montclair, NJ: Patterson Smith, pp. 287-288.

[50] Id. at 289.

[51] McKelvey, Blake (1977) *American Prisons—A History of Good Intentions*, Montclair, NJ: Patterson Smith, pp. 55-56.

[52] Takagi, Paul (1980) "The Walnut Street Jail: A penal reform to centralize the powers of the state," in Platt and Takagi (eds.) *Punishment and Penal Discipline*, Berkeley, CA: Crime and Social Justice Associates.

[53] See Lewis, note 41 above at 181-193.

[54] Id. at 188-193.

[55] Id.

[56] Id.

[57] Durham, Alexis M. III (1989) "Origins of interest in the privatization of punishment: The nineteenth and twentieth century American experience," *Criminology*, 27(1).

[58] Elvin, Jan (1985) "A civil liberties view of private prisons," *The Prison Journal*, Autumn-Winter 2, p. 51.

[59] See Logan, note 4 above at ch. 4.

[60] Cunniff, Mark A. (1985) "Privatization of corrections" in *Does Crime Pay?—An Examination of Prisons for Profit*, Washington, D.C.: AFSCME.

[61] Anderson, Patrick, Davoli, Charles R., Moriarty, Laura J. (1985) "Private corrections: Feast or fiasco?" *The Prison Journal*, 65(2), p. 34.

[62] See e.g., Martinson, note 15 above; see Lipton, Martinson, and Wilks, note 15 above.

[63] Walker, Samuel (1989) *Sense and Nonsense about Crime—A Policy Guide*; 2nd. ed. Pacific Grove, CA: Brooks-Cole, chs. 5 & 6.

[64] See Austin, note 12 above.

[65] See Lewis, note 41 above.

[66] Ayers, Edward L. (1986); McKelvey, Blake (1977); Sellin, J. Thorsten (1976) *Slavery and the Penal System*, New York: Elsevier.

[67] Sellin, J. Thorsten (1976) *Slavery and the Penal System*, New York: Elsevier, pp. 147-149.

[68] For an example of a model monitoring clause see Robbins, Ira P. (1988) *The Legal Dimensions of Private Incarceration*, Washington, D.C.: American Bar Association.

[69] See Robbins, note 27 above at 118.

[70] Medina v. O'Neill, 589 F. Supp. 1028 (1984).

[71] "Government for Sale—An Examination of the Contracting Out of State and Local services," Washington, D.C.: AFSCME.

[72] Donahue, John D. (1988) "Prisons for profit: Public justice, private

interests," Washington, D.C.: Economic Policy Institute.

[73] See General Accounting Office, note 6 at 3.

[74] Id. at 13.

[75] Id.

[76] American Correctional Association (1985) "Private sector operation of a correctional institution," Washington, D.C.: U.S. Department of Justice.

[77] See Logan, note 4 above at 91.

[78] See Donahue, note 72 above at 12.

[79] Court News Roundup (1986) *Judge's Journal*, Winter, p. 1.

[80] See Logan, note 4 above at 92-96.

[81] Id. at 117.

[82] Id.

[83] See Camp and Camp, note 3 above at 9.

[84] Kinkade, Patrick T. and Leone, Matthew C. (1992) "The privatization of prisons: The wardens' views," *Federal Probation*, 56(4).

[85] See Logan, note 4 above at 147.

[86] See Flanagan, note 31 above at 150.

[87] See Lewis, note 41 above at 264-265.

[88] Bowditch, Christine and Everett, Ronald S. (1987) "Private prisons: Problems within the solution," *Justice Quarterly*, 3(2).

[89] Quoted in Ryan, Ward, note 24 above at 35.

[90] See Sellin, note 67 above at ch. 11.

[91] Id. at 151.

[92] See Logan, note 4 above at 214-218.

[93] Based on Carleton, Mark T. (1971) *Politics and Punishment—The History of the Louisiana State Penal System*, Louisiana State University Press, pp. 16-58.

[94] Bentham, Jeremy (1969) *A Bentham Reader*, (ed.) Mack, Mary, New York: Pegasus, p. 200.

[95] Durham, Alexis M. III (1988) "Evaluating privatized correctional institutions: Obstacles to effective assessment," *Federal Probation*, 52(2).

[96] Council of State Governments, Urban Institute/Issues in Contracting for the Private Operation of Prisons and Jails, Final Report submitted to the National Institute of Justice, (1987), p. 114.

[97] Durham, Alexis M. III (1989) "The privatization of punishment: Justifications, expectations, and experience," *Criminal Justice Policy Review*, 3(1), p. 64.

[98] Hatry, Harry P., Brounstein, Paul J., and Levinson, Robert B. (1993) "Comparison of privately and publicly operated corrections facilities in Kentucky and Massachusetts," in Bowman, Hakim, and Seidenstat (eds.) *Privatizing Correctional Institutions*, New Brunswick: Transaction Publishers, p. 198.

[99] Logan, Charles H. (1993) "Well-kept: Comparing quality of confinement on private and public prisons," *Journal of Criminal Law and Criminology*, Feb.

[100] Id.

[101] Id.

[102] *The Morning Call* (1986) "Judge orders inmates from private prison," March 16, 1986, p. A4.

[103] *Judges' Journal* (1986) "Private prison declares bankruptcy," Winter 1986, pp. 1-2.

[104] This Focus is based upon Mason, Todd (1991) "Many for-profit jails hold no profits—nor even any inmates," *Wall Street Journal*, Jun. 18.

11

The Death Penalty

There is perhaps no more controversial correctional issue in criminal justice than capital punishment. The death penalty has inspired debate over the course of human history and continues to be the object of significant attention among citizens, scholars, and political leaders. Ironically, relative to other kinds of sanctions the death penalty actually involves a relatively small number of offenders. Although there are more than one million individuals currently held in American incarcerative institutions, at the middle of 1993 there were only about 2,700 convicted offenders on death row awaiting execution.[1] Less than 1 percent of the more than 13 million Crime Index offenses perpetrated annually involves homicide, the offense for which capital punishment is legally available. Furthermore, only a small subset of homicides involve circumstances that make possible a sentence of death rather than a term of imprisonment.

Why then, if so few crimes involve homicide, and so few murderers are offenders for whom capital punishment can be imposed, is there so much interest in and controversy over capital punishment? The answer may lie in the fact that the death penalty is viewed by most citizens as the severest possible sanction for the most heinous of crimes and is regarded as the ultimate expression of society's condemnation. The reality of the death penalty in modern America is that it is becoming an increasingly important sanction as growing numbers of death row inmates approach the end of the appeal process.

There are many issues associated with capital punishment. This chapter will focus on several matters that are pertinent to the current situation in the United States. After a brief overview of the major rationales for capital punishment and a sketch of the historical use of the sanction, we will examine its current status in law and in practice. This is followed by an analysis of the effects of capital punishment. The chapter will conclude with consideration of issues such as the economic costs of capital punishment, racism, and public views of the death penalty.

Rationales for Capital Punishment

There are three major rationales for the use of capital punishment. *Retribution* is perhaps the most theoretically complicated rationale. As John Cottingham has noted, there are numerous ways to understand retribution, including repayment, desert, and penalty.[2] For most modern analysts, however, retribution seems generally to refer to sanctions imposed in order to achieve justice. The offender is executed because he or she *deserves* the sanction for the crime. Death is the morally deserved penalty and may not be replaced by a lesser sanction.[3] The severity of the sanction is based upon the severity of the offense for which it is a response. With rare exceptions such as treason, in modern America this means homicide, although in the past Americans have used capital punishment for a wide range of offenses including kidnapping, theft, adultery, treason, and rape. Notions of the relative severity of crimes as they are related to the relative severity of penalties have changed over time, and capital punishment is generally no longer viewed by the courts as a proportional sanction for crimes other than homicide.[4]

The retributive rationale is essentially a backward-looking rationale. That is, application of the rationale to sentencing criminals requires looking back in time at what the offender has done rather than looking forward in time toward what the offender might do (specific deterrence, incapacitation, rehabilitation) or what effect a sanction might have on the future behavior of other individuals (general deterrence). Limiting considerations to what the offender deserves based on known past conduct does to some extent simplify the process of determining appropriate punishment. It is not necessary to make predictions about an offender's future dangerousness or about how other citizens will be affected by the punishment.

Critics of the retributive rationale argue that retribution itself does not require the death penalty, even for homicide offenders. According to this line of thought, unless all offenses are sanctioned with talionic punishments ("the punishment should match the crime not only in the degree of harm inflicted on its victim, but also in the mode and manner of its infliction: fines for larceny, physical beatings for battery, capital punishment for murder"),[5] it is not necessary to impose death on homicide offenders to achieve retributive objectives. Until society begins to assault those convicted of assault, and rob those who have robbed, there is no logical requirement that we kill those who kill.

Perhaps the most obvious forward-looking rationale for capital punishment is *incapacitation.* The interest here is in eliminating future threats of any kind. Advocates of this position are not satisfied with the claim that life imprisonment accomplishes the same objective, because escape is at least theoretically possible, and offenders might still commit homicide within the prison environment. Critics of incapacitation point out that for some kinds of homicides, such as those associated with organized criminal activities, the elimination of one individual merely creates opportunities for others to assume their place. An organized crime executioner or a drug ring enforcer who is executed will simply be replaced by another individual.

General deterrence is an extremely important justification for capital punishment. In general, this argument holds that the execution of offenders dissuades other potential murderers. This rationale for the death penalty is significant because if in fact the execution of one individual can restrain large numbers of other citizens from committing homicide, then the execution of a convicted offender serves to spare the lives of many innocent potential victims. We will return to the data on the deterrent effectiveness of capital punishment shortly.

As might be expected, ideological considerations influence the extent to which these various rationales have appeal. Retribution is likely to appeal to conservatives who believe in free will, rationality, and personal responsibility. Deterrence also appeals to conservatives who believe that individuals are rational beings who weigh the costs and benefits of various courses of action before acting. They argue that the death penalty influences such calculations. Incapacitation appeals to conservatives as well as to some liberals.

Advocates of liberal ideology have generally been significantly less enthusiastic about capital punishment. The liberal belief that the behavior of citizens reflects the impact of circumstances beyond the control of the individual has traditionally made it more difficult for many liberals to embrace such a severe penalty. Nonetheless, current data showing that about 70 percent of Democrats support the death penalty indicate that conservatives are far from alone in their enthusiasm for the death penalty.[6]

Historical Background

The death penalty has been in use from the very beginning of recorded legal history. The earliest known code of law is that of Ur-Engur in 2400 B.C. in Mesopotamia.[7] Records from 2350 B.C. suggest that capital punishment was used for some offenders, such as thieves and adulteresses. The sanction was to be by stoning, using stones inscribed with the offense committed.[8] Subsequent legal codes in Mesopotamia, such as the Code of Lipit-Ishtar (circa 1800 B.C.) and the Code of Hammurabi (1750 B.C.), also suggest that the penalty of death was not unusual. The Hammurabic Code is of special interest because it appears to be the first code to introduce the talionic principle. "The state's reaction to deviant behavior was essentially one of vengeance: death for death."[9] The Code specified the death penalty in 27 different clauses including death for house-builders whose structures collapsed killing an occupant, witchcraft, kidnapping, and theft when the convicted thief lacked the ability to pay restitution.[10]

More widely known is the Hebrew Law articulated in the Mosaic Code of the Old Testament (circa 1000 B.C.). The famous "eye for an eye" provision appears in Exodus 21:24-25, and for many citizens provides the moral basis for the death penalty. The Law of Moses identifies 36 capital crimes including such diverse offenses as adultery, breaches of religious law, assault, homicide, kidnapping, and treason. The law provided stoning, burning, and decapitation as means of execution.

The death penalty was also used in ancient Greece. The seventh-century Draconian Laws provided death for premeditated and voluntary homicide, while involuntary homicide and killing in anger were sanctioned with exile. To some extent this mirrors modern practices. A killer whose offense results from an argument which led to a fight, but which is not the result of premeditation, is not generally accorded capital punishment. In both ancient and classical Greece the social standing of the offender had some influence on the penalty for homicide.[11] Capital punishment was administered to some homicide offenders, but also to offenders such as thieves whom we would not consider for the penalty today.

The death penalty in Rome followed Greek tradition in that it was applied for a variety of offenses. Judges who took bribes, for instance, could be executed, as could thieves caught in the act at night.[12] Offender and victim class standing also had a role in the application of the death penalty and continued to be a factor at least until the time of Beccaria in the eighteenth century.

Capital punishment continued to be used throughout the Middle Ages, sometimes in unusual ways. The Burgundian Code, for instance, provided that a wife who deserted her husband would be executed by being buried alive in a bog.[13] She was to be buried from sight as just recompense for the shameful nature of her offense. For other crimes the methods of execution were sometimes left up to the offender's accuser, who could execute the offender in public.[14]

Capital punishment was an important part of penal practice in Europe through the early stages of the Industrial Revolution. By 1820 there were more than 200 offenses for which the death penalty was authorized in Great Britain. Most of these crimes did not involve homicide, but rather included a large number of acts that today we regard as relatively minor property offenses, such as shoplifting and forgery.[15]

Not surprisingly, the colonists from England adopted capital punishment after settling in the New World. There were, however, some differences between use of capital sanctions in the colonies and in the mother country. The Massachusetts Code of 1641, for example, provided capital punishment for idolatry, witchcraft, blasphemy, murder, manslaughter, poisoning, bestiality, sodomy, adultery, man-stealing (kidnapping), bearing false witness in a capital case, conspiracy, and rebellion. Burglary, theft, rape, and robbery, all capital crimes in England, were not accorded death in Massachusetts. The Massachusetts Code was based directly on the Old Testament, which does not provide death for such crimes.[16] The colonists were attempting to establish a society based upon the word of God, thus the close adherence to scripture and the divergence from English legal tradition.

The death penalty has continued to be used as a response to crime. Although it has been used in the twentieth-century United States for offenses ranging from homicide and rape to treason and kidnapping, it is now used almost exclusively as a sanction for homicide. Until the 1930s some states continued to hold public executions. Despite recent efforts in California to begin televising executions, in practice they usually remain closed to the general public.

In 1972 the United States Supreme Court, in Furman v. Georgia, ruled that the death penalty was being applied arbitrarily and was thus in violation of the Eighth and Fourteenth Amendments.[17] This ruling effectually put a temporary end to the death penalty until the states could redraft their statutes to provide procedural protections that would eliminate arbitrary imposition of the penalty. In 1976 Georgia's new statute was examined by the Court in Gregg v. Georgia and found to pass constitutional standards.[18] More than 70 percent of the states now have death penalty statutes that meet the standards articulated by the Court in the 1970s.[19]

The number of annual executions in the United States has varied significantly, from a high of 199 in 1935 to none during the years 1968 to 1976. Since the resumption of executions subsequent to Gregg v. Georgia, there have been more than 157 executions.[20]

Current Status

As of mid-1993, there were 2,729 inmates on death row.[21] Thirty-six states as well as the federal government currently have capital statutes, although there is wide variation in the extent to which such statutes are applied. Since the resumption of capital punishment subsequent to Gregg v. Georgia, Florida and Texas have been most energetic in using the death penalty, while many states, such as Utah, have rarely used it. Some capital states have not executed any offenders since *Gregg*.[22] The vast majority of death row inmates are sentenced in state rather than federal proceedings.

All but one of the offenders sent to death row since *Gregg* have been sentenced to death for homicide.[23] Although one Mississippi offender was placed on death row for rape of a child, it appears that the days of using the death penalty for other kinds of offenders are behind us. Despite the fact that states such as Montana provide capital punishment for offenses such as aggravated assault by a prison inmate who has been declared a persistent felony offender,[24] future executions will likely involve only homicide offenders.

Five methods for execution are used in the United States. Electrocution and the increasingly popular lethal injection are the methods of choice in most states. Lethal gas is available in seven states, hanging in three, and the firing squad in two states.[25]

The Supreme Court decisions of the 1970s prohibit mandatory capital sentences. Current death penalty practice requires a two-stage process. The first stage is the trial to determine guilt or innocence, and the second is a hearing to determine whether the death penalty is appropriate. Aggravating and mitigating factors must be considered in this second hearing, although the weight to be accorded to various factors by jurors was not set by the Supreme Court.

Examination of the characteristics of death row inmates makes clear that prisoners awaiting execution are not representative of the American population. Women, for instance, have rarely been executed. Ninety-eight percent of executions in the United States since 1638 have been of men.[26] This continues to be the case with only 34 of the 2,482 (1.4 percent) inmates on death row at the beginning of 1992 being women.[27]

Minorities are also over-represented on death row. At the beginning of 1992, about 50 percent of death row inmates were black, Hispanic, Asian, or Native American. Blacks accounted for 40 percent of prisoners awaiting executions, far more than their 12 percent proportion in the general population.[28]

Death rows hold disproportionate numbers of young offenders; about 70 percent of prisoners awaiting execution are less than 40 years of age. More than half had less than a high school education, while only 9.5 percent had any college experience.[29] Almost two-thirds of death row inmates had at least one prior felony conviction in addition to the offense for which they had been sentenced to death.[30]

America continues to utilize capital punishment as an important tool in the ongoing battle against crime. As Focus 11-1 indicates, the United States is not alone in its use of the death penalty. It does, however, stand alone among major industrialized western countries. Nonetheless, it appears clear that capital punishment in the United States will be utilized with increasing vigor in the years to come.

Focus 11-1
The Death Penalty Around the World

The United States is far from alone in its adoption of capital punishment. A study by Amnesty International revealed that 145 countries have legal provisions for capital punishment. This represents about 80 percent of all nations. Thirty-five countries do not have the sanction (20 percent).[31] The picture is a little bit more complicated than this, for 18 retentionist states do not use capital punishment for ordinary crimes, and 26 retentionist nations no longer actually impose the penalty. Thus about 40 percent of nations no longer use the death penalty as a punishment for common crimes such as homicide.[32]

In the Western Hemisphere there is considerable variation in practices. Canada has abolished the sanction, Mexico has it in some states but not others, and the rest of Latin America is characterized by a wide range of policies and practices. In some nations, such as Paraguay, the national constitution prohibits capital punishment for political crimes, but permits it for other kinds of offenses.[33] In practice, Paraguay no longer executes offenders and has become a de facto abolitionist nation.[34] El Salvador and Peru have abolished the death penalty,[35] while Chile and Guatemala continue to retain the sanction.[36] Some Latin American states, such as Brazil and Argentina, abolished capital punishment, restored it, then eliminated it once again.[37] In general, "the picture in South and Central America follows the long-term trend towards total abolition, interrupted at times of political instability, when military governments reimpose the death penalty for a variety of offenses against the state and public order."[38]

The countries thought by some to be closest in legal lineage to the United States, the western industrialized European nations, have essentially abandoned capital punishment except as a penalty for treason. Common criminals cannot be executed in Great Britain, France, Germany, Norway, the Netherlands, and Italy.[39] The Soviet Union continues to utilize the death penalty.

With few exceptions, African nations have retained the use of capital punishment. In some countries it is used for crimes other than homicide. In Kenya, Nigeria, and Zambia, for instance, it is the mandatory sanction for armed robbery.[40]

Eastern nations such as Japan, China, Malaysia, and Pakistan continue to use capital punishment, and it is an option in some parts of Australia. It is widely available in the Middle East, in nations such as Iran, Iraq, Jordan, and Israel.[41]

Some nations, like Cuba, abandoned capital punishment only to readopt it later on. Others, like New Zealand, adopted it but abandoned it when it failed to meet the objectives articulated by its proponents.[42] In many abolitionist nations movements regularly emerge to reinstate capital punishment. Great Britain, for instance, defeated efforts to reestablish the death penalty seven times in the period from abolition (1969) through 1987.[43]

Thus, most nations still employ capital punishment. With regard to crime rates, there appear to be few regularities among either retentionist or abolition states. Nations with relatively high crime rates, such as the United States, as well as those with low crime rates, such as Japan, permit capital punishment. During the last 25 years there does appear to be a shift toward abolition of the penalty, although some regions of the world, such as Africa, continue to be energetic in their support for and use of the death penalty.[44]

The Effects of Capital Punishment

In this section we look back at the major rationales for capital punishment and consider the evidence pertaining to those rationales. Retribution, deterrence, and incapacitation will each be discussed.

Retribution

Retribution is at once the easiest and the most difficult rationale to evaluate. It is simple to evaluate because it does not rely upon empirical data about post-execution events such as crime rates. The retributivist argues that capital punishment is just, irrespective of its impact on crime rates or other future events. Longtime death penalty opponent Professor Hugo Bedau notes, "There is a marvelous thing about retribution, which is that you don't have to know anything about the death penalty, how it works, about how much it costs. The retributive argument puts you on a lofty intellectual plane."[45]

Death penalty supporter Professor Ernest van den Haag shares Bedau's view on this matter. "There is no way of proving it right, as there is no way of proving it wrong. It's a moral matter."[46] Controversies over empirical methodology and interpretations of findings do not muddle the evaluative process.

On the other hand, the difficulty in evaluating the retributive value of capital punishment is that no indisputable metric for comparing crimes and punishments exists. Although popular discussions of capital

307

punishment often involve reference to the "eye for an eye" standard, in practice retributivists do not insist on strict application of the principle. As already noted, retributivists do not argue that robbers be robbed or that rapists be raped. The fact is that commensurate substitutes are routinely used. A misdemeanant may receive a 30-day jail term while a felon spends two years in a state prison. In modern America the common currency for serious crime is imprisonment. Various amounts of it are substituted for "in-kind" retribution.

It is possible, of course, to argue that homicide is an offense different in kind from other offenses, rather than merely in degree. Grand larceny and petit larceny are both theft differing only in the amount of financial loss. Homicide, according to this line of argument, is different than all other crimes because it involves the irreplaceable loss of human life. Unlike material losses, no restitution to the victim is possible. Because of this qualitative difference, some death penalty advocates argue that application of "in-kind" retribution is merited.

However, the reality is that only a small subset of homicide offenders have ever been executed in this country. Public opinion data reveal that even among those who strongly favor capital punishment, the death penalty is considered appropriate only for certain kinds of homicide.[47] Citizens are reluctant to execute, for instance, juvenile offenders and those who kill in the heat of passion.[48] Thus even among death penalty supporters the pure "eye for an eye" in-kind retribution is not always applied.

Further complicating the issue is the fact that only a subset of those who kill are actually sentenced to die. The Supreme Court has explicitly recognized this in its Furman v. Georgia decision. In that decision Justice Brennan wrote that

> [w]hen the punishment of death is inflicted in a trivial number of cases in which it is legally available, the conclusion is virtually inescapable that it is being inflicted arbitrarily. Indeed, it smacks of little more than a lottery system.[49]

Clearly the arbitrary imposition of a legally available punishment, be it the death penalty or any other sanction, will not produce the kind of justice retributivists are seeking. Although *Furman* was decided in 1972, it continues to be true that only a small subset of homicide offenders receive sentences of death.

There appear to be two solutions to this problem: either remove the arbitrariness from the sentencing process or adopt sanctions that do not result in arbitrary sentencing. The Supreme Court attempted to remove the arbitrariness by invoking procedural rules, such as the two-stage process, in its 1976 decisions.[50] Although some of the abuses typical of pre-*Gregg* processes were eliminated in subsequent capital trial processes, evidence submitted in the McClesky case suggests that capital punishment is still administered for reasons that have nothing to do with the crime or criminal record of the offender.[51]

Although defenders of capital punishment may agree that the system is not perfect, they may also argue that it is better to execute some of those deserving of death than to execute none of the deserving simply because it is not possible to assure that all deserving offenders receive death.

> Penalties themselves are not inherently discriminatory; distribution, the process which selects the persons who suffer the penalty, can be. Unjust distribution—either through unjust convictions or through unjust (unequal and biases) penalization of equally guilty convicts—can occur with respect to any penalty. The vice must be corrected by correcting the distributive process that produces it.[52]

The persuasiveness of this argument rests, in part, on whether the focus is on the impact of the system on individual offenders or on the body of offenders who are under consideration. Imagine, for instance, a system in which only blacks were executed for a particular type of crime even though whites committed the same kind of offense. Even if we agreed that, in theory, anyone who committed that crime, white or black, deserves death, would such a system violate our fundamental sense of justice? Would it be better to have a system that executed death-deserving blacks and never executed death-deserving whites than to have a system that accorded both the same level of penalty, albeit a less than deserved penalty?

In fact, this is exactly the situation as it formerly existed with regard to rape. Government historical data on executions for rape reveal 455 executions for rape, with 9 out of 10 of the executed convicts being black. Michael Radelet and Margaret Vandiver point out, "No cases are known in which any white man was executed for the rape of a black woman."[53] A study of more than 1,200 rape convictions in seven southern states revealed that 36 percent of blacks with white victims were sentenced to death, while only 2 percent of the offenders in the cases involving other offender-victim racial combinations received the death penalty.[54] This pattern of justice led to a variety of protests, the culmination of which was the United States Supreme Court decision in Coker v. Georgia, which outlawed the use of capital punishment for rape.[55]

General Deterrence

The body of research on general deterrence is now quite substantial. Irrespective of how one feels about capital punishment, it is quite remarkable that the public is so completely unaware of this body of research. This lack of awareness is even more striking in light of the fact that many citizens support capital punishment primarily because of its perceived deterrent potential.[56]

There are two main kinds of research on the deterrent effect of the death penalty. The first compares jurisdictions which have capital punishment with those that do not in terms of their respective homicide and crime rates. The second kind compares changes over time within jurisdictions in the imposition of capital punishment.

After decades of death penalty research it appears that there is little evidence that capital punishment has a discernable deterrent effect. A National Academy of Sciences analysis of deterrence found that the body of research on capital punishment did not establish the existence of a deterrent effect for the death penalty.[57]

The one major study that did find evidence of a significant deterrent effect was reported by economist Issac Ehrlich. He studied executions from the 1930s through 1969 and found that, on average, each execution deterred "between 7 and 8 murders."[58] These findings raised a firestorm of controversy, and other researchers immediately set out to examine Ehrlich's methodology and to try and replicate his results. During the ten years after the results of Ehrlich's research were made known numerous studies and analyses were published. This research identified a number of limitations and questionable methodological assumptions in Ehrlich's work and generally failed to detect the deterrent effect Ehrlich thought he had identified.[59] Research conducted in the last five years has also failed to find much evidence of a deterrent effect. A recent study of the five most active death penalty states, for instance, found that "[o]ne conclusion seems inescapable from the results presented here: Executions have failed to exert a consistent deterrent impact on homicides in the five states most likely to execute."[60] Another recent analysis looked only at felony murders, the kind most likely to be associated with the death penalty. This study also failed to uncover evidence supporting the deterrence argument.[61]

Research has even been conducted on the deterrent impact of capital punishment on *non*-capital felonies. Advocates of the death penalty have sometimes argued that executions have coattail effects that carry over onto non-capital crimes.[62] A 1991 analysis of this issue failed to find evidence that non-capital crimes were influenced by capital punishment.[63]

Thus current criminological evidence does not confirm the existence of a deterrent effect of capital punishment. This does not mean that no effect exists. It may be too small to measure or current measurement methods may simply be too crude to detect the effect. If social policy is to be based in part on scientific evidence, however, it is not easy to see how capital punishment can currently be justified on grounds of deterrence.

One final issue merits mention before moving on to incapacitation. The dispute over deterrence often focuses solely on whether an effect exists. For some advocates of capital punishment the existence of the effect would be sufficient to persuade them that capital punishment represents responsible social policy. This can be regarded as a strange deviation from the conventional standards we use to evaluate policy options. If it could be shown that teaching method A made it possible for 75 percent of students to read effectively within two years would we automatically adopt it? Of course not. We would want to compare the effectiveness of Method A with the effectiveness of teaching methods B, C, and D. Method D may be most effective and produce a 97 percent success rate. Naturally, we would chose Method D.

Unfortunately, public discussion of the deterrent value of capital punishment rarely adopts this standard comparative approach. Suppose capital punishment did deter, but only deterred one out of every 10,000 homicides. Would capital punishment as a social policy be as attractive an option as if it deterred half of all homicides? Of course not. The magnitude of the deterrent effect is probably more important than merely whether there is an effect. The overall costs of a system of capital punishment, in terms of economic expenses, executing the innocent, and consumption of judicial system time and resources, may simply not be worth a one in 10,000 deterrent effect. Although we would all agree that even that one innocent life is worth saving, those precious resources might be put to work in other ways to ultimately save many more lives (education, early delinquency detection, imposition of prison sentences on first-time serious offenders, for example).

On the other hand, if a deterrent effect of substantial impact were to be discovered, than it might be reasonable to anticipate that some current opponents of capital punishment would become more willing to adopt it as a social policy. Thus the debate over the mere existence of a deterrent effect probably misses the point. That the debate has assumed this form likely reflects in part the difficulty most researchers have had in detecting a deterrent effect of any sort. In light of the increasing numbers of executions, opportunities may soon exist which make possible new empirical analyses of the deterrence issue. If such studies begin to reveal deterrent effects, it will be important to commit serious attention to consideration of the magnitude of such effects.

Incapacitation

The incapacitation argument essentially states that an executed murderer ceases to represent a threat to society. Life imprisonment is not adequate because escape is possible, and other inmates and prison staff are at risk of victimization. This argument is probably the most straightforward appearing of the various justifications for capital punishment. Nonetheless, the issue is more complicated than it appears.

First, some kinds of homicide will not be prevented by eliminating the offender. Murders occurring in organized contexts, such as gang or organized crime homicides, may simply be perpetrated by individuals who take the offender's place in the organization. Organized crime "hit men" or drug industry-related "business enforcers" are good examples of offender types who will not be eliminated by executing those who do get caught and convicted. Although this represents a relatively small proportion of those convicted of murder, it is important to remember that only a small subset of homicide offenders legally eligible for the death penalty actually receive the sanction. The proportion of murderers who receive the death penalty who are instrumental, felony-related homicide offenders is thus much larger.

Second, evidence on the risks posed by death-sentenced inmates suggests that such risks are perhaps overestimated. When the Supreme Court commuted the death sentences of hundreds of offenders under sentence of death in the Furman v. Georgia decision, it created an opportunity to evaluate the danger represented by such criminals. A study of 558 such offenders revealed that homicide recidivism was a very small hazard. Four inmates and two prison guards were killed in prison by the more than 500 death-sentenced inmates examined in this study. Moreover, about 240 of these offenders were eventually returned to society. Almost 80 percent had not been returned to prison for any crimes at the time of the research. A single offender committed a second homicide subsequent to release. In summarizing this study, the researchers noted that

> [i]ncapacitation advocates would insist that the execution of every *Furman*-offender would have prevented the one subsequent murder referred to above. Further, the executions would have prevented six prison murders (four inmates and two guards). This evidence supports permanent incapacitation as a means to prevent future capital crimes. However, four inmates on death row at the time of Furman were innocent according to a study by Bedau and Radelet. These four individuals could possibly have been executed had it not been for Furman.[64]

In concluding they noted that

> [t]he data in this paper suggest that these prisoners did not represent a significant threat to society. Most have performed well in prison; those few who have committed additional violent acts were indistinguishable from those who have not.[65]

Finally, it is important to consider whether the small risks of homicide recidivism are worth the overall costs of maintaining a capital system. It is possible to argue that economic costs, as well as the risks to innocent convicts, may well exceed the benefits of incapacitation through execution. In addition, it is likely that the small risks of in-prison recidivism can be further reduced through properly managed facilities for life-sentenced convicts.

Although justice, deterrence, and incapacitation represent three major goals of capital punishment, there are other issues that merit consideration in formulating sound judgments about the value of the death penalty. Some of these issues have received little public attention. For instance, Robert Johnson argues that, by their very nature, death penalty systems dehumanize all the participants in the process: offenders, guards, and administrators. He suggests that the lengthy periods of confinement on death row represent an additional punishment that goes beyond what ought to be tolerated in a civilized society.[66]

Other issues have received substantial public exposure. We turn now to several of the more significant of these: the economic cost of capital punishment, racial discrimination, and public sentiment.

▓ *The Economic Cost of Capital Punishment*

Similar to the argument centering around incapacitation, consideration of the economic costs of capital punishment seems fairly straightforward. Citizens often express resentment about having to spend tax dollars to support and maintain convicted homicide offenders over the duration of their lifetimes. At approximately $30,000 per year, according to this reasoning, it will cost the taxpayers more than one million dollars to imprison an inmate for 40 years. For many citizens this represents a kind of secondary victimization.

As with most of the issues associated with capital punishment, the cost issue is not as simple as it appears. Criminal justice processes are quite different in capital cases than in non-capital cases. First, even when the law permits it, defendants facing the death penalty have little motivation to plead guilty. Typically, about 90 percent of criminal cases are resolved with a plea of guilt.[67] This saves an enormous amount of time and money. If even half of those defendants insisted on a trial, the criminal justice system would be overwhelmed. But in capital cases accused offenders insist on a trial ten times as often.[68] Naturally this dramatically increases the cost of processing such cases.

Beyond the reality of going to trial, such cases generally are longer, more complicated, involve more witnesses, and entail significantly more legal maneuvering. For instance, the number of legal motions increases by a factor of two to four in capital cases.[69] They typically involve longer, more expensive investigations, and often entail the use of expensive testimony provided by psychiatrists, forensic specialists, and other experts. Daily fees for such experts can range as high as $1,000 per day.[70]

Jury selection, presentation of arguments, jury instruction, and virtually all aspects of the trial process take more time, and thus consume more resources, than in non-capital trials. On average, capital proceedings generally take about three times longer than non-capital trials.[71]

The original trial to determine guilt or innocence is only the first of two constitutionally required proceedings in the post-*Furman* era. A separate hearing must be held to consider aggravating and mitigating circumstances in assessing whether the death penalty is warranted. This may involve hearing new witnesses and reviewing evidence and information not introduced in the trial. A New York study found that each death penalty case would cost state and county authorities $1.8 million in defense, prosecution, and court costs.[72] And these figures did not include the cost of appeals.

The appellate process involves multiple layers and, as is well understood by citizens, requires years to complete. In Kentucky, for example, offenders sentenced to death have a minimum of ten layers of appeals available.[73] Estimates of the cost of the appellate process indicate that hundreds of thousands of additional dollars will be spent before the judicial process is at an end.[74] Factoring in trial and appellate costs, the Ohio Public Defenders Office projected a $1 million dollar price tag per execution.[75] An analysis of Florida executions found that executions from 1979 through 1988 had cost the state $3 million each.[76]

Of course, these figures do not include the cost of maintaining death-sentenced inmates on death row over periods of years. Such facilities generally are more expensive to operate than conventional prison facilities because of the need for special security measures. A California estimate puts annual death row costs at about $40,000 per prisoner.[77]

Finally, the costs of processing capital cases do not represent the costs of executing offenders. Because many offenders have their conviction or sentence overturned during the appeal process, the actual cost per completed execution is necessarily higher. A 1986 analysis revealed that only ten percent of death penalty cases actually resulted in a death sentence. At $500,000 per capital trial, this means that it will cost the taxpayers of California about $5 million for each offender who receives the death penalty. In addition, not all offenders sentenced to death are actually executed. One California analysis revealed that all 55 death sentences in California at the time of the study were overturned in the appeal process. Resources expended on those cases did not, therefore, result in any executions.[78] Nonetheless, California continues to retain its death penalty statute. In other states, such as Kansas, cost considerations have provided sufficient motivation to defeat death penalty legislation (see Focus 11-2).

Focus 11-2
Death Penalty Price Too High For Kansas[79]

Kansas state senators voted for the death penalty when they knew the governor would veto it. But when they got a new governor, pro-death penalty, the senators decided they had better take a hard look at its price tag.

What they saw made them change their minds.

Faced with a sagging farm economy, the conservative

senators couldn't stomach the waste and expense of the modern-day American death penalty.

"I voted against it, and some people have tried to say I coddle criminals. Well, I don't coddle criminals," drawls Frank Gaines, a 16 year senate veteran, one of the last of a dying breed of populist Kansas stump orators.

"It costs a lot more money to have capital punishment, and frankly, I think life in prison is just as tough a penalty," says Gaines. "You just get yourself a confining building and put all them animals in there together. If it was me, I'd rather be put out of my damn misery than have to live like that."

Senators who voted no had nightmares of political disaster. After all, the new governor, Mike Hayden, had made support of the death penalty a major part of his campaign. And the voters gave him a solid victory.

But the backlash hasn't come.

"I never received as much mail as I did on that issue— but it was thank-you mail. That's real unusual," says Senate President Ross Doyen, who changed his mind after years of supporting the death penalty. "I think a lot of people say they favor it, but when you pin 'em down on the specifics, they're not so sure."

The most eye-opening specific was the bottom line: $11.5 million of the first year of the death penalty alone, according to the legislature's researchers.

"And those costs are deceptive," says researcher Mary Galligan. "they stack up over the years."

The Senate killed the death penalty initiative. Doyen, the Senate president, doesn't expect the issue to decide any future elections.

"Some people will be upset with you because you support it, and some will be upset because you don't. But it's no pendulum swinger."

"I think this issue is greatly overplayed."

Thus it is far from clear that the system of capital punishment costs taxpayers less money than a system of true life imprisonment. Of course, it is possible to streamline the appellate process, and a significant movement is emerging to accomplish this.[80] Yet, even if appeals could be cut in half, and it is far from obvious that Constitutional requirements would permit such a drastic reduction, costs would still be extraordinary. As noted above, the probability of an offender in a capital case insisting on a trial is ten times higher than in a non-capital case. Such costs, and at least some appeals, can never be eliminated. Moreover, expensive death rows would still be necessary.

It is, of course, possible to argue that the other benefits of capital punishment are such as to make the costs, whatever they might be, worthwhile. If one possesses a powerful moral commitment to capital punishment, for instance, then the costs may simply be what must be borne to achieve justice. On the other hand, it is important that citizens understand that capital punishment does not appear to be a cheaper way of handling capital offenders. Not only does a capital system seem to be more expensive than a non-capital system, the resources spent on capital punishment are not available for other enterprises that might ultimately have a more significant effect on the public safety and well-being.

Racial Discrimination

On September 25, 1991 Warren McClesky, convicted of killing a police officer in a robbery, was executed in the Georgia electric chair.[81] McClesky's execution was significant because it was the culmination of a 13-year legal battle in which the U.S. Supreme Court heard social scientific evidence indicating that race had an impact on the use of the death penalty in capital cases in Georgia. The research forming the basis of the racial discrimination claim was at that time the most sophisticated of a long line of research studies examining the influence of race on capital sentencing.

Analyzing death penalty traditions and practices for evidence of racial discrimination is a very complicated matter. It is not difficult to show that minorities, especially blacks, receive the death penalty to a degree well out of proportion with their prevalence in the population. As is the case for imprisonment, blacks are over-represented on death row—40 percent of death row inmates are black.[82] However, is this over-representation the result of racial discrimination in the criminal justice system or is it the result of differences in the nature of the crimes perpetrated by blacks and non-blacks?

A fairly substantial body of research has developed to examine this issue. Many early studies revealed that blacks were more likely than whites to be sentenced to death.[83] Many of these studies, were, however, flawed in that they did not take into account differences in the heinousness of the murder or the offender's prior record.[84]

More sophisticated recent studies have attempted to control for such variables and to look at the several places in the justice process where discrimination might have an impact on sentencing. A Florida study, for instance, found that the probability of a homicide being treated as a capital crime was greater when it involved a white victim and a black offender than when the victim was black or the offender white.[85] Studies of judicial sentencing have routinely found that both judges and juries are more likely to hand down death sentences when the victim was white.[86] A comprehensive assessment of 200 variables found that Georgia blacks who murdered whites had elevated risks of being given the death penalty.[87] A recent Kentucky analysis revealed that blacks accused of killing whites had the highest risks of being charged with a capital offense. Moreover, such offenders also had the highest probability of being sentenced to death.[88]

Although there are analysts who are reluctant to accept the validity of these findings,[89] the evidence has become increasingly clear that, in some jurisdictions and for some kinds of crimes, racial discrimination is still practiced. Even the Eleventh Circuit Court of Appeals, which heard and rejected Warren McClesky's discrimination-based appeal, assumed that the scientific evidence showing discrimination was valid. The U.S. Supreme Court did not dispute the finding of the Georgia study, although it found other grounds to reject McClesky's appeal.[90]

Have matters improved since the resumption of executions after the 1976 *Gregg* decision? In concluding their analysis of the McClesky case, Samuel Gross and Robert Mauro write:

> We do not claim that there have been no changes in patterns of capital sentencing since *Furman*. Very likely there have been changes, and it is possible that there has been a decrease in the prevalence of racial discrimination. . . . There may be less discrimination and less arbitrariness now, and for all the evidence shows, there may be more. The information on discrimination and on arbitrariness in capital sentencing for homicide was much sketchier in 1972 than it is in 1988, so comparisons are difficult, but to the extent that they can be made, they certainly show no marked improvement.[91]

Matters may have improved, but a recent federal study of racial disparity in death penalty sentencing revealed continuing evidence of discrimination.

> Our synthesis of the 28 studies shows a pattern of evidence indicating racial disparities in the charging, sentencing, and imposition of

the death penalty after the *Furman* decision. . . . Legally relevant variables, such as aggravating circumstances, were influential but did not explain fully the racial disparities researchers found. . . . To summarize, the synthesis supports a strong race of victim influence. The race of offender influence is not as clear cut and varies across a number of dimensions.[92]

Defenders of the death penalty point out that the discovery that application of a sanction is not entirely without flaws, such as racial discrimination, does not logically require the withdrawal of the sanction altogether. For instance, Gary Kleck's study of discrimination in sentencing for various crime types found evidence of discriminatory sentencing patterns for some crimes in some regions of the country.[93] But such discoveries have not led to cries to abandon fines, imprisonment, and other sanctions. In human institutions, according to this line of thought, there will always be difficulties in devising systems that operate with perfect fairness. Although it is important to strive to improve such systems, their lack of perfection is not adequate reason to discard them. If a system permits one deserving offender to go too lightly punished, the solution is not to make the punishment unfairly light for all, but to try and tighten the system to provide the proper level of severity for as many offenders as possible.

Critics of this view suggest that capital punishment is a special case. First, because death is a qualitatively different punishment, it merits special treatment. Second, because the death penalty is often regarded as the ultimate form of social condemnation of a just society, it is imperative that such a centerpiece be free from moral taint. An ultimate condemnation that comes down more heavily on minorities than on whites conveys a message of discrimination and injustice rather than of fairness.

Whatever view one holds regarding the proper approach to addressing racial discrimination, the *McClesky* decision indicates quite clearly that the Supreme Court is unlikely to play an active role in moving to correct racial injustice in the application of capital punishment in America. There is sufficient evidence to suggest that the application of the death penalty in some parts of the country is still not free from the effects of such discrimination. It appears, however, that the role the Court assumed in the *Furman* and *Gregg* era has significantly changed. Recent decisions suggest that it will be up to citizens and legislative bodies to insist on reforms that will tackle racial discrimination in capital sentencing.

Focus 11-3

Being Executed Twice:
Cruel and Unusual Punishment?

In 1944 a 15-year-old black youth named Willie Francis was arrested for the murder of a Louisiana pharmacist. A jury found Francis guilty and sentenced him to death in the electric chair.

His execution was scheduled for the spring of 1946. Standard execution procedures were followed in preparing for Francis' execution, and a small group of witnesses were on hand to witness the event. Francis was placed in the chair, and the electricity was turned on. Electricity passed into Francis, and he jerked in reaction. But he was not killed by the voltage. More current was sent into Francis, but again without lethal effect.

At this point Francis was taken from the chair, still alive and in good condition. This extraordinary event made national headlines. The state of Louisiana planned a second attempt to execute Francis, but he appealed to the U.S. Supreme Court. He argued that a second attempt to execute him constituted a violation of the Eighth Amendment prohibition against cruel and unusual punishment. Many citizens agreed with this position, and the Governor of Louisiana received thousands of letters asking him to commute the sentence to imprisonment.

In the majority opinion the Supreme Court pronounced that

> The cruelty against which the Constitution protects a convicted man is cruelty inherent in the method of punishment, not the necessary suffering involved in any method employed to extinguish life humanely. The fact that an unforeseeable accident prevented the prompt consummation of the sentence cannot, it seems to us, add an element of cruelty to a subsequent execution.[94]

By only a five to four margin, the Court rejected Francis' appeal. He was scheduled for a second execution, and this time was successfully electrocuted. This incident is distinctive because it raises serious questions, even among staunch

advocates of capital punishment, about the right of the condemned to a humane execution process.

What the Public Wants

It is possible to argue that in a democratic society policies designed to address important social problems should not be adopted without substantial public support. Certainly capital punishment, as the ultimate expression of society's condemnation for what most regard as the most terrible of crimes, represents a significant social policy. In the United States capital punishment is essentially a state, not a federal, matter and states are free to enact or not enact capital statutes. State gubernatorial campaigns routinely involve debate over the value of the death penalty. Thirty-six states have chosen to adopt capital punishment while the remainder have opted against it. Do such realities reflect public sentiment?

There exists a fairly lengthy body of information on basic death penalty preferences. Beginning in 1936, the Gallup poll has asked respondents, "Do you favor the death penalty for a person convicted of murder?" The numbers favoring capital punishment stabilized in the 60 percent range from the thirties until the mid-fifties when it began to decline. By 1966 the percent in favor reached bottom at 42. By the late 1970s it was back into the 60 percent range and by the late 1980s it was about 80 percent.[95]

These data provide a clear indication that public sentiment regarding the death penalty does vary over time, that such variation can be substantial, and that the vast majority of citizens currently seem receptive to capital punishment for murder. However, closer examination of the public view reveals some surprising findings.

First, Gallup poll data show that 62 percent of citizens believe that capital punishment is a deterrent to murder. Seventy-seven percent of death penalty supporters believe it is a deterrent.[96] As we have already seen, this perception is not supported by the scientific research currently available. This is significant because presumably the enthusiasm of some citizens for capital punishment would be reduced if they were aware of the research on deterrence. In fact, in one study about 16 percent of supporters indicated they would abandon their support for the death penalty if it were not a deterrent.[97]

In addition, when Gallup respondents were asked whether having true life imprisonment (without parole) available would influence their support for capital punishment, significant numbers of supporters said they would then oppose the death penalty. As the survey researchers note, "If both conditions—life without parole and proof of no deterrence—were present, the reduction would be to the 43 percent level."[98] An additional 11 percent indicated that their support of capital punishment was based on the cost of keeping murderers in prison. As discussed above, data exist indicating that it is more expensive to operate a system with capital punishment than to simply pay the costs of life imprisonment. Were this information commonly understood, presumably even more capital punishment advocates would elect to abandon their support for capital punishment.

Moreover, when citizens are asked about their support for the death penalty in specific kinds of cases, rather than in the abstract, the level of support decreases. For instance, a study of attitudes toward the death penalty for juveniles posed the following question:

> Ohio presently has the death penalty for adults convicted of murder. Would you favor or oppose the state passing a law to allow the death penalty for juveniles over 14 years of age convicted of murder?

About two-thirds of respondents opposed capital punishment for such murderers despite the fact that the U.S. Supreme Court has ruled that older juveniles may be put of death for murder.[99] (There have already been executions of offenders who were juveniles at the time of their crime.)

A survey of approximately 1,000 citizens asked respondents whether they would agree or disagree with a series of statements presenting different homicide scenarios. These statements are reproduced below.

1. I probably would recommend the death penalty even if the victim was a relative of the defendant and the murder occurred during a fight.
2. I probably would recommend the death penalty even if the crime had been committed under the influence of alcohol.
3. I probably would not recommend the death penalty even if the person had killed a storekeeper after an alarm sounded and he/she panicked trying to escape.

4. I probably would recommend the death penalty if the person killed his/her employer one week after he/she had been fired from his/her job.[100]

The percentages of respondents who would choose a death sentence for offenders in each of the scenarios are 52, 67, 78, and 79 respectively.[101] These responses indicate considerable variation in the willingness to use capital punishment as a sanction for murder. There is about a 50 percent increase in the percentage of respondents willing to use capital punishment for felony related or premeditated killing than for murders resulting from fights between relatives. In fact, the different degrees of homicide charges that can be brought (first, second, third degree) are to some extent a reflection of the seriousness with which various homicides are viewed. It is interesting to note, however, that 52 percent of respondents would use capital punishment to sanction a murder occurring during a fight between relatives. This kind of homicide is rarely charged as first degree murder, the level required in most jurisdictions to qualify as a capital crime.

This research shows how simple general questions about capital punishment do not reveal the complexities of public sentiment about the death penalty. Support or opposition to the death penalty varies with the kinds of homicides under consideration, the characteristics of the offender and victim, and the accuracy of perceptions regarding deterrence and economic costs of sanctioning offenders. It appears that a majority of citizens do support capital punishment under some conditions and given some assertions about its costs and effectiveness. However, dissemination of information about costs and deterrence, as well as enactment of laws providing true life prison terms, seems to have a significant impact on the level of public support for capital punishment.

The Future of the Death Penalty in America

As noted at the beginning of this chapter, the death penalty is important not only because it involves an ultimate penalty, but because it is regarded by many as society's most vigorous condemnation of unacceptable behavior. There are no other sanctions that have generated as much controversy in modern times as capital punishment, and it is unlikely that this will change in the future.

Whether capital punishment will continue to be used in the United States will probably not be determined by the scientific evidence on the effects of the penalty. The major professional association representing criminologists, the American Society of Criminology, who presumably should have the most insight into the nature of this evidence, passed the following resolution in 1987.

> Be it resolved that because social science research has demonstrated the death penalty to be racist in application and social science research has found no consistent evidence of crime deterrence through execution, the American Society of Criminology publicly condemns this form of punishment, and urges its members to use their professional skills in legislatures and courts to seek a speedy abolition of this form of punishment.[102]

How many citizens are aware that the nation's leading criminology professional organization has adopted this position? How many citizens are even aware that such an organization exists, never mind that it represents a group of experts whose professional judgments might be worth some consideration? When expertise in other areas is at issue, such expertise is routinely sought. For instance, the American Medical Association has had, and continues to have, an impact on the resolution of medicine-related issues in this country. Their views are often aggressively sought by policymakers. The same cannot be said for criminologists.

Why is such a source of expertise typically ignored? Part of the answer surely involves ideology. Citizens on both sides of the debate often have deep value-based emotional commitments to their assessment of the issue, commitments that may make re-evaluation of the evidence difficult. The fact is that citizens commonly and confidently believe they fully understand highly visible issues such as capital punishment. Such a belief, combined with the proper outrage they feel over the crimes committed by homicide offenders, may well lead them to endorse solutions that have yet to demonstrate anything like the kind of effectiveness demanded in other areas of policy. The NASA policy, associated with the O-ring failure, which resulted in the crash of the Challenger, was modified immediately. The absence of a clear impact of capital punishment on crime rates does not provoke the same level of public intolerance.

In a sense, it is possible to argue that the death penalty retains its popularity in part because of its glamour. It is certainly a distinctive penalty in terms of its threat to the basic human drive toward life. It is distinctive in that, once imposed, it cannot be remedied or reversed. It is part of an ancient tradition extending back into the earliest reaches of human legal history. Moreover, it is a penalty that apparently makes many people *feel* as though they have done something about a terrible problem, whether or not the problem is actually being addressed.

Such sentiments make possible the continuing interest in capital punishment as a remedy for serious crime. The previous Republican Administration in Washington lobbied energetically and successfully to expand the use of the death penalty for federal crimes, especially those involving drugs, as well as to limit habeas corpus appeals by death row inmates.[103] Although such responses to crime may have an immediate intuitive appeal, they do not represent solutions based on the information currently available to help us formulate realistic public policy. There is simply no evidence that adding the death penalty for violators of federal drug laws will have any impact whatsoever on violent drug offenders. Limiting appeals appears attractive to the citizen who is understandably frustrated with a system ill-designed to efficiently handle crime. But appeals are not in place without reason. More than 40 percent of habeas corpus appeals in capital cases result in reversal.[104] Of the 139 prisoners removed from death row in 1988, 75 percent were removed because their sentence was vacated or declared unconstitutional, or because the conviction itself was vacated.[105] "According to one count, from 1976 to 1989 more than 1,400 death penalty cases in the U.S. were reversed by appellate courts. About half of death sentences are being overturned on appeals."[106] The fact is, the courts do make errors in capital cases, and such errors are far from rare.

It is too soon to predict the course that will be taken by the current Administration, although President Clinton is on record as favoring the death penalty. Because of domestic economic issues, crime was not a major element in the 1992 Presidential campaign, thus there may be less political pressure on the Administration to take energetic action to address crime and punishment-related issues.

The irony of the whole debate is that ultimately it is likely that overall crime and homicide rates will be unaffected by the expansion or abolition of capital punishment. There simply are too many other factors that exert powerful influence on the movement of crime rates. Although advocates of capital punishment can maintain their enthusiasm for the sanction on retributive grounds, it is important to realize that there are costs. Economic resources and human energy spent on a capital system of unproven value in terms of crime control might better be put into other kinds of programs that, while not as glamorous, might stand a better chance of achieving crime reduction objectives.

Notes

[1] NAACP Legal Defense Fund, data supplied 7 Jun. 1993.

[2] Cottingham, John (1979) "Varieties of retribution," *Philosophical Quarterly*, 238.

[3] Kant, Immanuel (1973) "The metaphysical elements of justice," in Murphy, J.G. *Punishment and Rehabilitation*, Belmont, CA: Wadsworth.

[4] See, for instance, Coker v. Georgia, 433 U.S. 584 (1977). In this case the Supreme Court effectually outlawed use of the death penalty for rape offenders.

[5] Feinberg, Joel and Gross, Hyman (1975) *Punishment: Selected Readings*, Encino, CA: Dickenson Pub. Co., p. 4.

[6] Flanagan, Timothy J. and Maguire, Kathleen (1990) *Sourcebook of Criminal Justice Statistics—1989*, Washington, D.C.: U.S. Department of Justice, p. 168.

[7] Drapkin, Israel (1989) *Crime and Punishment in the Ancient World*, Lexington, MA: Lexington Books, p. 18.

[8] Id. at 18-19.

[9] Id. at 27.

[10] Johns, C.H.W., trans. (1911) *The Oldest Code of Laws in the World*, Edinburgh: T. & T. Clark.

[11] Sellin, J. Thorsten (1976) *Slavery and the Penal System*, New York: Elsevier.

[12] See Drapkin, note 7 above at 232.

[13] See Sellin, note 11 above at 34.

[14] Id.

[15] Koestler, Arthur (1957) *Reflections on Hanging*, New York: MacMillan.

[16] Powers, Edwin (1966) *Crime and Punishment in Early Massachusetts: 1620-1692*, Boston: Beacon Press.

[17] Furman v. Georgia 408 U.S. 238, 92 S. Ct. 2726, 33 L. Ed. 2d 346 (1972).

[18] Gregg v. Georgia 428 U.S. 153, 96 S. Ct. 2909, 49 L. Ed. 2d 859 (1976).

[19] Greenfeld, Lawrence (1992) "Capital Punishment 1991," Washington, D.C.: Bureau of Justice Statistics, p. 1.

[20] Id.

[21] See note 1 above.

[22] See Greenfeld, note 19 above.

[23] Id. at 1.

[24] Schlesinger, Steve, *Capital Punishment, 1986* (1987) Washington, D.C.: Bureau of Justice Statistics, p. 3.

[25] See Greenfeld, note 19 above.

[26] Allen, Harry E. and Simonsen, Clifford E. (1989) *Corrections in America*, New York: MacMillan, p. 325.

[27] See Greenfeld, note 19 above.

[28] Id. at 10.

[29] Id.

[30] Id. at 11.

[31] Hood, Roger (1989) *The Death Penalty—A World-Wide Perspective*, Oxford: Clarendon Press, pp. 7-8.

[32] Id. at 8.

[33] Id. at 134.

[34] See Hood, note 31 above at 26.

[35] Id.

[36] Id. at 27.

[37] Id.

[38] Id. at 27.

[39] Weichman, Dennis, Kendall, Jerry, and Bae, Ronald (1989) "The death penalty: An international view," *The Howard Journal*, 28(2), pp. 128-129.

[40] Id. at 129.

[41] Id. at 132.

[42] Newbold, Greg (1990) "Capital punishment in New Zealand: An experiment that failed," *Deviant Behavior*, 11.

[43] See Weichman, Kendall, and Bae, note 39 above at 126.

[44] See Hood, note 31 above at 8.

[45] Quoted in Dionne, E.J. (1990) "Capital punishment gaining favor as public seeks retribution," *Corrections Today*, 52(5), p. 180.

[46] Id.

[47] Durham, Alexis M. III, Elrod, H. Preston, and Kinkade, Patrick T. (1993) "Truth or Dare—Kill or Confine: What the Public Really Thinks about the Death Penalty," presented at the Western Society of Criminology annual meeting, Monterey, CA, Mar.

[48] Williams, Fran P., Gulick, David B., and Longmire, Dennis R. (1988)

"The public and the death penalty: Opinion as an artifact of question type," *Criminal Justice Research Bulletin*, 3(8).

[49] See *Furman*, note 17 above.

[50] See, e.g., Gregg v. Georgia, note 18 above.

[51] Baldus, David C., Pulaski, Charles, and Woodworth, George (1983) "Discrimination and arbitrariness in Georgia's charging and sentencing system: A preliminary report," unpublished manuscript, University of Iowa—College of Law). This research was submitted as evidence in the McClesky case (McClesky v. Kemp, 753 F.2d 877 (11th Cir. 1985)).

[52] van den Haag, Ernest (1975) *Punishing Criminals—Concerning a Very Old and Painful Question*, New York: Basic Books, p. 221; van den Haag, Ernest (1985) "The death penalty vindicates the law," *American Bar Association Journal*, 71, pp. 38-42.

[53] Radelet, Michael L. and Vandiver, Margaret (1986) "Race and capital punishment: An overview of the issues," *Crime and Social Justice*, 25, p. 98.

[54] Wolfgang, Marvin E. and Reidel, Marc (1973) "Race, judicial discretion, and the death penalty," *Annals of the American Academy of Political and Social Science*, 53.

[55] Coker v. Georgia, 433 U.S. 584 (1977).

[56] Zeisel, Hans and Gallup, Alec M. (1989) "Death penalty sentiment in the United States," *Journal of Quantitative Criminology*, 5(3).

[57] Blumstein, Alfred, Cohen, Jacqueline, and Nagin, Daniel (1978) *Deterrence and Incapacitation: Estimating the Effects of Criminal Sanctions on Crime Rates*, Washington, D.C.: National Academy of Sciences.

[58] Ehrlich, Issac (1975) The deterrent effect of capital punishment: A matter of life and death," *American Economic Review*, 65, p. 414.

[59] See, e.g., Bowers, William J. and Pierce, Glenn (1980) "Deterrence or brutalization: What is the effect of execution?" *Crime and Delinquency*, 26; McCahey, Richard M. (1980) "Dr. Ehrlich's magic bullet: Economic theory, econometrics, and the death penalty," *Crime and Delinquency*, 26; Forst, Brian (1983) "Capital punishment and deterrence: Conflicting evidence?" *Journal of Criminal Law and Criminology*, 74.

[60] Decker, Scott H. and Kohfeld, Carol W. (1990) "The deterrent effect of capital punishment in the five most active execution states: A time series analysis," *Criminal Justice Review*, 15(2), p. 190.

[61] Peterson, Ruth D. and Bailey, William C. (1991) "Felony murder and capital punishment: An examination of the deterrence question," *Criminology*, 29(3).

[62] Yunker, J. (1982) "Testing the deterrent effect of capital punishment: A reduced form approach," *Criminology*, 19.

[63] Bailey, William C. (1991) "The general prevention effect of capital punishment for non-capital felonies," in Bohm, R.M. *The Death Penalty in America: Current Research*, Cincinnati, OH: Anderson Pub.

[64] Marquart, James W. and Sorenson, Jonathan R. (1989) "A national study of Furman-commuted inmates: Assessing the threat to society from capital offenders," *Loyola of Los Angeles Law Review*, 23(1), p. 25.

[65] Id. at 28.

[66] Johnson, Robert (1990) *Death Work: A Study of the Modern Execution Process*, Belmont, CA: Brooks-Cole.

[67] Senna, Joseph J. and Siegel, Larry J. (1990) *Introduction to Criminal Justice*, New York: West Pub. Co., p. 402.

[68] Nakell, Barry (1978) "The cost of the death penalty," *Criminal Law Bulletin*, 14.

[69] New York State Defender's Association, Inc. (1982) *Capital Losses: The Price of the Death Penalty for New York State*, Albany, NY: New York State Defender's Association, Inc., p. 12.

[70] Blakely, Alan F. (1990) "The cost of killing criminals," *Northern Kentucky Law Review*, 18, p. 69.

[71] Id. at 71.

[72] See New York State Defenders Association, note 69 above at 26.

[73] Id. at 71.

[74] Id. at 76-77.

[75] Gray, Ian and Stanley, Moira (1989) *A Punishment in Search of a Crime—Americans Speak Out Against the Death Penalty*, New York: Avon Books, p. 43.

[76] Id.

[77] Moran, Richard and Ellis, Joseph (1986) "Price of executions is just too high," *Wall Street Journal*, Oct. 15, 1986, p. 34.

[78] Id.

[79] Drehle, Dave Von (1988) "Death penalty price too high for Kansas," *Miami Herald*, July 13, 1988, p. 12A.

[80] Dionne, E.J. (1990) "Capital punishment gaining favor as public seeks retribution," *Corrections Today*, Aug. p. 178.

[81] Applebome, Peter (1991) "Georgia inmate is executed after 'chaotic' legal move," *New York Times*, Sept. 26, 1991, p. A10.

[82] New York Times (1991) "40% on death row are black, new figures show," Sept. 30, p. A9.

[83] See, e.g., Johnson, Elmer H. (1957) "Selective forces in capital punish-

ment," *Social Forces*, 36; Zimring, Franklin E., Eigen, Joel, and O'Malley Sheila (1976) "Punishing homicides in Philadelphia: Perspectives on the death penalty," *University of Chicago Law Review*, 43.

[84] Kleck, Gary (1981) "Racial discrimination in criminal sentencing," *American Sociological Review*, 46.

[85] Radelet, Michael and Pierce, Glenn L. (1985) "Race and prosecutorial discretion in homicide cases," *Law and Society Review*, 19.

[86] See, e.g., Foley, Linda A. and Powell, Richard S. (1982) "The discretion of prosecutors, judges and jurists in capital cases," *Criminal Justice Review*, 7; Bowers, William (1983) "The pervasiveness of arbitrariness and discrimination under post-Furman capital statutes," *Journal of Criminal Law and Criminology*, 74.

[87] Baldus, David C., Pulaski, Charles and Woodworth (1983) "Comparative review of death sentences: An empirical study of the Georgia experience," *Journal of Criminal Law and Criminology*, 74.

[88] Keil, Thomas J. and Vito, Gennaro F. (1990) "Race and the death penalty in Kentucky murder trials: An analysis of post-Gregg outcomes," *Justice Quarterly*, 7.

[89] See, e.g., Wilbanks, William (1987) *The Myth of a Racist Criminal Justice System*, Monterey, CA: Brooks-Cole.

[90] Gross, Samuel R. and Mauro, Robert (1989) *Death and Discrimination—Racial Disparities in Capital Sentencing*, Boston: Northeastern University Press.

[91] Id. at 200.

[92] United States General Accounting Office (1990) "Death penalty sentencing—Research indicates pattern of racial disparities," Washington, D.C.: U.S. Government Accounting Office, Report GAO/GGD-90-57, pp. 5-6.

[93] See Kleck, note 84 above.

[94] Louisiana ex rel. Francis v. Resweber, 329 U.S. 459 (1947).

[95] Zeisel, Hans and Gallup, Alec M. (1989) "Death penalty sentiment in the United States," *Journal of Quantitative Criminology*, 5(3), pp. 285-286; Flanagan, Timothy J. and Maguire, Kathleen (1990) *Sourcebook of Criminal Justice Statistics—1989*, Washington, D.C.: U.S. Department of Justice, pp. 168-169.

[96] See Zeisel, Gallup, note 95 above at 289.

[97] Id. at 290.

[98] Id.

[99] Skovron, Sandra Evans, Scott, Joseph E., and Cullen, Francis T. (1989) "The death penalty for juveniles: An assessment of public support," *Crime and Delinquency*, 35(4), p. 552.

[100] Williams, Frank P., Gulick, David B., and Longmire, Dennis R. (1988)

"The public and the death penalty: Opinion as an artifact of question type," *Criminal Justice Research Bulletin*, 3(8), p. 4.

[101] Id.

[102]Petersilia, Joan (1990) "Death Penalty Resolution Debated and Endorsed," *The Criminologist*, vol. 15, no. 1, p. 1.

[103] Barr, William P. (1991) "Bush's crime bill: This time, pass it," *New York Times*, Sept. 24, 1991, p. A17.

[104] Young, Malcolm C. (1991) Letter to editor, *New York Times*, Oct. 4, p. A-16.

[105] Flanagan, Timothy J. and Maguire, Kathleen (1990) *Sourcebook of Criminal Justice Statistics—1989*, Washington, D.C.: U.S. Dept. of Justice, p. 629.

[106] Keve, Paul W. (1992) "The costliest punishment—A corrections administrator contemplates the death penalty," *Federal Probation*, 56(1), p. 12.

12

Failure, What Might Be Done, and What Corrections Simply Cannot Accomplish

Even the briefest examination of American newspapers and television newscasts makes clear that the correctional system is beset by a wide range of problems. In this book we have examined some of these problems as well as a number of the newest or most prominent solutions proposed to address these difficulties. After a discussion of the importance of ideology in corrections, we considered overcrowding and some of the hazards with which it is associated, the special challenges posed by diseases such as AIDS and tuberculosis, the difficulties presented by the increasing numbers of older offenders and women prisoners, the issue of deterrence, and the controversy regarding rehabilitation.

We also considered a variety of remedies to correctional problems. Alternatives to incarceration were described, including intensive supervision programs, home confinement, electronic monitoring, fines, restitution, community service, and day-reporting centers. Boot camps and correctional privatization, two of today's most highly publicized correctional innovations, were examined and evaluated. Finally, capital punishment was discussed, in part because of the symbolic importance of its place in the often volatile debate over effective responses to crime.

Our examination of these topics and issues was not designed to provide an exhaustive cataloging of the major crises and reforms in American punishment. Topics such as prison riots, correctional management, race and corrections, the juvenile correctional system, and a number of other subjects have not been covered. We have attempted to focus on some of the issues of greatest current importance; those that will be accorded significant discussion in the years to come in academic and practitioner circles as well as in the popular press. Our objectives in addressing each of these topics have been to communicate a basic understanding of each problem, provide an account of the nature of proposed correctional reforms, and, where possible, develop a sense of the effectiveness of the reforms currently being undertaken.

Having accomplished these objectives it is now time to stand back and consider the prospects for the near and distant future. Is there any reason to believe that the problems we have been examining will be resolved by the end of the current century? Is there any reason to believe that the next generation of students, criminologists, correctional practitioners, and politicians will not be discussing prison crowding, recidivism rates, the death penalty, correctional privatization, and the host of other issues that have been the subject of our attention?

Although it is typical for penal analysts to conclude their examinations of the correctional system with at least a token expression of optimism about the future, there is good reason to believe that many of the problems that we have considered will not be resolved in either the near or the distant future. There is an excellent basis for the belief that a number of factors will make it exceedingly difficult to do more than work around the edges of these problems. The remainder of this chapter will describe the basis for this pessimism, then provide a few suggestions which may have some value in developing an enlightened and effective response to crime.

What Have We Learned?

Despite the tripling of the prison population since the early 1970s, and the doubling during the 1980s, the message that there are substantial limitations on what imprisonment can accomplish has still not reached the upper levels of government. In January of 1992, then-Attorney General William P. Barr asserted, "The choice is clear . . . more prison space or more crime."[1] Barr held a conference in the spring of 1992 to discuss ways to expand the use of imprisonment as a response to crime.

And in the summer of 1992 he issued a series of recommendations to combat violent crime, again calling for more imprisonment.[2]

Enthusiasm for imprisonment is not limited to national leaders. Florida Governor Lawton Chiles has proposed adding 21,000 beds to the existing 50,000 in his home state. In justification of his proposal Chiles noted, "I can't stand the fact that Florida is Number 1 in violent crimes. If I had to push a peanut up Capitol Hill, I'd do that to provide safe streets for the people of Florida."[3] Florida State Corrections Secretary Harry Singleton vigorously expressed his support for the plan. "This is the building block. I've always said prisons are to keep people for the length of their sentence. I don't think we should manage the system by letting one out when we let one in."[4]

Of course, political memories sometimes run shallow and short. Just a few years ago then-Governor Bob Martinez expressed the same sentiments, with the result that 22,000 beds were added in the late 1980s, almost doubling Florida's prison capacity. Despite such an extraordinary and expensive measure, according to Governor Chiles, Florida is still leading the pack in terms of violent crime. Florida's experience is not unique. An analysis released by the Pennsylvania Commission on Sentencing concluded that although incarceration in Pennsylvania increased 32 percent from 1985 to 1991, violence rates increased 38 percent during the same period.[5] Some analysts might suggest that there is a lesson in all of this, and it is that simply repeating what was done in the 1980s will just not get the job done.

Of course, political leaders are under a variety of pressures to continue to publicly lobby for tougher and tougher responses to the crime problem. Moreover, when solutions fail, they have to explain why. Governor Douglas L. Wilder of Virginia points out that

> [i]t's absolutely insane the amount of money we spend on corrections. . . . What we have been doing is not right. But it is very difficult for politicians, and I am one of them, to say we have been wrong and that we've got to revisit, revise, and restructure the whole system.[6]

Wilder is correct, of course. The public wants strong and decisive measures. However, a better informed populace might make the kinds of restructuring envisioned by Wilder more feasible politically. We will return to this idea momentarily, but we now turn to consideration of the question of correctional effectiveness.

Correctional Effectiveness: What Does It Mean?

Citizens, academicians, and politicians routinely talk about effective correctional approaches. Arguments for longer prison sentences, fewer amenities for prison inmates, adoption of meaningful drug treatment, and a host of other approaches are frequently articulated in the media. A careful effort to listen to what is being said reveals several interesting points.

First, it is apparent that there is often little consensus regarding what "effectiveness" means. To some it means little more than taking offenders out of circulation. Others are interested in and hopeful about deterrent effects. Still others seek to rehabilitate criminals, reduce the cost of corrections, more fully engage the private sector in correctional operations, obtain justice, or secure restitution.

Second, citizens concerned with different goals will likely take different outcomes as evidence of effectiveness. For instance, a drop in the number of citizens who initially become involved with the law might be regarded as evidence of the effectiveness of general deterrence. Evidence of rehabilitation might be a decrease in the subsequent offending of treated offenders, or even an increase in various kinds of pro-social behavior (for example, proper parenting, maintenance of employment). Evidence of retributive effectiveness might be data showing that offenders serve close to 100 percent of their assigned penal sentence. Thus the nature of the evidence indicating correctional effectiveness will vary in accord with the character of the goal pursued.

Third, the reality is that most citizens are interested in more than a single goal. As a result, the process of determining correctional effectiveness is further complicated. Moreover, achievement of one goal may well come at the expense of another objective. For example, a correctional system that retains inmates through the full duration of their sentences may achieve retributive goals, yet may impede deterrent objectives. Inmates may be imprisoned beyond what is necessary to deter them from subsequent lawbreaking, and in so doing permit the prison socialization process to actually increase the adoption of pro-crime values (the "crime school" idea), thereby unraveling any good work that may have been done with regard to specific deterrence.

Finally, not only do citizens appear to have interest in a variety of goals for corrections, but the relative importance of such goals changes over time. Scrutiny of public opinion during the last 20 years makes clear that interest in various correctional goals has not remained static. While 73 percent of citizens surveyed in 1967 stated that rehabilitation was the primary correctional goal, in 1982 only 44 percent of citizens felt the same way.[7] By the end of the 1980s, it was still true that only a minority of citizens thought that rehabilitation was more important than punishment.[8] The decrease of interest in rehabilitation has been accompanied by an increase of interest in goals commonly associated with tougher anti-crime measures. There has been a significant increase in retribution in sentencing, in giving offenders what they deserve for their crimes rather than what they need to address the supposed conditions that resulted in their criminal involvement. Moreover, changes in the relative importance of goals mean changes in the kinds of evidence that will be regarded as most useful in evaluating correctional effectiveness.

In sum, American corrections has been expected to achieve a number of important goals, some of which have been in direct conflict. Additionally, different kinds of evidence have been regarded as valuable in assessing correctional effectiveness, and different analysts have often interpreted these data in very different ways. In light of this, it should not be surprising that the correctional system has been unable to achieve anything even approximating the level of effectiveness hoped for by citizens, politicians, and the academic community. The system's task is multifaceted, its resources are very limited, and measures of effectiveness are often controversial.

In thinking about correctional effectiveness, therefore, it is extremely important to be careful and precise in specifying both what is being sought and the kinds of information that will provide insight into whether the goal is being achieved. In fact, there appears to have been little of this kind of thinking in the public arena during the last two decades. We now turn to brief consideration of this recent period of penal reform.

Late Twentieth-Century Penal Reform

Perhaps the most visible expression of the national concern with crime can be found in the rhetoric of American presidents. In the 1972

Presidential campaign Senator George McGovern assured the country that "the No. 1 domestic priority of my administration" would be crime and the drug problem.[9] Richard Nixon, the Republican incumbent, was able to point to a brief overall decrease in crime, but nonetheless publicly pressured Congress to modify the law to toughen crime control strategies. He argued for expansion in the use of capital punishment, longer sentences for heroin pushers, and a major revision of the Federal Criminal Code.[10] Crime rates increased in 1973, and in a 1974 speech President Gerald Ford noted of crime that "[i]t can no longer be ignored. It can no longer be rationalized away. The time has come to act."[11]

Although a number of reforms were initiated in the mid and late 1970s, crime continued to be a hot issue. Many citizens were optimistic that the newly elected Reagan administration would be able to make significant progress in addressing the crime problem. Indeed, at the very outset of his first term in office Reagan appointed a commission to study serious crime. However, after eight years of the Reagan Administration, F.B.I. Crime Index rates were climbing. President George Bush's remarks in 1990 have a familiar ring. "It's time for Congress to act quickly and responsibly because the war on drugs and crime won't wait."[12] Senator Phil Gramm called for legislation to declare a "National Drug and Crime Emergency."[13]

What is especially interesting about the remarks of major political leaders such as Bush and Gramm is that they were made after a number of significant reforms were enacted. Specifically, sentencing structures were changed in many states and the federal government, doing away with the old indeterminate sentencing systems, ostensibly created tougher and more certain punishments for offenders. Mandatory minimum sentences were established for selected crimes. An offender sentenced to prison in many jurisdictions would know at the outset what his or her sentence would be, minus any good time that might be accumulated. Parole boards would no longer be able to release offenders early. Some states, such as Maine, did away with parole altogether.

Nonetheless, merely by looking at the pronouncements of major American political figures in the late 1980s and early 1990s, one would never conclude that such changes, apparently widely supported by citizens, politicians, and many academicians, had been implemented. According to our political leaders crime is still a major problem, and it continues to be imperative that we "take action now." One important difference exists, of course. Now our prisons are more packed then they have ever been, the incarceration rate is triple what it was during the 1972 Presidential campaign, and billions of dollars have been invested in a wide range of tough-minded correctional initiatives. Despite such changes, citizens continue to feel threatened. In 1975, 45 percent of citizens surveyed indicated that they were afraid to walk in their neighborhood. The figure in 1989 was an essentially identical 43 percent.[14]

Taken together, current crime rates, fiscal expenditures, and levels of public fear indicate that we are *worse* off now than we were in 1972. Moreover, the utterances of both politicians and citizens suggest quite clearly that the *perception* is that we are worse off now than 20 years ago. What has gone wrong? The grand expectations of the reformers of the 1970s have simply not been met, despite investment of considerable human effort and material resources into the reformed American system of punishment.

Why Have We Failed?

Many explanations have been articulated to account for the failure to reach correctional objectives. We will look briefly at several of these reasons. It is important to bear in mind that these explanations are not necessarily mutually exclusive.

The Poverty of the New Assumptions

The Neoclassical Revival discussed earlier in this book asserted the failure of correctional strategies that were based upon notions of "root causes," the tractability of human nature, the assumption that human behavior was not predicated primarily upon the exercise of free will, and the salience of social factors in explaining involvement in crime. The Revival insisted that humans are rational, employ such rationality in the exercise of free will, and are therefore responsible for their actions. The main function of the correctional system should not be, therefore, to rehabilitate, but to accord offenders what they deserve for their misconduct.

Critics of this perspective pointed out that whether this view of human nature accurately captures the essence of humanity, there is no reason to expect that giving offenders what they deserve will have any impact on future behavior of offenders or others, including future criminal behavior. The best result Neoclassicists could hope for would thus be a fair and just distribution of punishments in accord with desert.

Unfortunately, there is little evidence that this has occurred. Indeed, penal crowding has resulted in early release strategies that have further solidified the public belief that criminals are not getting what they deserve. Moreover, there is evidence that citizens themselves do not agree on the severity of the punishments, incarceration term lengths for instance, that should be given to various kinds of offenders.[15] Finally, surveys of citizens and politicians do not indicate that the most important correctional objective is giving offenders what they deserve. There seems to be considerably more interest in forward-looking utilitarian goals such as deterrence, rehabilitation, and incapacitation.[16]

Thus the assumptions of the Neoclassicists have perhaps been of relatively little value in stimulating development of the kinds of correctional policies that could be responsive to public preferences regarding crime.

Politics as Usual

It is remarkable that although the topic of crime persistently appears in campaign speeches, party platforms, and political advertisements, the nation seems to be forever embroiled in a crime crisis. How is it possible that the prominence of crime in the political firestorms that characterize our competitive electoral process has not led to sustained political action to deal with the problem?

Several possible explanations exist. First, it may be that although crime captures the public's attention and makes citizens angry, it really is not viewed by anyone as a solvable problem. Citizens may be mollified if they believe that the right approaches are being tried, irrespective of whether such strategies are ultimately effective. In recent times this has meant that politicians have had to persuade the public that they were tough, really tough, on crime. Thus Willie Horton-type ad campaigns, which utterly misrepresent reality, were adopted as instruments to accomplish this persuasion. A more recent example involves efforts by both the Republican administration and its Democratic critics to assign blame in the aftermath of the riots in Los Angeles. Similar blaming took place after the riots in Watts in 1963, yet the political will to correct the problems in L.A. was not sustained once the initial furor died down. Band-Aids were used rather than the major surgery needed to address the problems of the inner city. Politics seems to serve to satisfy voter urges rather than to set in motion processes that will adequately address problems.

As concern with crime increases, "legislative reform is aimed at crime bills which call for tougher responses including longer mandatory minimum sentences and the use of capital punishment for more crimes."[17] The *real* seriousness of such efforts can, however, be seen in the failure of such bills to include money to cover the costs of the reforms. For instance, Senator D'Amato of New York presented a crime bill requiring mandatory minimum ten-year sentences for drug crimes in which firearms were fired. When it was pointed out that his bill provided no new funds to cover the added costs to courts and prisons the Senator replied, "I could care a hoot about the fact that it may create a burden for the (federal) courts."[18] This expression of either sheer ignorance of the realities of crime control or of shameless political duplicity is far from rare and is certainly not confined to representatives from a single location on the ideological spectrum. Moreover, politicians are not alone in failing to understand the complexities of implementing meaningful correctional initiatives. Despite wanting to put more offenders behind bars, and to build prisons to accomplish this, citizens are often reluctant to foot the bill. A bond issue to provide a much-needed increase in prison capacity in New York, for instance, was rejected by voters.[19]

We do know from hard experience that tough laws passed without adequate financial support will simply create new problems. Tougher laws that have packed prisons in states such as Florida and Texas have simply led to early release policies that have defeated the original purposes of the toughening legislation. Recent estimates by the Texas Board of Criminal Justice indicate that the "average prison inmate in Texas serves less than 20 percent of his sentence."[20]

We also know that the political will to adequately support important penal reforms is often lacking. To be fair, some of this wavering may reflect conflicts within political ideological traditions. For instance, although Republicans have typically been viewed as the party of tough measures on crime, such as long prison sentences, they have also represented themselves as the stewards of fiscal conservatism. They have routinely criticized Democrats for the willingness to spend taxpayer dollars and expand government. Of course, this is exactly what we have witnessed with the recent expansion of the prison system—more expenditures and bigger government. On the one hand conservative politicians have an obligation to maintain the party's traditional "tough" posture toward crime, on the other they must assure the voters that increases in taxation are not on the horizon. Not an easy task.

Democrats have their own ideological contradictions, of course. The point is that part of the lack of political resolve may derive from paradoxes within the ideology upon which political action is based.

The Failure to Give Reform a Chance

In the larger historical span, the 20 years that have passed since the outset of the current penal reform initiative is a very short period of time. It can be argued that the failure of these reforms is only apparent, and that if given a reasonable amount of time, the reforms will prove successful.

The impatience characteristic of our political system has manifested itself in other areas. Lyndon Johnson's War on Poverty, for instance, was pronounced dead before a single decade had passed. However, the expectation that serious, long-standing problems such as poverty or crime would yield within a single political administration or even a decade or two is perhaps as perplexing as the fact that poverty and crime are at least as troubling now as they were in the early days of the nation.

The nature of our electoral political process creates ample opportunity to deny reforms of whatever variety a fair chance to succeed. Candidates for office typically develop popular appeal in part on their ability to criticize what the incumbent has done while in office. If the incumbent has decriminalized drugs, then the challenger must point out the error of that approach. If the incumbent has toughened sentencing, the challenger must point to the costs of imprisonment, overcrowding, and the neglect of the "causes" of crime. An incumbent who fails to focus on what has gone wrong will be in a poor position to persuade the electorate that what she or he offers is an improvement.

Thus politically based reforms must often, almost by their very nature, be short-lived. When a new crew takes over they must pursue, at least in part, the new agenda promised to the voters. Conditions in the American political climate, such as the frequency of elections, make it extremely difficult for the nation to commit energy and resources to a unified reform agenda over an extended period of time.

Interestingly enough, both conservatives and liberals are aware of this issue. When liberals denounced many of the reforms of the last 20 years as a failure, conservatives defended these reforms by insisting that they have not been given ample opportunity to produce results. Liberals rejected this defense, and accused conservatives of stalling and clinging to failed policy. Some liberals, however, were quick to use the same defense in the 1970s when rehabilitation came under attack. They asserted that rehabilitation had not been given an adequate chance to prove itself, and that expertise on what was effective was only beginning to become available. Conservatives responded by claiming that much of the twentieth century had been devoted to fruitless efforts to develop effective rehabilitative strategies.

Of course, nobody really knows what constitutes a fair trial period. What can be reasonably asserted is that frequent shifts in political power seem likely to forestall the possibility of any lengthy trial periods. If development and identification of truly effective solutions requires extensive time for fine-tuning, it may be very unlikely that political conditions will make the emergence of effective penal approaches possible.

Asking Too Much of the Penal System

Some critics have argued that America has maintained extraordinary faith in the correctional system even in the face of obvious failure. Indeed, Americans have attributed abilities to corrections that simply do not exist. Henry Pontell suggests that "our legal system was never designed to take on the entire task of social control. This seems true today, as the increased use of punishment has been revived as the "solution" to the crime problem."[21] In one sense, America has asked corrections to assume responsibility for problems well beyond the reach of its capabilities. The notion that merely threatening citizens with severe and certain punishment, or even actually applying such punishment, would address the myriad conditions that seem to be related to social misbehavior is really extraordinary. Parents, after all, do not rely solely upon punishment or the threat of punishment in their efforts to educate and train their children for responsible citizenship. They use a mix of positive inducement, teaching by example, creating opportunities, making resources available, providing explicit moral guidance, and a host of other methods to influence their children. It is therefore mystifying, according to this line of argument, why anyone would believe that punishment alone should be an effective agent for producing law-abiding behavior.

Solutions to the crime problem must embrace aspects of social functioning that make their indelible marks long before the individual develops behavioral practices which eventually put him or her into contact with the criminal justice system. The view that social conditions such as poverty, lack of educational opportunity, and unemployment, as well as conditions on the homefront, are responsible for significant amounts of crime fits well with this line of explanation. While we have expected too much of the correctional system, at the same time we have expected too little of other social institutions. It is no coincidence that the nation's poorest, most disadvantaged citizens have a disproportionately high likelihood of ending up in the correctional system. In Baltimore, for instance, more than half of young black males (aged 18 to 35) were under some form of justice system supervision (prison, jail, probation, parole) in 1991.[22] What citizens experience at home, in school, at work, and on the streets has more influence on lifelong behavior patterns than experiences that might be had within the correctional system. The high recidivism rates for state prisoners who have experienced punishment without being dissuaded from future involvement in crime are consistent with this viewpoint.

What Might Be Done

Significant portions of this book have been devoted to consideration of various strategies to deal with correctional challenges (for example, boot camps, intensive supervision, privatization, restitution). Having earlier suggested that at least some of these approaches may prove useful, it may seem odd that I should now write so gloomily about what has transpired and why the correctional system has not been successful in meeting many of its assigned obligations.

It is important to remember, however, that these approaches are currently being tried because of the shortcomings in what the correctional system has been able to accomplish. Moreover, some of the approaches discussed in earlier chapters may well have significant potential for success, but only if not limited by the more general kinds of factors discussed in the previous section.

It is clear that there remain numerous potential solutions that can be adopted to address correctional problems. Some are directly related to corrections. John DiIulio, for instance, suggests that efforts to improve upon the organization and management of prisons will address some of our concerns about corrections.[23] Norval Morris and Michael Tonry argue for a reconceptualization of the idea of punishment such that punishments served in the community are regarded not merely as alternatives to incarceration, but as sanctions in their own right.[24] As we have seen throughout this book, other analysts provide a variety of additional corrections-specific solutions.

Some analysts suggest that such specific reforms cannot be effective if they are unaccompanied by strategies to address general obstacles to enduring reform. Morris and Tonry describe six general types of obstacles: constitutional, legal, organizational, bureaucratic, ideological, and financial.[25] Although some of these obstacles involve the justice system itself, others involve related social institutions, legal restrictions, funding difficulties, limits associated with bureaucratic organizations, and political processes. They thus include, but are not limited to, specific problems of the correctional system.

The observations that follow below take a somewhat different tack. They assume that obstacles to successful corrections-specific reforms derive to no small extent from a more general problem: the inadequacy of the public's ability to influence correctional policymaking. In what follows, some suggestions for addressing this difficulty will be detailed. The focus of these observations is on general kinds of issues, which may seem to have relatively little to do with corrections in any narrow sense, but which may ultimately be more important than suggestions of more apparent direct relevance.

We begin with public education and detail the various kinds of information the public needs to possess to effectively address correctional problems. We then take up the education of political leaders and the development of public patience. The chapter concludes with some observations on the need to look beyond corrections for remedies to crime.

Education: What the People Need to Know

It is nothing short of astonishing that, given the amount of crime-related material in the electronic and print media, citizens know so very little about crime and punishment. Spectacular and anecdotal information abounds, but citizens lack systematic understanding of either the true dimensions of the crime problem or the severe limitations of the correctional system. There are a number of important kinds of information that citizens need to possess if they are going to assume positions of effective stewardship in bringing about meaningful change through the political process.

345

The Basis for Public Knowledge
of Crime and Justice

The public has little sense of the limitations of the information they possess. Although knowledge about crime and justice can derive from first or secondhand experience as a crime victim, average citizens get most of their information about crime and justice through newspapers, fiction on TV, in films and in books, and through so-called electronic newsmagazines. As numerous studies have shown, these information conduits too often focus on the glamourous or gruesome, and fail to portray accurately the real dimensions of either crime or the response to crime. Ray Surette notes that

> [i]n their coverage, the media offer explanations of crime that are direct and simple: lust, greed, immorality, jealousy, revenge, and insanity . . . media trials represent the final step in a long process of merging the news and entertainment—a process that has often resulted in multimedia and commercial news exploitation of these cases.[26]

Surette points out that "[i]t is no coincidence that similar crimes and criminals are depicted in entertainment and news, for the goals and needs of both are to assemble the largest audience possible to maximize readers, ratings, and revenue."[27] This is no minor matter, both because media coverage distorts the reality of crime and punishment, and because coverage of crime in entertainment and news results in beliefs and attitudes about crime and justice.

> Many have argued that the media's portrait of America and its social structure tend to become the accepted version of social reality. Over time people tend to perceive things the way the media portray them. The media thus play not only a reporting role but a defining role, establishing their audience's sense of reality; prescribing society's accepted norms, behaviors and boundaries; and forwarding the proper means of dealing with injustice.[28]

Surette argues that media portrayals focus on individual criminal culpability and result in public support for tough law and order-oriented policies that continue to rely on the standard institutions for addressing crime. "Entertainment and news portrayals that expound social change or structural causes of crime are rare."[29]

Thus at the very outset citizens need to understand the basis of their perceptions of the crime problem. They need to know that the information they receive is the product of a number of influences, not all of which are concerned with providing the most accurate information possible.

Public justice agencies also provide information, though typically it is channeled through the mass media. When the media do a crime story, most often they will turn to law enforcement spokespersons for information and interpretation.[30] Crime statistics are usually provided by representatives of law enforcement, although not always with happy results. For instance, the F.B.I.'s insistence on using the "Crime Clock" method of providing crime information is an excellent example of distortion. Computing the number of crimes per unit time is not a meaningful measure of crime because the population of the country has increased dramatically since the origins of the Crime Clock, while the number of seconds, minutes, and hours in a day has remained constant. A shortening of the time between crimes reflects, in part, the increase in the population of the country rather than dramatic increases in the crime rate. Despite this, the Crime Clock remains part of the F.B.I.'s public information approach, and visitors to the main office in Washington, D.C. can actually view an actual Crime Clock with flashing lights symbolizing the commission of each new crime.

While law enforcement spokespersons may be sought out because of some crime that has been committed, corrections officials are typically contacted when there has been a problem with the correctional system. Prison riots, furlough programs, early release of inmates and a host of other issues are typically the subject of media coverage of corrections.[31] Thus negative kinds of information about corrections seem to occupy the bulk of stories on corrections, with the expected negative public perception of the correctional system. Although there regularly appear media portrayals where law enforcement "gets their man," portrayals of correctional system success are rare.

Government efforts to improve public knowledge have been made. Justice agencies, such as the National Institute of Justice, have research and publication series that provide information about crime and justice. Unfortunately, the average citizen never sees or hears about what is contained in such reports. This is unfortunate because some of the reports, such as a report detailing the lack of evidence on the effectiveness of boot camps, contain important data that contradict information commonly presented in the popular media.

Of course, this is certainly not a problem limited to crime and punishment. Citizens have limited access to accurate information on all kinds of important matters, such as the movement of interest rates or political developments abroad. The thing that makes crime and punishment of special concern, however, is that considerable errant information is presented to citizens daily on crime and punishment, while relatively little such misinformation is provided on numerous other topics. When was the last time "Hard Copy" did a spectacular story on interest rates or political developments in Eastern Europe? Although there are many "infotainment" programs for crime (for example,"Top Cops," "America's Most Wanted," "Unsolved Mysteries,"), how many similar series are there devoted to the problems of poverty or the environment? Virtually none. As a consequence, the opportunities to convey errant information as part of the spectacularization of other social problems are much more limited than with crime.

Thus an important step in addressing the crime problem is assuring that the public has access to an accurate body of current information about crime and punishment. Perhaps one way to accomplish this would be to offer and require "Social Problems" type courses in the elementary, junior, and high schools. Such courses are routinely offered in college but might be more valuable if offered to all citizens, not merely those entering college.

A second approach might be development of locally based information clearinghouses that would represent a merger of public and private spheres, including the social science community. Such clearinghouses could develop both routine information dissemination mechanisms (newsletters, advertisements, local speeches to community groups, for example) and special information promotions on selected topics. To avoid self-serving selective dissemination of information, these clearinghouses would be independent of justice agencies in law enforcement, the courts, or corrections, as well as free of political affiliation.

Whatever remedial methods might be selected, current public education about crime and the correctional system is sadly inadequate and must be addressed. It is simply not realistic to expect meaningful changes in the manner in which correctional problems are addressed without a higher level of public awareness of the real dimensions of crime and punishment. Although such awareness alone does not assure the development of effective enduring solutions, it is difficult to see how a persistently misinformed public could ever provide the political basis for meaningful policy change.

Clarification of Correctional Goals

As we noted above, correctional goals sometimes conflict with one another. Indeed, some analysts attribute correctional failures in part to such goal incompatibility. Although in the abstract it is reasonable to want to achieve multiple objectives through the correctional system (incapacitation, justice, deterrence, rehabilitation, restitution, for example), in reality it may be impossible to do justice to all of them simultaneously. Worse, it may be impossible to do justice to *any* of them if too broad a focus is maintained.

Survey data described in earlier chapters suggest that citizens want to achieve multiple correctional objectives. Unfortunately, it is unlikely that such citizens have the faintest understanding of the difficulties of such an achievement. However, focus group studies do indicate that when citizens are made aware of correctional complexities, they are more than willing to modify their viewpoint to take such complications into consideration.[32]

Thus it is vital that information about the complicated nature of achieving correctional goals be communicated to the public. Again, the means described in the previous section might represent useful approaches to conveying this information. The chances of being able to channel correctional resources effectively, specify explicit measurable goals, conduct meaningful evaluation research, and fine-tune useful correctional approaches will be enhanced if the public has a realistic understanding of the complex interrelationships between correctional goals and objectives.

Understanding Correctional History

The philosopher Santayana wrote, "Those who cannot remember the past are condemned to repeat it." Somehow this solid observation seems not to have been taken to heart in the world of penal reform. The history of American corrections is to some extent a history of problems, new solutions, failures, and more solutions, some of which are the same old solutions. Almost without exception, new waves of reform come attended with much fanfare and little historical insight.

For instance, during the 1980s considerable interest emerged in privatizing the correctional system. Although some enthusiasts of privatization moderated their expectations, others viewed privatization as a panacea for all that ails the correctional system. Critics were equally varied, with the harshest critics regarding privatization as a shift to profit-motivated punishment that threatened fundamental citizen liberties in the crass pursuit of profit. For neither enthusiasts nor critics, however, was there much interest in looking for guidance at the extensive nineteenth-century experience with correctional privatization. In fact, many of the fears of critics are confirmed by the experience of the earlier period of privatization. This information might be useful in helping to avoid earlier errors, whether this involved abandonment of privatization or merely a more careful tooling of new privatization initiatives. The scant attention paid to this historical experience likely will result in mistakes that could be avoided, and may ultimately jeopardize an idea that might otherwise prove valuable.

How are citizens and their political leaders to make informed judgments about what reforms merit consideration if so little attention is paid to what has already transpired in the extensive American experience with punishment? Would not a company contemplating a change in business practices be interested in looking at how an earlier similar change affected productivity and profitability? Would not an individual giving thought to moving back to the big city, or returning to the farm, give consideration to his or her earlier experience for help in predicting whether such a return is a good idea? This commonsense notion of examining past experience to assist in making predictions about the future seems to have been ignored in the typical process of correctional reform.

Historians and social scientists could be of value in providing public information about previous reform projects. Penal historians are available to provide such information but have rarely been asked to participate in the correctional reform process in this capacity. This situation will probably not change as a result of pressure applied by scholars themselves. The initiative must come from enlightened citizens, politicians, and correctional officials. Of course, there is no political pressure or accountability to motivate such individuals to seek historically based guidance. There is little fear that critics of what turned out to be a failed reform will come back and cry out, "You mean you privatized the state prison system and did not even check with the historians at the state university first? Shocking!" Without some form of political accountability there is little likelihood that meaningful examinations of prior experience will be conducted.

Education: What the Politicians Need to Know

A 1992 survey revealed that 82 percent of Americans believed that the nation's political leaders were "out of touch."[33] Eighty-four percent felt that "it's time for politicians to step aside for new ones."[34] With regard to punishment, we have already seen that politicians are out of touch with the character of public opinion about crime and punishment. Studies have indicated, for instance, that politicians may seriously over-estimate the extent to which the public is interested in punitive, rather than rehabilitative, correctional goals.[35] To the extent that this is true, therefore, it should not be surprising that the public is dissatisfied with what the political leadership has managed to accomplish regarding crime and punishment. Politicians may be pursuing objectives that do not, despite the rhetoric, square with what Americans really want to do about crime.

How can politicians be educated about public attitudes, opinions, and preferences regarding corrections? In a democratic society one might expect that the education is provided by being tossed out of office during the next election. The truth, however, is that politicians are elected for a variety of reasons, some of which have to do with the many other issues besides crime, and others of which have nothing to do with issues at all (like party politics). Waiting for education to occur as a result of the electoral process is unlikely to prove productive. Other approaches are needed.

Perhaps the first step is to make the public itself aware of what its preferences are. Two factors suggest that this can be accomplished. First, refinements in survey technology, such as focus group and computer analysis techniques, indicate that the technical means to develop methodologically sound assessments of public preferences currently exist. Second, there appears to be significant public enthusiasm for information about public views as indicated by widely publicized survey initiatives regularly reported in media such as USA TODAY, TIME magazine, and the highly successful book The Day America Told the Truth. People are interested in what other people think about issues, thus motivating citizens to pay attention to the results of public attitude and preference surveys should not be problematic if information is not buried in obscure government reports or academic journals.

Making citizens aware of what the body politic thinks will make it much more difficult for politicians to misunderstand or misrepresent public sentiment. This awareness provides an *informational empowerment* enabling citizens to evaluate more effectively politicians who claim to be representing public wishes. Political leaders, understanding the data on public sentiment and the fact that the public itself now possesses an *informational identity* (a self-awareness of how it views various issues), will understand better what would now be the very real risks of ignoring public preferences. Presumably, at least some leaders will thus be motivated to pay closer attention to what the public is saying and make an effort to implement public desires. A politician who ignores the considerable public interest in correctional rehabilitation, for instance, would now face an informationally empowered constituency and be compelled to explain why he or she voted against providing funds for drug treatment facilities, inmate counseling centers, or prison education programs. It would be unrealistic to think such empowerment will end baseless political posturing about crime, but it should make it significantly more difficult and politically risky.

Developing Public Patience

Although everyone knows that Rome was not built in a day, the American political environment makes it difficult to accord modern reforms a reasonable opportunity to work. Citizens seem especially impatient when it comes to crime, perhaps because crime is so often cast by the media as little more than good guys versus bad guys. As noted earlier, this impatience is very unfortunate in light of the increasingly sophisticated technology for evaluating the effectiveness of reform. Both the ability to determine the level of success of a reform and the number of penal analysts insisting upon such methodologically sound research,[36] are greater now than they have ever been.

Can public patience with justice system reform be increased? Within the current quick-turnover electoral system dramatic increases in patience may be improbable. It is possible, however, that some of the educational reforms we have already discussed may indirectly influence public patience. To the extent that citizens understand the historical record, the distortions typically found in the media, the recurrence of political rhetoric about crime, the nature of public consensus regarding correctional goals, and the instrumental use of the correctional system as a whipping boy to further political campaigns, they may become more thoughtful and less reactive. With heightened understanding may come a more solid sense of the difficulties of implementing and carrying out meaningful changes and subsequently a more patient attitude toward penal reforms.

This may be wishful thinking, but it is not unprecedented. When citizens have been persuaded that significant time is required to address a problem, they have been willing to invest in the long haul. Real wars, not the kinds politicians routinely invoke against social ills, are an excellent example of the capacity of the citizenry to maintain a vigilant and energetic dedication to a plan designed to remedy some problem. It can be done, but typically only under extraordinary circumstances. With the continuing crisis in corrections, it may not be long before we find ourselves in just such extraordinary circumstances.

Looking Beyond Corrections

As noted earlier in this chapter, the correctional system has too often been regarded as a means of redressing deep-seated social and individual ills. The fact is that most of the individuals who end up in the deep end of the correctional system, the state and federal prisons, get there only after considerable prior involvement in crime. Perhaps because only a subset of such crimes result in detection, apprehension, and conviction, it is apparent that the resources of the correctional system simply do not seem to discourage a significant portion of offenders who do attract the system's notice. Offenders persist in their lawbreaking until they are funneled into the prison system.

Adults with long histories of involvement in crime, with little formal education, and who often experienced poorly structured upbringings, may be too entrenched into behavioral patterns for the correctional system to have much influence. Everyone is familiar with the old adage that it is impossible to teach an old dog new tricks. Most of us, correctly or incorrectly, believe that it is often very difficult to change the mind or habits of an older person. The point is that once individuals reach a certain stage in their personal development it is exceedingly difficult to achieve major changes in personality, attitude, or behavior. Consider the large number of middle and upper class non-criminal citizens who willingly elect to go through various kinds of often expensive psychotherapy of one variety or another *without* achieving dramatic effects. It is simply very difficult to reverse years of experience and socialization.

The frustration felt by many, if not most, citizens regarding the failures of the correctional system is understandable. What is less understandable is how citizens began to think that the correctional system could significantly influence behavior, through whatever means. Why should we expect the correctional system to be able to accomplish so much when so many other social institutions have failed? When family, schools, and churches are unable to inculcate law-abiding behavior, why should we be surprised if the correctional system also fails? In a sense, the popular conception of the correctional system is like a fairy tale. The big, bad criminal manages to defy all the constraints of conventional socialization and proceeds to victimize society. Up rides the correctional system, and the criminal somehow becomes law-abiding and a person of responsibility. In reality, this is a fairy tale gone awry, for as we know the crook eventually manages to regain freedom (release from prison), and returns to his or her previous prey-stalking exploits (recidivism rates). When this happens the hero becomes villain, and there is anger and frustration directed at both criminals and the correctional system.

Focus 12-1

Beyond Corrections: New York Reduces Prison Crowding by De-emphasizing Arrests of Street-Level Drug Dealers[37]

During the late 1980s, New York City faced one of the most serious institutional crowding crises in the country. Its jails and prisons were overflowing with inmates largely as a result of an ambitious anti-drug campaign that swept thousands of street dealers into the criminal justice system. In the belief that aggressive pursuit of such dealers would eventually have a withering effect on drug trafficking, a special Tactical Narcotics Team (TNT) was organized in 1988 to conduct neighborhood sweeps designed to put pressure on street level drug activity.

Initial public reaction to the teams was positive. The TNTs reassured the community that steps were being taken to address the drug problem. Ultimately, however, this approach did not resolve the drug problem in the city. The drug trade did not disappear. Moreover, aggressive, enforcement helped jam the city's incarcerative facilities with new inmates. Crowding, violence, staff morale problems, and a host of other dilemmas became increasingly problematic. Moreover, the cost of incarcerating these inmates was astronomical.

In 1989 New York City police made a record 94,490 drug arrests. The courts were packed with cases, and the city's incarcerative facilities were operating at 103 percent of capacity. In a desperate effort to free up prison space, some serious offenders were being allowed to plead to lesser charges. Some minor offenders were having their cases dropped altogether.

It became clear to both citizens and criminal justice officials that the focus on street dealers was not going to produce the results that had been anticipated. In the face of obvious failure, Police Commissioner Lee Brown decided to adopt an alternative approach. While not abandoning aggressive street-level enforcement altogether, more resources were shifted to pursuing higher-level drug offenders, and less effort was invested into making arrests of street dealers. In 1991 the police made only 69,606 drug arrests, a dramatic drop from the 1989 record high. This drop has been accompanied by subsequent decreases in court crowding. Moreover, New York City's correctional system is now operating at only 92 percent of capacity, the first time in several years that it has been under capacity. The city had even been using two barges to hold overflow inmates, but they now lie empty. The change in arrest policy has also resulted in savings running into the hundreds of millions of dollars.

New York's overcrowding problem has thus been eased, not by changes in correctional policy, but by a shift in law enforcement strategy. Recognition that arresting street-level offenders was not having the hoped-for impact on the drug problem led to adoption of a new focus on higher-level criminals. The correctional system has been a significant benefactor of this shift in enforcement priorities.

Correctional practitioners understand this problem. Although most practitioners can hardly be described as bleeding heart liberals, and although they possess a full understanding of the nasty personal nature of many offenders, they nonetheless understand that criminals are the result of more than just the exercise of free will in the pursuit of evil. In speaking about his job, one parole officer observed that

> [i]t's about helping punks, perverts, and predators, most of whom have no remorse for the harm they've inflicted on others, the innocent lives they've upset or ruined, or the hardship they work on the whole society. . . . You take any one of them, you read their jackets [folders containing criminal record and background information], and you say, "There but for the grace of God go I." Beaten and abused as kids. Many had no folks, or a father or somebody else in jail, a mother and every other adult they know except drug dealers on welfare, and always in poverty. Some are mentally retarded or borderline retarded, but the schools didn't take care of them.[38]

One correctional officer at a maximum security facility noted,

> What I do here . . . is protect, feed, and try to educate scum who raped and brutalized women and children; who robbed a convenience store and then, just for kicks, shot the old man and old lady who ran it; who didn't get paid for the drugs they sold and so killed to enforce the deal. . . . Of course, you have to feel a little sorry for these bastards. Nobody ever gave them a break. Nobody ever taught them right from wrong.[39]

If these correctional officials are right, then offenders become what they are through a variety of processes that are exerting influence long before the correctional system ever gets its hands on them. It is no shock, therefore, that there are significant limits to what the system can do. The parole officer quoted above made this clear in remarking that

> [y]ou can work your ass off for them—get them a job, help with their personal problems. Most will still do crime.[40]

By the time corrections takes over, for many offenders it is simply too late.

The public, of course, remains frustrated and angry. As with many forms of frustration and anger, however, at least one solution to these feelings is the development of a more realistic sense of what can actually be accomplished. Development of this understanding will lead to a better appreciation of the need to examine the functioning of other social institutions, and an understanding of the extent to which they all connect in influencing participation in criminal activity.

> If we have learned anything from the history of prison reform, it is that someday the rehabilitative ideal will return in some form, just as the current "just deserts" model is a throwback to retribution theories of the past. They will in all likelihood be a failure today, just as they were before. Prisons exist in society, and as long as society does not undergo a deep and radical structural transformation, there is little chance that institutions, especially coercive ones, will be qualitatively changed.[41]

At this point in time, with years of focus on the correctional system as a remedy for crime but little discernible positive effect, there ought to be plenty of motivation to begin to look beyond corrections for enduring answers to the persistent problem of crime.

Notes

[1] *National Prison Project Journal*, (1992) "Attorney General Barr holds "Corrections Summit" to promote imprisonment," 7(2), p. 3.

[2] Office of the Attorney General (1992) "Combating violent crime: 24 recommendations to strengthen criminal justice," Washington, D.C.: U.S. Department of Justice.

[3] Lavelle, Louis (1993) "Proposal would add 21,000 prison beds," *Tampa Tribune*, Florida/Metro, pp. 1 & 2.

[4] Id. at 2.

[5] Steffensmeier, Darrell (1992) "More PA prisoners did not reduce violent crime," *Overcrowded Times*, 3(6), p. 7.

[6] Hinds, Michael deCourcy (1992) "Feeling prisons' cost, governors weigh alternatives," *New York Times*, Aug. 7, p. A17.

[7] Flanagan, Timothy J. and Caulfield, Susan L. (1984) "Public opinion and prison policy: A review," *The Prison Journal*, 64, p. 42.

[8] Flanagan, Timothy J. and Maguire, Kathleen (1992) *Sourcebook of Criminal Justice Statistics—1991*, Washington, D.C.: U.S. Dept. of Justice, p. 210.

[9] Nordheimer, Jon (1972) "Wallace Joins Florida Race as Democrat," *New York Times*, Jan. 14, p. 1.

[10] Herbers, John, (1972) "President Urges Nation Help Keep His Office Strong," *New York Times*, Sept. 10, p. 1

[11] Hunter, Marjorie (1974) "Ford Presents Anticrime Program," *New York Times*, Sept. 25, p. 20.

[12] Criminal Justice Newsletter (1990) 21(3), p. 6.

[13] Criminal Justice Newsletter (1990), 21(3), p. 6.

[14] Jamieson, K. M. and Flanagan, T.J. (1989) *Sourcebook of Criminal Justice Statistics—1988*, Washington, D.C.: U.S. Department of Justice, p. 210.

[15] See, e.g., Blumstein, Alfred and Cohen, Jacqueline (1980) "Sentencing of convicted offenders: An analysis of the public's view," *Law and Society Review*, 14; Durham, Alexis M. III (1988) "Crime seriousness and punitive severity: An assessment of social attitudes," *Justice Quarterly*, 5.

[16] See, e.g., Cullen, Francis T., Skovron, Sandra E., Scott, Joseph E., and Burton, Velmar S., Jr. (1990) "Public support for correctional treatment: The tenacity of rehabilitative ideology," *Criminal Justice and Behavior*, 17(1); Penley, Victoria (1991) "Public opinion, punishment, and rehabilitation: A conver-

gence of ideologies," presented at the American Society of Criminology national conference, San Francisco, Nov.

[17] Benekos, Peter J. (1992) "Public Policy and Sentencing Reform: The Politics of Corrections," *Federal Probation*, 56(1), p. 8.

[18] Quoted in Benekos, note 17 above at 8.

[19] Sullivan, Larry E. (1990) *The Prison Reform Movement—Forlorn Hope*, Boston: Twayne Publishers, p. 130.

[20] Quoted in Benekos, note 17 above at 8.

[21] Pontell, Henry N. (1984) *A Capacity to Punish: The Ecology of Crime and Punishment*, Bloomington, Indiana, p. 3.

[22] Miller, Jerome (1992) "56 percent of young black males in Baltimore under justice system control," *Overcrowded Times*, 3(2).

[23] DiIulio, John J. (1991) *No Escape—The Future of American Corrections*, Basic Books.

[24] Morris, Norval and Tonry, Michael (1990) *Between Prison and Probation—Intermediate Punishments in a Rational Sentencing System*, New York: Oxford University Press, p. 224.

[25] Id. at 221-224.

[26] Surette, Ray (1992) *Media, Crime and Criminal Justice—Images and Reality*, Pacific Grove, CA: Brooks-Cole, p. 68.

[27] Id. at 75-76.

[28] Id. at 76.

[29] Id.

[30] Id. at 65-66.

[31] Id. at 67.

[32] Doble, John (1987) "Crime and punishment: The public's view," *The Public Agenda Foundation*.

[33] "Signs of the Times" (1992), USA TODAY, August 12, p. 9a.

[34] Id.

[35] See, e.g., Gottfredson, Stephen D., Warner, Barbara D. and Taylor, Ralph B. (1988) "Conflict and consensus about criminal justice in Maryland," in Walker and Hough (eds.) *Public Attitudes to Sentencing—Surveys from Five Countries*, Brookfield: Gower.

[36] See, e.g., see DiIulio, note 23 above at 263-265.

[37] Based on Treaster, Joseph B. (1992) "Police in New York shift drug battle away from street," *New York Times*, Aug. 3, p. 1.

[38] Quoted in DiIulio, note 23 above at 268-269.

[39] Id.

[40] Id. at 268.

[41] See Sullivan, note 19 above at 137.

POST SCRIPT

The Crisis Continues

As this book is going to press a number of events lend further credence to the somewhat pessimistic conclusions reached in the previous chapter. An article entitled "Prisons Running out of Cells, Money, and Choices" appeared in the national edition of the New York Times in May of 1993 and cited a number of unhappy realities.[1]

1. Crowding in Arizona has now made it necessary to move drunken driving convicts from jails to tents to make room for other inmates.
2. Illinois' decision to double-up inmates in cells has not solved its crowding problem, and by next year its prisons will hold 36,000 inmates in spaces originally constructed for 21,000.
3. Despite the fact that previous prison construction efforts have not stemmed crime in Texas, legislators in that state have adopted "the largest prison building program in United States history, aiming for a tripling of beds across 15 years to more than 80,000 by 1996."[2]

There are other significant current consequences of the failed prison-construction movement of the past decade. For instance, Arkansas was forced to cut 1,000 corrections jobs in an effort to control escalating prison-related costs. In South Carolina three new prisons sit empty because there is no money to pay for the correctional officers needed to operate the facilities.[3] Judges are becoming increasingly reluctant to impose long prison terms, especially for drug violations. Judge Spenser Williams, one of those judges and the editor of the Federal Judges Association Newsletter, notes

> We have more persons in prison per thousand than any other country in the world. We're building prisons faster than we are building classrooms. And still the crime rate is going up. The whole thing doesn't seem to be very effective."[4]

In the late spring of 1993 the Director of the Federal Bureau of Prisons announced that the Bureau's budget will have to double to more than $3.5 billion by 1997 just to manage crowding in its institutions.[5] Many states are continuing to experience similar economic crises.

Finally, the failures of America's incarceration policy are not limited to penal crowding and economic costs. Within a month of the director's budget announcement yet another study was published on the effectiveness of incarceration as a method of reducing violence. The study compared incarceration rates and age-adjusted violence rates and found that

> it is difficult to detect any overall relationship between incarceration and violence rates or to show that incarceration is a cost effective means of reducing violent crime. . . . Our analysis of the national data suggests that increasing incarceration levels have not reduced violent crime rates as predicted but, in fact, violence levels have been rising in recent years . . . the age-adjusted index violence rate has risen a sizeable 36 percent since 1980.[6]

In light of all this, and having discussed the case of Florida in previous chapters, a brief update might be useful in illustrating the continuing American fascination with imprisonment. As we have already seen, Florida's prison capacity was nearly doubled in the 1980s. According to one newspaper editorial, the outcome of this is that

> Florida ranks No. 1 in the nation in violent crime. It makes international headlines as tourists are beaten and murdered in broad daylight. Network news programs televise Florida's mean streets to the nation. Other countries advise their residents to stay out of Florida.[7]

One might think that, having tried massive prison construction and finding that the $1 billion dollar a year[8] system had not solved

Florida's problems, the governor and legislature would look elsewhere for solutions. Not so. During the spring of 1993 they were engaged in an ongoing battle to determine not *if* significant prison construction ought to be the linchpin of the latest solution to the state's crime problem, but rather *how much* construction there should be, and how it will be *financed*. Various proposals were floated during the spring, including Governor Lawton Chiles' plan to add 22,000 new beds.

Although conservatives have traditionally been supportive of prison construction programs, Chiles' plan to raise taxes to fund the construction did not please them. But desperate times call for desperate measures, and Chiles sought to defuse conservative discontent by proposing that the new prisons be funded through a 25-cent per pack tax on cigarettes. This "sin tax" approach created enormous controversy, and it became clear that it would not get through the legislature. Competing plans proliferated, including one that would attempt to make inmates defray the costs of prisons. It appeared that the state was headed for political gridlock, and a special legislative session was scheduled to address the prison construction issue.

But then a miracle happened. The headline in the May 23, 1993 Tampa Tribune proclaimed that the "State finds more money to pay for prison space."[9] The article reported that "[o]n the eve of a special legislative session on prison construction, state economists Sunday found enough money to build additional space for 10,000 prisoners without raising taxes or borrowing money. The money, $166.67 million, comes from lower estimates of the number of poor people seeking Medicaid and welfare benefits this year and next."[10]

So a political standoff was avoided. Chiles did not get all the beds he wanted, but he did get an immediate 20 percent increase in prison system capacity. Conservatives wary of new taxes were satisfied that no new taxes would be required. Less than a week after the new money was "discovered" the Tampa Tribune announced that "Florida approves massive prison expansion."[11]

But as it turns out, a "massive prison expansion" is simply not going to be of much value. State legislator Ron Silver notes, "I don't believe we've done what needed to be done. We just haven't done the job."[12] According to the Tampa Tribune, "The new prison beds are only about one-third of the 35,000-bed expansion the state needs, and the Legislature's action only delays for nine months the release of dangerous prisoners."[13] An early June editorial referred to the plan as "The Legislature's puny response to Florida's crime epidemic."[14] It is interesting that the paper could refer to the plan as both "massive" and "puny," but that reflects the current confused thinking about the role of prisons in addressing the crime problem.

A further irony is that during this historic week in Florida corrections, a conference of 700 criminal justice experts met in Tampa to consider correctional problems. A Tampa Tribune headline for a story on the conference proclaimed, "Experts say more prisons not the answer."[15] At this conference New York City's corrections commissioner argued that "[w]e must talk about more than just locking someone up and talk about prevention and treatment."[16] Criminal Justice Professor Todd Clear assessed the prison-building movement of the 1980s and concluded that "[w]hat we learned is that on the whole, the increase in punishments had little impact on crime, though it has dangerously overburdened the criminal justice system."[17] The President of the American Probation and Parole Association insisted, "We simply cannot afford to keep doing things the same old way."[18] But of course, less than 300 miles away in Tallahassee, state legislators were in the process of doing exactly that.

Finally, in the previous chapter we discussed the importance of public knowledge as a force in the development of effective correctional policy. It is interesting to note that although many of the news stories on the prison-building escapades of the legislature are reported in the papers on the front page under large banner headlines, the story on the corrections conference entitled "Experts say more prisons not the answer" not only appeared in a back section of the paper, but also on an inside page of that back section, and under a modestly sized headline. This article reported that correction experts were espousing views at *significant* variance with what the legislature was planning to do at virtually that very moment with millions and millions of dollars of taxpayer money. Why is this not news of sufficient importance to accord a prominent location in the paper? Such media treatment is all too typical, and it is thus not surprising that citizens are often woefully misinformed about correctional issues. As has been argued previously, unless the public becomes better informed about such problems there is significant reason to anticipate that Florida's approach to punishment-related problems will be replicated again and again, both in Florida and in other states as well.

Notes

[1] Clines, Francis X. (1993) "Prisons Running Out of Cells, Money, and Choices," *New York Times*, May 28, p. A1, B10.

[2] Id. at B10.

[3] Id.

[4] Frankel, Bruce (1993) "Judicial revolt over sentencing picks up steam," *USA Today*, May 3 p. 9a.

[5] Associated Press (1993) "'Get tough' laws hard on prisons, too," *Tampa Tribune*, May 13, p .12, Nation-World Section.

[6] Steffensmeier, Darrell and Harer, Miles D. (1993) "Bulging prisons, an aging U.S. population, and the nation's violent crime rate," *Federal Probation*, vol. 57, no. 2, pp. 9-10.

[7] Editorial (1993) *Tampa Tribune*, Jun. 1, p. 6, Nation-World Section.

[8] Lavelle, Louis (1993) "Prison reform stifled by political rhetoric," *Tampa Tribune*, May 23, p. 1, Florida-Metro Section.

[9] Chachere, Vickie (1993) "State finds more money to pay for prison space," *Tampa Tribune*, May 24, p. 1, Nation-World Section.

[10] Id.

[11] Chachere, Vickie (1993) "Florida approves massive prison construction," *Tampa Tribune*, May 28, p. 1, Nation-World Section.

[12] See Lavelle, note 7 above.

[13] Id.

[14] Editorial (1993), *Tampa Tribune*, Jun. 1, p. 6, Nation-World Section.

[15] Martinez, James (1993) "Experts say more prisons not the answer," *Tampa Tribune*, p. 3, Florida-Metro Section.

[16] Id.

[17] Id.

[18] Id.

Index